# Building the Self-Efficacy Beliefs of English Language Learners and Teachers

*Building the Self-Efficacy Beliefs of English Language Learners and Teachers* explores, juxtaposes, and bridges two fields of research that have developed separately: the self-efficacy beliefs of English language learners and the self-efficacy beliefs of English language teachers. The aim is to expand understanding in each field and highlight how the two areas can mutually inform each other. This should encourage fresh perspectives, providing direction for researchers, and improving learning, teaching, and teacher education.

Empirical research suggests that English language learners and teachers who believe they can fulfil a task are more likely to succeed than those who believe they cannot. Based on a deep understanding of how self-efficacy beliefs are formed and developed, this book illustrates how such beliefs can be supported and researched amongst English language learners and teachers. Bringing together the work of educators and researchers working in contexts including Algeria, Bulgaria, Canada, China, Iran, Israel, Japan, Norway, Türkiye, the United Arab Emirates, the United Kingdom, and the United States of America, this volume includes meta-analyses largely focusing on quantitative data and empirical studies employing qualitative approaches and mixed methods. Studies included examine factors impacting the development of language teachers' self-efficacy beliefs and investigate domain-specific dimensions of the self-efficacy beliefs of English language learners and teachers.

This rigorous and original volume will appeal to an international readership of scholars, teachers, teacher educators, and researchers with interests in language education, teacher education, TESOL, linguistics, and educational psychology.

**Mark Wyatt** is a Consultant in English language teaching.

**Farahnaz Faez** is a Professor in the Faculty of Education at The University of Western Ontario, Canada.

# Routledge Research in Language Education

The *Routledge Research in Language Education* series provides a platform for established and emerging scholars to present their latest research and discuss key issues in Language Education. This series welcomes books on all areas of language teaching and learning, including but not limited to language education policy and politics, multilingualism, literacy, L1, L2 or second language acquisition, curriculum, classroom practice, pedagogy, teaching materials, and language teacher education and development. Books in the series are not limited to the discussion of the teaching and learning of English only.

Books in the series include:

**Assessment of Plurilingual Competence and Plurilingual Learners in Educational Settings**
Educative Issues and Empirical Approaches
*Edited by Sílvia Melo-Pfeifer and Christian Ollivier*

**Early Childhood Language Education and Literacy Practices in Ethiopia**
Perspectives from Indigenous Knowledge, Gender, and Instructional Practices
*Edited by Kassahun Weldemariam, Margareth Sandvik and Moges Yigezu*

**Effects of Orthography on Second Language Phonology**
Learning, Awareness, Perception and Production
*Bene Bassetti*

**Ecological Perspectives in Early Language Education**
Parent, Teacher, Peer, and Child Agency in Interaction
*Mila Schwartz*

For more information about the series, please visit www.routledge.com/Routledge-Research-in-Language-Education/book-series/RRLE

# Building the Self-Efficacy Beliefs of English Language Learners and Teachers

New Perspectives for Research, Teaching and Learning

Edited by Mark Wyatt and Farahnaz Faez

NEW YORK AND LONDON

First published 2024
by Routledge
605 Third Avenue, New York, NY 10158

and by Routledge
4 Park Square, Milton Park, Abingdon, Oxon, OX14 4RN

*Routledge is an imprint of the Taylor & Francis Group, an informa business*

© 2024 selection and editorial matter, Mark Wyatt and Farahnaz Faez; individual chapters, the contributors

The right of Mark Wyatt and Farahnaz Faez to be identified as the author[/s] of the editorial material, and of the authors for their individual chapters, has been asserted in accordance with sections 77 and 78 of the Copyright, Designs and Patents Act 1988.

All rights reserved. No part of this book may be reprinted or reproduced or utilized in any form or by any electronic, mechanical, or other means, now known or hereafter invented, including photocopying and recording, or in any information storage or retrieval system, without permission in writing from the publishers.

*Trademark notice*: Product or corporate names may be trademarks or registered trademarks, and are used only for identification and explanation without intent to infringe.

ISBN: 978-1-032-45682-9 (hbk)
ISBN: 978-1-032-45933-2 (pbk)
ISBN: 978-1-003-37930-0 (ebk)

DOI: 10.4324/9781003379300

Typeset in Galliard
by MPS Limited, Dehradun

# Contents

List of Contributors — viii

1 Building English language learners' and teachers' self-efficacy beliefs — 1
   MARK WYATT AND FARAHNAZ FAEZ

**PART 1**
**Synthesizing the literature to expand understanding of language teachers' self-efficacy beliefs** — 19

2 Language teacher self-efficacy surveys: What have we learned? Where are we going? — 21
   MICHAEL KARAS, TAKUMI UCHIHARA, AND FARAHNAZ FAEZ

3 Language teachers' self-efficacy beliefs in the Turkish EFL context — 44
   FUNDA ÖLMEZ-ÇAĞLAR

**PART 2**
**Exploring factors impacting the development of English language teachers' self-efficacy beliefs** — 65

4 The formation of pre-service language teachers' self-efficacy beliefs: A case study — 67
   ZARINA MARKOVA

5  Novice EFL teachers' self-efficacy beliefs in the first year: An insight into the impact of task-, domain-, and context-specific factors upon perceptions of efficacy    87
NATALIE A. DONOHUE

6  Language teachers' self-efficacy beliefs evident in teacher–supervisor post-observation conferences in Iran    110
ZIA TAJEDDIN AND FERESHTEH TADAYON

7  Support for career-long development of language teachers' self-efficacy beliefs: Two Chinese EFL teachers' stories of professional development    126
RONGGAN ZHANG AND JUDITH HANKS

8  Growing teacher research efficacy beliefs through Exploratory Practice: An autoethnography    148
CHRIS BANISTER

## PART 3
**Investigating domain-specific dimensions of English language learners' and teachers' self-efficacy beliefs**    171

9  "I'm not a walking dictionary": Unpacking English language teachers' self-efficacy beliefs about teaching vocabulary    173
BEN NAISMITH AND LEO SELIVAN

10  An exploratory study on teachers' and learners' self-efficacy beliefs for English as a foreign language listening in Algeria    197
KELTOUM MANSOURI, SUZANNE GRAHAM, AND NAOMI FLYNN

11  Changes in the academic writing self-efficacy beliefs of students in transition from high school to an English medium instruction university programme in Japan    220
OLIVER HADINGHAM AND GENE THOMPSON

12 Exploring language self-efficacy beliefs and
technology-based learning strategies in an increasingly
digitalized world 241
NALAN ŞAN AND DERIN ATAY

# Epilogue 265

13 Researching the self-efficacy beliefs of language
learners and teachers: The roads ahead 267
FARAHNAZ FAEZ AND MARK WYATT

*Index* *277*

# Contributors

**Derin Atay** is a Professor of Applied Linguistics at Bahçeşehir University, Türkiye. Her research interests include the integration of 21st-century skills, active learning, global citizenship, student engagement in online education, and multicultural language education. She has published widely in indexed journals, conducted educational projects, and offered professional development seminars to teachers throughout Türkiye.

**Chris Banister** is a Senior Lecturer in English for Academic Purposes at Regent's University London, UK. He has previously worked as an English language teacher in the UK and Türkiye. A keen enquirer into his own classroom practice, Chris has published several book chapters and journal articles, including in *ELT Journal* and *Language Teaching Research*.

**Natalie Donohue**, PhD, is an Associate Professor in English Language and Didactics at Volda University College, Norway. She has taught English in Japan, Türkiye, and the UK and is now predominantly involved in language teacher training. Research interests include teacher motivation, self-efficacy, and cognition, with a particular focus on novice teachers.

**Farahnaz Faez** is a Professor of Applied Linguistics in the Faculty of Education at Western University, Ontario, Canada. Her research interests include second language pedagogy, language teacher education, language teacher self-efficacy, language teacher proficiency, and non-native English-speaking teachers. She is the Co-Editor of *TESL Canada Journal*.

**Naomi Flynn** is a Professor of Multilingual Education at the University of Reading's Institute of Education, UK. Her practitioner-oriented research is focused on enhancing teachers' pedagogy for pupils whose home language is not English through US–UK collaborative studies.

**Suzanne Graham** is a Professor of Language and Education at the Institute of Education, University of Reading, UK. She has researched and published widely in the fields of both language learner and language teacher self-efficacy, focusing particularly on self-efficacy beliefs in relation to second-language listening and reading comprehension.

**Oliver Hadingham** is a Researcher-practitioner with broad experience in teaching English as a medium of instruction (EMI) students at universities in Japan. He is interested in the usefulness of EMI support provision and the challenges faced by students in the transition to full English-medium content courses. He is studying for a doctorate at the University of Oxford, UK.

**Judith Hanks** is an Associate Professor of Language Education, University of Leeds, UK. She has worked in China, Italy, Singapore, and the UK. She leads MA TESOL and Teacher Education programmes and supervises PhD students investigating Exploratory Practice, professional development, and teacher education. Judith convenes the AILA Fully Inclusive Practitioner Research Network: https://www.fullyinclusivepr.com/

**Michael Karas** is an Assistant Professor in the Department of Applied Linguistics at Brock University, Ontario, Canada. His research interests include language teacher self-efficacy beliefs, learner silence, and research syntheses. He has taught in South Korea, China, and Canada.

**Keltoum Mansouri** is an Assistant Professor in the Department of English at the University of Oum El Bouaghi, Algeria. She gained a PhD from the Institute of Education, University of Reading, UK. Her main research interests are in the psychology of foreign language teaching and learning, more specifically in self-efficacy beliefs.

**Zarina Markova**, PhD, is a Chief Assistant Professor in the methodology of English language teaching at the South-West University Neofit Rilsky, Blagoevgrad, Bulgaria. She teaches language acquisition and English language teaching methodology, supervises teaching practice, and conducts state teacher certification examinations. She is a recipient of the 2016 FIPLV International Award.

**Ben Naismith** is an Assessment Scientist at Duolingo. Ben has worked in numerous contexts as a teacher, teacher trainer, materials developer, and researcher. He holds a PhD in Applied Linguistics from the University of Pittsburgh, USA. His research interests include second language acquisition, corpus linguistics, language assessment, and teacher education.

**Funda Ölmez-Çağlar** is currently a Research Assistant in the Department of Foreign Language Education at Akdeniz University, Türkiye. She holds a PhD in English Language Teaching from Hacettepe University, Türkiye.

Her research deals primarily with various aspects of the psychology of language learning and teaching.

**Nalan Şan** is an Instructor at Istanbul Technical University, and she is also studying for a PhD in Applied Linguistics at Bahçeşehir University, Türkiye. Her research interests include bilingual and self-regulated education, learning strategy training, continuous professional development, the interactive integration of digital education tools, and dialogic education.

**Leo Selivan**, of the David Yellin College of Education, Jerusalem, has worked as an English language teacher, senior teacher, examiner, trainer, and materials developer for almost 20 years. Today, he lectures on graduate and postgraduate courses for teachers and editors. He is the author of *Lexical Grammar* (CUP, 2018) and *Activities for Alternative Assessment* (Delta Publishing, 2021).

**Fereshteh Tadayon** is a PhD Candidate in Applied Linguistics at Allameh Tabataba'I University, Iran. Her main areas of research include teacher education, English as a Lingua Franca, and language testing.

**Zia Tajeddin** is a Professor of Applied Linguistics at Tarbiat Modares University, Iran. His main research areas include teacher education, L2 pragmatics, and EIL/ELF pedagogy. Zia co-edits the book series *Studies in Language Teacher Education* (Springer). He has published several books, most recently *Teacher Reflection: Policies, Practices and Impacts* (Multilingual Matters, 2022).

**Gene Thompson** is an Associate Professor in the Department of Global Business at Rikkyo University, Japan. His research on self-efficacy, exploring the interaction between learner and teacher self-beliefs and their behaviour, has appeared in the *International Journal of Bilingual Education and Bilingualism*, *System*, and *Asia Pacific Journal of Teacher Education*.

**Takumi Uchihara** is a Senior Assistant Professor at the Graduate School of International Cultural Studies at Tohoku University, Japan. His research interests include L2 vocabulary acquisition and research synthesis. He has been involved in meta-analysis projects on various topics related to applied linguistics including L2 teaching self-efficacy and vocabulary instruction.

**Mark Wyatt** is an Associate Professor of English at Khalifa University, UAE. He has researched self-efficacy beliefs for over 20 years, both in Nepal with English language learners and then with English language teachers in Oman, where he worked on a University of Leeds project. His articles have appeared in journals such as *System* and *TESOL Quarterly*.

**Ronggan Zhang** is a Research Fellow at the China Research Centre for Ethnic Teacher Education, Minzu University of Xingyi, China, having gained a PhD from the University of Leeds and 30 years' experience in language teaching and teacher training/mentoring. His research interests include understanding, and supporting teachers for, sustainable professional development over the span of a career.

# 1 Building English language learners' and teachers' self-efficacy beliefs

*Mark Wyatt and Farahnaz Faez*

## Introduction

The English language learner or teacher who believes that they *can* fulfil a task they value is more likely to succeed than one who believes they *cannot*. This simple idea, that is believing one *can-do* something that matters might increase the chance of a positive outcome (Faez et al., 2011), underpins the theory behind self-efficacy beliefs (Bandura, 1977). Bandura (1986, p. 21) has explained that "among the types of thoughts that affect action, none is more central or pervasive than people's judgements of their capabilities to deal effectively with different realities". Indeed, drawing on empirical findings, researchers such as Schunk (1991) and Graham and Weiner (1996) have argued that self-efficacy beliefs better predict success not only than other motivational constructs but also than a track record of achievements, skills, and knowledge.

Self-efficacy beliefs, which are strongly associated with the work of Albert Bandura, came to prominence in the 1970s at a time when psychologists were turning away from a behavioural view of learning to acknowledge the importance not just of the environment but also of personal factors, including cognition and affect, in shaping learning. More broadly, interest in the consciousness of the self can be traced back to William James, writing in the 1890s about the importance of self-esteem (Pajares & Schunk, 2005). Then, as these authors report, in the 1940s and 1950s, during the humanistic revolt against Behaviourism, Maslow's (1943) ideas about striving for self-actualization and Rogers' (1951) psychotherapeutic focus on the importance of attending to the "self" came to the fore. Various theories relating to selfhood subsequently developed, including self-concept (Shavelson et al., 1976) and self-worth (Harter, 1985), together with other expectancy for success constructs (e.g., Eccles, 1983).

Self-efficacy beliefs can be distinguished from other theories of self in various ways. Firstly, self-esteem relates to the attitudes one has towards oneself. So, self-esteem concerns affective and emotional reactions to one's

DOI: 10.4324/9781003379300-1

own sense of worthiness (Pajares & Schunk, 2005; Pintrich & Schunk, 1996). In contrast, self-efficacy beliefs are centred on a clear cognitive component, a judgement of capability to perform a specific task in a specific domain and context (Mercer, 2008; Pajares & Schunk, 2005). For example, a second language learner engaged in academic reading may feel more or less efficacious in skimming texts such as newspaper articles for gist, a self-evaluation that might be influenced by a range of situation-specific factors.

Meanwhile, self-concept includes both cognitive and affective components, incorporating both self-evaluation and feelings of self-worth (Mercer, 2008; Pajares & Schunk, 2005). So, for example, returning to the second language learner who is self-efficacious in skimming newspaper articles for gist in a particular setting, this self-belief might be a foundational element in helping the learner to have a positive self-concept of themselves as a reader in the second language. To explain: If they have generalized from success on different reading tasks, such as reading for gist, the learner might believe they are good at reading generally (a global self-efficacy belief). Furthermore, if they also believe that they are a good language learner with a growth mindset (Dweck, 2000) and so experience positive self-esteem, they might feel good about who they are (and so develop positive self-concept, in this case as a strong reader able to keep developing). Positive global self-efficacy beliefs and healthy self-esteem thus contribute to positive self-concept.

Self-efficacy beliefs are linked in Bandura's (1977) theory with outcome expectations, which are beliefs about the impact actions taken will have. Outcome expectations, which have been described as means-ends beliefs (Skinner, 1996), might relate quite closely in our field to beliefs about second language acquisition (Barcelos & Kalaja, 2011). For example, the second language learner who believes that skimming is a useful strategy that, enacted successfully, will lead to more effective reading performance, will likely have more positive outcome expectations for engaging in skimming than a learner who does not share this belief. However, if both learners share similar positive outcome expectations, of crucial importance in determining the likely degree of task fulfilment are their agent-means self-efficacy beliefs in impacting the quality and quantity of effort applied to the task. This point is as relevant to teachers as it is to learners. Wyatt (2018a) offers an illustrative matrix indicating how self-efficacy beliefs and outcome expectations can interact.

According to Bandura (1986), self-efficacy beliefs are influenced by four main sources. These include enactive mastery experiences gained from reflected-upon performance on similar tasks, vicarious experiences gained from observing or being told about others' successes, verbal persuasion in the form of feedback on performance, and physiological and emotional arousal gained through the senses. Bandura et al.'s (1977) early psychological research was with snake phobics who needed to experience or witness success in handling snakes or be convinced that they could do so to overcome their fears, and the positive language used to describe impactful sources (i.e., mastery, verbal persuasion) reflects this purpose, domain, and context. However, of course, the fit between self-efficacy beliefs and performance is not always optimal, and this can be seen in educational settings, for example. Learners or teachers might be over-efficacious (Wyatt, 2015) or possess illusional efficacy (Hiver & Dörnyei, 2017) that can lead to complacency and limit reflection and willingness to learn (Wheatley, 2005). Consequently, while the learner or teacher feeling themselves inefficacious might need sensitive mentoring that draws attention to their strengths and capacity to grow with a view to building self-efficacy beliefs, such an approach will not work in all situations with all teachers. Specifically, the over-efficacious teacher might sometimes benefit from looking more closely at the evidence, and so, perhaps from some kind of "interactive experience" with their mentor that seems to go beyond "verbal persuasion", hence Wyatt's (2016) use of alternative terminology.

Having introduced key concepts that inform this volume, we now provide a brief overview of how research into language learners' and teachers' self-efficacy beliefs developed. We then consider the characteristics of these research fields more closely, before introducing the various chapters in this book. We then offer concluding thoughts.

## The development of research into language learners' and teachers' self-efficacy beliefs

From its beginnings in the 1970s, research in self-efficacy beliefs has spread into a range of domains of human functioning, encompassing for example sports, health and dieting, business, technology, and education. However, curiously, in the field of education, as Wyatt (2021) explains, research into learners' and teachers' self-efficacy beliefs diverged from the beginning. This was partly because research into teachers' self-efficacy beliefs got off on the wrong track, claiming adherence to Bandura's (1977) ideas but actually conspicuously influenced by another construct, Rotter's (1966) locus of control (Klassen et al., 2011; Wyatt, 2014). However, after Bandura (1997) intervened to point out this misconceptualization, researchers into teachers' self-efficacy beliefs such as Tschannen-Moran and Woolfolk Hoy (2001) and Dellinger et al. (2008) developed quantitative instruments (and most of the research was quantitative at this time) that were better aligned with Bandura's (1986, 1997) theory. Meanwhile, within a separate thread of research in the late 20th century, into *learners'* self-efficacy beliefs in academic settings (Pajares, 1996), conceptualizations that did fit with Bandura's (1986) theory were more in evidence. However, even within this line of research, misconceptualizations on the part of individual researchers and survey developers were evident, as Pajares (1996) reports, and there were also tensions regarding the measurement of learners' self-efficacy beliefs in academic settings, bearing in mind that "particularized judgements of capability are better predictors of related outcomes than are more generalized self-beliefs" (p. 563). Some questions designed to elicit self-efficacy beliefs seemed insufficiently "particularized" at the time (Pajares, 1996), an issue that can unfortunately sometimes still be the case in different domains (Karas & Faez, 2021; Mills, 2014; Wyatt, 2022).

The two threads of research that emerged separately in the early 21st century, into language learners' self-efficacy (LLSE) beliefs and language teachers' self-efficacy (LTSE) beliefs, respectively, reflect their different pathways. For example, a sample item from a survey eliciting LLSE beliefs is as follows:

- "How sure are you that you can listen to and understand the main ideas of a conversation in which a tourist requests information and receives simple instructions in French?" (Mills et al., 2008, p. 292)

Contrast this with an item from a widely used survey eliciting LTSE beliefs:

- "How much can you do to get students to follow classroom rules in your English classroom?" (Chacón, 2005, p. 263)

The LLSE beliefs item here was developed in the foreign languages department of an American university to assess listening for gist (an important listening sub-skill). Meanwhile, the LTSE beliefs item was minimally adapted (adding the words "in your English classroom") from Tschannen-Moran and Woolfolk Hoy's (2001) "Teacher Sense of Efficacy Scale" (TSES). This instrument had been developed for use with pre- and in-service mainstream Kindergarten-Grade 12 (K-12) teachers in the United States. It remains popular, but its applicability to many second/foreign language classrooms around the world has been questioned (see Faez & Karas, 2017; Faez et al., 2021; Chapter 2 of this volume, for reviews), particularly in Confucian heritage cultures (Hoang & Wyatt, 2021; Thompson, 2020). Wyatt (2021, p. 296) defines LTSE beliefs "as these teachers' beliefs in their abilities to support language learning in various task-, domain- and context-specific cognitive, metacognitive, affective and social ways". Such a definition suggests the kind of potential synergy between the strands of research into LLSE and LTSE beliefs that can be found in other branches of motivation research that consider learners' and teachers' perspectives. This potential synergy should become evident as we consider the characteristics of the research that has been produced to date into LLSE and LTSE beliefs in more detail.

## Characteristics of the research to date on language learners' and teachers' self-efficacy beliefs

Various reviews of the literature on LLSE and LTSE beliefs have appeared in the last decade. Analyses of the research on LLSE beliefs have included Irie (2022), Mills (2014), Wang and Sun (2020), and Wyatt (2022). Meanwhile, reviews of the LTSE beliefs literature include Faez and Karas (2017), Faez et al. (2021), Hoang (2018), Thompson (2020), and Wyatt (2018a, 2018b, forthcoming). We first provide an overview of the literature on LLSE beliefs, before turning to LTSE beliefs.

### *Language learners' self-efficacy beliefs*

In a review of 46 LLSE beliefs studies set in second/foreign language contexts and produced in the 21st century, since the pioneering work of Mills (2004) and Wang (2004) and up until early 2020, Wyatt (2022) highlighted that:

- Powerful links between LLSE beliefs and self-regulated learning (SRL) strategies (Zimmerman, 2000) have been identified. This is to be expected since one of Bandura's (1986) key premises is that self-efficacious learners are likely to be more agentive in self-regulating their efforts. As Wyatt (2022) highlights, researchers working in various national contexts and with learners of all ages and levels have found that fuller use of SRL strategies, such as goal-setting, self-monitoring, and self-evaluating, correlate positively with LLSE beliefs.
- Positive, statistically significant, relationships between LLSE beliefs and the metacognitive, cognitive, and socio-affective learning strategies described by Oxford (1990) have also been identified in different contexts. These findings suggest, for example, that self-efficacious learners in areas such as reading skills also employ learning strategies that are likely to be beneficial to their reading skills development, such as planning, note-taking, inferring, and asking questions while maintaining a positive mindset.
- Different sources of efficacy-building information appear to impact LLSE beliefs in different ways, depending on the nature of the task and the cognitive processing of the information. For example, various studies have found that more anxious students, i.e., experiencing negative physiological and emotional arousal (Bandura, 1986), have also reported low LLSE beliefs. However, anxiety may not be such an issue if learners expect it in relation to a highly valued task and attend more closely to other kinds of efficacy-building experiences accordingly.
- Cutting-edge pedagogy has been employed to good effect in different contexts to boost LLSE beliefs for listening, reading, writing, and

speaking. For example, learners have been supported to engage more effectively in gist listening, absorbing details, interpreting opinions, and deciphering meaning while also benefiting from scaffolding to help them make links between the strategies employed and experiences of success (Graham, 2007; Graham & Macaro, 2008). As these researchers report, benefits from such an intervention included enhanced LLSE beliefs and improved scores in proficiency tests. Likewise, the introduction of word targets, reading circles, genre-based writing tasks, a project-based curriculum, and the integration of technology through the use of a virtual world platform have been found to boost LLSE beliefs for reading, writing, and speaking in contexts including Australia, Japan, Korea, and the United States, as Wyatt (2022) explains. Such research conducted by innovative educators demonstrates therefore the value of exploring LLSE beliefs as a task-, domain-, and context-specific construct, after Bandura (1977, 1986, 1997).

Meanwhile, in a review of 74 studies, including both English as first and second/foreign language contexts, Wang and Sun (2020) explored the relationship between language proficiency and LLSE beliefs, finding a small to medium effect size. Comparing students from Western, Middle Eastern, and East Asian cultures, the researchers found that students from non-Western cultures tended to be under-efficacious. An important implication is that teachers with such learners could perhaps do more to strengthen LLSE beliefs through creating an appropriately supportive environment in which there are opportunities to gain affirmative efficacy-building experiences.

### *Language teachers' self-efficacy beliefs*

Virtually all of the LTSE beliefs research to date has focused on teachers of a target language who themselves have been amongst its second language learners. However, despite being bilingual and potentially having inspiring personal histories of successful second language learning to share as role models, such teachers are frequently discriminated against in public discourse, sometimes pejoratively labelled "non-native speakers". "Native-speakerism" has been described by Holliday (2006, p. 385) as a "pervasive ideology [which is] characterized by the belief that 'native-speaker' teachers represent a 'Western culture' from which spring the ideals both of the English language and of English language teaching methodology". Native-speakerism has been vigorously challenged in recent decades. Unfortunately, however, it is still insidiously with us, as the following text from a recent blog illustrates:

> 80% of English teachers abroad in non-native English-speaking countries – particularly in public schools – are not native English speakers themselves

because there are simply not enough native English-speaking teachers to meet demand.

(Bentley, 2023)

Such native-speakerist attitudes can clearly unfairly threaten bilingual teachers' identities and livelihoods. When brought into educational contexts, these attitudes can create anxiety in bilingual teachers, since they imply a questioning of linguistic competence. The bilingual teachers facing such threats might then suffer from "imposter syndrome" (Dörnyei & Ushioda, 2011, p. 184). LTSE beliefs might be low.

Such a phenomenon explains why one of the key threads of the research into LTSE beliefs has explored their relationship with language proficiency (see Faez & Karas, 2017; Faez et al., 2021, for reviews). Faez et al.'s (2021) meta-analysis of 19 studies published between 2001 and 2018 found a moderate relationship between language proficiency and LTSE beliefs, with effects greatest in studies that used domain-specific instruments to assess LTSE beliefs (see Chapter 2 of this volume for a discussion of instrumentation). Many of these domain-specific instruments have been developed in East Asia (Wyatt, 2018b, forthcoming), where interaction between limited language proficiency and low LTSE beliefs in in-service teachers has previously been observed (Choi & Lee, 2016; Hiver, 2013). Research suggests that the effects of limited language proficiency may be even greater on the LTSE beliefs of pre-service teachers in East Asian contexts (Hoang & Wyatt, 2021).

However, fortunately, as Faez et al. (2021) highlight, once language proficiency has reached a certain threshold, other factors, including the teachers' pedagogical skills and the enactive mastery experiences that they derive from practising these skills, may be more influential in shaping LTSE beliefs and behaviour. Nevertheless, below a certain level, limited language proficiency and low LTSE beliefs may interact to stimulate avoidance behaviour to the detriment of the opportunities for learning the teachers provide within their environment. For example, quantitative and qualitative studies from Korea report on teachers feeling both inefficacious and anxious about their language proficiency, with these concerns contributing to them avoiding use of the target language in class (Choi & Lee, 2016; Hiver, 2013). Meanwhile, mixed methods research from Türkiye has suggested that teachers with higher levels of language awareness may also feel more efficacious in implementing contextualizing, incidental, and inductive grammar instruction practices than their less linguistically aware peers, who, in contrast, might be drawn more towards traditional, deductive grammar teaching methods that require less spontaneous language use in class (Wyatt & Dikilitaş, 2021). Similarly, research in various contexts has correlated high LTSE beliefs with a greater tendency to engage in communicative or task-based language teaching, as several reviews highlight (e.g., Faez et al., 2021; Thompson, 2020; Wyatt, 2018b).

One positive global development is that there is growing awareness that bilingual teachers of English do not necessarily require high levels of target language proficiency in general in order to do their jobs competently but instead require English-for-teaching (Faez et al., 2021; Thompson, 2020). A recent Canadian study, where levels of language proficiency tend to be high, found that teachers who identified as multilingual, regardless of their first language, reported higher LTSE beliefs overall than teachers who identified as monolingual so-called "native-speakers". As Karas and Faez (2021, p. 123) report: "This suggests that being proficient in more than one language and having successful language-learning experiences can enhance teachers' self-efficacy". If such findings are replicated, this might provide some confirmation that from teachers' perspectives, "the field [is] slowly [moving] away from monolingual and native-speakerist norms" (Karas & Faez, 2021, p. 123).

Besides issues concerning language proficiency and related attitudes, other trends in the LTSE beliefs literature include a focus on the dynamic changes observed over time in LTSE beliefs and the change processes themselves, shaped by different kinds of context-bound experience. Regarding the openness of LTSE beliefs to change, there were earlier misconceptions amongst researchers, with some erroneously seeing these beliefs as largely fixed (see Wyatt, 2014, for a discussion). However, it has long been recognized by many in the field that due to their specificity in relation to tasks, domains, and contexts, self-efficacy beliefs are "much more dynamic, fluctuating and changeable" (Pintrich & Schunk, 1996, p. 93) than more static and stable beliefs in individuals' complex belief systems (Pajares, 1992).

Studies that have explored changes in LTSE beliefs have done so with teachers at different levels in different contexts, using various methodological approaches. For example, amongst pre-service teachers in Türkiye and Vietnam, surveys have been administered at two or more different time points of practicum (sometimes stretching into induction) years to understand how LTSE beliefs fluctuate or change under the influence of different experiences (e.g., Atay, 2007; Hoang & Wyatt, 2021; Şahin & Atay, 2010). Such studies have cast light on the impact of different kinds of influence, enactive mastery and vicarious experiences and forms of mentoring, and the impact of contextual changes, such as progressing from microteaching in a relatively sheltered environment to teaching full-time in busy schools, on developing LTSE beliefs.

Meanwhile, longitudinal, qualitative case studies have been conducted with in-service teachers on a teacher education programme in Oman developing LTSE beliefs in different aspects of their work (e.g., Wyatt,

2010, 2013). Conceptual models (Wyatt, 2016; see also Markova, 2021, working with pre-service teachers in Bulgaria) have been developed, mapping how different kinds of reflected-upon experiences support growing practical knowledge and LTSE beliefs.

One trend in the research has been to focus on the impact of engaging teachers in researching their own practices. Cabaroglu (2014) reports on the benefits, in terms of LTSE beliefs development, of involving pre-service teachers in action research. Meanwhile, Wyatt and Dikilitaş (2016) report on in-service professional development that encouraged teachers to design practitioner research studies in their context. This involved the teachers in activities such as developing research questions, collecting and analysing data, and presenting their findings, in the process developing stronger teacher research self-efficacy (TRE) beliefs in different aspects of conducting practitioner research. Gaining self-efficacy beliefs in researching their own practices also supported growth in their LTSE beliefs, a positive pattern of development that Banister (2019) has similarly described introspectively from his own perspective as an emerging teacher-researcher.

It should be clear from this summary of the research that has been conducted into LLSE and LTSE beliefs so far that it carries various implications for practice. These implications inform different contributions to this volume. We introduce the different chapters now and then offer some concluding thoughts.

## The contents of the volume

The volume is divided into three parts. The first of these, *Synthesizing the literature to expand understanding of language teachers' self-efficacy beliefs*, includes two cutting-edge literature reviews. In Chapter 2, Michael Karas, Takumi Uchihara, and Farahnaz Faez analyse the quantitative survey instruments that have been used in LTSE beliefs research. Focusing on 83 studies from a range of contexts, including Iran, Türkiye, and the United States, they first provide an overview of the scales that have been used in LTSE beliefs research, classifying the instruments as either "Original TSES" (after Tschannen-Moran & Woolfolk Hoy, 2001), "Modified TSES" (e.g., Choi & Lee, 2016), or "Other Scales" (e.g., Wyatt & Dikilitaş, 2021). The chapter then considers LTSE levels based on these instruments and how these levels may have been impacted by demographic and methodological factors. The classification of LTSE beliefs as "high", "medium", or "low" in different studies is also discussed. There is a trend towards the development of more domain- and task-specific instruments, which the chapter highlights. It also focuses on key pedagogical implications for teacher educators, including the need to emphasize that English-for-teaching is required rather than high English language proficiency more generally.

Next, in Chapter 3, Funda Ölmez-Çağlar reviews the LTSE beliefs literature specifically in the Turkish EFL context, which, as noted above and elsewhere (Wyatt, 2018a, 2018b), is one of the most prominent sites of research into LTSE beliefs. The inclusion of a chapter such as this reflects how the field has developed, from reviews of teachers' self-efficacy beliefs more generally (Klassen et al., 2011) to specifically LTSE beliefs (e.g., Wyatt, 2018b) to specifically LTSE beliefs in a particular country. Ölmez-Çağlar analyses 76 studies from the Turkish EFL context that were published between 2007 and 2021. Over 40% of these studies were with pre-service teachers, which is one way in which the research in this context is strikingly different from that in others, such as Iran, where the focus is predominantly on in-service teachers (Wyatt, forthcoming). Other defining characteristics of the research in Türkiye include considerable interest in how LTSE beliefs develop longitudinally, shaped by different influences, as Ölmez-Çağlar reports, with domain-specificity also becoming a more prominent recent feature. Given the fluctuations of LTSE beliefs noted in longitudinal studies, Ölmez-Çağlar offers implications for teacher education.

The second part of the volume, *Exploring factors impacting the development of English language teachers' self-efficacy beliefs*, includes five chapters, all of which are qualitative. Although it can produce in-depth insights, qualitative research, which might involve "the use of narratives centred on teachers' lived experiences, and including their own images and metaphors" to access their perspectives (Wyatt, 2013, p. 240), is rare. This is the case, both in teachers' self-efficacy beliefs research in general education (Tschannen-Moran et al., 1998; Klassen et al., 2011) and in LTSE beliefs research in particular (Wyatt, 2018b). Of the 76 studies from Türkiye analysed by Ölmez-Çağlar in Chapter 3 of this volume, for example, only 1 is qualitative. We now introduce the five qualitative studies included here.

In Chapter 4, using data from observation schedules, lesson plans, a semi-structured interview, and coursework, Zarina Markova presents an in-depth qualitative case study of a Bulgarian pre-service teacher on a practicum. It is worth noting that, in the LTSE beliefs literature, this is only the third qualitative case study of an individual teacher we are aware of (after Wyatt, 2010, 2013) and the first of a pre-service teacher. Markova's focus is on exploring how the teacher's LTSE beliefs were formed, shaped by practicum experiences. Findings focus on how she overcame doubts in some areas of her work and cultivated high LTSE beliefs in others. Pedagogical implications highlight the importance of quality teacher education experiences involving key input and mentoring.

Chapter 5, by Natalie Donohue, is very rare in being focused on so-called native-speakers, who, as noted above and elsewhere (e.g., Wyatt, 2018b), have been a neglected group. Donohue presents a multi-case study of five novice teachers who had each taken a short initial teacher education course, specifically the Cambridge Certificate in Teaching English to Speakers of Other Languages (CELTA), before emigrating to other countries (China, Italy, Poland, and Vietnam) to begin teaching. Using interviews, questionnaires, and diary entries, Donohue charts their progress longitudinally, providing vignettes of each teacher and then a cross-case analysis focusing on task-, domain-, and context-specific dimensions of their LTSE beliefs growth. Factors such as the importance of social support in aiding development are highlighted, while implications for pre-service teacher education and in-service mentoring are raised.

In Chapter 6, the focus of the volume shifts from novice to in-service teachers, and specifically to a sample of 15 teachers and their 4 supervisors working in different private language schools in Iran. While Iranian private language school contexts are the focus of much LTSE beliefs research (Wyatt, forthcoming), the methodology employed tends to be predominantly quantitative. Zia Tajeddin and Fereshteh Tadayon's discourse analysis, which is centred on extracts of data from teacher-supervisor post-observation conferences, highlights the challenges in-service teachers in these private language institutes can face in maintaining positive LTSE beliefs. The supervision can be very directive, and implications from the study centre on the need for training for supervisors. Training would also benefit teachers to help them better negotiate the threats to their LTSE beliefs that they can unfortunately receive through post-observation conferences.

In Chapter 7, the attention shifts to China and to the development of two teachers' LTSE beliefs over their careers, explored from a person-oriented ecological sustainable perspective. Using observations, documentary analysis, questionnaires, and semi-structured interviews, Ronggan Zhang and Judith Hanks present narrative case studies that illustrate the fluid and context-sensitive nature of LTSE beliefs growth. In this study, self-perceptions of language proficiency seem to play a role in shaping LTSE beliefs, as they also seem to do elsewhere in East Asia (Hoang & Wyatt, 2021; Thompson, 2020). Interaction between LTSE beliefs and growth or fixed mindsets (Dweck, 2000) is also evident in these stories. An implication raised by the authors is that engaging with exploratory practice (EP) would be one way of helping such teachers in their professional development, strengthening their LTSE beliefs, and enhancing the quality of their lives.

Chapter 8, by Chris Banister, is an autoethnographic account of an exploratory practitioner's developmental journey while building stronger TRE beliefs. Banister explores three dimensions of his growth: 1) scaffolding learner-initiated puzzling (EP involves puzzling rather than problem-solving, and tends to involve learners as co-researchers); 2) integrating practice-as-research through use of potentially exploitable pedagogic activities; and 3) producing coherent oral reports of his research. Banister draws upon a variety of artefacts while analysing his growth in these three areas and reflecting on how his TRE beliefs have changed over time. Pedagogical implications for other teachers contemplating practitioner research are offered.

The third part of the volume, *Investigating domain-specific dimensions of English language learners' and teachers' self-efficacy beliefs*, includes four chapters, all of which employ mixed methods. As noted above and discussed in Chapter 2, there is an increasing trend towards domain-specific LTSE beliefs research. There is evidence of crossover between research into learners and teachers too, in that one of these chapters (Chapter 10) concerns both LTSE and LLSE beliefs; the second author, Suzanne Graham, has written much on LLSE beliefs (Graham, 2007; Graham & Macaro, 2008). Chapters 11 and 12, both on LLSE beliefs, are second-authored by researchers notable for their work on LTSE beliefs (e.g., Atay, 2007; Thompson, 2020), although these researchers have previously published on LLSE beliefs as well.

As to the chapters in this section, Chapter 9, authored by Ben Naismith and Leo Selivan, addresses a glaring gap in the LTSE beliefs literature, a lack of previous research regarding these beliefs about vocabulary teaching, even though grammar teaching (e.g., Wyatt & Dikilitaş, 2021) and literacy have received attention. After reviewing the literature, Naismith and Selivan introduce their survey designed to elicit LTSE beliefs for vocabulary teaching techniques and for teaching different aspects of vocabulary knowledge, and teachers' lexical awareness. There were 142 valid responses to their survey and 7 of the participants took part in follow-up semi-structured interviews. Supported by factor analysis, findings provide rich insights into vocabulary LTSE beliefs, and there are pedagogical implications, for example with regard to providing support in the "grey area" of semi-fixed expressions.

In Chapter 10, we transition from vocabulary to listening, which has also been neglected to date in LTSE beliefs research, and to the most under-researched continent in LLSE/LTSE beliefs research: Africa (Wyatt, 2018b, 2021). In an Algerian context, Keltoum Mansouri, Suzanne Graham, and Naomi Flynn report on exploring the relationships between 10 teachers' LTSE beliefs for providing listening instruction and 186 university students' LLSE beliefs for listening and these learners' levels of proficiency for listening. Correlational analysis is used to explore the relationships, and semi-structured interviews provide additional insights. It is evident that more input on teaching listening, particularly regarding metacognition and strategy use, is needed in teacher education in this national context. Meanwhile, Algerian learners also need more support in developing awareness of listening processes and strategies and more encouragement to build stronger LLSE beliefs. As the authors highlight, similar research is needed in other contexts.

In Chapter 11, the focus shifts to academic writing LLSE beliefs in Japan. In an English Medium Instruction (EMI) environment where students are making the sometimes difficult transition from high school to university, Oliver Hadingham and Gene Thompson trace the development of LLSE beliefs for academic writing in English longitudinally over the first semester of an undergraduate social sciences degree. Drawing upon a locally developed "EMI Writing Self-efficacy Scale" administered to 40 students at four time-points throughout the semester, journal entries completed by each of the same students and semi-structured interviews with a smaller sample, Hadingham and Thompson highlight fluctuating patterns of development, which their qualitative data help them interpret. Implications regarding the provision of academic language support, which might include greater strategy training to reduce anxiety, encourage growth mindsets, and boost LLSE beliefs, are highlighted by the authors.

Finally, in Chapter 12 attention shifts back to Türkiye and the inclusion of technology-based learning strategies on a hybrid (online and face-to-face) English course for undergraduates to support the development of LLSE beliefs. Nalan Şan and Derin Atay administered Wang et al.'s (2013) "Questionnaire of English Self-Efficacy" which assesses LLSE beliefs for all four skills, and An et al.'s (2021) "Self-regulated English Learning Strategies Questionnaire". In total, 84 students completed these surveys. The researchers also conducted 6 focus group interviews with 30 of these students. Şan and Atay identified a modest but statistically significant positive correlation between LLSE beliefs and strategy use, a relationship which their qualitative data offer further insights on. Implications the authors highlight include the need to encourage learners to engage deeply with technology in language learning as this will likely strengthen their LLSE beliefs in skills areas including listening.

Having previewed the chapters, we now offer some concluding thoughts.

## Concluding thoughts

Self-efficacy beliefs have been the subject of numerous journal articles in the last few decades, during which time the research has increasingly become more domain-specific, with the self-efficacy beliefs of language learners and language teachers emerging as distinct fields in the 21st century. However, while there have been ground-breaking articles in the past decade, little of the research has been published in book form, a format which can help readers make connections between studies and within and across research areas. Moreover, there has been little research pulling together the two fields (the self-efficacy beliefs of language learners and teachers). By presenting this edited book, we aim to:

- Cast a broader spotlight on the research area than is possible through journal articles alone.
- Bring together experts from around the world, who are looking to use self-efficacy beliefs theory to improve the quality of language learning and teaching and teacher education.
- Encourage the development of fresh perspectives, with readers able to garner insights from the fields of both LTSE and LLSE beliefs research.
- Draw upon the various contributions in the volume to propose a research agenda that will appear in the epilogue.

## References

An, Z., Wang, C., Li, S., Gan, Z., & Li, H. (2021). Technology-assisted self-regulated English language learning: Associations with English language self-efficacy, English enjoyment, and learning outcomes. *Frontiers in Psychology, 11*, 3763. https://www.frontiersin.org/articles/10.3389/fpsyg.2020.558466/full

Atay, D. (2007). Beginning teacher efficacy and the practicum in an EFL context. *Teacher Development, 11*(2), 203–219. http://www.tandfonline.com/doi/abs/10.1080/13664530701414720

Bandura, A. (1977). Self-efficacy: Toward a unifying theory of behavioural change. *Psychological Review, 84*(2), 191–215.

Bandura, A. (1986). *Social foundations of thought and action: A social cognitive theory*. Prentice-Hall.

Bandura, A. (1997). *Self-efficacy: The exercise of control*. Freeman.

Bandura, A., Adams, N.E., & Beyer, J. (1977). Cognitive processes mediating behavioural change. *Journal of Personality and Social Psychology, 35*(3), 125–139. 10.1037/0022-3514.35.3.125

Banister, C. (2019). Rebuilding practitioner self-efficacy through learner feedback. In A. Slimani-Rolls & R. Kiely (Eds.), *Exploratory practice for continuing professional development* (pp. 135–151). Palgrave Macmillan.

Barcelos, A.M.F., & Kalaja, P. (2011). Introduction to *beliefs about SLA revisited*. *System, 39*, 281–289. 10.1016/j.system.2011.07.001

Bentley, J. (2023, Feb. 24). How large is the job market for English teachers abroad? International TEFL Academy blog. Accessed 12 Jun. 2023 from: https://www.internationalteflacademy.com/blog/how-large-is-the-job-market-for-english-teachers-abroad

Cabaroglu, N. (2014). Professional development through action research: Impact on self-efficacy. *System, 44*, 79–88. https://www.sciencedirect.com/science/article/pii/S0346251X14000645

Chacón, C.T. (2005). Teachers' perceived efficacy among English as a foreign language teachers in middle schools in Venezuela. *Teaching and Teacher Education, 21*, 257–272. 10.1016/j.tate.2005.01.001

Choi, E., & Lee, J. (2016). Investigating the relationship of target language proficiency and self-efficacy among nonnative EFL teachers. *System, 58*, 49–63. https://www.sciencedirect.com/science/article/pii/S0346251X1600035X

Dellinger, A.B., Bobbett, J.J., Olivier, D.F., & Ellett, C.D. (2008). Measuring teachers' self-efficacy beliefs: Development and use of the TEBS-Self. *Teaching and Teacher Education*, 24(3), 751–766. https://www.sciencedirect.com/science/article/pii/S0742051X07000339

Dörnyei, Z., & Ushioda, E. (2011). *Teaching and researching motivation* (2nd ed.). Longman.

Dweck, C.S. (2000). *Self-theories: Their role in motivation, personality and development*. Taylor & Francis.

Eccles, J. (1983). Expectancies, values and academic behaviors. In J. T. Spence (Ed.), *Achievement and achievement motives* (pp. 75–146). Freeman.

Faez, F., & Karas, M. (2017). Connecting language proficiency to (self-reported) teaching ability: A review and analysis of research. *RELC Journal*, 48(1), 135–151. 10.1177/0033688217694755

Faez, F., Karas, M., & Uchihara, T. (2021). Connecting language proficiency to teaching ability: A meta-analysis. *Language Teaching Research*, 25(5), 754–777. 10.1177/1362168819868667

Faez, F., Majhanovich, S., Taylor, S.K., Smith, M., & Crowley, K. (2011). The power of "Can Do" statements: Teachers' perceptions of CEFR-informed instruction in French as a second language classrooms in Ontario. *Canadian Journal of Applied Linguistics*, 14(2), 1–19. https://journals.lib.unb.ca/index.php/CJAL/article/view/19855/21653

Graham, S. (2007). Learner strategies and self-efficacy: Making the connection. *Language Learning Journal*, 35(1), 81–93. 10.1080/09571730701315832

Graham, S.J., & Macaro, E. (2008). Strategy instruction in listening for lower-intermediate learners of French. *Language Learning*, 58(4), 747–783. 10.1111/j.1467-9922.2008.00478.x

Graham, S., & Weiner, B. (1996). Theories and principles of motivation. In D.C. Berliner & R.C. Calfee (Eds.), *Handbook of educational psychology* (pp. 63–84). Simon and Schuster Macmillan.

Harter, S. (1985). Competence as a dimension of self-evaluation: Toward a comprehensive model of self-worth. In R. Leahy (Ed.), *The development of the self* (pp. 55–121). Academic Press.

Hiver, P. (2013). The interplay of possible language teacher selves in professional development choices. *Language Teaching Research*, 17(2), 210–227. 10.1177%2F1362168813475944

Hiver, P., & Dörnyei, Z. (2017). Language teacher immunity: A double-edged sword. *Applied Linguistics*, 38(3), 405–423. https://eric.ed.gov/?id=EJ1157605

Hoang, T. (2018). Teacher self-efficacy research in English as a foreign language contexts: A systematic review. *Journal of Asia TEFL*, 15(4), 976–990. 10.18823/asiatefl.2018.15.4.6.976

Hoang, T., & Wyatt, M. (2021). Exploring the self-efficacy beliefs of Vietnamese pre-service teachers of English as a foreign language. *System*, 96(102422), 1–14. 10.1016/j.system.2020.102422

Holliday, A. (2006). Native-speakerism. *ELT Journal*, 60(4), 385–387. 10.1093/elt/ccl030

Irie, K. (2022). Self-efficacy. In T. Gregersen & S. Mercer (Eds.), *The Routledge handbook of the psychology of language learning and teaching* (pp. 100–110). Routledge.

Karas, M., & Faez, F. (2021). Self-efficacy of English language teachers in Ontario: The impact of language proficiency, teaching qualifications, linguistic identity, and teaching experience. *The Canadian Modern Language Review, 77*(2), 110–128. 10.3138/cmlr-2020-0012

Klassen, R.M., Tze, V.M.C., Betts, S.M., & Gordon, K.A. (2011). Teacher efficacy research 1998-2009: Signs of progress or unfulfilled promise? *Educational Psychology Review, 23*, 21–43. https://link.springer.com/article/10.1007/s10648-010-9141-8

Markova, Z. (2021). Towards a comprehensive conceptualisation of teachers' self-efficacy beliefs. *Cambridge Journal of Education, 51*(5), 653–671. 10.1080/0305764X.2021.1906844

Maslow, A.H. (1943). A theory of human motivation. *Psychological Review, 50*(4), 370–396. 10.1037/h0054346

Mercer, S. (2008). Learner self-beliefs. *ELT Journal, 62*(2), 182–183. 10.1093/elt/ccn001

Mills, N.A. (2004). *Self-efficacy of college intermediate French students: Relation to motivation, achievement, and proficiency* [Unpublished doctoral dissertation]. Emory University.

Mills, N. (2014). Self-efficacy in second language acquisition. In S. Mercer & M. Williams (Eds.), *Multiple perspectives on the self in SLA* (pp. 6–22). Multilingual Matters.

Mills, N., Pajares, F., & Herron, C. (2008). A reevaluation of the role of anxiety: Self-efficacy, anxiety, and their relation to reading and listening proficiency. *Foreign Language Annals, 39*(2), 276–295. 10.1111/j.1944-9720.2006.tb02266.x

Oxford, R. (1990). *Language learning strategies.* Newbury House.

Pajares, F.M. (1992). Teachers' beliefs and educational research: Cleaning up a messy construct. *Review of Educational Research, 62*(3), 307–332. http://journals.sagepub.com/doi/abs/10.3102/00346543062003307

Pajares, F. (1996). Self-efficacy beliefs in academic settings. *Review of Educational Research, 66*(4), 543–578. 10.3102/00346543066004543

Pajares, F., & Schunk, D.H. (2005). Self-efficacy and self-concept beliefs: Jointly contributing to the quality of human life. In H.W. Marsh, R.G. Craven, & D.H. MacInery (Eds.), *New frontiers for self-research* (pp. 95–122). Information Age Publishing.

Pintrich, P.R., & Schunk, D.H. (1996). *Motivation in education: Theory, research and applications.* Prentice Hall.

Rogers, C.R. (1951). *Client-centered therapy.* Constable.

Rotter, J. (1966). Generalized expectancies for internal versus external control of reinforcement. *Psychological Monographs, 80*(1), 1–28. https://psycnet.apa.org/record/2011-19211-001

Şahin, F.E., & Atay, D. (2010). Sense of efficacy from student teaching to the induction year. *Procedia – Social and Behavioral Sciences, 2*(2), 337–341. 10.1016/j.sbspro.2010.03.021

Schunk, D.H. (1991). Self-efficacy and academic motivation. *Educational Psychologist*, *26*, 207–231. https://psycnet.apa.org/doi/10.1207/s15326985ep2603&4_2

Shavelson, R.J., Hubner, J.J., & Stanton, J.C. (1976). Self-concept: Validation of construct interpretations. *Review of Educational Research*, *46*(3), 407–441. 10.3102/00346543046003407

Skinner, E.A. (1996). A guide to constructs of control. *Journal of Personality and Social Psychology*, *71*(3), 549–570. 10.1037/0022-3514.71.3.549

Thompson, G. (2020). *Exploring language teacher efficacy in Japan*. Multilingual Matters.

Tschannen-Moran, M., & Woolfolk Hoy, A. (2001). Teacher efficacy: Capturing an elusive construct. *Teaching and Teacher Education*, *17*(7), 783–805. 10.1016/S0742-051X(01)00036-1

Tschannen-Moran, M., Woolfolk Hoy, A., & Hoy, W.K. (1998). Teacher efficacy: Its meaning and measure. *Review of Educational Research*, *68*(2), 202–248. 10.3102/00346543068002202

Wang, C. (2004). *Self-regulated learning strategies and self-efficacy beliefs of children learning English as a second language* [Unpublished doctoral dissertation]. Ohio State University.

Wang, C., Schwab, G., Fenn, P., & Chang, M. (2013). Self-efficacy and self-regulated learning strategies for English language learners: Comparison between Chinese and German college students. *Journal of Educational and Developmental Psychology*, *3*(1), 173–191. https://www.ccsenet.org/journal/index.php/jedp/article/view/26477

Wang, C., & Sun, T. (2020). Relationship between self-efficacy and language proficiency: A meta-analysis. *System*, *95*, 102366. 10.1016/j.system.2020.102366

Wheatley, K.F. (2005). The case for reconceptualizing teacher efficacy research. *Teaching and Teacher Education*, *21*(7), 747–766. 10.1016/j.tate.2005.05.009

Wyatt, M. (2010). An English teacher's developing self-efficacy beliefs in using groupwork. *System*, *38*(4), 603–613. https://www.sciencedirect.com/science/article/pii/S0346251X10001120

Wyatt, M. (2013). Overcoming low self-efficacy beliefs in teaching English to young learners. *International Journal of Qualitative Studies in Education*, *26*(2), 238–255. http://www.tandfonline.com/doi/abs/10.1080/09518398.2011.605082

Wyatt, M. (2014). Towards a re-conceptualization of teachers' self-efficacy beliefs: Tackling enduring problems with the quantitative research and moving on. *International Journal of Research and Method in Education*, *37*(2), 166–189. http://www.tandfonline.com/doi/abs/10.1080/1743727X.2012.742050

Wyatt, M. (2015). Using qualitative research methods to assess the degree of fit between teachers' reported self-efficacy beliefs and their practical knowledge during teacher education. *Australian Journal of Teacher Education*, *40*(1), Art 7, 1–30. http://ro.ecu.edu.au/ajte/vol40/iss1/7/

Wyatt, M. (2016). "Are they becoming more reflective and/or efficacious?" A conceptual model mapping how teachers' self-efficacy beliefs might grow. *Educational Review*, *68*(1), 114–137. http://www.tandfonline.com/doi/abs/10.1080/00131911.2015.1058754

Wyatt, M. (2018a). Language teachers' self-efficacy beliefs: An introduction. In S. Mercer & A. Kostoulas (Eds.), *Language teacher psychology* (pp. 122–140). Multilingual Matters. http://www.multilingual-matters.com/display.asp?K=9781783099450

Wyatt, M. (2018b). Language teachers' self-efficacy beliefs: A review of the literature (2005–2016). *Australian Journal of Teacher Education*, 43(4), 92–120. 10.14221/ajte.2018v43n4.6

Wyatt, M. (2021). Research into second language learners' and teachers' self-efficacy beliefs: Making the connections. *TESOL Quarterly*, 55(1), 298–307. https://onlinelibrary.wiley.com/doi/full/10.1002/tesq.3010

Wyatt, M. (2022). Self-efficacy. In S. Li, P. Hiver & M. Papi (Eds.), *The Routledge handbook of second language acquisition and individual differences* (pp. 207–219). Routledge. https://www.taylorfrancis.com/chapters/edit/10.4324/9781003270546-17/self-efficacy-mark-wyatt

Wyatt, M. (forthcoming). Language teachers' self-efficacy beliefs (2010–2020): A systematic review. In Z. Tajeddin & T.S.C. Farrell (Eds.), *Handbook of language teacher education: Critical reviews and research syntheses*. Springer.

Wyatt, M., & Dikilitaş, K. (2016). English language teachers becoming more efficacious through research engagement at their Turkish university. *Educational Action Research*, 24(4), 550–570. http://www.tandfonline.com/doi/abs/10.1080/09650792.2015.1076731

Wyatt, M., & Dikilitaş, K. (2021). English language teachers' self-efficacy beliefs for grammar instruction: Implications for teacher educators. *The Language Learning Journal*, 49(5), 541–553. 10.1080/09571736.2019.1642943

Zimmerman, B.J. (2000). Self-efficacy: An essential motive to learn. *Contemporary Educational Psychology*, 25, 82–91. 10.1006/ceps.1999.1016

Part 1

# Synthesizing the literature to expand understanding of language teachers' self-efficacy beliefs

# 2 Language teacher self-efficacy surveys

What have we learned? Where are we going?

*Michael Karas, Takumi Uchihara, and Farahnaz Faez*

## Introduction

Much of language teacher self-efficacy (LTSE) research has involved the use of surveys (Wyatt, 2018). Early LTSE research (e.g., Chacón, 2005; Shim, 2001) utilized general education measures to capture language teachers' confidence in their teaching capabilities, but as the field has developed, more recent studies have generated their own more domain-specific scales (e.g., Thompson & Woodman, 2019). This growth in research has precipitated numerous syntheses in LTSE research as a way to further understand the growing literature. Syntheses of LTSE research have taken broad overviews of the field (Wyatt, 2018, forthcoming), looked at LTSE in foreign language (FL) contexts (Hoang, 2018), and even examined the relationship between proficiency and self-efficacy (Faez & Karas, 2017; Faez et al., 2021). Following this line of work, this chapter presents a synthesis of surveys used in LTSE research. It begins with an overview of scales used in LTSE research. Next, it focuses on teachers' levels of self-efficacy based on these scales and considers how demographic and methodological variables may impact these levels. Finally, it investigates how levels of self-efficacy can be classified as "high", "medium", or "low" based on these previous results.

## Literature review

Early LTSE work was heavily influenced by general education. As such, it followed the quantitative tradition in general teacher self-efficacy work and utilized self-efficacy scales as the primary means to assess LTSE. The most prominent scale used is the Teachers' Sense of Efficacy Scale (TSES) created by Tschannen-Moran and Woolfolk Hoy (2001). Developed at Ohio State University, the TSES consists of short-form 12-item and long-form 24-item versions that assess teacher self-efficacy across 3 subscales of Student Engagement, Classroom Management, and Instructional Strategies. LTSE researchers have utilized the TSES in many studies in its original form or by slightly changing the wording of items to make the scale more applicable to language teaching or even altering the subscales themselves. However, more recent research has seen researchers develop their own self-efficacy scales to move beyond the field's reliance on general education measures.

The heavy use of general education scales in LTSE has generated discussion about how specific scales need to be and what exactly they are measuring. Ideally, self-efficacy scales should include task-specific items that are context- and domain-specific (Bandura, 1997). However, when LTSE researchers rely on general measures, some of this specificity is lost. The TSES subscales address many issues that are common to any teaching context, but they do not address many of the specifics of language teaching. This is best displayed by showing examples of items and how they have developed over time. For example, the first item on the TSES for Instructional Strategies is:

- To what extent can you use a variety of assessment strategies? (Tschannen-Moran & Woolfolk Hoy, 2001, p. 800).

While this item addresses the issue of assessment, it is not specific to language teaching and there is no focus on specific assessment items, making it more of a global item (Wyatt, 2016). To make items more domain-specific, authors have added words/phrases to make TSES items more focused on the language classroom. For example, Chacón (2005) adjusted the above item to:

- How much can you use a variety of assessment strategies in your English classroom? (Chacón, 2005, p. 263).

These types of changes are frequent across studies that use the TSES as researchers attempt to enhance the specificity of items for their studies and provide participants with more information to assess their abilities. In our view, this type of change does not drastically change the meaning of the item, which is why studies like Chacón's (2005) that make minor adjustments are categorized as "Original TSES" (described further below) in this synthesis.

Alternatively, in order to address teaching tasks specific to their studies, authors have added/removed items from the TSES to make the scale more appropriate for their contexts. Choi and Lee (2016) do this but maintain the TSES factor structure. For example, they add the following item to the Classroom Management subscale of the TSES:

- I can create an atmosphere that encourages students to use English freely (Choi & Lee, 2016, p. 62).

Other studies add new subscales to the TSES to address context-specific issues, e.g., Praver (2014), who added the subscale of "Dealing with Supervisors" in Japan. Meanwhile, others remove TSES subscales not pertinent to their contexts, e.g., Best (2014), who removed the Classroom Management subscale. While these studies still use the TSES, these modifications are greater as they either alter the subscales/factors themselves with different items or even alter the entire scale structure with new subscales. These types of studies were categorized as "Modified TSES" in the analysis.

Studies that have moved beyond the TSES show how authors have addressed more specific issues in language teaching. While the assessment item noted above falls under "Instructional Strategies" on the TSES, domain-specific scales have focused much more on Assessment. Akbari and Tavassoli (2014) dedicate a subscale to Efficacy in Classroom Assessment and Materials, while Karas (2019) has a subscale for Assessment on its own. A sample item is:

- I can connect assessments to stated learning objectives (Karas, 2019, p. 90).

In using this, along with five other Assessment items, Karas (2019) provides an example of how researchers can focus on different teaching areas and explore them in-depth. Alternatively, in studies such as Zhang (2018), which focus on specific elements of L2 teaching, in this case pronunciation, we see items specified to match skill areas beyond general L2 instruction. Again, using assessment as an example, one sample item reads:

- I can assess students' pronunciation learning outcomes through multiple tasks, such as reading tasks, spontaneous interaction, presentations, etc. (Zhang, 2018, p. 146).

Both Karas (2019) and Zhang (2018) provide examples of how studies have strived to make L2 self-efficacy scales more domain- and task-specific. Karas (2019) focuses on general L2 teaching across six subscales, while Zhang (2018) enhances specificity and focuses on pronunciation instruction, a more specific domain of L2 teaching. Similarly, Wyatt and Dikilitaş (2021) focus on grammar instruction. For studies that generate their own items, there is a clear effort to address the more context-, domain-, and task-specific elements of LTSE.

Wyatt (2016) notes that often quantitative research on LTSE presents global self-efficacy scores, which are generated from task-specific items. These global scores, which are part of the focus of this study, are less predictive of actual behaviour but still useful to assess teachers' overall self-efficacy more broadly. These levels of self-efficacy are reported as numerical values, with most studies following Tschannen-Moran et al.'s (1998) theoretical interpretation of self-efficacy that has higher scores as an indication of enhanced teacher self-efficacy.

However, it is not easy to interpret what these levels of self-efficacy mean. When looking at descriptive levels of self-efficacy, studies often note self-efficacy subscale scores in comparison with each other (i.e., which subscale is higher or lower than the other) or describe overall scores in a general manner (e.g., "relatively high", Choi & Lee, 2016, p. 55). Since studies use different scales and measures, it is not always easy to determine if a self-efficacy score is actually "high" or "low" as some form of comparison is required. This synthesis sought to address this by looking at levels of self-efficacy across LTSE studies to see what might be considered higher or lower levels of self-efficacy.

## Methodology

This study is guided by the following research questions:

1 What scales have been used in LTSE research?
2 Based on these scales, what are the levels of self-efficacy for teachers?
3 How do different demographic and methodological variables affect levels of self-efficacy?
4 Based on these levels, what can be considered "high", "medium", and "low" self-efficacy?

In order to find suitable manuscripts, literature searches were conducted with major databases: Linguistics and Language Behaviour Abstracts (LLBA), ProQuest Education, and ProQuest Dissertations. Searches were also conducted on Google and Google Scholar. Finally, previous syntheses (e.g., Faez et al., 2021; Wyatt, 2018, forthcoming) on LTSE were reviewed for studies.

This study took an inclusive approach and included as many suitable manuscripts as possible. This allows for the examination of a large number of manuscripts, and research quality is for the reader to decide (Norris & Ortega, 2006). Studies were included if they met the following criteria:

1 The study focused on language teachers and/or prospective language teachers. Teachers of other subjects were not included. Studies that included teachers of different subjects (i.e., not language teachers) with English language learners were also excluded.
2 The study included a quantitatively based LTSE scale. Mixed methods studies were also included. Studies that used general self-efficacy scales that look at human functioning more broadly were excluded.

3 Sufficient statistical information was included in the study to allow for analysis. For example, descriptive statistics of levels of self-efficacy needed to be included in the study.
4 The study was written in English. While we would have liked to include literature in other languages, we were unable to do so.

*Coding scheme*

Studies were coded for the following categories:

- Identification (year, type of publication, methodology – quantitative or mixed methods),
- Study location
  - FL vs. second language (SL),
  - type of school (primary, secondary, postsecondary, private, language teacher education [LTE] programme), number of schools, and target language,
- Participants (number, gender, pre-service vs. in-service, age, experience, degree level, degree type, first language [L1], and native speaker status), and
- Measure of self-efficacy (scale type, scale points, number of items, item phrasing, number of subscales, language, reliability, and use of factor analysis).

*Analysis*

Analysis for the first research question involved reviewing the numerous scales used in LTSE research and categorizing them. For research questions 2, 3, and 4, looking at levels of self-efficacy, analysis focused on using descriptive statistics. Means and standard deviations of levels of self-efficacy were recorded when provided or calculated by hand. Some studies provide overall scores for the entire scale. Other studies only provide subscale scores or even only individual item scores. Whenever possible, reported scores were used, but some scores were calculated by hand using means of subscales and/or items. These were then converted into percentages for comparison. Thus, below, mean percentage scores, standard deviations, and 95% confidence intervals (CIs) are provided.

Some studies included pre- and post-test designs. For analysis, the most recent result was used to avoid using two scores from the same group of participants. This may have raised the level of self-efficacy as some studies included significant differences between pre- and post-tests. However, not all studies showed differences and there is evidence that self-efficacy can even decrease after interventions (e.g., Kissau, 2012). Thus, while we acknowledge there may be a training effect, the most recent self-efficacy score was used for analysis when calculating the overall scores. For the final research question that looked to understand levels of self-efficacy as high, medium, or low, all scores were included to have a full view of the range of scores included in this sample of studies.

## Results

### Study sample information

This sample included a total of 83 studies. Across these studies, the sample included 15,508 participants ($M$ = 187, $SD$ = 229) across a total of 246 schools ($M$ = 9.11, $SD$ = 18.4 per study that provided this information). The majority of studies took place in Iran ($n$ = 29), followed by Türkiye ($n$ = 13), the United States ($n$ = 12), China ($n$ = 4), and Japan ($n$ = 4), as well as a host of other locations (e.g., Venezuela, Ethiopia, Thailand, and Croatia). The teachers had a mean experience of 8.47 years of teaching ($SD$ = 6.32). See Table 2.1 for further study sample information.

### Language teacher self-efficacy scales

The first research question sought to determine which LTSE scales have been utilized. Without question, the most commonly used scale remains the TSES from Tschannen-Moran and Woolfolk Hoy (2001). A total of 50 studies utilized the TSES in virtually its original form with little to no modification.

*Table 2.1* Study sample information

| | |
|---|---|
| Methodology | Quantitative ($n$ = 50) |
| | Mixed methods ($n$ = 33) |
| Type of publication | Journal articles ($n$ = 66) |
| | Dissertations ($n$ = 14) |
| | Conference proceedings ($n$ = 2) |
| | Book chapter ($n$ = 1) |
| Context | Foreign language ($n$ = 69) |
| | Foreign/second language ($n$ = 8) |
| | Second language ($n$ = 6) |
| Language focus | English ($n$ = 69) |
| | Mixed languages ($n$ = 9) |
| | French ($n$ = 3) |
| | Spanish ($n$ = 1) |
| | Chinese ($n$ = 1) |
| Teachers | In-service ($n$ = 67) |
| | Pre-service ($n$ = 11) |
| | Mixed ($n$ = 5) |

These were categorized as "Original TSES" as they utilized the TSES with no modifications or made minor changes like in the Chacón (2005) example noted above. On top of this, a further 15 studies used the TSES but made significant modifications to it by adding/removing items or even adding and removing different subscales. As these changes were more substantial, this group was categorized as "Modified TSES", such as the Choi and Lee (2016) example noted above. Thus, in this sample, a total of 65 studies (78%) used the TSES in some form, and this does not even include studies that drew inspiration from TSES items for their own surveys (e.g., Thompson & Woodman, 2019). However, it should be noted that some studies that used the TSES and were classified into these two TSES categories also used other scales. For example, Swanson (2012) uses the TSES in its original form (i.e., Original TSES) but also uses the Second/Foreign Language Teacher Efficacy Scale (S/FLTES) developed by the author (Swanson, 2010a).

The final group consisted of 18 studies that used different surveys but did not use the TSES. This group was labelled as "Other Scales" as they utilized a different scale/subscale beyond the TSES and did not use the TSES with any of its original factors. The examples of Karas (2019), Zhang (2018), and Wyatt and Dikilitaş (2021) discussed above fall into this category. Thus, for the total 83 studies, there were 50 Original TSES, 15 Modified TSES, and 18 Other Scales included in this synthesis. (Please see https://www.researchgate.net/publication/375952459_LTSE_Synthesis_-_Included_Studies for a full list of the 83 studies so categorized.) Those of the 83 studies explicitly mentioned in this chapter have been asterisked in the references.

It should be noted that the classification of scales is not simple. As already mentioned, if a study included the TSES, it was grouped into one of the TSES categories. Of the 18 studies in the Other Scales category, 3 use a previously designed measure (Karimvand, 2011; Liu & Wang, 2021; Shim, 2001), 2 studies have a broader focus beyond LTSE but created self-efficacy subscales for their studies (Kormos & Nijakowska, 2017; Nishino, 2012), while another 2 focused on sub-areas of language teaching (grammar, Wyatt & Dikilitaş, 2021; pronunciation, Zhang, 2018). Table 2.2 highlights newly developed scales that broadly focus on LTSE; the studies cited above are not included in this table as they use previous measures or have a more specific focus beyond general language teaching. However, as noted, at times, researchers have created their own scales but also used the TSES. Thus, Table 2.2 describes newly formed LTSE measures with 10 studies from the Other Scales category and 2 studies from the TSES categories (Kissau, 2012; Swanson, 2012) that generated new measures while using the original TSES.

*Common scales/subscales across studies*

Looking at the newly developed scales and subscales (Table 2.2), it is interesting to note some of the similarities across these new measures. For

Table 2.2 Newly formed LTSE scales

| *LTSE scale and source | Description | Subscales (No. of items in brackets) |
|---|---|---|
| Teacher efficacy (Chiang, 2008) | To our knowledge, the first LTSE scale not based on a general measure. A study-specific scale developed in Taiwan with 30 items and no subscales. | • NA |
| Second/foreign language teacher efficacy scale (S/FLTES) (Swanson, 2010a, 2012) | Originally developed by Swanson (2010a), it consisted of two subscales with 10 items, but a third was added in the 2012 study (Culture) for 14 total items. Scale developed with North American language teachers. | • Teacher as facilitator (6)<br>• Content knowledge (4)<br>• Culture (4) |
| Efficacy (Faez & Valeo, 2012) | A study-specific scale with 20 items drawn from the local teacher accreditation requirements of adult ESL teachers in Ontario, Canada assessing LTSE with no subscales. | • NA |
| Exploratory items (Kissau, 2012) Also used in Kissau & Algozzine (2014) | A 5-item scale utilized alongside the TSES in Kissau's studies. Items were generated by the author in the United States. | • NA |
| English Language Teachers' Sense of Self-Efficacy Scale (EL-TSES) (Yaman et al., 2013) | Developed in Türkiye, the scale includes 22 items across 4 subscales. | • Observing and Assessing the Language Development (7)<br>• Cooperating with the School, Personnel, Colleagues, Family, and Society (3)<br>• Organizing Appropriate Methods and Techniques for a Suitable Classroom Atmosphere (8)<br>• Professional Development (3) |

| | | |
|---|---|---|
| ELT teacher efficacy instrument (ELTEI) (Akbari & Tavassoli, 2014) Also adapted by Kaygisiz et al. (2018) | Utilizing vignettes and developed in Iran, the 32-item scale consists of 7 subscales. | • Efficacy in Classroom Management and Remedial Action (8)<br>• Efficacy in Classroom Assessment and Materials (5)<br>• Efficacy in Skill and Proficiency Adjustment (7)<br>• Efficacy in Teaching and Correcting Language Components (5)<br>• Efficacy in Age Adjustment (3)<br>• Efficacy in Social Adaptation (2)<br>• Core Efficacy (2) |
| European portfolio for student teachers of languages (EPOSTL) (Bergil & Sarıçoban, 2017) | The EPOSTL was developed by the Council of Europe and adapted for Bergil and Sarıçoban's (2017) study in Türkiye with 195 items. It is not clear how many items per subscale. | • Context<br>• Methodology<br>• Resources<br>• Lesson Planning<br>• Conducting a Lesson<br>• Independent Learning<br>• Assessment of Learning |
| Teacher efficacy (Cooke & Faez, 2018) | Focused on French as a Second Language (FSL) teachers in Canada, this scale consists of 24 items across 4 subscales drawn from a document that outlined areas of competency required for effective FSL instruction in Canada. | • General Teaching Methodology (8)<br>• L2 Pedagogy (8)<br>• Language Proficiency (5)<br>• Cultural Knowledge (3) |
| English language teacher self-efficacy scale (EL-TSES) (Karas, 2019) | Drawing on data from English teachers around the globe, the scale has 26 items drawn from various TESOL standards documents across six subscales. | • Classroom Proficiency (7)<br>• Learner-Focused Instruction (3)<br>• Assessment (6)<br>• Language Instruction (4)<br>• Culture (3)<br>• Materials (3) |

(*Continued*)

Table 2.2 (Continued)

| *LTSE scale and source | Description | Subscales (No. of items in brackets) |
|---|---|---|
| Japanese teacher of English efficacy scale (JTE-TES) (Thompson & Woodman, 2019) | Created in the Japanese context, the scale has 15 items across 5 subscales. | • Using English (4)<br>• Communicative Teaching (3)<br>• Teamwork (3)<br>• Student Achievement (3)<br>• Managing Workload (2) |
| EFL teachers' self-efficacy beliefs (Hoang & Wyatt, 2021) | Drawing on items from the TSES and study-specific items, this 23-item scale has 6 subscales. Scale developed in Vietnam. | • Motivational English Instruction (8)<br>• Developing English teaching materials (4)<br>• Communicative English (3)<br>• Managing Classroom Activities (3)<br>• Managing Misbehaviors (2)<br>• Teaching Exam Oriented English (3) |
| Self-efficacy in application of professional standards for K-12 Chinese Language Teachers (Polin, 2021) | A 15-item scale with no subscales drawn from professional standards document for K-12 Chinese teachers in the United States. | • NA |

* For some scales, there was a specific intention to name the measure (e.g., Akbari & Tavassoli, 2014), but other studies simply used "self-efficacy" or general terms to describe the measure.

example, many scales have attempted to incorporate proficiency in some way. Early studies measured self-efficacy and proficiency with different scales (Faez et al., 2021), but Swanson (2010a) attempted to incorporate proficiency as part of self-efficacy with the Content Knowledge subscale. Others have followed, with subscales such as L2 Self-Confidence (Nishino, 2012), Language Proficiency (Cooke & Faez, 2018), Oral English Use (Lee, 2009), Classroom Proficiency (Karas, 2019), and Using English (Thompson & Woodman, 2019). All of these address the importance of language proficiency for LTSE in some manner. Some of these studies still use general proficiency measures as well in their studies (e.g., Karas, 2019). However, with these new measures, many attempt to address the interconnected nature of L2 teaching and target language proficiency as language serves as both the medium and content of instruction (Freeman, 2017; Richards, 2017). From this perspective, one's self-efficacy to enact various classroom tasks must also be investigated in relation to one's ability to complete that task in the target language.

There are other similarities across subscales. For example, Nishino (2012), Hoang and Wyatt (2021), and Thompson and Woodman (2019) have measures that deal with communicative language teaching (CLT). CLT, while popular in western contexts, is still a teaching approach that some teachers can find difficult as it requires a high level of proficiency and much focus on student-centred classroom activities, which some teachers can find intimidating. Materials development also features in some studies. For both Karas (2019) and Hoang and Wyatt (2021), subscales on material development and use emerged after factor analysis, and materials also feature in Akbari and Tavassoli (2014). Culture also features prominently, as language and culture are heavily intertwined. Swanson (2010a) originally did not have a Culture subscale on the S/FLTES, but it was added and confirmed by factor analysis in a later study (Swanson, 2012). Other studies have again followed suit and utilized subscales that address culture in some way: Cultural Instruction (Parks, 2021); Culture (Karas, 2019); and Cultural Knowledge (Cooke & Faez, 2018).

Other subscales are similar to some of the subscales found in the TSES. Classroom management features prominently in Akbari and Tavassoli (2014) as well as Hoang and Wyatt (2021). Instruction is dealt with in different ways. Kissau (2012) utilized five Exploratory Items that focused on general L2 instruction, while Cooke and Faez (2018) included items under L2 Pedagogy. For Karas (2019), these items were listed under Language Instruction. Wyatt and Dikilitaş's (2021) study focusing on grammar instruction had items that align with factors generally associated with inductive and deductive grammar instruction. Zhang's (2018) study on pronunciation broke items down based on general instructional strategies but also based on segmental and suprasegmental elements. Thus, while there are nuances across studies, instruction has certainly been addressed with new scales/subscales and with many more

L2 teaching-specific items. Measures that are comparable to the TSES subscale of Student Engagement are also found, although perhaps not as commonly. For example, Karas (2019) includes Learner-Focused Instruction as a subscale. As can be seen, LTSE researchers have created many new scales and subscales that address various L2 teaching tasks.

*Levels of self-efficacy*

The second and third research questions investigate teachers' levels of self-efficacy and how methodological and demographic variables may impact these levels. This analysis looked at comparisons of studies that used similar scales but sought to look at potential differences/similarities across self-efficacy levels when comparing different measures.

*Original TSES*

A total of N = 50 studies with $k$ = 57 effect sizes utilized either the short ($k$ = 20) or long-form ($k$ = 37) TSES with its original factor structure and items. Most studies utilized the 9-point Likert scale ($k$ = 26) used in the original TSES study (Tschannen-Moran & Woolfolk Hoy, 2001), while others used a 5-point scale ($k$ = 25). All of Swanson's (2010a, 2010b, 2012, 2013, 2014) studies utilized a 101-point Likert scale (i.e., 0–100) ($k$ = 5) while Huangfu (2012) was the sole study to use a 6-point Likert scale. Most studies appeared to use the original English language version of the scale ($k$ = 46), while others used the Turkish version ($k$ = 5) or had the TSES translated into Chinese ($k$ = 1), Thai ($k$ = 1) or Farsi ($k$ = 1). In this category, all items were phrased as questions as in the original TSES (e.g., To what extent ... ?).

Internal consistency estimates were not always reported, but the mean Cronbach alpha ($M$ = .87, $SD$ = .07, CI [.85, .89]) for the overall TSES further supported the TSES's high internal consistency across studies. The mean Cronbach alphas for the TSES subscales were also strong for Student Engagement ($M$ = .81, $SD$ = .06, CI [.79, .84]), Classroom Management ($M$ = .84, $SD$ = .06, CI [.81, .87]), and Instructional Strategies ($M$ = .82, $SD$ = .06, CI [.80, .85]), indicating the subscales showed high internal consistency as well. Ten studies ($k$ = 10) using the original TSES employed some form of factor analysis as well, with results further enhancing the TSES's solid 3-factor structure.

Looking at the total Original TSES sample, the adjusted percentage score for the overall scale was $M$ = 75.5 ($SD$ = 10.9, CI [72.6, 78.4]). The subscale scores were similar for the studies that used the Original TSES: Student Engagement ($M$ = 74.5, $SD$ = 8.11, CI [71.9, 77.2]), Classroom Management ($M$ = 77.1, $SD$ = 12.3, CI [74.1, 80.1]), and Instructional

*Table 2.3* A comparison of the 12-item and 24-item scales

|  | Student engagement | Classroom management | Instructional strategies | Overall TSES score |
|---|---|---|---|---|
| 12-item TSES | M = 74.9<br>SD = 10.9<br>CI [69.3, 80.5] | M = 77.7<br>SD = 13.0<br>CI [71.0, 84.4] | M = 79.9<br>SD = 12.6<br>CI [73.4, 86.3] | M = 75.9<br>SD = 13.9<br>CI [69.4, 82.4] |
| 24-item TSES | M = 74.3<br>SD = 5.35<br>CI [71.9, 76.6] | M = 76.7<br>SD = 4.86<br>CI [74.5, 78.8] | M = 76.2<br>SD = 6.14<br>CI [73.5, 78.9] | M = 75.3<br>SD = 9.09<br>CI [72.3, 78.3] |

TSES subscale results based on 12-item ($k$ = 17) and 24-item ($k$ = 24) scores. Overall TSES results based on 12-item ($k$ = 20) and 24-item ($k$ = 37) scores.

Strategies ($M$ = 77.8, $SD$ = 11.8, CI [74.7, 80.9]). Table 2.3 outlines the comparison of the 12-item and 24-item scales. The 24-item scale was used more frequently compared to the 12-item scale, but the results across the overall scale and subscale scores are very similar. However, the standard deviation was larger for the short-form studies, suggesting there is a wider range of self-efficacy scores within the short-form studies.

Comparing studies that used a 5-point Likert scale ($k$ = 25) with studies using the original 9-point Likert scale ($k$ = 26), there was little difference in the overall means for 5-point ($M$ = 74.6, $SD$ = 10.7, CI [70.2, 79.0]) and 9-point scales ($M$ = 75.0, $SD$ = 12.0, CI [70.1, 79.9]), suggesting scale length did not impact these studies. However, for Swanson's studies that utilized a 101-point Likert scale, the mean score was higher ($M$ = 82.2, $SD$ = 2.67, CI [78.8, 83.6]), indicating there may be an impact when utilizing wider-ranging scales.

Looking at scale points in regard to the TSES subscales, there was some difference in the mean scores for studies that used a 5-point Likert scale ($k$ = 18) and studies that used a 9-point Likert scale ($k$ = 15): Student Engagement ($M$ = 73.3 vs. $M$ = 75.2), Classroom Management ($M$ = 74.8 vs. 78.4), and Instructional Strategies ($M$ = 74.9 vs. 77.5), with studies using 9-point Likert scales having slightly higher means. Similar to overall results, studies that used the larger 101-point Likert scale showed higher means across the TSES subscales (SE $M$ = 77.3, CM $M$ = 80.9, IS $M$ = 88.3), with Instructional Strategies being notably higher.

Regarding study location, many locations only appeared one time (e.g., Venezuela, Ethiopia) in the data set, but there was sufficient data for comparison between Iran, Türkiye, and the United States (see Table 2.4). Studies from Iran showed lower means across the overall scale and TSES subscales compared to results from Türkiye and the United States. This gap was especially noteworthy for Instructional Strategies, as teachers in the United States showed much higher levels of self-efficacy on this subscale.

34  *Michael Karas et. al*

*Table 2.4* A comparison of Iran, Türkiye, and the United States

|  | Student engagement | Classroom management | Instructional strategies | Overall TSES score |
|---|---|---|---|---|
| Iran | M = 70.7<br>SD = 12.1<br>CI [63.0, 78.4] | M = 72.8<br>SD = 13.5<br>CI [64.3, 81.4] | M = 71.4<br>SD = 12.8<br>CI [63.3, 79.5] | M = 72.3<br>SD = 14.2<br>CI [66.3, 78.3] |
| Türkiye | M = 78.2<br>SD = 5.68<br>CI [73.4, 82.9] | M = 79.3<br>SD = 6.31<br>CI [74.0, 84.6] | M = 79.6<br>SD = 6.48<br>CI [74.2, 85.0] | M = 79.2<br>SD = 5.31<br>CI [75.1, 83.2] |
| United States | M = 77.6<br>SD = 2.47<br>CI [75.0,80.2] | M = 82.5<br>SD = 7.4<br>CI [74.7, 90.2] | M = 87.9<br>SD = 2.12<br>CI [85.7, 90.1] | M = 82.4<br>SD = 2.68<br>CI [80.0, 84.9] |

TSES scores by location. Subscale scores based on Iran ($k$ = 12), Türkiye ($k$ = 8), and the United States ($k$ = 6). Overall scores based on Iran ($k$ = 24), Türkiye ($k$ = 9), and the United States ($k$ = 7).

Finally, there was little difference between effects with in-service teachers ($k$ = 46, $M$ = 75.3, $SD$ = 12, CI [71.7, 78.8]) and pre-service teachers ($k$ = 8, $M$ = 76.7, $SD$ = 3.83, CI [73.5, 79.9]), although it is interesting to note that the pre-service teacher mean was marginally higher.

*Modified TSES*

There were $n$ = 15 studies, with $k$ = 18 effect sizes, that made significant modifications to the TSES and thus warranted inclusion in this category. This category again saw variation in the scale points used for the surveys. Some used a 9-point scale ($k$ = 5), a 6-point scale ($k$ = 4), or a 5-point scale ($k$ = 6), while Parks (2021) used a 10-point scale. Interestingly, this category also saw further variation in the wording of self-efficacy items. As the authors made changes to the items in this category, they also made further modifications to the wording of items, utilizing questions ($k$ = 8), "I can" statements as advocated by Bandura (2006) ($k$ = 3), or "other" statements (e.g., I feel prepared; I am confident, etc.) ($k$ = 4).

Despite the modifications, the scales still showed strong overall internal consistency for the whole scale (Cronbach alpha $M$ = .88, $SD$ = .08, CI [.83, .93]) and for the modified subscales of Student Engagement ($M$ = .78, $SD$ = .07, CI [.72, .85]), Classroom Management ($M$ = .78, $SD$ = .07, CI [.70, .85]), and Instructional Strategies ($M$ = .80, $SD$ = .09, CI [.72, .89]).

The overall score for this sample was $M$ = 74.6, $SD$ = 11.1, CI [69.0, 80.1]. Looking at the TSES subscales, the scores were in a similar range: Student Engagement ($M$ = 72.8, $SD$ = 14.6, CI [65.6, 75.1]), Classroom Management ($M$ = 75.6, $SD$ = 8.77, CI [70.9, 80.3]), and Instructional Strategies ($M$ = 74.9, $SD$ = 12.4, CI [68.8, 81.1]). The lower Student

Engagement score is partially impacted by the scores in Praver (2014), as both native and non-native teachers in this study reported low confidence to engage with students. The sample was insufficient to conduct analysis based on the short and long-form scales and by study location.

*Other scales*

Comparison in this category was more difficult and often not possible because many of the measures have only been used a single time or focus on completely different LTSE domains. There were $k = 9$ "Study-Specific Scales" that broadly focused on L2 teaching self-efficacy that allowed for some comparison. These $k = 9$ scales that generally focused on L2 teaching self-efficacy had a mean Cronbach alpha of $M = .92$, $SD = .06$, CI [.87, .97], indicating high internal consistency. However, only $n = 4$ studies utilized factor analysis to generate their scales (Hoang & Wyatt, 2021; Karas, 2019; Thompson & Woodman, 2019; Yaman et al., 2013). Akbari and Tavasoli's (2014) scale also showed good consistency across two studies (Akbari & Tavassoli, 2014; Kaygisiz et al., 2018) ($M = .85$, $SD = .02$, CI [.65, 1.04]) and both studies utilized factor analysis. Thus, similar to TSES internal consistency scores, more domain-specific L2 measures also show strong internal consistency. Levels of self-efficacy are presented in Table 2.5.

*Levels of self-efficacy across scales*

Table 2.5 shows the comparison of the different levels of self-efficacy across different scales. It is interesting to note that the Original TSES and Modified TSES all have very similar overall adjusted mean scores. These scales, despite the range of modifications, are still originally based on a general education measure. On the other end, with scales developed specifically for L2 teacher self-efficacy, with the exception of Akbari and Tavasoli's (2014) scale which has only been used twice, the means seem to be higher. The table also includes the scales developed by Swanson (2012)

*Table 2.5* A comparison of the different levels of self-efficacy across different scales

| Scale | Mean | SD | 95% CI | Studies k | Sample |
|---|---|---|---|---|---|
| Original TSES | 75.5 | 10.9 | [72.6, 78.4] | $k = 57$ | Chacón (2005) |
| Modified TSES | 74.6 | 11.1 | [69.0, 80.1] | $k = 18$ | Choi & Lee (2016) |
| S/FLTES | 87.1 | 3.53 | [83.4, 90.8] | $k = 6$ | Swanson (2014) |
| ELTIS | 71.2 | 3.38 | [40.8, 102.0] | $k = 2$ | Akbari & Tavassoli (2014) |
| Exploratory Items | 83.6 | 6.68 | [67.0, 100.0] | $k = 3$ | Kissau (2012) |
| Study-Specific Scales | 79.3 | 7.01 | [73.9, 84.0] | $k = 9$ | Thompson & Woodman (2019) |

Adjusted mean scores of different scale groupings.

and Kissau (2012) that were used alongside the TSES. These scales also show higher means compared to the TSES. Thus, it appears that as teachers assess their self-efficacy with domain-specific LTSE measures, the scores appear to be higher. However, these results should be interpreted with caution. For the S/FLTES, these studies use a 101-point scale, which seems to impact the level of self-efficacy somewhat, and no overall scores were provided in S/FLTES studies. Furthermore, for studies that use the TSES, they often utilize questions for self-efficacy items. However, for the other scales, there was more of a diversity of options as some used questions, "I can" statements, or different statements altogether. Thus, while it is noteworthy to descriptively highlight the higher means for language-specific scales, this result could be due to a variety of factors not accounted for in this analysis.

*Categorizing levels of self-efficacy*

Based on these self-efficacy scores, the final research question explored if it is possible to have L2 teacher self-efficacy benchmarks that could offer researchers an indication if the reported levels of self-efficacy in their study are "high", "medium", or "low". This analysis inspected all of the scales combined. When looking at all of the overall scales, including all pre-tests and post-tests, and including the TSES, Modified TSES, and the "Other Scales", the mean is $M = 75.2$, $SD = 10.9$, and CI [73.2, 77.1]. The quartiles are also highly concentrated with 25th = 72.6, 50th = 77.2, and 75th = 81.8. Thus, no matter what the scale, it appears likely that many self-efficacy scores are in the 70–80 range, and if scores are below this, they could be considered low, and if they are above, they may be considered high.

The next analysis examined the specific subscales, including the TSES, Modified TSES, and the new subscales created with new scales. While overall self-efficacy is more abstract, the subscales represent a more focused domain of global self-efficacy around specific L2 teaching areas. For subscales, the scores were virtually the same ($M = 75.5$, $SD = 12$, CI [74.1, 77.0]). The 25th percentile was 72.8, 50th percentile was 77.1, and the 75th percentile was 82.2. Again, it appears that most subscale scores are between 70 and 80, after being converted to percentages.

## Discussion

The results of this synthesis coincide with the results in Wyatt (2018) in that the TSES remains the dominant scale used in LTSE research. Many studies have made modifications to the TSES, but many continue to use the TSES in its original form. The TSES 3-factor structure remains strong as many studies have confirmed it with different participant groups and subsequent factor analyses. While this attests to one of the TSES's strengths and can be appealing for researchers, it is important to consider the full implications of using the TSES. The TSES items were developed in the context of K-12 education in the United States and many items are quite global (Wyatt, 2016). The TSES is not domain-specific to language teaching and many important tasks for language teachers are not covered. It is also important to consider cultural implications as items may not be appropriate for all contexts and the presentation of TSES items may have the unintentional impact of imposing pedagogical norms on teachers and unduly promoting certain elements of teaching over others (Wyatt, 2021). Considering how much the TSES has been used, it is important for researchers to now fully examine the benefits and drawbacks of the tool. Considering the results of this study, what is left to be learned from the TSES for LTSE researchers? We do not advocate for researchers to not use the tool but rather argue researchers need to fully understand the TSES beyond its factor structure and use the tool only if it is truly informative for their study as there are now a plethora of new scales that have been developed specifically for/by LTSE researchers.

Many of these new scales can be used "as is", but we encourage researchers to utilize scales based on their study purpose and context, and if required, create new subscales or scales to fit their research. From the new scales noted in Table 2.2, we see distinct new subscales that address more focused areas of L2 teaching that the TSES and other general measures do not cover. New studies can experiment with these subscales and potentially use measures from a variety of studies to generate a "new" instrument. However, researchers should also feel encouraged to create their own scales if needed as there are now numerous studies that outline LTSE scale development for other researchers to follow. While factor analysis can be complicated and requires a large group of participants, we encourage researchers to utilize it when creating a scale along with measures of internal consistency (e.g., Cronbach alpha). However, there should also be a focus on the specific items to ensure they are clear, focused, and relevant to the teachers who are assessing their self-efficacy. A strong factor structure for a scale is important, but task-specific items that are clear and relevant to teachers are also necessary, especially to enhance the pedagogical implications for quantitative LTSE work. Research that focuses on even more specific elements of L2 teaching such as pronunciation (Zhang, 2018) and grammar (Wyatt & Dikilitaş, 2021) is also promising and can further enhance the practicality of quantitative LTSE work.

The levels of self-efficacy were often very similar. Few differences were noted between scores with the TSES. While the differences were not vast, more domain-specific scales that focused on specifics of L2 teaching seemed to show higher levels of self-efficacy. For example, this was seen with the

S/FLTES, Kissau's (2012) Exploratory Items, and the "Study-Specific" scales. This matches the results from Faez et al.'s (2021) meta-analysis looking at the relationship between proficiency and self-efficacy. In that meta-analysis, more domain-specific L2 scales showed higher correlations with proficiency compared with the TSES. Thus, similarly, it seems that when scales are more domain-specific and address more specific L2 teaching tasks, the levels of self-efficacy appear higher. However, as noted, this should be interpreted with caution as other elements (e.g., Likert Scale, participants) could also be at play.

Comparing across groups was not always possible due to the different measures. However, for the Original TSES, it was interesting to note the differences between Iran, Türkiye, and the United States in terms of overall scores. Using the TSES, there were notable differences across these three groups. Efficacy levels were reported to be higher in the United States than in Türkiye and Iran. One possible explanation for the difference may be cultural and contextual factors playing a role, which has been reported by teachers in general education (Klassen et al., 2009). Klassen et al. (2009) noted clear differences between teachers from East Asia and North America, and Praver (2014) also noted cultural elements in his study comparing Japanese and foreign English teachers in Japan. Cultural elements must be interpreted with caution, but it is important to note these results as researchers assess self-efficacy across different groups.

Finally, regarding the levels of self-efficacy, the scores were very concentrated between 70 and 80 for the overall scores and the subscale scores. These are only percentages, but it was interesting to note the tight range of the scores. Thus, scores between 70 and 80 appear to be somewhat common. Scores below this range may be considered "low" and scores above could be considered "high", but again, these are loose categorizations.

**Pedagogical implications**

Researchers have long noted the lack of pedagogical implications from quantitative (language) teacher self-efficacy research (Wheatley, 2005; Wyatt, 2014). This is an issue with these studies as it is not always easy to discern pedagogical implications from survey work, especially when looking at global scores. However, a look at some of the new scales does offer some insights.

The first noteworthy element is proficiency. Many studies seem to grapple with how to include proficiency as it is a key competency for language teachers (Richards, 2010). While some scales approach proficiency from a general proficiency perspective (i.e., not in relation to specific teaching tasks), many new scales address proficiency within efficacy items. For example, Lee (2009), Thompson and Woodman (2019), and Karas (2019) all include subscales that address proficiency but from a perspective that aligns with what Freeman et al. (2015) term "English-for-teaching". In other words, these studies ask teachers to assess their capabilities to teach *with* the language of instruction. This is something that is noteworthy for LTE. Teachers' proficiency in the language they teach remains a key skill for teachers, but LTE programmes should also emphasize the skill needed to teach in the language of instruction. As researchers have noted, this teacher language moves beyond linguistic capability and includes pedagogical and discursive ability as well (Richards, 2017). These newer measures may be helpful for all teachers as it may be useful for them to reflect on their abilities to enact various teaching tasks in the language of focus.

The emergence of factors related to materials is also noteworthy. In Karas (2019), Hoang and Wyatt (2021), and Akbari and Tavassoli (2014), after factor analysis, subscales related to materials emerged. This is noteworthy for language teacher educators and language teachers. Often, materials can be generic, uncreative, and inappropriate for different contexts (Bao, 2018), and teachers themselves need to skillfully adapt/adjust materials for their classrooms. The emergence of these factors perhaps indicates that it may be worthwhile for LTE programmes and professional development initiatives to emphasize material selection, adaptation, and/or creation as this appears to be an area for L2 teacher self-efficacy.

Similar to materials, it was interesting to note culture emerged across numerous studies after factor analysis as well (e.g., Karas, 2019; Swanson, 2012). LTE programmes likely already include cultural elements in their programmes as culture and language instruction are inseparable, but these results reaffirm the importance of addressing culture in language instruction.

Finally, enhancing the specificity of items may make quantitative LTSE work more practical for language teachers. Wyatt (2014) has noted that when items are from a more global perspective, this can be difficult to fully understand what teachers are actually evaluating when completing scales. However, looking at the L2 domain-specific scales and the even more specific language competency scales from Zhang (2018) and Wyatt and Dikilitaş (2021), we find more task-specific items for teachers to interpret. There are numerous other areas for LTSE researchers to explore (e.g., vocabulary, listening, etc.), and scales that have an even greater focus could be useful to assist teachers in determining specific L2 teaching areas/tasks in which they are highly efficacious, or areas/tasks where they may seek to improve and build more confidence.

## Conclusion

The synthesis of language teacher efficacy surveys presented in this chapter provides useful findings about the development of such surveys for future studies. There are now ample scale options for LTSE researchers to consider, and we encourage researchers to explore these new measures, potentially alongside nuanced qualitative measures that offer deeper understandings.

## References

*Akbari, R., & Tavassoli, K. (2014). Developing an ELT context-specific teacher efficacy instrument. *RELC Journal*, 45(1), 27–50. 10.1177/0033688214523345

Bandura, A. (1997). *Self-efficacy: The exercise of control*. W.H. Freeman and Company.

Bandura, A. (2006). Guide for constructing self-efficacy scales. In F. Pajares & T. Urdan (Eds.), *Self-efficacy beliefs of adolescents* (pp. 307–337). Information Age Publishing.

Bao, D. (Ed.) (2018). *Creativity and innovations in ELT materials development: Looking beyond the current design*. Multilingual Matters.

Bergil, A.S., & Sariçoban, A. (2017). The use of EPOSTL to determine the self-efficacy of prospective EFL teachers: Raising awareness in English language teacher education. *Journal of Language and Linguistic Studies*, 13(1), 399-411. https://dergipark.org.tr/en/pub/jlls/issue/36109/405469

Best, B. (2014). A study of elementary school Thai English teachers' perceived English proficiency and self-reported English teaching efficacy (Master's dissertation). *Language in India*, 14(7), 75–195.

*Chacón, C.T. (2005). Teachers' perceived efficacy among English as a foreign language teachers in middle schools in Venezuela. *Teaching and Teacher Education*, 21, 257–272. 10.1016/j.tate.2005.01.001

*Chiang, M.H. (2008). Effects of fieldwork experience on empowering prospective foreign language teachers. *Teaching and Teacher Education*, 24(5), 1270–1287. 10.1016/j.tate.2007.05.004

*Choi, E., & Lee, J. (2016). Investigating the relationship of target language proficiency and self-efficacy among nonnative EFL teachers. *System*, 58, 49–63. 10.1016/j.system.2016.02.010

*Cooke, S., & Faez, F. (2018). Self-efficacy beliefs of novice French as a second language teachers: A case study of Ontario teachers. *Canadian Journal of Applied Linguistics*, 21(2), 1–18. https://www.erudit.org/en/journals/cjal/1900-v1-n1-cjal04434/1057963ar.pdf

Faez, F., & Karas, M. (2017). Connecting language proficiency to (self-reported) teaching ability: A review and analysis of research. *RELC Journal*, 48(1), 135–151. 10.1177/0033688217694755

Faez, F., Karas, M., & Uchihara, T. (2021). Connecting language proficiency to teaching ability: A meta-analysis. *Language Teaching Research*, 25(5), 754–777. 10.1177/1362168819868667

*Faez, F. & Valeo, A. (2012) TESOL teacher education: Novice teachers' perceptions of their preparedness and efficacy in the classroom. *TESOL Quarterly*, 46(3), 450–471. 10.1002/tesq.37

Freeman, D. (2017). The case for teachers' classroom English proficiency. *RELC Journal*, 48(1), 31–52. 10.1177/0033688217691073

Freeman, D., Katz, A., Gomez, P.G. & Burns, A. (2015). English-for-teaching: Rethinking teacher proficiency in the classroom. *ELT Journal*, 69(2), 129–139. 10.1093/elt/ccu074

Hoang, T. (2018). Teacher self-efficacy research in English as foreign language contexts: A systematic review. *Journal of Asia TEFL*, 15, 976–990. 10.18823/asiatefl.2018.15.4.6.976

*Hoang, T., & Wyatt, M. (2021). Exploring the self-efficacy beliefs of Vietnamese pre-service teachers of English as a foreign language. *System*, 96(102422), 1–14. First published online 25/11/2020. 10.1016/j.system.2020.102422

*Huangfu, W. (2012). Effects of EFL teachers' self-efficacy on motivational teaching behaviors. *Asian Social Science*, 8(15), 68. 10.5539/ass.v8n15p68

*Karas, M. (2019). *English language teacher self-efficacy beliefs* [Unpublished doctoral dissertation]. Western University.

*Karimvand, P.N. (2011). The Nexus between Iranian EFL Teachers' self-efficacy, teaching experience and gender. *English Language Teaching*, 4(3), 171–183. 10.5539/elt.v4n3p171

*Kaygisiz, S., Anagun, S.S., & Karahan, E. (2018). The predictive relationship between self-efficacy levels of English teachers and language teaching methods. *Eurasian Journal of Educational Research*, 18(78), 183–202. https://dergipark.org.tr/en/pub/ejer/issue/42563/512870

*Kissau, S. (2012). Perceptions of self-efficacy for two types of second language methods instruction. *Computer Assisted Language Learning*, 25(4), 295–317. 10.1080/09588221.2011.587436

*Kissau, S., & Algozzine, B. (2014). The impact of mode of instructional delivery on second language teacher self-efficacy. *ReCALL*, 27(2), 239–256. 10.1017/S0958344014000391

Klassen, R.M., Bong, M., Usher, E.L., Chong, W.H., Huan, V.S., Wong, I.Y.F., & Georgiou, T. (2009). Exploring the validity of a teachers' self-efficacy scale in five countries. *Contemporary Educational Psychology*, 34, 67–76. 10.1016/j.cedpsych.2008.08.001

*Kormos, J., & Nijakowska, J. (2017). Inclusive practices in teaching students with dyslexia: Second language teachers' concerns, attitudes and self-efficacy beliefs on a massive open online learning course. *Teaching and Teacher Education*, 68, 30–41. 10.1016/j.tate.2017.08.005

*Lee, J.A. (2009). *Teachers' sense of efficacy in teaching English, perceived English language proficiency, and attitudes toward the English language: A case study of Korean public elementary school teachers* [Unpublished doctoral dissertation]. The Ohio State University.

*Liu, H., Chu, W., & Wang, Y. (2021). Unpacking EFL teacher self-efficacy in livestream teaching in the Chinese context. *Frontiers in Psychology*, 12. 10.3389/fpsyg.2021.717129

*Nishino, T. (2012). Modeling teacher beliefs and practices in context: A multi-methods approach. *The Modern Language Journal*, 96(3), 380–399. 10.1111/j.1540-4781.2012.01364.x

Norris, J.M., & Ortega, L. (2006). The value and practice of research synthesis for language learning and teaching. In. J.M. Norris & L. Ortega (Eds.), *Synthesizing research on language learning* (pp. 3–50). John Benjamins Publishing.

*Parks, P. (2021). *Should I stay, or should I go? A mixed method study of pre-service English second language teacher efficacy-identity development in Quebec.* [Unpublished doctoral dissertation.].

Polin, L.G. (2021). *Self-efficacy and professional development activities and needs of Chinese language teachers in secondary schools in North Carolina: An explanatory sequential mixed methods study* [Unpublished doctoral dissertation]. University of North Carolina.

*Praver, M. (2014). *Japanese university English language teachers' self-efficacy beliefs: A mixed methods approach* [Unpublished doctoral dissertation]. Temple University.

Richards, J.C. (2010). Competence and performance in language teaching. *RELC Journal*, 41(2), 101–122. 10.1177/0033688210372953

Richards, J.C. (2017). Teaching English through English: Proficiency, pedagogy and performance. *RELC Journal*, 48(1), 7–30. 10.1177/0033688217690059

Shim, J.W. (2001). *The teacher efficacy beliefs of Korean teachers of English as a foreign language* [Unpublished doctoral dissertation]. The Ohio State University.

*Swanson, P. (2010a). Teacher efficacy and attrition: Helping students at introductory levels of language instruction appears critical. *Hispania*, 93(2), 305–321.

*Swanson, P. (2010b). Efficacy and language teacher attrition: A case for mentorship beyond the classroom. *NECTFL Review*, 66, 48–72.

*Swanson, P. (2012). Second/foreign language teacher efficacy and its relationship to professional attrition. *The Canadian Modern Language Review*, 68(1), 78–101. 10.3138/cmlr.68.1.078

*Swanson, P. (2013). From teacher training through the first year on the job: Changes in foreign language teacher efficacy. *Electronic Journal of Foreign Language Teaching*, 10(1), 5–16. http://e-flt.nus.edu.sg/v10n12013/swanson.pdf

*Swanson, P. (2014). The power of belief: Spanish teachers' sense of efficacy and student performance on the National Spanish Examinations. *Hispania*, 97(1), 5–20.

*Thompson, G. & Woodman, K. (2019). Exploring Japanese high school English teachers' foreign language teacher efficacy beliefs. *Asia-Pacific Journal of Teacher Education*, 47(1), 48–65. 10.1080/1359866X.2018.1498062

Tschannen-Moran, M., Woolfolk Hoy, A., & Hoy, W.K. (1998). Teacher efficacy: Its meaning and measure. *Review of Educational Research*, 68(2), 202–248. 10.3102/00346543068002202

Tschannen-Moran, M., & Woolfolk Hoy, A. (2001). Teacher efficacy: Capturing an elusive construct. *Teaching and Teacher Education*, 17, 783–805. 10.1016/S0742-051X(01)00036-1

Wheatley, K.F. (2005). The case for reconceptualizing teacher efficacy research. *Teaching and Teacher Education*, 21(7), 747–766. 10.1016/j.tate.2005.05.009

Wyatt, M. (2014). Towards a re-conceptualization of teachers' self-efficacy beliefs: Tackling enduring problems with the quantitative research and moving on. *International Journal of Research and Method in Education*, 37(2), 166–189. 10.1080/1743727X.2012.742050

Wyatt, M. (2016). "Are they becoming more reflective and/or efficacious?" A conceptual model mapping how teachers' self-efficacy beliefs might grow. *Educational Review*, 68(1), 114–137. 10.1080/00131911.2015.1058754

Wyatt, M. (2018). Language teachers' self-efficacy beliefs: A review of the literature (2005–2016). *Australian Journal of Teacher Education*, *43*(4), 92–120. 10.14221/ajte.2018v43n4.6

Wyatt, M. (2021). Research into second language learners' and teachers self-efficacy beliefs: Making the connections. *TESOL Quarterly*, *55*(1), 296–307. 10.1002/tesq.3010

Wyatt, M. (forthcoming). Language teachers' self-efficacy beliefs: A systematic review. In. Z. Tajeddin & T.S.C. Farrell (Eds.), *Handbook of language teacher education: Critical reviews and research syntheses*. Springer.

*Wyatt, M., & Dikilitaş, K. (2021). English language teachers' self-efficacy beliefs for grammar instruction: Implications for teacher educators. *The Language Learning Journal*, *49*(5), 541–553. 10.1080/09571736.2019.1642943

*Yaman, Ş., Inandi, Y., & Esen, G. (2013). A regression study: English language teachers' general and professional sense of self-efficacy. *Education & Science/Egitim ve Bilim*, *38*(170), 335–346.

*Zhang, B. (2018). *English language teachers' required knowledge and self-efficacy beliefs about pronunciation instruction* [Unpublished master's thesis]. University of Western Ontario.

# 3 Language teachers' self-efficacy beliefs in the Turkish EFL context

*Funda Ölmez-Çağlar*

## Introduction

Teachers' self-efficacy (TSE) beliefs have long been a prominent research area in mainstream education while language teachers' self-efficacy (LTSE) beliefs have started to draw second/foreign language (L2) researchers' attention more recently, particularly in the past two decades. During this time, LTSE beliefs have been researched from different perspectives by researchers from a wide range of national contexts, and L2 researchers in Türkiye have made a notable contribution to this line of research (Wyatt, 2018a, 2018b). A substantial body of research in the Turkish English as a foreign language (EFL) context has so far scrutinized the efficacy beliefs of pre-service teachers (e.g., Yüksel, 2014), in-service teachers (e.g., Ortaçtepe & Akyel, 2015), or both (e.g., Uztosun, 2016) through quantitative (e.g., Yaylı & Ekizler, 2015), qualitative (e.g, Wyatt & Dikilitaş, 2016), or mixed methodologies (e.g., Şahin & Atay, 2010).

Self-efficacy beliefs are important in life in that believing in the personal capacity to achieve a goal or complete a predetermined task is a prerequisite for at least endeavouring to gain success in that action (Bandura, 1997). This also holds true for educational contexts where TSE or LTSE beliefs impact various aspects of teaching and learning. However, despite bearing similarities to TSE beliefs in many aspects, LTSE beliefs have idiosyncratic characteristics as well. One such characteristic is the impact of how competent L2 teachers feel for teaching the target language, which may also change for those who are native and non-native speakers, particularly if the latter group feels stigmatized (Wyatt, 2018a) (see also Chapter 1 of this volume for a discussion). Researching LTSE beliefs using instruments developed for TSE beliefs in mainstream education remains the predominant trend in Türkiye, as in many other national contexts (see also Chapter 2 of this volume). Yet, following global research trends, L2 research in Türkiye has also started to emphasize the domain-specific nature of LTSE beliefs more recently. This chapter aims to uncover what has been learned from

DOI: 10.4324/9781003379300-4

previous research in Türkiye and provides a research synthesis of LTSE beliefs in the Turkish EFL context.

## Literature review

As in any other human action, teachers' self-perceived potentials or capabilities influence different aspects of their teaching processes. Based on the Social Cognitive Theory (Bandura, 1986), as real agents of their actions, individuals hold certain beliefs about their capacities for undertaking any action, and these might affect their emotions, motivations for the action, and the action itself. In other words, individuals' actions are impacted by how efficacious they feel about carrying out those actions. Major sources of self-efficacy beliefs are rooted in individuals' personal experiences of performing those actions (i.e., enactive mastery experiences), observations of others' performances and self-evaluations through comparison (i.e., vicarious experiences), the encouragement they get from other people (i.e., verbal persuasion), and how they feel physically and emotionally at the time of self-evaluation (i.e., physiological and affective states) (Bandura, 1986, 1997).

Not surprisingly, individuals' own accomplishments or failures stand out as the most robust source of self-efficacy beliefs for teachers in educational settings, though not necessarily for novice teachers who might not have sufficient past experience for developing efficacy beliefs (Tschannen-Moran & Woolfolk Hoy, 2007). The importance of experience means that teachers' earlier performances, achievements, or failures in similar contexts tend to appear as a primary source of TSE beliefs. In addition, observing and learning about others' experiences, getting feedback from others about various aspects of teaching, and physiological and emotional states in relation to teaching can help to consolidate or weaken TSE beliefs based on self-evaluation using these sources. Information on self-efficacy gathered from these sources is processed cognitively during self-evaluation based on the specific instructional task and context (Tschannen-Moran et al., 1998). Therefore, it is crucial to highlight that TSE beliefs have domain-, task-, and context-specific characteristics (Tschannen-Moran & Woolfolk Hoy, 2001; Wyatt, 2018a, 2018b).

With their impact on various aspects of teaching as well as their context-, task- and domain-specific characteristics, TSE beliefs have been researched extensively in mainstream education for decades. Although research into LTSE beliefs is more recent, these beliefs are increasingly examined in a wide variety of national contexts, as clearly seen in a recent global review (Wyatt, 2018a). LTSE beliefs research conducted so far has focused on various issues such as the sources of these beliefs (e.g., Phan & Locke, 2015), their links with L2 teachers' language proficiency and pedagogical strategies (e.g., Chacón, 2005), and personal qualities like emotional intelligence (e.g., Moafian & Ghanizadeh, 2009). L2 researchers have also traced changes in LTSE beliefs over time (e.g., Wyatt, 2013) and as a result of teacher educational practices (e.g., Swanson, 2013).

Following research trends in mainstream education, a majority of LTSE beliefs studies have made use of Tschannen-Moran and Hoy's (2001) Teachers' Sense of Efficacy Scale (TSES) or a slightly adapted version for L2 teachers (e.g., Chacón, 2005). While this instrument elicits a holistic view of efficacy beliefs, more recent LTSE beliefs research has dealt with particular domains of L2 teaching such as grammar instruction (e.g., Wyatt & Dikilitaş, 2021). As evident from Wyatt's (2018a) review of LTSE beliefs research, L2 researchers from Türkiye have contributed significantly to this research line. However, despite this contribution, there appears to be limited research reviewing current understandings and accumulated knowledge of LTSE beliefs in this particular national context. Given that this context differs considerably from other sites where LTSE beliefs have been researched (e.g., Iran and the United States), a dedicated literature review is needed. To elaborate on the understanding of LTSE beliefs here, this research synthesis explores L2 research trends in relation to LTSE beliefs in the Turkish EFL context. As such, this chapter offers insights into these beliefs from the perspective of pre- and in-service EFL teachers in Türkiye. The next section provides a methodological overview of this research synthesis.

## Research methodology

The current research synthesis, as a "systematic secondary review of accumulated primary research results" (Norris & Ortega, 2006, p. 4), meticulously reviews studies on LTSE beliefs conducted in Türkiye. As to the national context, English is taught as a foreign language here. Children start to learn English in the second grade in state schools, but an earlier start is also possible in private schools. The English course is an inherent part of the curriculum throughout elementary school, middle school, and high school, although total class hours for the course can vary considerably and range from 2 to 20 hours per week. Students continue learning English at university as well. Not surprisingly though, students' exposure to English is mostly limited to the classroom context in instructional language settings, particularly due to its EFL status. English teachers are therefore the primary source of English input for students, an insight which highlights the importance of their self-efficacy beliefs for the whole process of English language teaching (ELT) and learning.

The current review includes previous research into Turkish pre- and in-service EFL TSE beliefs. Regarding their teacher education, EFL teachers graduate from four-year undergraduate ELT programmes at faculties of education in Türkiye. As well as pedagogical and field-specific courses, the undergraduate ELT curriculum involves a one-year teaching practicum. In their final year, pre-service teachers take two practicum courses, one per semester. They first observe in-service EFL teachers teaching at schools under the Ministry of National Education and then practise teaching under the supervision of both the classroom teachers (i.e., mentor teachers) in practicum schools and their academic supervisors. It is also possible for graduates of other related departments (e.g., English Language and Literature) to get a certificate for ELT through a one-year intensive programme in faculties of education and then get appointed as teachers of English. The English proficiency of both ELT students and students of other related departments is tested before admission to undergraduate programmes. Graduates subsequently take a field-specific test concerning ELT, as part of a more comprehensive test, before being appointed by the Ministry of Education as teachers of English at state schools.

As to the steps taken for the research synthesis, the review incorporated various forms of published research into LTSE beliefs in the Turkish EFL context, namely, journal articles, conference proceedings, book chapters, and unpublished dissertations. Relevant research was located through Google scholar, citation indexes, and the CoHE (Council of Higher Education) National Thesis Center. The studies were included in the review without any prior exclusion criteria regarding their methodology, quality, or publication details. The review aimed for exhaustive sampling and was therefore broadly inclusive in identifying relevant research for the synthesis, as suggested by Lipsey and Wilson (2001) and Norris and Ortega (2006). It covers only studies published as full texts in English between 2007 and 2021, with a sampling of only pre- and in-service EFL teachers in Türkiye. To focus solely on the LTSE beliefs of EFL teachers, it excludes studies that involve broader samples of teachers, such as those that include teachers of other languages or subjects other than English.

The resulting literature review consists of 76 studies.[1] While the majority of these studies were published as journal articles ($n$ = 37), others were found in full-text conference proceedings ($n$ = 2), book chapters ($n$ = 1), master's theses ($n$ = 28), or PhD dissertations ($n$ = 8). In cases of overlaps between published articles and theses/dissertations, the published works were included in the review, excluding the previous versions of the studies in theses/dissertations. The studies included in the review were thoroughly analysed, with a table used as a starting point. For each study, key information was written in each column: Author(s), year, source, title, research focus, aim, research questions, methodology, sample, instruments, major findings, and limitations. The table was repeatedly reviewed, filtered, arranged, rearranged, and annotated to support the uncovering of recurring themes and the classification of the studies. The next section provides key findings of 15 years of LTSE research conducted in the Turkish EFL context, considering the educational levels at which participants were teaching, major research methodologies, and the research focus of the studies.

## Results

### Major research trends considering samples and methodological approaches

The first step was to consider who the research was conducted with and how. Major trends in relation to the research samples and the adopted methodological approaches are summarized in Table 3.1.

An evaluation of the study samples reveals that 50% of the reviewed studies ($n$ = 38) focused on the efficacy beliefs of in-service EFL teachers. Next, research examining the beliefs of pre-service teachers makes up another 41% of reviewed studies ($n$ = 31). Some studies appear to have explored the LTSE beliefs of both groups, but these were much more limited in number (9%). As to the methodological approaches adopted for these studies, the majority of all reviewed studies had either a mixed methods (51%) or a quantitative research design (47%). Surprisingly, only one study (Wyatt & Dikilitaş, 2016) made use of a qualitative approach.

Of all quantitative and mixed methods studies, over two-thirds of them (51 out of 75) used the TSES (Tschannen-Moran & Woolfolk Hoy, 2001) as a fundamental data collection tool. The TSES was either administered in its original form, using its long or short version, or with its validated Turkish version (Capa et al., 2005). The TSES aims to assess TSE beliefs in general based on three dimensions (i.e., student engagement, instructional strategies, and classroom management), but without specific reference to any content area such as ELT. Consequently, an adapted version of the TSES for teachers of English, such as Chacón's (2005), was preferred by some researchers (e.g., İnceçay & Keşli Dollar, 2012; Ortaçtepe & Akyel, 2015). In fact, and as also discussed in Chapter 2 of this volume, Chacon's (2005) version of the TSES represents minimal adaptation, as the items were slightly modified by adding phrases like "learning English" and "in your English class" to make it more appropriate for an EFL teaching context.

Table 3.1 An overview of LTSE beliefs research in the Turkish EFL context (2007–2021)

| Sample | Methodology | | | |
| --- | --- | --- | --- | --- |
| | Quantitative | Mixed methods | Qualitative | Total |
| Pre-service teachers | 13 | 18 | – | 31 |
| In-service teachers | 19 | 18 | 1 | 38 |
| Both | 4 | 3 | – | 7 |
| Total | 36 | 39 | 1 | 76 |

While using the TSES to measure the efficacy beliefs of pre- or in-service EFL teachers, some studies attempted to complement the data collection process with other instruments like interviews (e.g., Sevimel & Subasi, 2018) to focus more on LTSE beliefs specific to language teaching (see examples below). Researchers in other studies appeared to prefer constructing their own instruments to measure overall efficacy for L2 teaching (e.g., Üstünbaş & Alagözlü, 2021) or self-efficacy for specific domains of L2 teaching like grammar instruction (e.g., Wyatt & Dikilitaş, 2021). For instance, to measure pre- and in-service EFL TSE, Üstünbaş and Alagözlü (2021) used their own scale involving four components: Planning, teaching, assessment, and professional development. With slight changes in wording, the same items were used for both pre-service (e.g., *How well do you believe you will be able to respond to students about the function of a specific language form?*) and in-service EFL teachers (e.g., *How well can you respond to students about the function of a specific language form?*) (Üstünbaş, 2020, pp. 162–164). As this all demonstrates, quantitative data collection tools have a prominent role in LTSE beliefs research in Türkiye.

However, as well as surveying LTSE beliefs using scales and questionnaires as a major tool, researchers have also employed one-to-one or focus group interviews, reflection papers or journals, and observation forms. Among the instruments used to explore LTSE beliefs, interviews have been the second most frequently used instrument after scales and questionnaires. Indeed, of all reviewed studies, 26 made use of interviews. In many mixed methods studies, interviews were conducted with a smaller group of participants, usually as a follow up to the quantitative data collection. In these studies, efficacy information was mostly elicited through open-ended questions asked during one-to-one interviews. For instance, Can and Daloğlu (2021, p. 499) asked some general questions like "Why do you evaluate yourself as such?" to identify the sources of efficacy beliefs and questions such as "Which strategies increase your self-efficacy?" to encourage participants to elaborate on change processes. Following a somewhat different route, Ucar and Yazıcı Bozkaya (2016, p. 19) looked for critical incidents and guided the interviewees with more specific questions like "What do you do when you faced a challenging situation in the classroom?" and "How do you react when your students are confused?"

Focus-group interviews were preferred in studies aiming to get deeper insights into various aspects of the LTSE beliefs of participants as a whole group, such as while exploring the potential sources of LTSE beliefs (Sevimel & Subasi, 2018), or scrutinizing the factors affecting pre-service EFL TSE beliefs during the practicum period (Atay, 2007). Using focus-group discussions as a follow up to the TSES, Atay's (2007) study uncovered various factors influencing changes in LTSE beliefs, such as increased awareness of teaching competence, and the influence of beliefs about learning and teaching; such findings highlight that beliefs about second language acquisition can intersect with LTSE beliefs. The study also revealed other factors like the influence of cooperating teachers (i.e., mentoring and providing verbal persuasion), the impact of established practices in teaching, and institutional characteristics of the practicum school (i.e., the particular context).

Of all studies under review, six research studies involved reflective journals or reflection papers as a data collection tool. For instance, besides measuring self-efficacy beliefs using the TSES three times during the practicum period, Yüksel (2014) also asked pre-service EFL teachers to write reflection papers to elaborate on how the practicum period impacted their LTSE beliefs.

However, of all reviewed studies, only three included observations in the data collection process. For example, in their study on pre-service EFL TSE in relation to their classroom management and readiness, İnceçay and Keşli Dollar (2012) utilized an observation scheme they developed for their study to triangulate observed practices with self-reported beliefs. To sum up, reflection and observation have been used, but only to a limited extent in LTSE beliefs research, although both can provide further and fuller insights into LTSE beliefs.

### *An overview of major research themes*

The current review revealed that LTSE beliefs research conducted in the Turkish EFL context has focused on four major themes. The research trends concerning the studies' major areas of focus are summarized in Table 3.2.

*Table 3.2* LTSE beliefs research in the Turkish EFL context based on major areas of focus

| Major focus | n | Sample themes |
| --- | --- | --- |
| LTSE beliefs in relation to different factors | 47 | LTSE beliefs in relation to socio-demographic factors; English proficiency; pedagogical strategies; teacher stress; burnout; emotional intelligence; teacher motivation |
| Development of LTSE beliefs | 15 | Development of LTSE beliefs through teaching practicum; research engagement |
| LTSE beliefs about specific domains of teaching and L2 instruction | 11 | LTSE beliefs for grammar instruction; writing instruction; classroom management |
| Comparison of LTSE beliefs | 3 | Pre-service vs. in-service EFL teachers |

## LTSE beliefs in relation to different factors

An analysis of the 76 studies based on their major areas of focus showed that the majority of these studies explored LTSE beliefs in relation to various factors. Among these, socio-demographic factors were among the most frequently researched variables examined along with LTSE beliefs. In total, 14 studies included in the review appeared to explore the efficacy beliefs of EFL teachers (pre-service, in-service, or both) based on socio-demographic factors such as teaching experience ($n = 11$), latest graduation degree and subject area ($n = 7$), gender ($n = 7$), and age ($n = 3$). While investigating one or several of these factors, most of these studies used the original form of the TSES in English (Tschannen-Moran & Woolfolk Hoy, 2001) or its validated Turkish version (Capa et al., 2005) as the major instrument for data collection. Working on quantitative data, they tested for a possible difference in global efficacy scores and/or in the three subscale scores (i.e., student engagement, instructional strategies, and classroom management) based on these socio-demographic factors. A few studies focusing on global differences used an adapted version of the TSES for teachers of English ( e.g., Can & Daloğlu, 2021) or developed their own instruments for the same purpose (Güven & Çakır, 2012).

Most of the studies scrutinizing the LTSE beliefs of in-service teachers in relation to their teaching experience ($n = 7$) uncovered that teachers with greater experience (usually measured at intervals of three or five years) felt more efficacious as well. Such research even reported strong correlations (e.g., Can & Daloğlu, 2021), and only a few studies (e.g., Tunç Yüksel, 2010) found no change in self-efficacy beliefs based on teaching experience. However, these findings should be interpreted cautiously since the quality and quantity of experience might vary greatly across different contexts, and even the way researchers deal with teaching experience as a variable can have an impact on the results as well.

Apart from socio-demographic factors, researchers also dealt with the links between LTSE beliefs and other teacher-related factors such as teacher burnout ($n = 5$), stress ($n = 2$), emotional intelligence ($n = 2$), motivation for teaching (n = 2), and teacher beliefs, e.g., pedagogical and epistemological beliefs ($n = 2$). As expected, LTSE beliefs were found to correlate negatively with teacher burnout. For instance, having found a moderate negative correlation between in-service EFL teachers' efficacy for teaching in general and burnout levels, Mızrak (2019) underscored how empowering teacher efficacy might be in helping to reduce teacher burnout.

Positive links were uncovered between LTSE beliefs and teacher motivation by similarly computing global efficacy scores using the TSES. Going beyond the correlations between LTSE beliefs and teacher motivation, Taşçı (2019) found that in-service EFL TSE beliefs predict teacher motivation. Following a different route with pre-service EFL teachers, Ölmez Çağlar (2019) revealed that stronger possible language teacher selves (i.e., ideal and ought-to language teacher selves) predict higher motivation for teaching, which in turn predicts greater teacher self-efficacy. Besides these studies, one study was found for each of the following teacher-related factors and their links with LTSE beliefs: Critical thinking dispositions, democratic values, goal orientations, mindsets, professional identity, and teaching concerns. As expected, LTSE beliefs appeared to correlate negatively with teaching concerns (Yaylı & Ekizler, 2015) and positively with critical thinking dispositions (Yüksel & Alcı, 2012). On the other hand, the hypothesis that teachers with growth mindsets would feel more efficacious in teaching was not supported very strongly, as only a low correlation was found between LTSE beliefs and mindsets (Yılmaz, 2020). However, growth mindsets can be particularly important for teachers with low LTSE beliefs, since low self-efficacy beliefs do not necessarily cause problems when accompanied by a growth mindset (Wyatt, 2018a).

The teacher-related factors elucidated in relation to LTSE beliefs also involved a few variables specific to L2 teaching such as teachers' English proficiency ($n = 6$), foreign language teaching anxiety ($n = 2$), and the status of the EFL teachers as native or non-native speakers ($n = 1$). The studies researching LTSE beliefs in relation to in-service EFL teachers' English proficiency collected some form of quantitative data, and almost all made use of Chacón's (2005) minimally adapted version of the TSES for teachers of English and her measure of self-reported English proficiency. The studies ($n = 6$) reported finding significant links between teachers' LTSE beliefs and English proficiency, similar to findings reported in Faez et al. (2021). As Chacón (2005) did, four of these studies investigated teachers' pedagogical strategies as well. Of all reviewed studies, only one (Serin, 2019) investigated the LTSE beliefs of EFL teachers based on their status as native or non-native speakers of English.

This particular mixed methods study (Serin, 2019) employing the TSES with no adaptations specific to teaching English revealed a significant difference between the self-efficacy beliefs of native and non-native speakers. The non-native-speaker teachers of English reported having greater self-efficacy for teaching, as Karas and Faez (2021), in a Canadian context, have similarly found. Using her interview data, Serin (2019) highlighted non-native and native-speaking teachers' differing views of teacher efficacy. While being a non-native speaker was not perceived as a cause of inferiority for teaching English for the former group and L2 proficiency was seen only as a part of LTSE, the native-speaking teachers defined teacher efficacy differently and regarded speaking the students' mother tongue as an important aspect of teacher self-efficacy. This indicated that the native-speaking teachers recognized the value of being bilingual.

Besides such variables, other factors examined in relation to LTSE beliefs were concerned with classroom practices. As reported earlier, four studies explored LTSE beliefs together with teachers' English proficiency and pedagogical strategies in tandem. The pedagogical strategies were gauged using self-report quantitative measures like Chacón's (2005) and/or Eslami and Fatahi's (2008) instruments, which show to what extent teachers are inclined to use pedagogical tasks and strategies concerning the grammar-translation method (GTM) or communicative language teaching (CLT). Five more studies focused specifically on the relations between LTSE beliefs and classroom practices. These similarly made use of self-report measures to scrutinize the respondents' teaching practices. For instance, Doğan (2020) employed Choi and Lee's (2018) modified version of the TSES and their measure of pedagogical practices, through which L2 teachers report their communicative and non-communicative teaching practices. His research showed that LTSE beliefs had a positive moderate correlation with CLT practices while no correlation was found with non-communicative practices. In this sense, the results of his research were directly in line with those of Choi and Lee's (2018) study with EFL teachers in South Korea since LTSE beliefs were found to be positively correlated with communicative teaching, but not with non-communicative teaching practices.

*Development of LTSE beliefs*

A second key area of focus for LTSE beliefs research in the Turkish EFL context has been their developmental process. Of all reviewed studies, 15 investigated how the LTSE beliefs of pre-service ($n$ = 12; all mixed methods) and in-service EFL teachers ($n$ = 3) were constructed over time through teacher educational practices using the original TSES or an adapted version of this measure (with only 3 exceptions). Most of the research into pre-service teachers' LTSE beliefs ($n$ = 10) gauged the development of these beliefs through the teaching practicum in their final year as undergraduate student teachers. For instance, Atay (2007) traced the developmental process of pre-service teachers' LTSE beliefs using a pre- and post-test during the one-year practicum period as well as focus group discussions. Through the results, she was able to evidence the domain-specific development of efficacy beliefs since the participants had a significant decrease in their self-efficacy for instructional strategies while showing an increase in self-efficacy for classroom management and student engagement. To provide further insights into the development of LTSE beliefs of pre-service teachers in another longitudinal study, Yüksel (2014) tracked their global self-efficacy for teaching by administering the TSES three times during students' final year. She revealed a decrease at the end of the first semester, during which pre-service teachers observed mentor teachers' lessons as part of the teaching practicum, and an increase at the end of the second semester, during which they had a chance to teach lessons under supervision. The qualitative data gathered through reflection papers highlighted pre-service teachers' own teaching experiences in the form of enactive mastery experiences as the most influential efficacy-building source for them during the practicum period. Adding a further dimension to this line of research, Şahin and Atay (2010) examined the developmental trajectories of self-efficacy beliefs by including both practicum and induction years. Data collected using the TSES before and after student teaching as well as after the induction year indicated an initial increase during the teaching practicum and then a decrease after the induction year. The researchers underscored, with reference to the qualitative data, that there was a certain need for more teaching practice to strengthen self-efficacy beliefs. The above studies of pre-service EFL teachers evidence the dynamicity and fluctuations of teacher self-efficacy in this national context.

Other studies have investigated the development of LTSE beliefs of pre-service teachers by focusing specifically on the impact of peer mentoring, peer feedback, and mentor feedback during the practicum period using mixed methods. Peer mentoring and feedback have been underlined as useful sources of LTSE beliefs. For instance, upon assigning the pre-service EFL teachers into two different groups and making a comparison of traditional and peer mentoring practices in his study, Çapan (2017) concluded that peer mentoring helped pre-service teachers to reduce their teaching concerns and further strengthen efficacy beliefs. Again with senior student teachers, Cabaroglu (2014) studied the influence of action research engagement on the development of LTSE beliefs. After finding a positive impact, she recommended incorporating action research into pre-service language teacher education as a way of reinforcing efficacy. Other studies have elucidated the way LTSE beliefs can be developed by way of some other teacher educational practices with different cohorts of pre-service teachers, not just senior student teachers. Focusing on the impact of the flipped classroom approach in an undergraduate classroom management course with sophomores as part of a quasi-experimental study, Kurt (2017) highlighted the advantages of flipped learning as an efficacy-building approach for student teachers. Kurt (2017, p. 218) concluded that the flipped class makes it possible to realize "a pedagogical shift to create a student-centred, individualised learning environment" as an essential aspect of effective teaching and learning in the 21st century.

Compared to these research studies of pre-service teachers, the studies concerning the development of in-service EFL TSE beliefs have been quite limited ($n = 3$). However, in their quantitative study with 50 in-service EFL teachers, Ortaçtepe and Akyel (2015) explored to what extent the teachers strengthened their efficacy and classroom practices through a professional development programme. For data collection, they reported using several methods: Chacón's (2005) adapted version of the TSES for self-efficacy, an observation scheme that allows for quantifying teachers' classroom practices regarding CLT as well as a self-report measure of CLT practices. The results revealed that the professional development programme exerted a positive impact on both self-efficacy and CLT-based teaching practices. Meanwhile, of all studies under review, the only qualitative study focused on three in-service EFL teachers' self-efficacy beliefs development. The teachers grew by becoming engaged in research as part of continuous professional development in a tertiary-level instructional context (Wyatt & Dikilitaş, 2016). The teachers appeared to strengthen their self-efficacy beliefs by getting involved in teacher research.

*LTSE beliefs about specific domains of teaching and L2 instruction*

A total of 11 studies have specifically focused on pre- and in-service EFL teachers' efficacy for various domains of teaching like classroom management, technology integration, web-based teaching, and different dimensions of L2 instruction, such as writing, grammar instruction, and teaching English to young learners (TEYL). Among these, teacher efficacy for integrating technology in English lessons has been the focus of five studies. This was evident as a theme, especially in recent years. Studies have reported finding links between TSE for technology- or web-based instruction and their use/knowledge of technologies/web in teaching. For instance, Dinçer's (2020) study of tertiary-level EFL teachers drew upon self-report quantitative measures. It reported that TSE for technology integration significantly predicted their technological pedagogical content knowledge (TPACK) levels in relation to EFL teaching. However, as seen in the above study, the explored relationships of teacher efficacy were usually limited to the knowledge level (e.g., TPACK) rather than to classroom practice.

Several reviewed studies specifically looked for self-efficacy for classroom management. İnceçay and Keşli Dollar (2012), for instance, collected data using various methods: A quantitative instrument involving the classroom management items under Chacón's (2005) adapted version of the TSES, a classroom observation scheme, and a scale for teacher readiness, particularly for classroom management. Self-efficacy for classroom management was positively correlated with self-report readiness scores. However, neither self-efficacy nor readiness scores were significantly correlated with observation scores for classroom management. Since the participating pre-service teachers' self-reported classroom management and readiness scores did not match up with their classroom behaviours, classroom management was highlighted as a domain requiring substantial procedural knowledge and practice.

There have only been three studies regarding the LTSE beliefs for specific domains of L2 teaching. In Onbaşı's (2014) study of tertiary-level EFL teachers' efficacy in writing instruction and student perceptions, the items in the TSES were adapted specifically for writing classes in a tertiary-level EFL context. The self-report questionnaire data and follow-up teacher interviews were integrated with student data regarding teacher performance in writing instruction and students' writing scores. The researcher reported consistency between self-reported teacher efficacy and student perceptions. Compared to teachers with low self-efficacy beliefs, those with high self-efficacy beliefs reported having a larger array of strategies and techniques for writing instruction, and their students appeared to demonstrate greater writing achievement.

In another study, Uztosun (2016) focused on a group of pre- and in-service teachers' self-efficacy for TEYL using a questionnaire he developed for the study to identify the problems they were trying to cope with. He identified, for example, that the pre-service teachers in the study felt least efficacious for using materials appropriate to young learners, while the in-service teachers felt least efficacious in differentiating between children with different developmental features.

Meanwhile, focusing on tertiary-level in-service EFL TSE for grammar instruction in particular, Wyatt and Dikilitaş's (2021) mixed methods study elucidated the links between grammar instruction self-efficacy, teachers' self-reported practices of grammar teaching, grammatical awareness, and self-reported English proficiency. A distinctive feature of this study was that as class observation was not feasible with teachers from 19 universities in different cities, the researchers employed the lesson description technique instead and asked the participants how they would teach a given grammar topic. Having gained an elaborate understanding of classroom practices, the researchers revealed three clusters of grammar teachers and, most importantly, positive links between greater self-efficacy, greater grammatical awareness, and practices of discovery learning in grammar teaching.

*Comparison of LTSE beliefs*

Of the studies under review, only two compared the efficacy beliefs of pre- and in-service EFL teachers. The first by Dolgun and Caner (2018) compared 75 pre-service and 105 in-service EFL teachers' self-efficacy beliefs using the validated Turkish version of the TSES in its long form. They found high and almost equal global efficacy scores for these two groups as well as in subscales of self-efficacy for classroom management and instructional strategies, although they reported some differences between the two groups through an item-by-item analysis as well. More recently, Üstünbaş and Alagözlü (2021) conducted a mixed methods study to compare the LTSE beliefs and metacognitive awareness of these two groups. Upon administering their own scale to measure self-efficacy for teaching English, they found no significant difference between self-efficacy scores of the two groups, although these groups differed in their levels of metacognitive awareness.

Other studies provide additional insights. For example, although their major aim was not to compare pre- and in-service teachers' efficacy but to reveal links between LTSE beliefs and teaching concerns (as reported earlier), Yaylı and Ekizler (2015) revealed that in-service EFL teachers had significantly higher efficacy compared to pre-service teachers in terms of both overall efficacy and self-efficacy in the three different dimensions of the TSES. Following another route, Çakır and Alıcı (2009) compared pre-service EFL teachers' self-perceived efficacy with instructors' judgements of their competence; the self-perceived efficacy scores were significantly higher than the instructors' evaluations.

## Discussion

As can be seen above, LTSE beliefs research has developed into a separate domain-specific area of TSE research and gained momentum, especially in the last decade in Türkiye. Through a synthesis of research-based contributions to the understanding of LTSE beliefs from the Turkish EFL context, the current review has revealed that most of the studies conducted in Türkiye employed either a mixed methods or quantitative design. In contrast, a qualitative design was used only in one study (Wyatt & Dikilitaş, 2016), although such an approach can be valuable. Indeed, future qualitative research might provide further and deeper insights into LTSE beliefs in this national context. The research conducted in Türkiye has followed similar research trends with LTSE beliefs research in other contexts (Wyatt, 2018a) by using global teacher efficacy measures, especially Tschannen-Moran and Woolfolk Hoy's (2001) TSES as the dominant instrument for learning about the self-efficacy beliefs of teachers of English. Although some studies have attempted to adapt the scale for the EFL teaching context, the reviewed research might have missed idiosyncratic LTSE beliefs specific to the domain of L2 instruction in Türkiye. As a validated measure, the TSES allows for the comparison of both national and international results. However, as Wyatt (2018a) highlights, since the questions might seem overly general, respondents might answer a question in the TSES in a variety of ways by thinking of different instructional tasks.

Most of the reviewed studies in this research synthesis appeared to explore LTSE beliefs in relation to various teacher-related factors and classroom practices. In many of the studies, the emerging positive links of global efficacy scores with various factors like emotional intelligence and their negative links with factors like teacher stress and burnout were not surprising, as they were not in other contexts either (Wyatt, 2018b). Yet, the current review also sheds light on a neglected area, as notwithstanding recent research by Karas and Faez (2021) in an English as a Second Language (ESL) environment, there has been a relative "dearth of research conducted with native-speaker teachers of English in EFL contexts" (Wyatt, 2018a, p. 112). One of the studies in this review (Serin, 2019) highlighted that not being able to speak the students' mother tongue may undermine native-speaking EFL teachers' self-efficacy. Furthermore, the non-native-speaking teachers' high self-efficacy and lack of concern for native-speaker norms in L2 teaching in this study were promising findings in light of debates about the status of English as a global language, considering World Englishes perspectives (Jenkins, 2006). However, an additional explanation for the non-native-speaker teachers' high self-efficacy, as highlighted by Serin (2019), is that the teachers may have been feeling competent about their L2 proficiency due to teaching students with lower proficiency levels at K-12 schools. Karas and Faez (2020) have reported similar findings in a Canadian ESL context. Nevertheless, there may also be a methodological explanation. Although the aforementioned analysis of differences between the two groups of teachers was based on teacher interviews in Serin's (2019) mixed methods study, the underlying reason for the significant difference in efficacy scores of the two groups might have been the use of a global teacher efficacy measure without any specific reference to teaching English.

As to the relationship between LTSE beliefs and classroom practices, the dichotomous nature of the classroom practices measures used in this research line, both in Türkiye (e.g., Doğan, 2020) and in other contexts (e.g., Eslami & Fatahi, 2008), might have had an influence on the results. Guided to choose either communicatively or grammatically oriented teaching practices, the participants in these studies might have been more inclined to choose the former as opposed to opting for traditional L2 teaching practices like the GTM, which carries negative associations. The line of research into specific domains of LTSE beliefs like technology integration, writing, and grammar instruction in EFL classes underlines the interrelationships between self-efficacy in these domains and teacher practices. Although reconsidering the idiosyncratic features of LTSE beliefs seems worthwhile, especially by scrutinizing dimensions of LTSE beliefs specific to L2 instruction, these studies are quite limited in number. Further research might therefore provide deeper insights into domain-specific LTSE beliefs.

A particularly distinctive contribution to the worldwide LTSE beliefs literature made by research conducted in the Turkish EFL context has been through studies focusing on the development of LTSE beliefs. Varying developmental trajectories of the three dimensions of global teacher efficacy

(Atay, 2007) and fluctuations during the teaching practicum (Yüksel, 2014) evidence the domain-specific and dynamic nature of LTSE beliefs.

The growth of LTSE beliefs through supervised teaching has underlined mastery experiences as a primary source of efficacy, in line with Bandura's theory (Bandura, 1986, 1997). However, the self-reported high self-efficacy of pre-service teachers at this stage requires meticulous scrutiny. Given that self-perceived efficacy may also be inconsistent with an independent evaluation (Çakır & Alıcı, 2009; İnceçay & Keşli Dollar, 2012), it is essential to underscore that high self-efficacy, especially in the form of over-efficaciousness, might also be problematic. Most importantly, over-efficaciousness can hamper willingness for teacher development and openness to learning (Wheatley, 2005).

However, in the current review, there is clear evidence for the dynamicity of LTSE beliefs in the growth of pre-service EFL TSE during the practicum followed by a decrease in the induction year. The underlying reason for the decline after the induction year may be the reality shock teachers usually experience at the start of their career (Caspersen & Raaen, 2014) owing to a complex group of challenges ranging from lesson planning and organization to issues related to teacher identity development (Farrell, 2006). This suggests that a smooth and refined transition from student teaching to teaching through an appropriate theory-practice balance in teacher education and further teaching practices can positively reflect on LTSE beliefs. As evidenced by research, professional development programmes (Ortaçtepe & Akyel, 2015), including those incorporating research engagement (Cabaroglu, 2014; Wyatt & Dikilitaş, 2016), can play a key part in teacher development and in consolidating LTSE beliefs. Along with the dynamic development of LTSE beliefs, this implies that well-structured teacher education programmes and teacher practices can help L2 teachers feel more efficacious.

## Pedagogical implications and conclusions

Overall, the current research synthesis consolidates understanding of LTSE beliefs by providing evidence that these beliefs are complex and domain-specific constructs that are in close interrelationships with a wide array of factors and display non-linear developmental trajectories. The results imply that an equilibrium between theory and practice in pre-service education may help teachers to develop more realistic LTSE beliefs and minimize the risk of a reality shock at the start of teaching in schools.

For a smooth transition from student teaching to teaching, this chapter suggests a thorough evaluation of pre-service teacher education curricula and then systematic and well-structured refinements. As Faez and Valeo (2012) recommend, aligning the components of teacher education programmes with novice teachers' needs at each stage can be an effective strategy. Based on a needs analysis, providing pedagogical and psychological guidance in relation to shifting roles from students to teachers may help novices feel more efficacious.

Moreover, due to the idiosyncratic nature of every learning and teaching context, the inclusion of domain- and task-specific, context-based, and problem-oriented inquiries in L2 classrooms can be effective for improving teacher efficacy. For instance, by making use of action research in real classrooms during the practicum, pre-service teachers can become more informed and better prepared for classroom realities as they inquire, reflect on, and learn how to deal with specific problems and work on areas for further development (Cabaroglu, 2014).

As the teaching and learning journey is never complete, guiding teachers throughout their teaching careers through continuous professional development practices can reflect positively on their efficacy as well. For example, developing action plans through a situated analysis of their own classrooms can be useful for in-service EFL teachers. Furthermore, engaging in action research can be beneficial for in-service EFL teachers in terms of helping them gain further practical knowledge and develop positive self-efficacy beliefs (Wyatt & Dikilitaş, 2016). In addition, professional development programmes involving awareness-raising tasks about past teaching experiences, reflective teaching practices, interaction between colleagues, reading activities, seminars, and workshops can boost LTSE beliefs (Ortaçtepe & Akyel, 2015). As well as encouraging practitioner research, well-organized professional development programmes involving continuous mentor and peer feedback can help teachers to reflect more realistically on their teaching performances, realize their potentials, and take informed steps forward. These refinements in pre- and in-service EFL teacher education programmes may overall help to advance LTSE beliefs.

### Note

1 The studies cited in this chapter have been asterisked in the references.

### References

*Atay, D. (2007). Beginning teacher efficacy and the practicum in an EFL context. *Teacher Development, 11*(2), 203–219. 10.1080/13664530701414720

Bandura, A. (1986). *Social foundations of thought and action: A social cognitive theory.* Prentice-Hall.

Bandura, A. (1997). *Self-efficacy: The exercise of control.* Freeman.

*Cabaroglu, N. (2014). Professional development through action research: Impact on self-efficacy. *System, 44*(1), 79–88. 10.1016/j.system.2014.03.003

*Can, S., & Daloğlu, A. (2021). University prep school instructors' self-efficacy perceptions. *Journal of Language and Linguistic Studies, 17*(1), 493–516.

Capa, Y., Cakiroglu, J., & Sarikaya, H. (2005). The development and validation of a Turkish version of the Teachers' Sense of Efficacy Scale. *Education and Science*, *30*(137), 74–81.

Caspersen, J., & Raaen, F. D. (2014). Novice teachers and how they cope. *Teachers and Teaching: Theory and Practice*, *20*(2), 189–211. 10.1080/13540602.2013.848570

Chacón, C. T. (2005). Teachers' perceived efficacy among English as a foreign language teachers in middle schools in Venezuela. *Teaching and Teacher Education*, *21*(3), 257–272. 10.1016/j.tate.2005.01.001

Choi, E., & Lee, J. (2018). EFL teachers' self-efficacy and teaching practices. *ELT Journal*, *72*(2), 175–186. 10.1093/elt/ccx046

*Çakır, Ö., & Alıcı, D. (2009). Seeing self as others see you: Variability in self-efficacy ratings in student teaching. *Teachers and Teaching: Theory and Practice*, *15*(5), 541–561. 10.1080/13540600903139555

*Çapan, S. A. (2017). *Reciprocal peer mentoring in pre-service ELT practicum in terms of teaching concerns and teacher efficacy beliefs* [Unpublished doctoral dissertation]. Çukurova University.

*Dinçer, R. (2020). *Exploring predictive power of in-service EFL instructors' technology integration self efficacy beliefs on their TPACK levels* [Unpublished master's thesis]. Bahçeşehir University.

*Doğan, Ç. (2020). *The relationship between English teachers' self-efficacy beliefs and their classroom practices: A southeastern case from Turkey* [Unpublished master's thesis]. Gaziantep University.

*Dolgun, H., & Caner, M. (2018). Self-efficacy belief profiles of pre-service and in-service EFL teachers. *Mehmet Akif Ersoy Üniversitesi Eğitim Fakültesi Dergisi*, *48*(4), 602–623. 10.21764/maeuefd.335597

Eslami, Z. R., & Fatahi, A. (2008). Teachers' sense of self-efficacy, English proficiency, and instructional strategies: A study of nonnative EFL teachers in Iran. *TESL-EJ*, *11*(4), 1–19. https://files.eric.ed.gov/fulltext/EJ898136.pdf

Faez, F., Karas, M., & Uchihara, T. (2021). Connecting language proficiency to teaching ability: A meta-analysis. *Language Teaching Research*, *25*(5), 754–777. 10.1177/1362168819868667

Faez, F., & Valeo, A. (2012). TESOL teacher education: Novice teachers' perceptions of their preparedness and efficacy in the classroom. *TESOL Quarterly*, *46*(3), 450–471. 10.1002/tesq.37

Farrell, T. S. C. (2006). The first year of language teaching: Imposing order. *System*, *34*(2), 211–221. 10.1016/j.system.2005.12.001

*Güven, S., & Çakır, Ö. (2012). A study on primary school English teachers' self-efficacy beliefs. *Education and Science*, *37*(163), 43–52.

*İnceçay, G., & Keşli Dollar, Y. (2012). Classroom management, self-efficacy and readiness of Turkish pre-service English teachers. *ELT Research Journal*, *1*(3), 189–198.

Jenkins, J. (2006). Current perspectives on teaching World Englishes and English as a lingua franca. *TESOL Quarterly*, *40*(1), 157–181. 10.2307/40264515

Karas, M., & Faez, F. (2020). What level of proficiency do teachers need to teach English in different settings? Perceptions of novice teachers in Canada. *TESL-EJ*, *24*(2), 1–21.

Karas, M., & Faez, F. (2021). Self-efficacy of English language teachers in Ontario: The impact of language proficiency, teaching qualifications, linguistic identity, and teaching experience. *The Canadian Modern Language Review, 77*(2), 110–128. 10.3138/cmlr-2020-0012

*Kurt, G. (2017). Implementing the flipped classroom in teacher education: Evidence from Turkey. *Educational Technology & Society, 20*(1), 211–221. 10.2307/jeductechsoci.20.1.211

Lipsey, M. W., & Wilson, D. B. (2001). *Practical meta-analysis*. Sage.

*Mızrak, P. (2019). *An exploratory study on the relationship between teacher burnout and teacher self-efficacy among English language instructors* [Unpublished master's thesis]. Bolu Abant İzzet Baysal University.

Moafian, F., & Ghanizadeh, A. (2009). The relationship between Iranian EFL teachers' emotional intelligence and their self-efficacy in Language Institutes. *System, 37*(4), 708–718. 10.1016/j.system.2009.09.014

Norris, J. M., & Ortega, L. (2006). The value and practice of research synthesis for language learning and teaching. In J. M. Norris & L. Ortega (Eds.), *Synthesizing research in language learning and teaching* (pp. 3–50). John Benjamins.

*Onbaşı, M. (2014). *EFL instructors' self-efficacy in relation to student achievement and student perception of instructors' efficacy in teaching writing* [Unpublished master's thesis]. Marmara University.

*Ortaçtepe, D., & Akyel, A. S. (2015). The effects of a professional development program on English as a foreign language teachers' efficacy and classroom practice. *TESOL Journal, 6*(4), 680–706. 10.1002/tesj.185

*Ölmez Çağlar, F. (2019). *Relationships among possible selves, motivations and self-efficacy beliefs of senior student teachers of English* [Unpublished doctoral dissertation]. Hacettepe University.

Phan, N. T., & Locke, T. (2015). Sources of self-efficacy of Vietnamese EFL teachers: A qualitative study. *Teaching and Teacher Education, 52*, 73–82. 10.1016/j.tate.2015.09.006

*Serin, N. (2019). *Self-efficacy beliefs of English language teachers: To be or not to be a nonnative speaker* [Unpublished master's thesis]. Bahçeşehir University.

*Sevimel, A., & Subasi, G. (2018). The factors affecting teacher efficacy perceptions of Turkish pre-service English language teachers. *The Journal of Language Teaching and Learning, 8*(1), 1–17.

Swanson, P. B. (2013). From teacher training through the first year on the job: Changes in foreign language teacher efficacy. *Electronic Journal of Foreign Language Teaching, 10*(1), 5–16.

*Şahin, F. E., & Atay, D. (2010). Sense of efficacy from student teaching to the induction year. *Procedia – Social and Behavioral Sciences, 2*, 337–341. 10.1016/j.sbspro.2010.03.021

*Taşcı, Ç. (2019). *A multivariable examination of the relationships between EFL instructors' self-efficacy beliefs and motivation in higher education* [Unpublished doctoral dissertation]. Middle East Technical University.

Tschannen-Moran, M., & Woolfolk Hoy, A. (2001). Teacher efficacy: Capturing an elusive construct. *Teaching and Teacher Education, 17*(7), 783–805. 10.1016/S0742-051X(01)00036-1

Tschannen-Moran, M., & Woolfolk Hoy, A. (2007). The differential antecedents of self-efficacy beliefs of novice and experienced teachers. *Teaching and Teacher Education*, 23(6), 944–956. 10.1016/j.tate.2006.05.003

Tschannen-Moran, M., Woolfolk Hoy, A., & Hoy, W. K. (1998). Teacher efficacy: Its meaning and measure. *American Educational Research Association*, 68(2), 202–248.

*Tunç Yüksel, B. (2010). *Teacher efficacy beliefs of Turkish EFL teachers: A study with Turkish EFL teachers working at state primary schools* [Unpublished master's thesis]. Anadolu University.

*Ucar, H., & Yazıcı Bozkaya, M. (2016). Pre-service EFL teachers' self-efficacy beliefs, goal orientations, and participations in an online learning environment. *Turkish Online Journal of Distance Education*, 17(2), 15–29. 10.17718/tojde.66088

*Uztosun, M. S. (2016). Pre-service and in-service English teachers' efficacy beliefs about teaching English at primary schools. *Elementary Education Online*, 15(4), 1191–1205. 10.17051/io.2016.80068

Üstünbaş, Ü. (2020). *Pre-service and in-service English language teachers' self-efficacy beliefs and metacognitive awareness* [Unpublished doctoral dissertation]. Hacettepe University.

*Üstünbaş, Ü., & Alagözlü, N. (2021). Efficacy beliefs and metacognitive awareness in English language teaching and teacher education. *Bartın University Journal of Faculty of Education*, 10(2), 267–280. 10.14686/buefad.828035

Wheatley, K. F. (2005). The case for reconceptualizing teacher efficacy research. *Teaching and Teacher Education*, 21(7), 747–766. 10.1016/j.tate.2005.05.009

Wyatt, M. (2013). Overcoming low self-efficacy beliefs in teaching English to young learners. *International Journal of Qualitative Studies in Education*, 26(2), 238–255. 10.1080/09518398.2011.605082

Wyatt, M. (2018a). Language teachers' self-efficacy beliefs: A review of the literature (2005–2016). *Australian Journal of Teacher Education*, 43(4), 92–120. 10.14221/ajte.2018v43n4.6

Wyatt, M. (2018b). Language teachers' self-efficacy beliefs: An introduction. In S. Mercer & A. Kostoulas (Eds.), *Language teacher psychology* (pp. 122–140). Multilingual Matters.

*Wyatt, M., & Dikilitaş, K. (2016). English language teachers becoming more efficacious through research engagement at their Turkish university. *Educational Action Research*, 24(4), 550–570. 10.1080/09650792.2015.1076731

*Wyatt, M., & Dikilitaş, K. (2021). English language teachers' self-efficacy beliefs for grammar instruction: Implications for teacher educators. *The Language Learning Journal*, 49(5), 541–553. 10.1080/09571736.2019.1642943

*Yaylı, D., & Ekizler, F. (2015). Pre- and in-service EFL teachers' sense of efficacy and teaching concerns. *Journal of Language Education and Research*, 1(1), 44–64.

*Yılmaz, A. (2020). *An investigation into the relationship between English preparatory teachers' mindsets and their self-efficacy beliefs* [Unpublished master's thesis]. İstanbul Sabahattin Zaim University.

*Yüksel, G., & Alcı, B. (2012). Self-efficacy and critical thinking dispositions as predictors of success in school practicum. *International Online Journal of Educational Sciences*, 4(1), 81–90.

*Yüksel, H. G. (2014). Becoming a teacher: Tracing changes in pre-service English as a foreign language teachers' sense of efficacy. *South African Journal of Education*, 34(3), 1–8. 10.15700/201409161104

# Part 2
# Exploring factors impacting the development of English language teachers' self-efficacy beliefs

# 4 The formation of pre-service language teachers' self-efficacy beliefs
## A case study

*Zarina Markova*

### Introduction

Teachers' self-efficacy (TSE) beliefs research has evolved from research into self-efficacy beliefs in general. Self-efficacy beliefs have been defined as "beliefs in one's capabilities to organize and execute the courses of action required to produce given attainments" (Bandura, 1997, p. 3). They have attracted considerable research interest over recent decades. Self-efficacy beliefs are agent-means beliefs, i.e., beliefs about the capacity to take an action, and in Bandura's (1986) theory, they interact with outcome expectations, which are means-ends beliefs (Skinner, 1996), i.e., beliefs about the impact the action will have.

Language TSE beliefs have been brought into focus comparatively recently, with the increasing recognition of the specificity of the language teaching domain, where language is both the subject matter and the medium of instruction. The self-efficacy beliefs of pre-service language teachers (PLTSE), however, are still underexplored (Hoang, 2018; Wyatt, 2018). Studies have generally examined the changes of PLTSE beliefs during the practicum (Atay, 2007; Cabaroglu, 2014a; Hoang & Wyatt, 2021) and shed light on their sources (Hoang & Wyatt, 2021; Yüksel, 2014), but have not provided a more detailed description of how these beliefs and sources interact with pre-service language teacher knowledge. This is surprising given the general agreement that a better understanding of the formation and development of PLTSE beliefs can support both teacher educators and prospective teachers themselves (Wyatt, 2018). Even more surprisingly, PLTSE beliefs appear not to attract much interest in research contexts other than Türkiye (Wyatt, 2018). This chapter aims to address this gap by presenting a case study of the formation of a pre-service language teacher's sense of self-efficacy during her English practicum in a Bulgarian context.

DOI: 10.4324/9781003379300-6

## Literature review

Studies investigating changes in PLTSE beliefs over the practicum typically use, adapted or not, the Teachers' Sense of Efficacy Scale (TSES), developed by Tschannen-Moran and Woolfolk Hoy (2001) and measuring TSE beliefs concerning three fields of teaching activity: Classroom management, instructional strategies, and student engagement. Findings have generally yielded uneven growth of PLTSE beliefs across these different fields. For example, in Türkiye, Atay (2007) and Şahin and Atay (2010) reported a significant strengthening in PLTSE beliefs in areas related to classroom management and student engagement and a weakening (Atay, 2007) or lack of significant growth (Şahin & Atay, 2010) regarding instructional strategies. Similarly, in a Vietnamese context, Hoang and Wyatt (2021) found statistically significant gains in PLTSE beliefs about classroom management and student engagement. However, an exception to this pattern is a study in Türkiye by Cabaroglu (2014a), where large and statistically significant gains in all three areas of PLTSE beliefs were reported, possibly due to the additional engagement of the participants in action research activities. Only one of the reported studies (Hoang & Wyatt, 2021) goes beyond the use of the TSES, in additionally including self-developed items, to address domain-specific PLTSE beliefs (see Chapter 2 of this volume for a discussion of instrumentation). Its results reveal significant growth in PLTSE beliefs about motivational English instruction, and lack thereof related to beliefs about developing English teaching materials and teaching communicative English (Hoang & Wyatt, 2021), thus suggesting that such beliefs are less open to influence during the practicum. Possible explanations can be connected with either the insufficient task-specificity of the survey items or pre-service teachers' inclination to focus more on classroom management and students' motivation as prerequisites for effective language learning than on the language teaching tasks themselves (Hoang & Wyatt, 2021). The latter interpretation is in tune with the findings regarding broader instructional strategies reported on by Atay (2007) and Şahin and Atay (2010) and noted above. Deeper exploration of the processes of PLTSE beliefs growth through a qualitative lens could throw more light on aspects of these processes which quantitative approaches are less well-equipped to explore.

There is still a relatively limited number of studies using qualitative data as part of a mixed-methods approach to investigating PLTSE beliefs. Those studies that do use qualitative data do so to focus predominantly on the sources of PLTSE beliefs. For example, in agreement with Bandura's (1997) conceptualization, enactive mastery experiences have been found to be a major source of PLTSE beliefs (Hoang & Wyatt, 2021; Yüksel, 2014). They have been reported to influence pre-service language teachers' general pedagogical skills in various ways. These include: Dealing with misbehaving students (Cabaroglu, 2014a; Hoang & Wyatt, 2021), managing classroom activities (Hoang & Wyatt, 2021; Parks, 2021), giving effective instructions (Yüksel, 2014), and engaging language learners (Atay, 2007; Cabaroglu, 2014a; Hoang & Wyatt, 2021; Yüksel, 2014). When enactive discipline-specific mastery experiences are discussed, this is mostly done in connection with pre-service teachers' target language knowledge and skills (Atay, 2007; Yüksel, 2014) but also with their abilities to support struggling students through the use of the mother tongue (Parks, 2021). Findings show that although enactive mastery experiences are not always positive, they bear the potential, through reflection, to turn into valuable real-life lessons (Cabaroglu, 2014a; Hoang & Wyatt, 2021; Parks, 2021). However, a key point is that PLTSE beliefs are more likely to grow when student teachers are given the freedom to experiment, fail, reflect, and revise rather than when their mentors maintain tight control over their classrooms (Parks, 2021).

Vicarious experiences as a main source of PLTSE information are usually discussed in connection with the opportunities (or lack thereof) to observe mentors' teaching. Such observational information is related to developing general pedagogical skills like engaging learners and maintaining a productive classroom atmosphere (Atay, 2007; Cabaroglu, 2014b). However, such vicarious experiences also support language teaching skills such as using the target language as a medium for instruction (Atay, 2007; Cabaroglu, 2014b), grammar and vocabulary teaching, correcting learners, using teaching materials and activities to develop communicative skills (Atay, 2007; Cabaroglu, 2014b). Again, vicarious experiences do not always have a positive impact on PLTSE beliefs – often they are reported to cause self-efficacy doubts and disappointment with the level of mentor teaching and established classroom practices (Atay, 2007; Cabaroglu, 2014b). In these cases, reflection is alluded to as a process pre-service teachers have to go through to solve their teaching dilemmas (Cabaroglu, 2014b).

Interactive experiences[1] are another main source of information prospective language teachers draw on when forming their PLTSE beliefs. They are generally related to feedback, both verbal and non-verbal, from mentors (Atay, 2007; Hoang & Wyatt, 2021; Parks, 2021; Yüksel, 2014), peers (Yüksel, 2014), and students (Parks, 2021; Yüksel, 2014). An interesting finding across studies is that pre-service language teachers' perceptions of how successful an enactive experience is tend to come from their students' reactions, not from a mentor's or supervisor's feedback (Atay, 2007; Parks, 2021). Similarly to enactive mastery and vicarious experiences, interactive experiences can influence PLTSE beliefs both positively and negatively. A certain degree of resilience (Parks, 2021) is needed to consider criticism as an impetus for reflection and growth (Hoang & Wyatt, 2021). Corrective feedback, however, can lose its potential to transform if pre-service language teachers do not feel supported by significant others (Yüksel, 2014), or by peers or students (Parks, 2021).

Affective states, as the fourth source of self-efficacy information, seem to have less influence on PLTSE beliefs since they tend to be mentioned by fewer survey respondents as a key source (Hoang & Wyatt, 2021; Yüksel, 2014). They are often seen in relation to the processing of efficacy information from other sources (Yüksel, 2014) and can be positive and negative (Hoang & Wyatt, 2021; Yüksel, 2014). Pre-service language teachers may be able to control negative affective states once they become immersed in enactive mastery experiences (Yüksel, 2014).

The most striking finding emerging from this literature review is that, unlike research into the LTSE beliefs of in-service teachers (Wyatt, 2016), so far most studies of PLTSE beliefs do not seem to have looked for connections between changes in PLTSE beliefs, the sources of PLTSE beliefs information, and reflection. Explanations could be found in the lack of qualitative case study research methodology employed, which has been used to trace change in in-service teachers (e.g., Wyatt, 2013), and the research questions themselves. These research questions have focused predominantly on comparison between pre-practicum and post-practicum PLTSE beliefs, their relation to perceived language proficiency, and sources of PLTSE beliefs information. Yet, it is still curious given, first, Bandura's (1997) assertion that reflective thought is crucial in the formation of self-efficacy beliefs and, second, teacher educators' conviction that reflection is central to pre-service teachers' learning and development (Freeman, 2016; Walsh & Mann, 2015).

Two notable exceptions from this observation are Cabaroglu's (2014a) study, which explores how pre-service language teachers' engagement in action research influences their self-efficacy beliefs, and Parks' (2021) research on pre-service second language teachers' efficacy-identity development. Both studies suggest the reflection process enhances PLTSE beliefs, no matter whether it is structured and guided by a teacher educator (Cabaroglu, 2014a) or occurs naturally among pre-service teachers in their peer groups (Parks, 2021). This points to the need for further exploration of the role of reflection in the formation of PLTSE beliefs, especially in light of more general TSE beliefs research (Markova, 2021; Wheatley, 2002; Wyatt, 2016) emphasizing concerns about the over-focus on positive TSE beliefs, and the neglect of TSE doubts as a catalyst for teacher learning. The present chapter aims to address these issues further by reporting findings of a qualitative case study focusing on the formation of PLTSE beliefs.

### Research context

The case study participant was in her early twenties and was pursuing an English teaching qualification while studying Applied Linguistics at a

Bulgarian university where I am employed as a teacher educator. After an initial introductory year, the programme includes a two-year theoretical part consisting of courses in the field of education, psychology, and foreign language teaching (FLT). The final year of the programme gives practical experience: Observation of 15 lessons in a state or a municipality school,[2] team-teaching of 15 lessons, and a 10-week practicum when pre-service teachers work together with a school mentor and are supervised by a university teacher educator. The teaching certificate is obtained after the successful completion of the programme and the state practice exam, which involves teaching and self-evaluating a lesson before a board of three university-based teacher educators and the school mentor. My involvement with the programme starts during the third year, when I teach courses on "Methodology of Foreign Language Teaching", "Language Acquisition and Foreign Language Teaching", and "Teaching English to Young Learners", and continues throughout the final year. This allows me natural opportunities to collect data, for example through analysing students' assignments or lesson plans, and my research (with a larger group, of which I say more below) built on these opportunities.

## Research methodology

The study sought answers to the following research question:

How did a prospective language teacher form her self-efficacy beliefs during the practicum?

Within a qualitative case study approach (Stake, 1995), data collection instruments included:

1 Observation schedule. This instrument focused attention on the aims of the observed lesson, and how they were reflected in the procedure and classroom interaction. To stimulate reflection, it included additional questions like "What have you learned from this observation? Which aspect of the observed lesson do you feel most/least confident about?[3] Why?"
2 Lesson plan. Its sections are related to aims, procedure, and classroom management, and a section on anticipated problems and possible solutions to them to stimulate exploration of potential pitfalls and strategies to avoid or manage them. This template was introduced during the courses in FLT when pre-service teachers gained practice in using it for different lesson types. For the purposes of this study, several more questions were included to prompt reflection on aspects of a lesson causing PLTSE doubts, ways to overcome them, and, correspondingly, aspects of a lesson associated with greater feelings of security and higher TSE beliefs.
3 Semi-structured interviews. These interviews followed the principle of hierarchical focusing (Tomlinson, 1989). Common questions included:

Whose idea was this (with a particular teaching task in mind)? How did you come up with it? Why did you think it could solve the problem? How did you consider its implementation during the lesson? Could you possibly describe the steps of your argumentation? Are you satisfied with the result? In what terms? Do you feel more confident about this task now? What have you learned from this experience? The questions did not necessarily follow this order to enable a smooth flow of the interview. Additional probing questions were asked when needed.

4 Assignments, self-assessment of coursework as well as assessors' comments for evidence of developing cognitions and reflection were also analysed.

Employing these data collection instruments allowed data triangulation for verification and validation of the qualitative analysis (Patton, 1999). For example, the observation schedules might point to feelings of insecurity which (if present) could be explored further during the practicum. The lesson plans, with their sections on anticipated problems and possible solutions, could provide data about situations of practice (Schön, 1983) that the case study participant felt uncertain about, and how she intended to deal with them. She could follow her mentor's advice or procedures suggested in the teacher's book, but could also follow her own way of handling the uncertainty. The next section of the lesson plan explicitly focused on TSE beliefs and any doubts about her own abilities to cope with taxing teaching situations. The data from the semi-structured interview could throw more light on her cognitions and PLTSE beliefs before and after conducting the lessons. Finally, her assignments, self-assessment, and my comments on them would allow me to compare and complement the data collected through the first three instruments.

## Data collection and analysis

Data collection occurred mostly over the lesson observation stage in November 2020 and the teaching practice in March–June 2021. Normally, the practicum takes place in schools in the city where the university is based; in 2020–2021, however, due to COVID-19 restrictions for the different regions of the country, most (14 out of 17) prospective teachers preferred to conduct their observations and teaching practice in their hometown schools, which were smaller; more opportunities for face-to-face teaching were expected. They still had local, school-based mentors to cooperate with, but my communication with them was online, predominantly asynchronous, with the pre-service teachers sending their observation schedules and lesson plans and receiving personal feedback by email. We gathered three times in a virtual classroom – once for instructions and twice for general feedback on common teaching problems and concerns during the lesson observation stage and the teaching practice stage. Within this period, I collected and analysed 119 observation schedules and 230 lesson plans submitted by 14 prospective teachers.[4]

My analysis of the observation schedules involved two perspectives. From a teacher educator's standpoint, I examined the extent to which the aims of an observed lesson were understood, lessons were learned from each observation and, as a whole, how deep was the reflection. As a researcher, I was additionally interested in PLTSE beliefs and doubts that emerged across my students' writing, how (or whether) they were connected with growth in their professional knowledge, whether remedies for coping with doubts were applied, and if so, how realistic they were. I analysed the lesson plans in a similar way: As an educator focusing on features such as well-defined and realistic lesson aims; coherence between them, the teaching activities, and the interaction patterns; good balance in terms of different language skills; judicious use of the coursebook; and well-argued anticipated difficulties and solutions. As a researcher, I paid additional attention to the depth of reflection related to LTSE doubts and ways to deal with them, to high LTSE beliefs, and whether a relationship between professional knowledge and LTSE beliefs or doubts was described or hinted at. I also checked for consistency in each pre-service teacher's reflections across her observation schedules and lesson plans.

Among the teachers whose descriptions were exhaustive enough and revealed interesting examples of their growth (or lack thereof) in LTSE beliefs and/or professional knowledge, four were chosen to be interviewed. Before the interviews, all four student teachers expressed willingness to participate in the research and signed an informed consent, which promised anonymity in line with ethical guidelines.

The interviews themselves took place during the last week of June and the first of July 2021 (after the practicum), lasted about an hour, were conducted and recorded online, via BigBlueButton, and were transcribed shortly afterwards. To avoid issues with recall, the interviewees had the opportunity to consult their observation schedules and lesson plans. My analysis of the interview data involved checking:

- the consistency between a student teacher's interview data, and the data from her observation schedules and lesson plans,
- whether and how the themes emerging from the content of the first two instruments were developed and elaborated on,
- whether new themes were mentioned or alluded to, and if so, how they were connected to the previous ones.

After the pre-service teachers' state exam, the synthesized data were sent by email for member checking to confirm the fair interpretation of their thoughts and feelings. For space limitations, here I report on one case, Bozhura's (pseudonym used).

I started working with Bozhura in her third university year, as a tutor of the courses FLT Methodology and Teaching English to Young Learners. She came across as amiable and hard-working, always taking notes. Bozhura readily took part in the discussions, and, after experiencing initial difficulties (e.g., in the first draft of her assignment in FLT Methodology), developed her analytical skills over time with grit and patience following the tutor's scaffolding. Bozhura's practicum was in a basic education school in a mountainous village in south-western Bulgaria where she taught lower secondary classes of between 16 and 22 boys and girls.

When presenting the results of the case study, the data coding system shown in Table 4.1 is followed.

*Table 4.1* Data codes

| Pre-service teacher's pseudonym | Data source | Number |
| --- | --- | --- |
| Bozhura | Observation schedule (O) | 1–7 |
| | Lesson plan (LP) | 1–10 |
| | Interview (I) | 1 |
| | Course assignments (CA) | 7 |
| | Self-assessment (SA) | 6 |

## Results

### Cultivating high PLTSE beliefs

The dominant PLTSE beliefs and doubts emerging from Bozhura's reflections on her practicum were domain-specific. Her observation schedules and lesson plans exhibited comparatively high TSE beliefs related to teaching new target language, be it grammar, vocabulary, or function. This may have been because of a perceived sense of security of "the rules which have to be followed" (O1) and "the plenitude of opportunities to present the new language, especially when it comes to vocabulary or function" (O2). This was indeed visible in all her lesson plans, abundant with illustrations of colourful flashcards, photos, tables, and graphs, which she intended to use as visual aids to contextualize the target language and enhance students' understanding (LP1-10). Bozhura's high TSE beliefs concerning teaching new target language items were backed up by competence in lesson planning, and preparation and use of ELT materials – areas of pre-service language teacher's competence investigated in previous research (Cabaroglu, 2014b; Hoang & Wyatt, 2021). Corresponding PLTSE beliefs were not mentioned explicitly in the lesson plans, perhaps because Bozhura's thoughts were focused more on other aspects of classroom implementation. Yet, supplementary ELT materials were judiciously and consistently applied throughout the lesson plans, which hinted at a high degree of self-efficacy in this area – an assumption confirmed during the interview. According to Bozhura, her PLTSE beliefs about planning a lesson and developing ELT materials stemmed from her interactive experiences during the university courses in FLT (I). Adhering to the maxim "By failing to prepare you are preparing to fail" (I), she quickly internalized strong outcome expectations (Bandura, 1977), which helped her work hard to achieve enactive mastery experiences when preparing the corresponding course assignments, as she confirmed in interview. These outcome expectations, in turn, enhanced her PLTSE beliefs. Continuous effort during her practicum additionally strengthened these beliefs, as she explained (I); previous PLTSE research has reported similar findings (Cabaroglu, 2014a).

The references to high PLTSE beliefs regarding grammar teaching, however, merit more exploration. The illustrations in several observation schedules (O1-3) and lesson plans (LP3-4) depicted a contextualized, but still deductive, approach. This was not in full harmony with the rest of Bozhura's work, which showed sufficient knowledge and use of communicative language teaching tasks, and suggested she was a "contextualizing/ interactive/communicative" teacher (Wyatt & Dikilitaş, 2021). Since previous research provides evidence that contextualization is a key grammar teaching component such teachers identify with (Wyatt & Dikilitaş, 2021), it was interesting to see Bozhura's rationale for the deductive aspects of her choice of approach (LP3-4). She connected this with her mentor's impact, through both vicarious and interactive experiences, which made her reflect on which approach to use: The strictly deductive one would make her students more at ease in comparison to discovery-oriented, inductive grammar teaching, which would be new to the students, she explained in interview. Dilemmas of this kind are reported in other studies of the pre-service teachers' practicum (Cabaroglu, 2014b). In Bozhura's case, what happened in the end was a trade-off between her professional knowledge and contextual factors "because they [students] already seemed a bit stressed out because interns don't often come to our school, and I wanted them to feel better, in their comfort zone somehow", she reported. Still, the result was an enactive mastery experience and, correspondingly, strengthened her PLTSE beliefs.

However, additionally, possible PLTSE doubts about inductive grammar teaching could also have influenced Bozhura's decision as she did not hesitate to introduce meditation and transition activities, also unfamiliar to students, in the very first lesson. Her reasoning was informed by the vicarious experiences of observing her mentor's work, which reinforced her awareness that students need a "break from repetitive tasks" (I). Bozhura, however, had already developed strong means-ends and PLTSE beliefs in this area through reflection on course content and interactive experiences, and through enactive mastery experiences in considering the implementation of meditation and transition activities (CA4) during her studies. The first enactive mastery experiences at school only strengthened PLTSE beliefs in this area and she continued applying such activities in all her lessons (LP1-10), she confirmed (I).

Another interesting example of growth is the way Bozhura built her self-efficacy about formative assessment – an area of concern in other pre-service language teachers' contexts too (Atay, 2007). Self-assessment was part of Bozhura's courses in FLT (SA1-6), and it must have been convincing as an interactive experience, since she immediately decided to apply it in the future (I). Bozhura's lesson plans (LP2, LP9) provide evidence for such use in developing her students' writing skills: Self-assessment in writing recipes (LP2) and peer-assessment in writing animal descriptions (LP9). The implementation of these forms of assessment confirmed her expectations that they would be unfamiliar to students: "Well, at first they stared amazed, maybe because this had not been applied before, but I explained what they had to do step by step, I also explained why I was doing it". These enactive mastery experiences strengthened her self-efficacy beliefs in using alternative assessment. They also enhanced her teacher knowledge, namely, awareness of her students' history of learning English (I).

The data so far suggest that Bozhura's PLTSE belief formation paths share several characteristics:

1 They were conceived during the theoretical part of her teacher preparation programme, through reflection on course content and interactive experiences leading to enactive mastery experiences in her work on course assignments. Thus, she developed self-efficacy for learning to perform (Schunk, 1996).
2 Corresponding means-ends beliefs about the effectiveness of different language teaching tasks were added to the growing system of her professional knowledge and beliefs.
3 The tasks themselves became part of her future teaching repertoire as possible ready-made solutions which Schön (1983) terms "Technical Rationality".
4 These tasks were thoughtfully integrated in her teaching. They were applied as solutions to problems anticipated after reflection on language learning principles and/or after gaining vicarious experiences from observing her mentor's lessons. Her students' emotional well-being was a serious factor informing her decisions at this stage.
5 The application of these tasks not only led to enactive mastery experiences, which in turn caused higher PLTSE beliefs and outcome expectations, but also enhanced her teacher knowledge.

As a whole, the data on Bozhura's high PLTSE beliefs indicate there was a considerable degree of fit (Wyatt, 2015) between them and her professional knowledge and confirm the observation that high self-efficacy beliefs can lead to competent performances only when they are accompanied by the requisite knowledge and ability (Schunk, 1996).

*Overcoming PLTSE doubts*

Bozhura repeatedly reported low TSE beliefs associated with freer speaking tasks (O1-2, LP1, LP6, LP10). They were caused by vicarious experiences of observing her mentor teaching and were attributed to means-ends doubts about the effectiveness of open (but not closed) pair work. She felt open pair work inhibited both the shyer students – "a girl so nervous that she almost started crying" (O2) – and the struggling ones – "There are students who can express themselves well in English and those who still have difficulties" (LP6). Similar problems with students' speaking skills have been observed in rural Bulgarian classrooms (Ivanova, 2016). In Bozhura's case, however, uncertainties seemed to be additionally confirmed by insecurities about her personal lexicon (O1-2, LP1). "While the children were describing what they did during the summer, there were questions like: How to say *делфинариум/вятърна мелница/медуза*[5] in English?", she wrote in her second observation schedule, and also "When it comes to speaking, students always ask numerous questions, and you have to be very well prepared to answer adequately" (LP1). PLTSE doubts related to aspects of language proficiency are reported in other studies (Atay, 2007). Generally, there is a danger such doubts lead teachers to resort to avoidance strategies, which deprive students from participating in communicative activities (Wyatt & Dikilitaş, 2021).

This was not the case with Bozhura, though, as her lesson plans showed sufficient evidence of her planning to achieve the opposite (LP2, LP6, LP8-10). For example, in a lesson called "Strong, fit and healthy!", her 13/14-year-old students were to be given illustrations of different sports which they had to describe to a partner explaining whether and why they liked the corresponding sport. Language support including keywords and phrases was to be provided on the board (LP6). In a lesson about health issues with 10/11-year-old students, health problems were to be discussed in closed pairs in a similar way. Bozhura might have had her agent-means doubts (Skinner, 1996) about utilizing closed-pair work, but they did not deter her from applying the appropriate interaction patterns to achieve her aims. She had strong means-ends beliefs about the effectiveness of closed-pair work because of enactive mastery experiences as a foreign language learner: "when I studied English, I experienced it myself, and I could see that it was effective. So, I already had an idea of the results" (I). These beliefs were additionally strengthened through enactive mastery and interactive experiences at the university (CA2, CA4, SA3).

The interview data reveal that Bozhura's agent-means doubts about using closed pairs to develop speaking skills were partly influenced by her vicarious experiences of observing her mentor's interaction patterns and the subsequent awareness that the students might feel awkward working in closed pairs for the first time (I). These uncertainties were at the same time intertwined with more general classroom management doubts – "I worried about the discipline, the noise, the students' reaction" (I). Similar preservice teachers' concerns have been voiced in other contexts (Cabaroglu, 2014a, 2014b), and low PLTSE beliefs about classroom management skills at the beginning of the practicum are commonly reported across studies (Atay, 2007; Cabaroglu, 2014a; Hoang & Wyatt, 2021).

Despite her doubts, Bozhura was determined: "I had concerns, but then, I had concerns about any task since I didn't have enough experience. I was never sure what might happen, but I decided to take a risk" (I). She overcame her doubts through careful preparation and reflection. Unlike reported examples of a posteriori reflection (Cabaroglu, 2014a, 2014b), however, Bozhura deliberated in advance on such details of the organization of the closed-pair activity as teacher instructions, pair formation, her position in the classroom during the different stages, interaction with students (I). Then she took the decision to "combine the students in such a way that a student with better speaking skills would work with a student who had difficulties, so that the more fluent student could help the other with the task", as she explained in the interview. Bozhura's preparation seems to have borne fruit as task control was perceived, which resulted in a positive enactive mastery experience:

> I think it was OK. To some extent it was a bit difficult because, as I said, they resort to Bulgarian, but I tried to remind them "let's say it in English now, let's try", and I helped them when they needed it. Generally, there were no problems during the class.

Similar proactive behaviour allowed Bozhura to overcome the doubts about her personal lexicon. She spent a lot of time reflecting "on every single [lesson] step" – an iterative process where she "tried to anticipate as much as possible all the questions the students could have, how [she] could answer them, what language [she] would need" (I). In this way, she accumulated a corpus of presumable words before each lesson to feel "well-prepared". Only then did Bozhura feel she "gained some confidence" and was ready to enter the classroom (I). Such a strategy for boosting perceived language proficiency has been reported in Bulgarian research on pre-service teachers' cognitions (Velikova, 2013). In Bozhura's case, it was effective as it led to positive enactive mastery experiences, and, with time, to some increase in her beliefs that her language competence was sufficient for teaching (I).

Another area where Bozhura had continuous PLSTE doubts was time management (LP2-3, LP8-9). Reflection was needed to understand why an apparently straightforward teaching task linked to mastery experiences of learning to perform (CA 3-6) was causing her doubts (I). Having identified the cause – insufficient awareness of her students' language knowledge and skills, and of their attitudes to learning English – she first decided to follow her German tutor's advice and, as an approximation, to multiply twice the time she would need to do all the lesson tasks. After more reflection, she decided to keep this calculation in mind, but still prepare materials to individualize instruction – "more challenging for the fast learners and easier for the rest" (I). This strategy led to pleasing enactive mastery experiences in class but did not strengthen much her PLTSE beliefs about time management (I).

In addition to evidence regarding Bozhura's cognitions, the interview data also contained multiple references to her emotions causing physiological arousal (Bandura, 1977): "I felt happy", mentioned several times throughout the interview; "I was in my element", "I simply loved what I was doing". Apparently, apart from the developed reflective skills and preliminary teaching knowledge, love for teaching (Hargreaves, 2005) also aided Bozhura in overcoming her language teaching doubts.

The features in Bozhura's paths to overcoming her PLTSE doubts that stand out are as follows:

1 The time of their origin depended on the level of their specificity: More specific, task-oriented doubts addressing closed-pair speaking activities, or time management started when she faced real classroom teaching, whereas more global domain doubts related to personal language proficiency probably originated earlier and thus were more fixed (Pajares, 1992).
2 Her PLTSE doubts went hand in hand with high means-ends beliefs about the effectiveness of the corresponding tasks. These beliefs were conceived through reflection, interactive and enactive mastery experiences of learning to perform, and were integrated in her professional knowledge and beliefs.
3 The PLTSE doubts were caused by perceived lack of knowledge and skills to live up to the expected standards or by an awareness that the employment of the corresponding tasks in her teaching context may be problematic.
4 To overcome doubts, Bozhura engaged in reflection involving hypotheses and mental experiments. Her students' language development and emotional well-being influenced her reasoning during this stage.

5 These mental efforts resulted in enactive mastery experiences in class, which enhanced her PLTSE beliefs and teacher knowledge.
6 The mastery experiences regarding her personal lexicon and time management, though, were not considered convincing enough to eliminate teaching doubts, probably because the related teaching tasks differed from lesson to lesson and thus prevented the generalization of PLTSE beliefs. To compensate for this, Bozhura continued with her reflections before each of her lessons, thus accumulating useful linguistic and methodological knowledge.
7 Her persistence in this process was supported by altruistic motives: Love for students and the teaching profession.

## Discussion

The case study results indicate an uneven start in the formation of Bozhura's PLTSE beliefs. At the beginning of her practicum, she felt self-efficacious about certain teaching tasks, and less so about others. The reported high self-efficacy beliefs relate to language instructional strategies, an area where mixed-methods research has produced differing results: From significant growth in perceived self-efficacy regarding motivational English instruction (Hoang & Wyatt, 2021) and in general more positive pedagogical PLTSE beliefs about instructional strategies (Cabaroglu, 2014a) to significant weakening of the latter (Atay, 2007).

There are overlapping concerns about domain-specific teaching tasks, such as the alternative assessment of writing skills and grammar teaching, perceived as important by both Bozhura and some Turkish pre-service teachers (Atay, 2007). This is the only similarity, however, as, unlike her Turkish counterparts, Bozhura reported high self-efficacy beliefs concerning these tasks.

Such discrepancies could be related to differences in teacher education programmes, but also to mentors' attitudes and behaviours towards prospective teachers. While Bozhura's mentor gave her support and freedom to experiment and learn, a stance reported in other studies too (Atay, 2007; Parks, 2021), such an attitude should not be taken for granted, as the same studies reveal.

The evidence regarding Bozhura's feelings of self-inefficacy corresponds more with the reports on PLTSE doubts. Her concerns about time management can be viewed in light of the findings of low PLTSE beliefs about broader classroom management skills at the start of the practicum (Atay, 2007; Cabaroglu, 2014a; Hoang & Wyatt, 2021). Bozhura's perception of deficits in her language competence and its relation to her LTSE beliefs about speaking tasks also resonates with research results across language teaching contexts (Faez & Karas, 2017; Faez et al., 2021; Hoang & Wyatt, 2021).

As regards the PLTSE sources, similarly to previous research (Hoang & Wyatt, 2021; Yüksel, 2014), enactive mastery experiences, vicarious experiences, and interactive experiences have been found to inform the formation of self-efficacy beliefs. A caveat to this observation is that part of Bozhura's enactive mastery experiences is related to learning to perform, an aspect not new in educational contexts (Schunk, 1996) that can also be expected in teacher preparation programmes but has not been discussed in the PLTSE beliefs literature so far. With respect to the fourth source of LTSE beliefs, the only affective state mentioned by Bozhura has been related to love for students and teaching, echoing research findings in a different context (Hoang & Wyatt, 2021).

The results reveal that the formation of Bozhura's PLTSE beliefs differed depending on their degree. However, they always involved high means-ends beliefs integrated, through reflection on language pedagogy materials, vicarious and interactive experiences, in her teacher knowledge. This finding relates Bozhura to teacher C (where she was initially feeling less efficacious but persisted) or teacher E (where she felt efficacious from the outset), as suggested by Wyatt's (2018) matrix of the interaction between efficacy and outcome expectations, and indicates potential for learning and development.

Bozhura's high PLTSE beliefs started their formation during her teacher preparation programme, when, depending on the tasks, she developed self-efficacy for performing or for learning to perform (Schunk, 1996), the former about lesson planning and preparing ELT materials, the latter regarding the use of peer- and self-assessment, and transition and mediation activities. These tasks were incorporated in Bozhura's future teaching repertoire as "Technical Rationality" (Schön, 1983), and implemented during her practicum after reflection on how they could be applied to her teaching context. The resulting enactive mastery experiences strengthened her high PLTSE and means-ends beliefs. In many ways, this PLTSE beliefs formation path follows Fives' extended model of teacher self-efficacy (2003), where information from the sources of LTSE beliefs affects pedagogical knowledge and beliefs, which then influence the way the teaching task is analysed. The result is enactive mastery experiences and consequently enhanced TSE beliefs and teacher knowledge. The data on Bozhura's implementation of deductive grammar teaching indicate, however, that a boost in teacher knowledge is not always guaranteed. Although she may have had her valid reasons for using this approach, repeated success in applying it may lead to exaggerated LTSE beliefs, impediment to reflection, and lack of fit between these beliefs and teacher knowledge – all of which pertain to teacher F (a teacher who becomes complacent) (Wyatt, 2018).

This potential danger was more unlikely when self-inefficacy was perceived. In Bozhura's case, it resulted from uncertainties about the implementation of language teaching tasks associated with high means-ends beliefs. To overcome her self-efficacy doubts, Bozhura engaged in a process of inquiry (Dewey, 2008, Chapter 11), where she first specified their causes, next hypothesized a possible solution, then visualized its implementation with particular students in mind and, if needed, considered more solutions to apply. Finally, she tested her solution in the classroom, which led to enactive mastery experiences and, correspondingly, to synchronized growth between PLTSE beliefs and teacher knowledge (Wyatt, 2015), a prerequisite for future competent performances (Schunk, 1996). This process of PLTSE beliefs formation entails reflection throughout its stages and thus resembles more the action research sequence described by Cabaroglu (2014a) than the "trial-error-reflect" line (Parks, 2021), where reflection is limited to "reflection-as-repair" (Freeman, 2016).

The pattern of the formation of perceived self-efficacy emerging from this case study shares several characteristics with two models of LTSE beliefs (Markova, 2021; Wyatt, 2016). These characteristics include the link between the development of LTSE beliefs and teacher knowledge, the emphasis on the importance of doubts and reflection in this process, and the recognition of the role of contextual factors, moral reasoning (Richardson, 2018), and affective states. Additionally, the findings suggest a considerable degree of overlap between the dimensions of teacher knowledge growth reported in Bozhura's case and in Wyatt's model of LTSE beliefs (2016), but also a difference regarding the place of reflection – when it comes to the teaching task it is before its performance, not after it. The data also indicate that reflection involves mental experiments that may necessitate going back and forth in the reflective cycle until a feasible solution to the teaching task is found (Markova, 2021). Such variations between the case study data and the expected patterns of the two models may be attributed to differences in research contexts (in-service vs pre-service teacher education, professional development through action research vs learning to teach during the practicum), but also to data collection instruments. Bozhura's a priori reflection may have been induced by the lesson plan structure she had to adhere to, particularly the section on anticipated problems and possible solutions, which required consideration of teaching tasks perceived as more challenging, identification of their causes, and evaluation of potential ways of dealing with them. To her credit, she applied herself to strictly following this structure and thus provided rich data on her cognitions while preparing to teach. This aspect of her development could also explain the findings illustrating her proactive engagement in reflection even when the teaching tasks were associated with high means-ends and LTSE beliefs, which does not corroborate the corresponding cycle in the second model (Markova, 2021). What becomes clear is the need for more exploration in this area of LTSE beliefs research to deepen our understanding of the formation and growth of these beliefs.

## Conclusions and pedagogical implications

Case studies are very rare in the LTSE beliefs literature (Wyatt, 2022), even more so in pre-service language teacher education, and, through exploring change processes in-depth, this case study provides rich insights. Nevertheless, it is also important to acknowledge limitations. First, the findings reflect the formation of LTSE beliefs of a prospective English language teacher obtaining her degree from a Bulgarian university and conducting her practicum in a village school. Therefore, they may not be generalizable to other contexts. Second, the data collection instruments include self-reports, a common limitation of such studies (Faez & Karas, 2017; Wyatt, 2014). Third, the interview focused on past events and, although every effort was made to ensure sufficiently good recall, this could have skewed the data. To mitigate these limitations, the nature and intent of the study were carefully explained, assessment was separated from data collection as much as possible, and finally, data triangulation was employed.

With these limitations in mind, the following conclusions can be drawn. First, the overall successful formation of Bozhura's PLTSE beliefs can be attributed to personal qualities like conscientiousness, patience, reflexivity, and attentiveness. However, also important were contextual factors such as constructivist aspects of the teacher education programme, which enabled her to develop a reflective stance and accumulate useful professional knowledge, attitudes, and beliefs. Tutoring and mentoring, which scaffolded this process, were influential. All of these factors combined to prevent strong negative feelings of inadequacy during the practicum and contributed to persistence in overcoming agent-means doubts.

Several pedagogical implications emerge from this study. First, Bozhura's case confirms the importance of sound professional knowledge for enhancing PLTSE beliefs. This knowledge can be acquired through balanced theoretical input on language learning combined with the exploration of practice-oriented teaching activities.

Throughout this process, reflective skills should be consistently nurtured. At present, the importance of reflection in L2 teacher education appears to be well-recognized, but the facilitation of it too often remains rather mundane (Walsh & Mann, 2015). During the practicum, reflection predominantly involves reflection-on-action aimed at improvement, which reduces its value (Freeman, 2016). Instead, student teachers can be encouraged to analyse, hypothesize and test hypotheses *in action*, under a tutor's and/or mentors' supervision.

Next, it can be beneficial to provide a focus on perceived self-efficacy, its formation, and development during language teacher education. Such a focus can raise prospective teachers' awareness of the significance of adequate LTSE beliefs, the potential of LTSE doubts, the necessity of a good degree of fit between beliefs and teacher knowledge (Wyatt, 2015), and the need to cultivate reflective skills. All of these elements could foster a more positive attitude to inevitable pitfalls and prevent discouragement.

Last, this study again confirms the importance of the mentor as both a supporter and a role model, and the necessity of cooperation between ministries of education, universities, and schools towards mentor education. Such education could promote individual partnerships between mentors and prospective teachers aiming to resolve practice-oriented, personally meaningful educational problems, and foster both sides' motivation (Lamb & Wyatt, 2019) and commitment to the language teaching profession in general.

## Notes

1 Used instead of "social persuasion" as a more general term, especially in educational contexts where the received input from others is more often intended to stimulate reflection than to persuade (Wyatt, 2016). I view interactive experiences as taking place during the practicum, but also during the theoretical courses. They could involve students, peers, mentors, and tutors.
2 The school level can be chosen according to preferences and availability. It is not uncommon for a pre-service English language teacher to teach both primary and lower secondary students at a basic education school.
3 For practical reasons, I used "confident" instead of "self-efficacious" in the observation schedule, the lesson plan template, and the interview.
4 The three pre-service teachers who did their practicum in the university city were not included in this batch as they taught predominantly online.
5 dolphinarium/windmill/jellyfish.

## References

Atay, D. (2007). Beginning teacher efficacy and the practicum in an EFL context. *Teacher Development*, *11*(2), 203–221. 10.1080/13664530701414720

Bandura, A. (1977). Self-efficacy: Toward a unifying theory of behavioral change. *Psychological Review*, *84*(2), 192–215. 10.1016/0146-6402(78)90002-4

Bandura, A. (1986). *Social foundations of thought and action: A social-cognitive theory*. Prentice-Hall.

Bandura, A. (1997). *Self-efficacy: The exercise of control*. Macmillan.

Cabaroglu, N. (2014a). Professional development through action research: Impact on self-efficacy. *System*, *44*, 79–88. 10.1016/j.system.2014.03.003.

Cabaroglu, N. (2014b). Re-visiting the theory and practice gap through the lens of student teacher dilemmas. *Australian Journal of Teacher Education*, *39*(2), 89–149. 10.14221/ajte.2014v39n2.10

Dewey, J. (2008). *Democracy and education*. Project Gutenberg. Retrieved on 11th July 2022 from https://www.gutenberg.org/files/852/852-h/852-h.htm

Faez, F., & Karas, M. (2017). Connecting language proficiency to (self-reported) teaching ability: A review and analysis of research. *RELC Journal*, *48*(1), 135–151. 10.1177/0033688217694755

Faez, F., Karas, M., & Uchihara, T. (2021). Connecting language proficiency to teaching ability: A meta-analysis. *Language Teaching Research, 25*(5), 754–777. 10.1177/1362168819868667

Fives, H. (2003). *Exploring the relationships of teachers' efficacy, knowledge, and pedagogical beliefs: A multimethod study* [UMD Theses and dissertations]. http://hdl.handle.net/1903/3

Freeman, D. (2016). *Educating second language teachers.* Oxford University Press.

Hargreaves, A. (2005). The emotions of teaching and educational change. In. Hargreaves, A. (Ed.), *Extending educational change* (pp. 278–290). Springer.

Hoang, T. (2018). Teacher self-efficacy research in English as a foreign language contexts: A systematic review. *The Journal of Asia TEFL, 15*(4), 976–990. 10.18823/asiatefl.2018.15.4.6.976

Hoang, T., & Wyatt, M. (2021). Exploring the self-efficacy beliefs of Vietnamese pre-service teachers of English as a foreign language. *System, 96*, article 102422 10.1016/j.system.2020.102422.

Ivanova, I. (2016). The status of speaking and communication in EFL classroom. *Annual of Konstantin Preslavsky University of Shumen. Faculty of the Humanities. Vol. 27A*, (pp. 45–52). Konstantin Preslavski University Press.

Lamb, M., & Wyatt, M. (2019). Teacher motivation: The missing ingredient in teacher education. In S. Mann & S. Walsh (Eds.), *The Routledge handbook of language teacher education* (pp. 522–535). Routledge.

Markova, Z. (2021). Towards a comprehensive conceptualisation of teachers' self-efficacy beliefs. *Cambridge Journal of Education, 51*(5), 653–671. 10.1080/0305764X.2021.1906844

Pajares, M. F. (1992). Teachers' beliefs and educational research: Cleaning up a messy construct. *Review of Educational Research, 62*(3), 307–332. 10.3102/00346543062003307

Parks, P. (2021). *Should I stay, or should I go? A mixed method study of pre-service English second language teacher efficacy-identity development in Quebec* [Unpublished doctoral dissertation]. McGill University. https://escholarship.mcgill.ca/collections/theses?locale=en

Patton, M. Q. (1999). Enhancing the quality and credibility of qualitative analysis. *Health Services Research, 34*(5), 1189–1208.

Richardson, H. S. (2018, Fall). Moral reasoning. In E. N. Zalta (Ed.), *The Stanford encyclopedia of philosophy.* Retrieved on 31st January 2023 from https://plato.stanford.edu/archives/fall2018/entries/reasoning-moral

Şahin, F. E., & Atay, D. (2010). Sense of efficacy from student teaching to the induction year. *Procedia – Social and Behavioral Sciences, 2*(2), 337–341. 10.1016/j.sbspro.2010.03.021

Schön, D. (1983). *The reflective practitioner: How professionals think in practice.* Basic Books.

Schunk, D. (1996, April 8–12). *Self-efficacy for learning and performance* [Paper presentation] American Educational Research Association. Conference 1996, New York, USA. https://eric.ed.gov/?id=ED394663

Skinner, E.A. (1996). A guide to constructs of control. *Journal of Personality and Social Psychology, 71*, 549–570. 10.1037//0022-3514.71.3.549

Stake, R. (1995). *The art of case study research*. Sage.

Tomlinson, P. (1989). Having it both ways: Hierarchical focusing as research interview method. *British Educational Research Journal*, 15(2), 155–176. 10.1080/0141192890150205

Tschannen-Moran, M., & Woolfolk Hoy, A. (2001). Teacher efficacy: Capturing an elusive construct. *Teaching and Teacher Education*, 17(7), 783–805. 10.1016/S0742-051X(01)00036-1

Velikova, S. (2013). Using the European Portfolio for Student Teachers of Languages (EPOSTL) to scaffold reflective teacher learning in English language teacher education. In J. Edge & S. Mann (Eds.), *Innovations in pre-service education and training for English language teachers* (pp. 201–216). British Council UK.

Walsh, S., & Mann, S. (2015). Doing reflective practice: A data-led way forward. *ELT Journal*, 69(4), 351–362. 10.1093/elt/ccv018

Wheatley, K. F. (2002). The potential benefits of teacher efficacy doubts for educational reform. *Teaching and Teacher Education*, 18(1), 5–22. 10.1016/S0742-051X(01)00047-6

Wyatt, M. (2013). Overcoming low self-efficacy beliefs in teaching English to young learners. *International Journal of Qualitative Studies in Education*, 26(2), 238–255. http://www.tandfonline.com/doi/abs/10.1080/09518398.2011.605082

Wyatt, M. (2014). Towards a re-conceptualization of teachers' self-efficacy beliefs: Tackling enduring problems with the quantitative research and moving on. *International Journal of Research and Method in Education*, 37(2), 166–189. http://www.tandfonline.com/doi/abs/10.1080/1743727X.2012.742050

Wyatt, M. (2015). Using qualitative research methods to assess the degree of fit between teachers' reported self-efficacy beliefs and their practical knowledge during teacher education. *Australian Journal of Teacher Education*, 40(1), 117–144. 10.14221/ajte.2015v40n1.7

Wyatt, M. (2016). "Are they becoming more reflective and/or efficacious?" A conceptual model mapping how teachers' self-efficacy beliefs might grow. *Educational Review*, 68(1), 114–137. 10.1080/00131911.2015.1058754

Wyatt, M. (2018). Language teachers' self-efficacy beliefs: An introduction. In S. Mercer & A. Kostoulas (Eds.), *Language teacher psychology* (pp. 122–140). Multilingual Matters.

Wyatt, M. (2022). Learning to use a qualitative case study approach to research language teachers' self-efficacy beliefs. In K. Dikilitaş & K. M. Reynolds (Eds.), *Research methods in language teaching and learning* (pp. 9–23). Wiley Blackwell.

Wyatt, M., & Dikilitaş, K. (2021). English language teachers' self-efficacy beliefs for grammar instruction: Implications for teacher educators. *The Language Learning Journal*, 49(5), 541–553. 10.1080/09571736.2019.1642943

Yüksel, H. G. (2014). Becoming a teacher: Tracing changes in pre-service English as a foreign language teachers' sense of efficacy. *South African Journal of Education*, 34(3), 1–8. 10.15700/201409161104

# 5 Novice EFL teachers' self-efficacy beliefs in the first year

An insight into the impact of task-, domain-, and context-specific factors upon perceptions of efficacy

*Natalie A. Donohue*

## Introduction

The first year of teaching is often seen as the most difficult, requiring much adaptation, flexibility, and learning to adjust to a new role (Farrell, 2016). Language teaching, and particularly English language teaching (ELT), may be considered unique in terms of the variety of tasks, domains, and contexts involved, leading to a range of additional potential challenges. One way of measuring how novice teachers navigate this formative period in their career is through their self-perceptions of efficacy. Self-efficacy beliefs represent the extent to which one judges oneself capable of completing a particular task (Bandura, 1997). Embedded in social cognitive theory, self-efficacy offers a theoretical framework of motivation for the analysis of teachers' cognitions relating to tasks associated with their profession. Skaalvik and Skaalvik define this construct as it applies to teachers as "an individual teacher's beliefs in their own ability to plan, organize, and carry out activities that are required to attain given educational goals" (2010, p. 1059).

Researching teachers' – and particularly novice teachers' – perceptions of efficacy is an important area of inquiry for many reasons. Whilst self-efficacy doubts can stimulate development (Wheatley, 2002; Wyatt, 2015), excessive self-efficacy can hamper such development (Ončevska Ager & Wyatt, 2019; Wheatley, 2002). Self-efficacy beliefs have been linked to motivation (Skaalvik & Skaalvik, 2019), persistence (Bandura, 1997), engagement (Skaalvik & Skaalvik, 2019), and resilience (Gu & Day, 2007). Bandura (1997) argues that self-efficacy is more susceptible to fluctuations whilst novice teachers build experience and confidence within their role.

There are four recognized sources associated with self-efficacy beliefs: Mastery experiences; physiological feedback; vicarious experiences; and verbal persuasion. Input from each of these sources can either positively or negatively impact upon a person's sense of self-efficacy (Bandura, 1997). Bandura proposes mastery experiences to be the most powerful influence

DOI: 10.4324/9781003379300-7

for teachers, yet, as novice teachers lack a wealth of mastery experiences to draw upon (Reeve, 2018), the other three sources of self-efficacy information are expected to have greater importance. However, self-efficacy is a complex construct, influenced not only by these four sources but also by the nature of tasks and the context in which they are enacted (Bandura, 1997; Tschannen-Moran & Hoy, 2001).

Whilst these factors may be more or less influential at particular stages of a teacher's career, no one single source determines perceptions of efficacy. Instead, self-efficacy is constructed through complex internal evaluation of all sources (Bandura, 1997). Most notably, self-efficacy encompasses *perceived* competence, resulting from "cognitive processing of diverse sources (e.g., other people's opinions, feedback, evaluation, encouragement or reinforcement; past experiences and training; observing peers; information about appropriate task strategies)" (Dörnyei & Ushioda, 2011, p. 17). Put simply, self-efficacy theory allows not only for consideration of teacher education and the impact it may have upon baseline perceptions of self-competence, but also how the experiences and feedback a teacher receives once in-service can influence judgements of efficacy. Therefore, it is a particularly useful framework for application in longitudinal studies of novice teachers and their transition into teaching.

*Novice teachers' self-efficacy beliefs*

Self-efficacy is particularly applicable when examining novice teachers; teacher efficacy has been described as "a changeable and developing construct that fluctuates with experience, knowledge, and interpretation of contextual factors" (Fives & Alexander, 2004, p. 333). The early years of teaching can be particularly trying, replete with new experiences and challenges. Research has indicated that whilst teachers' self-efficacy (TSE) beliefs stabilize over time (Tschannen-Moran & Johnson, 2011), they are typically in a state of flux in the early years and more susceptible to change (Bandura, 1997). Some research suggests novice teachers can overestimate their self-efficacy beliefs before experiencing a "reality shock" once moving in-service (Tschannen-Moran & Hoy, 2007), whilst other studies show that following a steady strengthening during pre-service training, self-efficacy beliefs can undergo a significant weakening in the transitional stage to in-service teaching (Hoy & Spero, 2005; Klassen et al., 2014). Consequently, it is vital to consider teacher preparation programmes and to what extent they can prepare novice teachers for their subsequent professional roles.

Once in-service, the extent to which an individual over- or underestimates their abilities has "consequences for the courses of action they choose to pursue and the effort they exert in those pursuits" (Hoy & Spero, 2005, p. 344). Possessing a high degree of self-efficacy can be a powerful tool in helping novice teachers deal with challenges; they can initiate change if their perceived efficacy is sufficient (Wyatt, 2018; Klassen et al., 2014). However, excessive self-efficacy can deter critical examination of one's abilities and practices (Ončevska Ager & Wyatt, 2019), inevitably impacting upon professional development. A lack of self-efficacy, conversely, typically leads to negative cognitions and emotions that can inhibit successful performance (Bandura, 1997).

It is also noteworthy that "teachers do not feel equally efficacious in all teaching situations" (Wheatley, 2002, p. 6); rather, perceptions of self-efficacy are task-, domain-, and context-specific (Bandura, 2001). Nevertheless, much existing research into TSE concerns global efficacy (Tschannen-Moran & Hoy, 2001; Wyatt, 2015), without sufficient attention given to the particular activity or setting, and key "microanalytical" considerations (Pajares, 1996). A contributing factor to this situation is the lack of qualitative research in the area (Wyatt, 2015). Thus far, most research into TSE has been quantitative in nature, with self-efficacy being typically measured through self-reporting on Likert-scale questions (Wheatley, 2002; Klassen et al., 2011). This fails to fully account for the complex judgements and interpretations which can contribute to perceptions of self-efficacy, including the influence of vital microanalytical considerations (Wheatley, 2002; Wyatt, 2015). To truly recognize and reflect the detailed and shifting nature of novice TSE beliefs and "emergent themes of individual importance to teachers" (Wyatt, 2018, p. 128), qualitative methods are necessary.

*Language teachers' self-efficacy beliefs research*

Language teacher self-efficacy (LTSE) research also lacks both qualitative and longitudinal insight. Wyatt (2018) provides a review of LTSE beliefs, identifying 98 studies between 2005 and 2016, which include journal articles, book chapters, and postgraduate theses. In total, 85 of the studies involved some quantitative data compared to only 13 with a purely qualitative focus. This indicates a lack of breadth in understanding LTSE beliefs from a qualitative perspective. The dynamic nature of self-efficacy is also routinely overlooked (Wyatt, 2015, 2018), and there remains a gap in the LTSE beliefs literature with regards to the complex transition of novice teachers from pre-service education to in-service teaching.

Teacher education naturally plays a key role in shaping teachers' confidence and self-efficacy levels as they begin teaching and potentially in impacting their resilience when facing unexpected circumstances or challenges in the classroom (Ončevska Ager & Wyatt, 2019). For ELT specifically, it is worth acknowledging the variety of routes into the profession: Some teachers may have tertiary-level degrees, whilst others may have as little as an online certificate or no training whatsoever. Drawing upon research from TSE more generally, it is possible to speculate that those with less teacher preparation may perceive lower levels of efficacy when they begin teaching. Identifying the nature of LTSE beliefs held at the conclusion of a teacher education programme and observing whether there are any significant shifts in these beliefs over time can help inform teacher educators (Wyatt, 2015).

An enduringly popular route into ELT for many – traditionally native English speakers – is short initial teacher education courses (SITECs), such as the Cambridge Certificate in Teaching English to Speakers of Other Languages (CELTA). SITECs offer internationally recognized teaching certification for the private sector in a very short period of time: typically four weeks full-time, or across six months part-time. They consist of a practical teaching element (at least eight hours) combined with theory-based assignments. Due to a lack of context-specific content, this certification theoretically allows trainees to subsequently seek employment globally. Over the years, criticism has been levelled at the CELTA, and other SITECs, but there is evidence that the majority of CELTA courses are well-designed and taught and that participants are generally satisfied with the quality (Anderson, 2016; Kiely & Askham, 2012). However, it cannot be assumed that novice teachers trained through such time-limited courses will feel efficacious in relation to the different task-, domain-, and context-specific factors they may encounter in-service.

Indeed, despite SITECs being intended as a "basic toolkit" (Hobbs, 2013), Senior (2006) claims that "a considerable number [of novice teachers] start teaching feeling that their teaching skills and subject-matter knowledge are inadequate for the task" (p. 51). For instance, to consider task-specific impacts on self-efficacy, the time constraints inherent to SITECs may lead to task-specific efficacy doubts in relation to grammar teaching. Both Anderson (2016) and Howard (2018) note that inexperienced native-speaking[1] candidates are more likely to report deficiencies in grammar and language awareness. Alternatively, a native-speaking novice teacher may feel more efficacious in teaching pronunciation.

Similarly, domain-specific impacts upon self-efficacy may emerge for SITEC-trained novice teachers in that the content and expectations of the particular subject (for example communicative English as opposed to academic English) or a particular student profile (children compared to adults) may result in different perceptions of efficacy. This is pertinent in light of findings that expatriate EFL teachers can often be required to teach unfamiliar courses (Medgyes & Kiss, 2019), and that there is an increased likelihood that they will be asked to teach young learners once employed (Anderson, 2016; Senior, 2006). SITECs predominantly focus on the teaching of adults, but it is generally accepted that young learners require alternative teaching approaches. A consequence is that SITEC-trained novice teachers may have lower perceptions of efficacy with this student profile.

Context-specific factors are also likely to influence novice TSE beliefs. One major attraction of SITECs is that the certification is internationally recognized and candidates are not subsequently bound to a specific geographical region. However, once in-service, they may face differing cultural and professional expectations, especially if they had undertaken teacher education in a different context and constructed self-efficacy beliefs tailored to a specific group or teaching style. This was evident in Borg's (2008) study of three CELTA-trained novice teachers. One participant felt unable to utilize the skills and knowledge learnt in the course due to the perceived clash between the skills and knowledge acquired and the established teaching approach and expectations of the school. Meanwhile, another felt strongly that although the course gave her the skills necessary to teach, it did not adequately prepare her for the realities and challenges of teaching monolingual classes. Additionally, context-specific factors including available resources, supervisory support, time pressure, and autonomy have been found to play a significant role in relation to the self-efficacy beliefs of novice teachers (Tschannen-Moran & Hoy, 2007).

A final aspect to consider in relation to novice LTSE beliefs is access to social support once in-service. Access to a collaborative professional environment, wherein novice teachers can reflect and develop their practice alongside more experienced colleagues, can increase their self-efficacy beliefs (Zonoubi et al., 2017), while appreciation from colleagues can help develop their sense of competence, self-efficacy levels, and self-esteem (Wyatt, 2013). Indeed, in a study by Hoy and Spero (2005), teachers with higher levels of efficacy at the end of their first year also indicated they had received higher levels of support than those who had lower efficacy. Conversely, negative social experiences such as limited autonomy or working within an unsupportive workplace environment can diminish self-efficacy beliefs and motivation (Yuan & Zhang, 2017). SITEC-trained expatriate novice teachers may not always have access to support in the workplace (Howard, 2018; Medgyes & Kiss, 2019), and without it they can face challenges in relation to lesson planning, delivering lessons, classroom management, and identity development (Farrell, 2015).

Nevertheless, a study by Kiely and Askham (2012, p. 508) reported that trainees were confident in their knowledge at the end of their SITEC, and "though the skills may have been raw, and the knowledge fragile, they had a clear and confident sense of what good practice involves". However, in terms of microanalytical considerations, the range and variety of tasks, domains, and contexts found across ELT may result in additional challenges for SITEC-trained novice teachers. A lack of sufficient social support may hinder novice EFL teachers in building self-efficacy beliefs once in-service. To summarize, there is a clear gap in the literature when it comes to empirical data on the self-efficacy of SITEC-trained novice teachers, though their self-efficacy beliefs may be challenged. The following study seeks to address this gap by exploring the impact of task-, domain-, and context-specific factors on novice EFL teachers' perceptions of efficacy in their first year of teaching.

## Research methodology

This study formed part of a larger doctoral research project, which investigated expatriate novice EFL teacher motivation and self-efficacy beliefs in the first year of teaching. To address two of the significant gaps in LTSE research discussed above, this study utilized a longitudinal, qualitative case-study design. Five participants were recruited in total, two of whom were followed for the entirety of their first year and three of whom were followed for their first six months of teaching. All had English as their native language. These participants had each completed a CELTA course prior to emigrating to a different country to begin their teaching career, thereby representing a group of language teachers facing a complex array of social, cultural, and contextual challenges as they simultaneously adapted to a new professional role. As can be seen in Table 5.1, the participants (pseudonymized) came from different educational and professional backgrounds, with varying reasons for choosing to complete a CELTA qualification. Following their respective CELTA courses, each novice teacher took up employment in an EFL context, either in one or more private language schools or in a freelance capacity.

*Table 5.1* Overview of participants

| Participant | Background | EFL context | Reasons for choosing CELTA |
|---|---|---|---|
| Sean (1 year) | BA Spanish and TEFL certificate | Vietnam (1 school) | To travel and save money for translation qualifications |
| James (1 year) | BA Fine Art and online TEFL certificate | Italy (3 schools and private tutoring) | To earn money in Italy whilst studying aspects of agriculture |
| Molly (6 months) | BA French and History of Art | China (1 school) | To travel while teaching |
| Rupert (6 months) | Quantity Surveyor | Poland (freelance) | Sustainable career after relocating with family |
| Emma (6 months) | Student recruiter at an American university | Vietnam (1 school) | To move abroad and teach English |

Qualitative data were primarily collected through multiple in-depth interviews, monthly questionnaires, and weekly diary entries, although email correspondence and retrospective reflections provided additional data for some participants. Interviews were conducted post-CELTA, after six months of teaching, and – for Sean and James – at the end of their first year. Weekly diary entries provided insight into experiences and issues which the individual teachers felt were most relevant that week, including, for instance, particular successes and challenges, any critical incidents, and information about specific lessons. To help mitigate any missing diary entries, a monthly questionnaire (see Appendix) provided supplementary data, containing primarily open-ended questions, with a few closed questions to allow participants to self-evaluate their efficacy levels. Questions changed little from month to month and explored, for example, participants' perceptions of their efficacy across different aspects of teaching, reflections on their development as teachers, and any changes in their workplace environment. Data collected from both the diary entries and questionnaires helped to form subsequent interview guides for each individual participant. Interviews offered opportunities to further probe into the novice teachers' experiences and elicit retrospective and prospective accounts of their trajectories as English teachers. The interviews were then transcribed verbatim, with interpretative phenomenological analysis chosen to guide data analysis due to its suitability for detailed analysis of a small number of participants and qualitative data in particular (Smith, 2017).

Within the confines of this chapter, it is not possible to outline and analyse the self-efficacy beliefs of each novice teacher participant in relation to every aspect of their teaching, nor were there sufficient data on each element from every participant to make an accurate assessment of this. Therefore, only the most salient themes from each participant will be considered, reflecting what the novice teachers themselves found most pertinent to discuss in their contributions. Nevertheless, it is clear from these findings that greater consideration should indeed be given to task-, domain-, and context-specific self-efficacy, echoing calls from other contemporary researchers (Wheatley, 2002; Wyatt, 2018).

## Results

This section first considers the five participants collectively due to the similarity in reflections on their respective CELTA courses. Thereafter, each participant is discussed individually, so that the nature and dynamism of their self-efficacy beliefs, as they navigated their first year of teaching, can be highlighted.

## Post-CELTA

Almost all participants reflected positively on their CELTA courses. Whilst acknowledging that time constraints limited what could be covered, they were pragmatic in their expectations, showing awareness that there was still much yet to learn about ELT. James' comments reflected those shared by Sean, Emma, and Molly: "there would not have been *time* to incorporate more ... it's fairly 'stripped down' already to the basics ... I think for the time that it was, yeah, it was useful" (James, 1st interview). Rupert, conversely, was the only participant critical of his CELTA course, particularly regarding its lack of "a focus on aspects of the language which as a native speaker are *innate*, but aren't really explicitly understood and explainable" (Rupert, 1st interview). Noteworthy here, however, is that Rupert was the only participant to envisage EFL teaching as a long-term career choice and, additionally, the only one to complete the CELTA part-time. These factors may have contributed to higher expectations of the course.

All participants reported confidence in their global efficacy to teach English after their course. Emma, for instance, stated: "I remember feeling at the end ... like 'yeah, I feel like a teacher'" (Emma, 1st interview). Rupert also perceived high global efficacy due to his native English-speaker status. When their beliefs were probed more deeply, however, certain caveats emerged amongst the participants, particularly regarding grammar teaching (linked to task-specific efficacy), and the possibility of teaching young learners (linked to domain-specificity). These concerns, along with others, arose to varying extents across participants, depending on context and teaching role.

### Sean

Once in-service, Sean's global efficacy for teaching was challenged by multiple task-, domain-, and context-specific factors. His teaching role involved assessing groups of four or five students on their progress after self-studying multimedia-based material, something he had not been prepared for on the CELTA (domain-specific). Sean had to provide "hot error correction" (task-specific), whereby he had to identify errors and correct them immediately – a task which represented challenges which were further compounded by his self-perceived lack of grammar knowledge.

Sean initially had limited access to professional development or social support within his role but was proactive in making concerted efforts to self-study and address his weaknesses and, by his third month, reported improved ability to help "students zero in on their weaknesses and strengthen them" (3rd-month questionnaire). However, his self-efficacy for this task was not always stable, and in his second interview, he admitted he still found this task "difficult" sometimes and would like specific training in this area.

A pivotal moment for Sean came following a promotion after seven months. This new role involved assessing students on a one-to-one basis, allowing him to cater to his students' needs more easily: "For the first time in my 6 months of being here I feel like I'm teaching and passing on something to the students which is a great feeling and has helped me develop my teaching skills" (7th-month diary entry). He also gained access to professional development and a supportive collegial team following the promotion, which further increased his self-efficacy perceptions in assessing students and correcting errors. Furthermore, perceiving that his students often lacked basic grammatical understanding, Sean volunteered to teach weekly grammar classes, stating: "I've realised that for grammar they need an actual teacher to teach them the grammar because they don't understand it otherwise" (10th-month diary entry). This suggests he perceived sufficient self-improvement in his own language awareness to feel comfortable offering himself as this "actual teacher".

Indeed, in his third interview, Sean reported satisfaction in overcoming his challenges, reporting high global efficacy for teaching overall: "I feel like I can teach English at a high standard to any level as I have had so many classes over my time here" (3rd interview). However, he also raised concerns in future teaching scenarios, including teaching reading and writing skills and teaching large classes, showing that despite evincing high global efficacy for teaching in general, this efficacy would not necessarily extend to unfamiliar tasks and domains.

### *James*

James, working across several schools and tutoring privately, faced alternative challenges to Sean. Post-CELTA, he indicated concerns over lack of resources and having much preparation to do beforehand, and about teaching children because of a lack of experience. Once in-service, these worries were not unfounded and he struggled with fluctuating self-efficacy in lesson planning (task-specific) and teaching young learners (domain-specific) throughout the year.

James initially indicated high task-specific efficacy beliefs for lesson planning when offering intense private tuition to one student, but by the end of his first month, his self-perceptions had shifted: "I'm still learning the basics of English and without proper preparation it's difficult to deliver a high level of instruction" (1st-month questionnaire). He reported particular difficulty in lesson planning for young learners in language schools – reiterating his lack of experience in this domain. James became reliant on the textbooks and resources available but conceded that he struggled with "adapting material from the course books to encourage conversation, especially with younger learners" (2nd-month questionnaire).

After three months, James perceived himself "becoming more confident and preparing better for lessons" (3rd-month questionnaire). When he found a successful activity, for instance using cloze tasks, he frequently incorporated it into his teaching. However, he subsequently became "flummoxed" when access to resources unexpectedly changed. This was particularly challenging when he was asked to teach an intensive one-month course at a local primary school in his fifth month, where he was expected to create his own syllabus: "it [was] more of a challenge to organise a lesson where you had almost zero physical resources" (2nd interview). Reflecting on this experience, James acknowledged both successes and challenges, but still felt a lack of confidence in teaching young learners. He also received very little advice from colleagues.

In fact, James was lacking in consistent access to supportive colleagues. Nevertheless, he was influenced by his staffroom observations, characterizing colleagues as doing minimum planning and preparation, which subsequently influenced his own engagement and self-perceptions: "I'm just above that, I hope, but I'm not far from it" (2nd interview).

Despite this admission, James showed signs of developing efficacy in lesson planning and teaching in the second half of the year. For instance, although conceding it could still be difficult to find enough material for lessons, he mitigated this by utilizing different coursebooks when planning. Subsequently, by the end of his first year, due to recent successful mastery experiences – and receiving more hours at fewer schools – James indicated higher perceptions of self-efficacy for both lesson planning and for teaching adults, perceiving himself more "able to plan better for adults/find more interesting material from [the] school's resources" (9th-month questionnaire). He remained somewhat ambivalent, however, about teaching young learners, stating he would "be curious to go back to teaching children because I see it as a challenge, but I'd want to do some kind of training first" (3rd interview).

*Molly*

During the CELTA, Molly found the practical aspect very difficult and anxiety-provoking, but subsequently praised the course for increasing her confidence in lesson planning and teaching: "I felt like I'd improved loads" (1st interview). However, she simultaneously noted worries about teaching monolingual, monocultural students and young learners.

Once in-service, Molly faced significant challenges from the outset, both within her teaching role, and regarding living in China. She characterized some of her first lessons as "disasters", reporting problems with miscommunication with a co-teacher, lack of knowledge of how to teach particular grammar points, and students struggling with content. These negative initial experiences appeared to directly impact her efficacy for teaching more generally and she reported being unable to teach the next lesson because she "started crying uncontrollably 30 mins before" (1st diary entry).

Molly was consistently influenced by praise and feedback (verbal persuasion) from colleagues, reporting that she had been told "my instructions and gestures and demo-ing were really strong so the stuff I can work on will be more 'in-depth, advanced' things like pacing and tracking participation. I was very excited to hear this" (1st-month diary entry). However, several weeks after this, she received feedback which indicated she "didn't understand the aims of the activities" she was running, and she "didn't actually teach the students" (6th-month reflection), which significantly impacted her perceptions of efficacy. Again, through colleagues' feedback, Molly was able to identify appropriate methods to address these concerns.

Indeed, Molly appeared to receive a substantial amount of social support from colleagues which helped her address other challenges she faced. For instance, classroom management of young learners emerged as an issue, but after discussing this "at length" with colleagues, she implemented some new strategies and saw "improvement in all but one student" (3rd-month questionnaire). She acknowledged significant progress in this area over time, noting after six months that classroom management "no longer causes me anxiety, mainly thanks to experience and advice from colleagues" (6th-month reflection).

However, after a period of limited contact and inconsistent contributions, Molly withdrew from the study. She conceded she was struggling with work-related stress and lack of motivation: "I'm teaching very low-level English and am frustrated by this ... I find that the majority of my planning & effort goes into classroom management/game planning, which is not what I'm interested in" (8th-month email). This suggests that her global efficacy for teaching was negatively impacted not just through physiological feedback but also because of the domain-specific impact of teaching young learners.

### Rupert

Rupert acknowledged a lack of task-specific efficacy regarding grammar teaching post-CELTA but aimed to rectify this through self-study. Whilst searching for work, he specifically sought domains in which he perceived himself to have higher teaching efficacy, such as in teaching adults and Business English. However, he was limited in his options as a freelance teacher in a small city and ended up predominantly teaching children.

Within his first few months of teaching, Rupert was continually critical of his own teaching abilities, despite showing evidence of doing needs analyses, tailoring his teaching to students' needs, and longer-term planning. He reported "inconsistency" throughout his teaching, noting some successes, but also acknowledging challenges he faced: "some lessons go very well, language is explored and new lexis introduced etc. Others go terribly, especially those with the younger learners and maintaining discipline" (4th-month questionnaire).

Whilst he was somewhat able to mitigate perceived deficiencies in grammar knowledge through self-study, with respect to domain-specific concerns around teaching young learners and context-specific factors, he sought the support and advice of colleagues. For instance, in an end-of-year reflection, he acknowledged contextual challenges which clashed with his CELTA training, including that his Polish students were resistant to pair and group work, and they "want to speak to a native speaker and not to another student". Being a freelance teacher, however, he had limited access to the support he wanted. When he did receive advice, he often accepted it, even if it clashed with his own teaching beliefs and negatively impacted his self-perceptions of efficacy: "I try my best to do as the [Directors of Studies] say, even when their advice/requirements go against what was taught on the CELTA course" (2nd-month questionnaire). Throughout his contributions, Rupert regretted the lack of social support he had in dealing with the challenges he faced: "I can rely only on myself. And it is hard at times" (4th-month questionnaire). He ended his first year of teaching conceding "I don't believe I matched up to my initial expectations" (end-of-year reflection).

*Emma*

Perhaps because of already securing a teaching job in Vietnam before her post-CELTA interview, Emma commented on aspects of teaching she was most looking forward to, such as teaching adults and not anticipating much lesson planning. Yet, despite explicitly vocalizing her newfound identity as a "teacher", once in-service, Emma quickly began to doubt her abilities, which she attributed to a lack of induction and being unaware of the expectations of the school (context-specific). She had accepted a job in the same company as Sean and was also required to "assess" students and provide immediate error correction. She noted a lack of confidence in these areas because the CELTA "didn't teach us assessment, so it's all very new to me" (1st-month diary entry).

A particularly significant moment for Emma was observing a fellow teacher failing his probationary period because – in her understanding – his lessons were not "fun" enough. This vicarious experience resulted in her questioning her own teaching abilities as well as the school's expectations: "I'm not really sure if my instruction is that good. I can't tell if the focus of my [school] is on students having fun/feeling good or learning" (1st-month questionnaire). She also felt conflicted about how much error correction to give, believing that too much was frustrating for students and affected their fluency and confidence in speaking.

Emma initially felt unable to seek support from colleagues, reporting: "I don't feel comfortable asking for support or telling them the hard time that I am having" (1st-month questionnaire). Yet, once having passed her own probation, influenced by positive feedback from her manager, she stated: "I'm feeling more and more confident" (3rd-month questionnaire). However, she reiterated conflict over the school's expectations of lessons: "while I want my classes to be fun, it's still difficult to have fun as a priority over education".

After five months, Emma's contributions continued to indicate frustration about prioritizing "fun" over learning and so much hot error correction: "I don't fully agree with what is being asked of me currently" (5th-month diary entry). Additionally, despite having built efficacy in assessing students, this was reduced when she was unexpectedly told her fail rates were too low. These issues – among others – impacted her so much that she decided "I will not stay until the end of my contract in [4 months]" (5th-month questionnaire).

However, it subsequently appeared that the social support she received from colleagues impacted positively upon her perceptions of efficacy: "we have been trying as a team to kind of come together as far as how much feedback or correction we're giving" (2nd interview). This support also included encouragement from her manager to give training to other teachers and by the end of her first six months of teaching, Emma reflected positively on her development: "I don't feel like I'm an expert teacher but I definitely feel a lot more confident in a lot of areas". Although context-related issues remained, verbal persuasion and mastery experiences helped increase her global efficacy.

## Discussion

This section considers more deeply the dynamic nature of novice TSE beliefs characterized by fluctuations in self-perceptions due to task-, domain-, and context-specific factors. It draws out the most common factors shared amongst the participants. The notable impact of social support upon self-efficacy perceptions is also discussed.

### Task-specific

Each novice teacher in this study could be seen to experience shifts in their efficacy due to task-specific factors. The most prominent are shown in Table 5.2.

Table 5.2 Task-specific impacts influencing participants' self-efficacy

| Participant | Task-specific impact on self-efficacy | Shifts over time | Positively influential factors | Negatively influential factors |
|---|---|---|---|---|
| Sean | Error correction/ grammar teaching/ language awareness | Steadily increasing throughout his 1st year | Self-study; mastery experiences; formal professional development (following promotion) | Lack of pre-service training |
| James | Lesson planning | Fluctuating throughout his 1st year | Mastery experiences; access to resources | Vicarious experience (observations of colleagues); losing access to resources |
| Rupert | Grammar teaching/ language awareness | Increasing throughout his 1st year, but still perceived deficiencies | Self-study | Lack of pre-service training |
| Emma | Error correction | Consistently low throughout first five months, increasing in 6th month | Social support; mastery experiences | Lack of pre-service training; expectations of the school |

For instance, particularly evident across Sean, Rupert, and Emma's cases were fluctuating self-perceptions in their abilities related to language awareness, wherein they found it difficult identifying errors and correcting them (Sean and Emma) or explaining grammatical structures and answering students' questions (Rupert). Whilst each teacher recognized a lack of explicit knowledge in this area following their CELTA, echoing Anderson (2016) and Howard (2018), only Sean and Rupert attempted to address perceived gaps in their knowledge through self-study. Positive mastery experiences also helped to increase each teacher's self-efficacy beliefs over time, although only Sean perceived a significant improvement in this area by the end of his first year.

A pervasive task-specific impact on self-efficacy for James was lesson planning and his self-perceptions continuously fluctuated throughout his contributions. Whilst heavily reliant on the resources available at his schools, he acknowledged that his planning was not at the level he expected, and unexpectedly losing access to resources at times negatively impacted his self-perceived ability to plan engaging lessons. He was additionally influenced by observations of his colleagues putting little effort into their planning. However, by the end of his first year, successful mastery experiences appeared to have increased his task-specific efficacy for lesson planning.

*Domain-specific*

Throughout this study, two prominent domain-specific impacts upon self-efficacy emerged: Teaching young learners and "assessing" rather than teaching, as shown in Table 5.3.

The former influenced the perceptions of self-efficacy of James, Rupert, and Molly, both in terms of classroom management and the teaching content. CELTA courses typically provide minimal instruction in how to teach young learners, and, indeed, these participants noted concerns about teaching this student profile post-CELTA. Whilst mastery experiences helped James and Rupert build some efficacy in this area, both wished for advice from colleagues which they were unable to access. Unfortunately, as Medgyes and Kiss (2019) and Howard (2018) highlight, SITEC-trained novice teachers may not always have access to supportive workplace environments. Conversely, the feedback which Molly received from colleagues appeared to be fundamental in forming her perceptions of efficacy for teaching children, echoing Zonoubi et al.'s (2017) findings. Although she experienced both significant stress and negative mastery experiences, feedback she received seemed to enable her to persevere despite her challenges.

"Assessing" rather than "teaching" their students was an unexpected domain-specific factor which influenced both Sean's and Emma's perceptions of efficacy. Further supporting Medgyes and Kiss' (2019) claim that

102   Natalie A. Donohue

Table 5.3 Domain-specific impacts influencing participants' self-efficacy

| Participant | Domain-specific impact on self-efficacy | Shifts over time | Positively influential factors | Negatively influential factors |
|---|---|---|---|---|
| Sean | "Assessing" rather than teaching | Steadily increasing | Mastery experiences; formal professional development (following promotion) | Lack of pre-service training |
| James | Teaching young learners | Fluctuating, but still low at the end of his 1st year | Mastery experiences | Lack of pre-service training; lack of advice from colleagues |
| Molly | Teaching young learners | Fluctuating, but particularly low at the end of six months | Feedback from colleagues | Lack of pre-service training; physiological feedback (stress); mastery experiences |
| Rupert | Teaching young learners | Fluctuating | Mastery experiences | Lack of pre-service training; lack of advice from colleagues |
| Emma | "Assessing" rather than teaching | Fluctuating with a notable decrease in 5th month, followed by an increase | Mastery experiences; feedback from colleagues | Lack of pre-service training; feedback from manager |

expatriate teachers are often required to teach unfamiliar courses, neither had been prepared for assessing students on the CELTA course, and, while neither overtly critiqued the CELTA for this, they nonetheless struggled to various degrees adapting to this facet of their role. Mastery experiences over time helped both teachers build their self-efficacy; Sean also benefited from professional development. For Emma, however, feedback from colleagues impacted her both positively and negatively, negatively when she was unexpectedly told after five months by her manager that her "fail" rates were too low, but positively when she was able to seek support and advice from her colleagues on how to rectify this.

*Context-specific*

Although multiple context-specific impacts on self-efficacy emerged across the participants' data, Rupert's and Emma's experiences of contextual expectations appeared to have particularly significant impacts on their self-efficacy over time, as shown in Table 5.4.

Like Borg's (2008) CELTA-trained participants, Rupert found that CELTA-promoted methods sometimes clashed with the expectations of the local context, with teacher-fronted instruction expected in Poland. While experimenting with different approaches provided mastery experiences and offered some reconciliation, Rupert also unsuccessfully sought advice from local colleagues and felt increasingly isolated in navigating contextual expectations. So desperate was he for support from other teachers that he compromised his own teacher beliefs and training to incorporate requests from his manager, despite this also hampering his development of self-efficacy.

Emma's perceptions of efficacy were impacted by her school's apparent expectation to promote "fun" over learning, which, likewise, clashed with her CELTA training and teacher beliefs. Observing a colleague failing probation because of unsuccessfully meeting the school's expectations,

*Table 5.4* Context-specific impacts influencing participants' self-efficacy

| Participant | Context-specific impact on self-efficacy | Shifts over time | Positively influential factors | Negatively influential factors |
|---|---|---|---|---|
| Rupert | Contextual expectations of the role of the teacher and student | Consistently low | Mastery experiences | Clash with pre-service training; lack of advice from colleagues; feedback from manager |
| Emma | Prioritizing "fun" over learning/expectations of school | Consistently low | Support from colleagues | Clash with pre-service training; observation of colleague |

despite appearing to be a competent teacher, compromised Emma's developing efficacy for teaching and she consistently questioned her own abilities to meet these expectations throughout the remainder of the study. However, in the face of such internal conflict, support from colleagues and managers fortunately seemed to bolster her self-confidence (Tschannen-Moran & Hoy, 2007).

*Social support*

A striking theme throughout this dataset is the impact of social support on the novice teachers' self-perceptions of efficacy. There was variable access to social support across the group, and those with less (James and Rupert) were more likely to report issues with planning, teaching, and classroom management, echoing Farrell's (2015) findings. Conversely, despite facing significant challenges relating to self-efficacy, those with greater access to social support (Molly and Emma) indicated higher confidence and self-esteem in dealing with these challenges, a finding that mirrors Wyatt (2013).

Many social factors could be either positive or negative influences: Feedback from managers; access to social support in the workplace generally; and observation of colleagues. For instance, a collaborative workplace environment was a positive influence (Sean, Molly, and Emma), whilst feelings of isolation negatively impacted perceptions of efficacy (James and Rupert). Furthermore, social support could be seen as either mitigating or compounding the influence of task-, domain-, and context-specific factors upon novice TSE. Both Sean and Emma noted the positive effect advice from colleagues had upon their ability to correct errors (task-specific) when assessing students (domain-specific), highlighting the importance of novice teachers having access to a supportive, collaborative workplace (Zonoubi et al., 2017). However, Rupert and James struggled with isolation and, in their teaching of young learners (domain-specific) for instance, it could be argued that they exhibited diminished self-efficacy and motivation without adequate support (Yuan & Zhang, 2017). Molly was heavily influenced by feedback from colleagues, eventually appearing to become reliant on their interpretations of her abilities to inform her own perceptions of efficacy. However, despite access to social support, Molly displayed such low global self-efficacy that it led to negative cognitions and emotions, hindering her abilities to perform her role successfully (Bandura, 1997).

## Pedagogical implications and conclusions

This study documents five novice EFL teachers' shifting perceptions of self-efficacy in their first year of teaching whilst concurrently highlighting the variation in LTSE – both individually and collectively – relating to task-, domain-, and context-specific factors. It illustrates shifts in LTSE beliefs in response to various stimuli, including pre-service education, in-service experiences, and social support. Concordant with existing research, the accounts of these novice teachers show that perceptions of efficacy are neither stable nor linear (Fives & Alexander, 2004; Bandura, 1997), instead fluctuating in response to the participants' experiences in the classroom and wider workplace, or feedback received from colleagues.

Following their CELTA course, each novice teacher indicated high perceptions of global efficacy, whilst simultaneously acknowledging that they still had gaps to address in their knowledge and skills. Most participants were pragmatic in their expectations of such a time-constrained course and reflected positively upon the content, as previous research has also found (Anderson, 2016; Kiely & Askham, 2012). Additionally, it was notable that participants did not blame their limited pre-service education for the challenges faced in-service. While no significant alterations to the course content were suggested, it is unclear whether SITECs provide sufficient information to trainees about the reality of EFL teaching in the private sector and the variation found in terms of job responsibilities, social support, and in-service training. This is touched upon in an article by Donohue et al. (2023), which focuses in more depth on two of the participants discussed here (Sean and James), illustrating the potential impact that SITECs can have upon the identity construction and subsequent professional engagement of novice EFL teachers. Donohue and colleagues also highlight the significant role that motivation plays in identity formation – a concept that could be seen as neglected on such short pre-service courses. Consequently, SITECs could potentially improve in raising awareness of task-, domain-, and context-specific factors which may influence self-efficacy beliefs once candidates move in-service, and in highlighting the importance of continuing professional development, together with the benefits of accessing social support in the workplace.

Echoing findings by Hoy and Spero (2005) and Klassen et al. (2014), each novice teacher evidenced some measure of weakening self-efficacy relating to the task-, domain-, and context-specific nature of their role once in-service. This was generally followed by some degree of growth over time, although there were fluctuations, influenced by microanalytical considerations, the four sources of efficacy information, and access to social support. In line with Bandura (1997), these findings demonstrate that a novice language teacher's self-efficacy beliefs are clearly susceptible to influence during the first year of teaching.

Social support and workplace atmosphere emerged as particularly influential factors in shaping novice EFL teachers' perceptions of efficacy. In line with the TSE and LTSE beliefs literature, these findings confirm that the absence of social support negatively impacts novice teachers' perceptions of efficacy (Farrell, 2015), whilst access to support can increase it, despite significant prevailing challenges (Wyatt, 2013). Therefore, language schools could consider offering mentoring opportunities to novice teachers to help them adapt to their new role and context, and help them integrate more successfully into their workplace environment. Furthermore, such schools could facilitate access to in-service training, in problematic areas such as teaching young learners or dealing with contextual challenges. In reality, though, it may be unrealistic to expect widespread changes within the private EFL sector, particularly if expatriate SITEC-trained teachers are more likely to consider EFL teaching as a short-term career (Donohue et al., 2023).

In summary, this study highlights that self-perceptions of efficacy are closely bound with the nature of teaching tasks the novice teachers complete, the type of students they teach, and their working contexts. Consequently, this chapter joins other contemporary research in calling for less focus on holistic levels of self-efficacy and greater consideration of task-, domain-, and context-specific dimensions of self-efficacy beliefs in empirical studies. If LTSE beliefs research is to be useful to curriculum designers, teacher educators, and educational administrators, it is crucial that more attention should be given to micro-considerations relating to task, domain, and context, both over time and from a qualitative perspective (Wheatley, 2002; Wyatt, 2015).

## Note

1 Despite the terms "native" and "non-native" being acknowledged as problematic (see, for instance, Faez [2011] and Selvi [2014]), they remain pervasive in contemporary literature. I, too, recognize that these labels can be reductive and inherently loaded with privilege, but lack the scope here to focus explicitly on this issue, and therefore, for consistency, these terms are used throughout this chapter.

## References

Anderson, J. (2016). Initial teacher training courses and non-native speaker teachers. *ELT Journal*, *70*(3), 261–274. 10.1093/elt/ccv072

Bandura, A. (1997). *Self-efficacy: The exercise of control*. W. H. Freeman.

Bandura, A. (2001). Social cognitive theory: An agentic perspective. *Annual Review of Psychology*, *52*(1), 1–26. 10.1146/annurev.psych.52.1.1

Borg, M. (2008). Teaching post-CELTA: The interplay of novice teacher, course and context. In T.S.C. Farrell (Ed.), *Novice language teachers: Insights and perspectives* (pp. 104–117). Equinox.

Donohue, N.A., Lamb, M.V., & Borg, S. (2023). 'CELTA as "a safety net": EFL teachers' identity development and professional engagement in their first year'. *The European Journal of Applied Linguistics and TEFL*, *12*(1), 51–70.

Dörnyei, Z., & Ushioda, E. (2011). *Teaching and researching motivation* (2nd ed.). Routledge.
Faez, F. (2011). Are you a native speaker of English? Moving beyond a simplistic dichotomy. *Critical Inquiry in Language Studies*, *8*, 378–399. 10.1080/154 27587.2011.615708
Farrell, T.S.C. (Ed.) (2015). *International perspectives on English language teacher education: Innovations from the field*. Springer.
Farrell, T.S.C. (2016). *From trainee to teacher: Reflective practice for novice teachers*. Equinox.
Fives, H., & Alexander, P.A. (2004). Another piece in the achievement puzzle. In D.M. McInerney & S. Van Etten (Eds.), *Big theories revisited* (pp. 329–360). Information Age Publishing.
Gu, Q., & Day, C. (2007). Teachers' resilience: A necessary condition for effectiveness. *Teaching and Teacher Education*, *23*, 1302–1316. 10.1016/j.tate.2006.06.006
Hobbs, V. (2013). 'A basic starter pack': The TESOL Certificate as a course in survival. *ELT Journal*, *67*(2), 163–174. 10.1093/elt/ccs078
Howard, E.A. (2018). Building foundations on sand: Certified TEFL teachers' shifting identity through practice. *Studia Paedigogica*, *23*(2), 159–174. 10.5817/SP201 8-2-9
Hoy, A.W., & Spero, R.B. (2005). Changes in teachers' efficacy during the early years of teaching: A comparison of four measures. *Teaching and Teacher Education*, *21*, 343–356. 10.1016/j.tate.2005.01.007
Kiely, R., & Askham, J. (2012). Furnished imagination: The impact of pre-service teacher training on early career work in TESOL. *TESOL Quarterly*, *46*(3), 496–518. 10.1002/tesq.39
Klassen, R., Durksen, T.L., & Tze, V.M.C. (2014). Teachers' self-efficacy beliefs: Ready to move from theory to practice? In P.W. Richardson, S.A. Karabenick, & H.M.G. Watt (Eds.), *Teacher motivation: Theory and practice* (pp. 100–115). Routledge.
Klassen, R., Tze, V.M.C., Betts, S., & Gordan, K. (2011). Teacher efficacy research 1998-2009: Signs of progress or unfulfilled promise? *Educational Psychology Review*, *23*, 21–43. 10.1007/s10648-010-9141-8
Medgyes, P., & Kiss, T. (2019). Quality assurance and the expatriate native speaker teacher. In J. de Dios Martinez Agudo (Ed.), *Quality in TESOL and teacher education: From a results culture towards a quality culture* (pp. 94–102). Routledge.
Ončevska Ager, E.O., & Wyatt, M. (2019). Supporting a pre-service English language teacher's self-determined development. *Teaching and Teacher Education*, *78*, 106–116. 10.1016/j.tate.2018.11.013
Pajares, F. (1996). Self-efficacy beliefs in academic settings. *Review of Educational Research*, *66*(4), 543–578. 10.3102/00346543066004543
Reeve, J. (2018). *Understanding motivation and emotion* (7th ed.). Wiley Custom.
Selvi, A. F. (2014). Myths and misconceptions about nonnative English speakers in the TESOL NNEST) movement. *TESOL Journal*, *5*, 573–611. 10.1002/tesj.158
Senior, R. (2006). *The experience of language teaching*. Cambridge University Press.

Skaalvik, E.M., & Skaalvik, S. (2010). Teacher self-efficacy and teacher burnout: A study of relations. *Teaching and Teacher Education*, *26*(4), 1059–1069. 10.1016/j.tate.2009.11.001

Skaalvik, E.M., & Skaalvik, S. (2019). Teacher self-efficacy and collective teacher efficacy: Relations with perceived job resources and job demands, feeling of belonging, and teacher engagement. *Creative Education*, *10*, 1400–1424. 10.4236/ce.2019.107104

Smith, J.A. (2017). Interpretative phenomenological analysis: Getting at lived experience. *The Journal of Positive Psychology*, *12*(3), 303–304. 10.1080/17439760.2016.1262622

Tschannen-Moran, M., & Hoy, A.W. (2001). Teacher efficacy: Capturing an elusive construct. *Teaching and Teacher Education*, *17*, 783–805. 10.1016/S0742-051X(01)00036-1

Tschannen-Moran, M., & Hoy, A.W. (2007). The differential antecedents of self-efficacy beliefs of novice and experienced teachers. *Teaching and Teacher Education*, *23*(6), 944–956. 10.1016/j.tate.2006.05.003

Tschannen-Moran, M., & Johnson, D. (2011). Exploring literacy teachers' self-efficacy beliefs: Potential sources at play. *Teaching and Teacher Education*, *27*(4), 751–761. 10.1016/j.tate.2010.12.005

Wheatley, K.F. (2002). The potential benefits of teacher efficacy doubts for educational reform. *Teaching and Teacher Education*, *18*, 5–22. 10.1016/S0742-051X(01)00047-6

Wyatt, M. (2013). Motivating teachers in the developing world: Insights from research with English language teachers in Oman. *International Review of Education*, *59*(2), 217–242. 10.1007/s11159-013-9358-0

Wyatt, M. (2015). Using qualitative research methods to assess the degree of fit between teachers' reported self-efficacy beliefs and their practical knowledge during teacher education. *Australian Journal of Teacher Education*, *40*(1), 117–145. 10.14221/ajte.2015v40n1.7

Wyatt, M. (2018). Language teachers' self-efficacy beliefs: An introduction. In. S. Mercer & A. Kostoulas (Eds.), *Language teacher psychology* (pp. 122–140). Multilingual Matters.

Yuan, R., & Zhang, L.J. (2017). Exploring student teachers' motivation change in initial teacher education: A Chinese perspective. *Teaching and Teacher Education*, *61*, 142–152. 10.1016/j.tate.2016.10.010

Zonoubi, R., Rasekh, A.E., & Tavakoli, M. (2017). EFL teacher self-efficacy development in professional learning communities. *System*, *66*, 1–12. 10.1016/j.system.2017.03.003

## Appendix: Sample questions from the monthly questionnaire

3. Are you satisfied with the following aspects of your job this month:

| | |
|---|---|
| *-teaching* | YES/NO |
| WHY/WHY NOT_____ | |
| *-lesson planning* | YES/NO |
| WHY/WHY NOT_____ | |
| *-doing administration* | YES/NO |
| WHY/WHY NOT_____ | |
| *-other aspects of your job (please specify)* | YES/NO |
| WHY/WHY NOT_____ | |

5. What has been a success this month?

6. What has been a challenge this month?

8. Has anything happened this month that you felt unprepared for following your teacher training? How did you deal with it?

12. Have there been any instances this month where you felt you needed support within your teaching establishment? Did you get it? Who did you get it from, e.g., DoS, teacher colleagues, admin staff, etc.?

# 6 Language teachers' self-efficacy beliefs evident in teacher–supervisor post-observation conferences in Iran

*Zia Tajeddin and Fereshteh Tadayon*

## Introduction

Post-observation conferences (POCs) tend to be scheduled by supervisors after classroom observations for debrief conversations focused on teachers' teaching practices (Baecher et al., 2018). Talk in POCs tends to centre on the pedagogy of language teaching and, as such, entails discussions of teachers' pedagogical beliefs and practices. POCs typically feature teachers' self-evaluation of and reflection on lessons observed. However, although such practices are resisted by supervisors concerned by judgementoring practices (Malderez, 2015), traditionally, in many contexts, the main space for POC talk is taken by the supervisor, who can offer a critical evaluation of the teaching and directive suggestions for the teachers' instructional improvement (Copland, 2010; Copland et al., 2009). The positive–negative–positive feedback sandwich associated with a directive approach can provide support for teachers' self-efficacy beliefs and so enhance the self-confidence teachers hold about their capabilities. However, directive supervision, rather than alternatives such as collaborative supervision, can unfortunately also have a very negative effect on teachers' self-efficacy beliefs; evaluative POCs can be "fraught with risk which may damage, rather than nurture, the [teacher's] fragile enthusiasm, and commitment to continuous improvement" (Riera, 2011, p. 54). Teachers who suffer such experiences can feel victimized, depressed, and ready to leave the profession (Farrell, 2015; Gebhard, 1984). Consequently, in the face of directive supervision, teachers might position themselves in various ways to protect their self-efficacy beliefs. In this light, this chapter aims to explore POCs in an Iranian context as a mediation space to explore the challenges to and expression of language teachers' self-efficacy (LTSE) beliefs.

First, though, to define terms, LTSE beliefs are these teachers' beliefs in "their abilities to support learning in various task- and context-specific cognitive, metacognitive, affective and social ways" (Wyatt, 2010, p. 603). This is a line of research that draws upon Bandura's (1986) Social Cognitive

DOI: 10.4324/9781003379300-8

Theory and his definition of self-efficacy beliefs: "people's judgements of their capabilities to organize and execute courses of action required to attain designated types of performance" (p. 391). Research into self-efficacy beliefs developed in various domains in the late 20th century, such as teaching (see Klassen et al., 2011, for a review), and then, in the early 21st century, as strands of the research became more field-specific, in relation to language teachers (Wyatt, 2018). Contexts where LTSE beliefs have been much researched include Türkiye (see Chapter 3 of this volume) and Iran, where much of the research has been quantitative in nature and survey-based (see Faez et al. [2021], and Chapter 2 of this volume for reviews of the methodology).

Bandura (1997) postulated that teachers' self-efficacy is nourished by four main sources: (a) mastery experiences (teachers' success or failure in performing a specific task), (b) vicarious experiences (their observation of others' performances), (c) social persuasion (positive or negative feedback from others), and (d) psychological and affective states (their affective states such as stress, anxiety, and excitement when performing tasks). Among these sources, social persuasion is provided by significant "others", including students, peer teachers, supervisors, managers, and teacher educators. Supportive or evaluative feedback and judgements from these significant others can potentially boost or undermine teachers' self-efficacy beliefs in their teaching capabilities, depending on the extent to which cognitive processing takes place (Bandura, 1997). Of crucial importance, then, is the quality of the teacher's reflection on potentially efficacy-building experiences.

Given the centrality of reflection, models of LTSE beliefs growth (e.g., Markova, 2021; Wyatt, 2016) highlight the role it plays in the process of efficacy building. The importance of reflection is underscored by recent empirical research conducted in the Iranian context. Using survey instruments including one designed by Tschannen-Moran and Woolfolk Hoy (2001), Moradkhani et al. (2017) found a significant correlation between reflective qualities and LTSE beliefs scores. On the basis of their findings, they concluded: "EFL teachers who are more engaged in reflective practices are more efficacious in encouraging students to participate in classroom activities, applying efficient and various teaching techniques, and dealing with management-related issues" (Moradkhani et al., 2017, p. 5).

If they can stimulate reflection, therefore, POCs are likely to play a positive role in building LTSE beliefs. This suggests that developmental talk during POCs is needed. Such talk can beneficially encourage teachers to draw on their perspectives in self-reflecting on their observed teaching practices, considering their own needs and interests rather than any evaluative criteria (Walsh & Mann, 2019). However, feedback in POCs is often evaluative, prompting teachers to carry out a personal audit of the weaknesses and strengths of their teaching practices, with their supervisors' role being that of providing corrective feedback (Kurtoglu-Hooton, 2010). In such a scenario, supervisors might take longer turns, initiating topics while teachers merely provide limited responses (e.g., Donaghue, 2015; Louw et al., 2016). Such supervisory practices have been identified in different contexts. For instance, having examined average turn lengths, topic initiations, interruptions, and redirections, Hyland and Lo (2006) concluded that teachers mostly had a passive role in POCs, while their supervisors tended to interrupt teachers and take on the role of a dominant interactant. Similarly, Copland (2012) found that supervisors tended to be authority figures, controlling the discourse. Such behaviour in POCs is unlikely to support a strengthening of LTSE beliefs, and might in fact have a very different effect, with teachers experiencing stress and anxiety, i.e., physiological arousal negatively, with unfortunate consequences for their LTSE beliefs, as vignettes in Farrell (2015) and Gebhard (1984) illustrate.

However, although POCs have obvious potential to impact LTSE beliefs, if the feedback is processed and reflected upon, relatively few LTSE beliefs studies (e.g., Ortaçtepe & Akyel, 2015; Phan & Locke, 2015; Wyatt, 2010, 2013, 2015) have made use of observational data and data from POCs. Moreover, the discourse within POCs has rarely been analysed in detail by LTSE beliefs researchers, although there are exceptions (e.g., Wyatt, 2008). Consequently, to address this gap, this chapter reports on an empirical study in which a set of 15 POCs was analysed for the ways in which English language teachers in Iran expressed their self-efficacy (inefficacy) beliefs while being supported to reflect or challenged by their supervisors.

## Research methodology

This study was situated in four different private language institutes located in different cities in Iran. Each institute is well-established, with over 10 years' experience of offering English language courses. The selection of these institutes was based on their voluntary participation in our study. After the second author contacted many institutes, 4 supervisors and 15 in-service teachers from these 4 institutes agreed to participate and signed a written consent form. The consent form ensured the anonymity and confidentiality of their recorded voices during POCs. Regarding supervisors' backgrounds, they each had 8–10+ years' experience in their roles. The in-service teachers each had at least five years' teaching experience. Their ages ranged from 29 to 45; they consisted of 14 females and 5 males; they were all native Persian speakers. The four supervisors, two males and two females, held doctoral degrees in Teaching English as a Foreign Language (TEFL), and the teachers held master's degrees in TEFL.

Primarily, supervisors have the responsibility of improving the quality of in-service teachers' instruction (Sadeghi & Richards, 2016). In Iran's highly centralized foreign language education system, there has been little consensus on any unified curricula for teacher training (e.g., Bagherzadeh & Tajeddin, 2021; Pishghadam & Saboori, 2014; Tajeddin & Norouzi, 2022), and teacher quality tends to be variable. In the context of private language institutes, supervisory observation has remained an essential part of the evaluation of in-service teachers' classroom performance, and every institute runs its own teacher supervision and feedback sessions. In fact, supervisors have the right to prescribe to teachers a set of rules or suggestions, and teachers need to abide by the rules if they aspire to keep their jobs safely and gain promotion (Akbari et al., 2006). This situation has been the case in different Iranian language institutes, where supervision is often seen as a top-down and evaluative process rather than a collaborative inspection of classroom instruction (Gholaminejad, 2023).

In the present study, four supervisors provided us with some general information, such as in-service teachers' experience and teaching background. The main rationale behind the observations they conduct is to gain insights into whether the in-service teachers are teaching according to the institute's expectations and are qualified for pay raises or promotion to teach at higher levels. Regarding the POC's place in the system, as explained by supervisors, there are no specific professional development courses informed by the input from observations and POCs. There is also no official or unified procedure among supervisors for POCs, and each is conducted informally in a separate session. The observation process is conducted at the supervisor's discretion, and the supervisors are entrusted to conduct POCs as individual meetings between the supervisor and the teacher.

The data used in this study consisted of audio-recorded POCs of each supervisor holding a one-on-one debriefing session with each observed teacher. All teachers were contacted to ask for permission for their POC talk to be recorded and signed the consent form. Prior to the POCs, the teachers were informed ahead of the schedule, and supervisors arranged the date and time at least a week beforehand. After each observation, each supervisor set up individual POCs. These debriefing sessions were held shortly after the observed lesson. Audio data from 15 feedback sessions were gathered, with each teacher involved once. These feedback sessions ranged from 20 to 50 minutes in duration.

There were no specific evaluative criteria used for each POC, as each supervisor was working in a different language institute. As noted above, conducting POCs at regular intervals was part of the supervisors' responsibility. All interactions took place in either English or Persian, and those in Persian were translated into English. Each POC started with the supervisor's general evaluation of the lesson observed before various aspects of the lesson were discussed. Sometimes the supervisor concluded the POC by highlighting strengths and suggesting strategies for more effective teaching. The supervisor completed an observation form assigned by their language institutes.

We analysed the data thematically (Braun & Clarke, 2006), following established procedures in transcribing, coding, rereading, and recoding, focusing on those segments of POCs that related to the expression of teachers' self-efficacy beliefs, while considering supervisor talk and paying attention to positioning. Drawing on positioning analysis (Bamberg, 1997) helped us explore how teachers and supervisors projected their perspectives and managed tensions. Positioning analysis helped us understand both supervisors and teachers as "located in conversations as observably and subjectively coherent participants in jointly produced storylines" (Davies & Harré, 1999, p. 48). So, this framework helped us see how supervisors and teachers were positioned and positioned each other in discursive practices. We now present our findings, focusing on salient excerpts from the dataset.

## Findings

In the section below, we look at some of the excerpts from POCs that illustrate teachers expressing their self-efficacy beliefs in different ways. We explore these under three general categories that reflect both our reading of the teachers' self-efficacy beliefs literature (e.g., Tschannen-Moran & Woolfolk Hoy, 2001) and emergent themes. The three sections are (a) instructional strategies (i.e., teaching skills and subskills), (b) feedback, and (c) student engagement.

### Teachers' self-efficacy beliefs about instructional strategies

All the POCs commenced with teachers given some opportunity to comment on their lessons. For example, in excerpt #1, the supervisor asks for the teacher's view on the lesson taught and the relevant strategies employed. The teacher explains the instructional strategies she applied to teach "so do I, me neither" using different pictures. By taking a long turn and providing full responses, the teacher demonstrates that she is self-efficacious:

### Excerpt #1

Supervisor: ok, the session I observed. So, you didn't send me the lesson plan. So please tell me what have you done and what you think about it.

Teacher: so, I started with a picture of mine showing my friends. I told them to look at it we have a lot in common, I'm a teacher and she's a teacher. We love coffee. Some things like this elicit their

> *opinions to teach 'so do I', 'me neither'. They shared their ideas, But I noticed they hadn't understood them very well. One or two times was hard because they wouldn't understand. So, I repeat the words more times.*

Sometimes supervisors could be quite negative. In excerpt #2, the supervisor criticizes the teacher's strategies for classroom interaction. As the excerpt shows, the teacher is contradicted at the beginning and is negatively positioned by the supervisor, who is questioning her ability. However, the teacher self-efficaciously positions herself as a competent teacher who would know how to elicit the students' opinions, and so is offering resistance. She then changes the subject.

**Excerpt #2**

Supervisor: *no, the interaction was teacher-student, you were just interacting with students, not students with each other. I think they were paired at the beginning of the session but weren't so in this activity in which they should have talked about themselves.*
Teacher: *yes, the students should have interacted with each other because they were upper-intermediate students, so they did not tell that, to me, it has no problem. I also taught them the word "wreck" and asked for their opinions if they knew anything.*

In excerpt #3, we see more judgementoring. The supervisor quickly shifts from praising the teacher's grammar instruction to questioning her competence in teaching listening. The teacher positions herself self-efficaciously by highlighting that the issue observed is with the institute's lack of the required facilities that she can nevertheless address through sound pedagogical practices:

**Excerpt #3**

Supervisor: *I enjoyed your class. Your teaching technique about grammar was very useful for students. But I'm wondering why you didn't have speakers for listening. You know students' listening doesn't get better if the audio files don't have high quality.*
Teacher: *yes, it's the institute's problem. In this situation, I use my cellphone for the listening part and put chairs in a way so they can hear the audio files very loudly and clearly. Also, this form of sitting helps them have more conversations with each other.*

In excerpt #4, the supervisor reveals immediately to the teacher that a negative judgement about the lesson has already been made. Indeed, the supervisor makes the kind of statement that could in some cases crush a teacher's self-efficacy beliefs. However, the supervisor then repositions herself from being the sole authority to a sympathizing mentor, who has had the same kind of experience (being warned in advance to minimize her teacher talking time by a previous supervisor). In making this transition, the supervisor nevertheless displays a patronizing attitude with regard to the teacher's teaching performance. From the teacher's words, it seems that she has not behaved very efficaciously while being observed, conscious of the presence of the supervisor and offering her students fewer explanations than she would usually have. Discussing the lesson, she then indicates that she has obediently tried to follow the supervisor's instructions, before offering a very modest defence, which appears to mollify the supervisor.

**Excerpt #4**

Supervisor: *You've spoonfed them and talked a lot, showing that you haven't done your needs analysis accurately.*
Teacher: *yes, sometimes I was quiet. You know one of the students would distract me.*
Supervisor: *I know, one aspect of teaching is character. But only for a short time you had them speak.*
Teacher: *yeah, I did that. But students thought that I had some problems that I couldn't speak.*
Supervisor: *yes, I had this experience where my mentor told me to remain quiet and give students time to speak.*
Teacher: *in some activities, I stayed silent. in the case of a few students in the class, I interfere and share my ideas with them so I talk more.*
Supervisor: *Ok then.*

In excerpt #5, we see a similar pattern, in that the supervisor immediately questions the teacher's competence. The teacher attempts to explain his actions and indeed indicates that he has obeyed previous instructions. The supervisor's initial questions suggest, actually, that he has paid little attention to the lesson observed. However, there is then a shift to more abstract questions, which are harder to answer. The teacher is being put on the spot. So, this supervisor positions himself as the sole authority of the POC talk, while the teacher is positioned as the one who is in need of help. The teacher is required to follow a particular sequence of teaching imposed by the supervisor, who ends the session with the longest turn to emphasize dominance. Such directive supervisory behaviour that is akin to bullying is of course extremely demotivating for teachers to experience, as noted above and in the literature (Farrell, 2015; Gebhard, 1984).

**Excerpt #5**

Supervisor: *yes, you've written them on the board, but you didn't have any task for asking them to practice. Or did you?*
Teacher: *I gave them some cards for practice, [I] try not to be book bound as you said before.*
Supervisor: *yes, not to be book-bound. You told them some things. What was it?*
Teacher: *yes, it was the context for this session.*
Supervisor: *Ok, tell me what's the purpose of teaching reading?*
Teacher: *indirectly teaching them something new?*
Supervisor: *no, the purpose of teaching reading?*
Teacher: *so, to remember something about the topic of reading?*
Supervisor: *yes, but it wasn't there. All the time you were speaking about a reading topic and there was no production. they were just listening to exposure they got from you.*
Teacher: *ok.*

*Teachers' self-efficacy beliefs about giving feedback*

In addition to attending to teachers' instructional strategies, all supervisors evaluated feedback provided by teachers on students' task performance. In response, teachers rarely articulated powerful self-efficacy beliefs regarding their methods of providing feedback. In excerpt #6, for example, the supervisor intensely challenges the teacher's approach to providing feedback, positioning himself as the authority and the teacher as relatively inexperienced and incompetent. The teacher accepts the criticism, offering little resistance.

**Excerpt #6**

Supervisor: *You've focused so much on their errors. I don't think it's necessary because they get demotivated after a while and feel embarrassed. You know that learning takes time, so give them time to practise freely.*
Teacher: *yes, it was because of the personality of some learners who were generally shy and unwilling to learn.*
Supervisor: *yeah, but you should teach them and give feedback based on their personality so they don't get embarrassed. If you continue correcting them directly, they lose their motivation for learning.*

118  *Zia Tajeddin and Fereshteh Tadayon*

However, this kind of unchecked dominance was not the case all the time. Sometimes, teachers resisted the supervisor's hegemonic talk by refusing to accept pedagogic practices or by challenging their supervisor's view of classroom practice. In excerpt #7, for example, the teacher self-efficaciously interjects to participate in the dialogue, seek clarification, and justify his pedagogy.

**Excerpt #7**

Supervisor: *in one listening activity you had students make notes, not required for their levels.*
Teacher: *[The teacher interrupts the supervisor] ... so we had. At the beginning of the listening activity in the book, they put the words in order and made notes while listening.*
Supervisor: *but ask them to verbalize and talk about something they've heard.*
Teacher: *you mean to ask them to give me an oral summary?*
Supervisor: *Ask them (Wh) questions so that they can talk more and giving feedback is easier to do.*
Teacher: *I preferred writing while listening so I can give them detailed feedback than asking them to speak, but there was no time left to do that.*
Supervisor: *if you had had, that would have been better.*
Teacher: *for five minutes if I can, I tell them to write keywords.*

*Teachers' self-efficacy beliefs about student engagement*

In relation to engaging students, the findings reveal that teachers tended to have positive self-efficacy beliefs. They felt competent in raising their students' motivation and self-confidence for learning. In excerpt #8, for example, the teacher highlights positive self-efficacy beliefs in motivating students from a range of backgrounds and proficiency levels. In this excerpt, the supervisor encourages the teacher's approach to engaging students, allows space for the teacher to position herself as self-efficacious and agentive in this regard, and, in the final turn, functions as a co-analyst, inviting further reflection. Such motivating supervisory practices can help teachers build stronger self-efficacy beliefs.

**Excerpt #8**

Supervisor: *one point is that you provided a competitive activity, and two by two could do that creatively.*

Teacher: *yes, but it wasn't a race.*
Supervisor: *yeah, I know. It seemed that the students would like it very much.*
Teacher: *yes, my reason is that I don't prefer to ask individual students from the very first because raising their self-confidence is much more important than anything. So, group work would help them because some are lower, others are higher, and some are from different L1 backgrounds.*
Supervisor: *yes, and you improvised an activity in the middle of the lesson, that was so creative, I think.*

A few teachers were able to assume the identity of an empathetic, self-efficacious teacher, catering to students' needs and problems. In excerpt #9, the supervisor supports the teacher's approach to engaging students by focusing particular attention on the teacher's instructional strategies. This allows the teacher to expand on these learner-centred strategies efficaciously.

**Excerpt #9**

Supervisor: *the next point was how you've actively involved students although some students were silent. You were well able how to give examples and help them understand grammatical points better.*
Teacher: *yes, I'm sympathizing with students. As some of them have some personal problems, so I try to keep them engaged and active, and I teach them more points than the book to show that I respect their learning in my class.*

However, some supervisors, seeking to maintain the position of dominant interactants, questioned teachers' theoretical knowledge base, which could undermine their self-efficacy beliefs. In excerpt #10, after the teacher has drawn upon her practical knowledge to justify her pedagogy, the supervisor implies that more relevant theoretical knowledge regarding underlying psychological factors and learning is required. The teacher needs to defend herself.

**Excerpt #10**

Supervisor: *in most of the activities, you made them stand up and sit in circles.*
Teacher: *about this, you know students don't like to stand up.*
Supervisor: *yeah, it's hard and stressful for them.*
Teacher: *they're shy and skip these group activities, but I do this so they become more sociable.*

Supervisor: *Right. You should do it in a way so they don't hurt or get upset. If you studied how psychological factors affect students' learning, you would know it very well.*

Teacher: *yes, I studied psychology and second language learning and I know it.*

Supervisory practice implying that a teacher lacks a justifiable rationale for her engagement with students is also evident in excerpt #11. Here the supervisor provides advice but is rebuffed. The teacher positions herself as a knowledgeable and self-efficacious interactant in this POC, and the supervisor has almost no response.

**Excerpt #11**

Supervisor: *some of the students' levels are higher while others are lower. Better to have a closer connection with the lower ones by bringing them to sit closer to you. It's not bad? So, you can dominate the class better.*

Teacher: *but my opinion is that lower-level students need to boost their self-confidence, I don't like to bring them closer so they feel inferior. I go next to them but do not give them a space near my desk so they feel inferior to others.*

Supervisor: *no, I don't mean to tell them directly so they understand why you would ask them to sit closer to you.*

Teacher: *yeah, but they realize why I would do that.*

Supervisor: *hmm*

**Discussion**

As can be seen from the analysis above, the teachers in these Iranian private language institutes faced some challenges during POCs from the largely directive supervision they received. Consequently, partly as a result of their supervisors' stance and turn-taking practices, these teachers were rarely able to express positive LTSE beliefs. In some cases, where teachers were bullied, positioned as needing help, or asked to follow the must-be teaching sequence imposed by the dominant supervisor, they were gaining the kinds of experiences that could weaken LTSE beliefs.

However, it should be emphasized that the sample of POCs analysed in this study was self-selected through institutes volunteering to participate and cannot therefore be considered representative of private language institutes in Iran. Nevertheless, the reality that supervisors are too often mainly authoritative and evaluative rather than having a facilitative role in teachers' pedagogical practices has also been discussed in some other studies (e.g., Copland, 2008, Hyland & Lo, 2006; Vásquez, 2004). This situation may be particularly true of Iran. For example, while the supervisors' role in North American contexts has undergone changes to become more developmental (Bailey, 2006), Agheshteh and Mehrpur (2021) have posited that the dominant approach to supervision in the Iranian EFL supervision context has remained prescriptive and directive. In the Iranian context, where the hierarchical nature of the teacher–supervisor relationship is very evident, it is perhaps unsurprising that many teachers hold quite negative attitudes towards being observed, as Gholaminejad (2023) has found.

Nevertheless, our findings reveal that at times teachers were able to hold to positive LTSE beliefs in some aspects of their work, namely, in their use of instructional strategies (e.g., teaching grammar), in providing feedback (e.g., written feedback), and in engaging students (e.g., keeping students motivated). Added to this is their commendable self-efficacy to grapple with an institute's lack of facilities, their refusal to accept questionable pedagogic practices, and their rejection of their supervisors' positioning of them as incompetent, unknowledgeable, or inexperienced teachers. It should be pointed out that, at times too, supervisors did seek to stimulate reflection on pedagogical practices they valued (e.g., with regard to engaging learners). In this way, the developmental talk in some of the POCs could lead to efficacy building of a positive nature.

## Pedagogical implications and conclusions

Various implications arise from this study. The first concerns supervisory practices. Findings suggest that the supervisors in this study would benefit from greater critical awareness as to the impact their behaviour in POC feedback sessions might have. They need to be more open to providing the kind of developmental support through dialogic work that can foster growth (Walsh & Mann, 2015). So, there is a need for in-service professional development courses for supervisors to alert them as to their role in POCs. More attempts should be made to raise supervisors' awareness of what they do and how they interact with teachers. So, courses are needed to both provide input and encourage introspection so that supervisors can become more aware of their positionings and of their role in supporting growth in the LTSE beliefs of the teachers they supervise. Although supervisors also have other important roles in teacher supervision that involve explicitly communicating their intentions, expectations, and the consequences of their supervisory practices (Johnson & Golombek, 2020), too little attention is paid to the developmental aspects of their work, and this needs to change. Regulators of private language institutes in Iran who could organize in-service professional development for supervisors should take note.

A second implication concerns the teachers who appear to be the targets of evaluative supervisory feedback. In-service teacher education could help make teachers better prepared for POCs by including a module on the aims of teacher observation and POCs as a space for dialogic interaction between teachers and supervisors. Teachers could become better aware of opportunities and challenges inherent to POCs and learn how to engage with their supervisors in agentic ways that enable them to contribute self-efficaciously. Over time, this could contribute to the culture of supervision becoming more collaborative. In the short term, this change could strengthen teachers' beliefs in their own capabilities and prompt these teachers to engage more fully in their own professional development (Lazarides & Warner, 2020). This would be highly worthwhile. As Fackler et al.'s (2021) review of studies shows, teachers' self-efficacy beliefs, when strengthened, are associated with numerous desirable outcomes like good student performance and a positive classroom climate.

A third implication is that private language institutes in Iran could focus more on encouraging peer observation as a professional development strategy. Engaging in peer observation can enhance LTSE beliefs (Mousavi, 2014), particularly if this strategy is followed by supportive debriefing sessions that avoid judgementoring.

Besides these pedagogical implications, there are also implications for further research. As noted above, relatively few studies in the LTSE beliefs literature have analysed POCs, even though these events can provide valuable means for teachers to gain interactive efficacy-building experiences they can reflect upon and develop through. Data from POCs could be triangulated with observational data to gain richer insights, as in studies set in other contexts (e.g., Phan & Locke, 2015; Wyatt, 2013). Indeed the absence of observational data was a necessary limitation of the current study (given that the four sites of the research were located in different parts of the country). Further research could additionally draw on other sources of data, such as post-POC reflection diaries, to explore teachers' and supervisors' perspectives. Furthermore, changes could be explored over time, considering development over a series of POCs, perhaps through a longitudinal, qualitative case study, an approach that remains rare in LTSE beliefs research (Wyatt, 2022). Such case study research could focus on the development of individuals. It follows that there are many possible future directions.

## References

Agheshteh, H., & Mehrpur, S. (2021). Teacher autonomy and supervisor authority: Power dynamics in language teacher supervision in Iran. *Iranian Journal of Language Teaching Research*, 9(1), 87–106. 10.30466/ijltr.2021.120977

Akbari, R., Gaffar Samar, R., & Tajik, L. (2006). Developing a classroom observation model based on Iranian EFL teachers' attitude. *Journal of Faculty of Letters and Humanities*, *49*(198), 1–38. https://www.sid.ir/En/Journal/ViewPaper.aspx?ID=90104

Baecher, L., Browne Graves, S., & Ghailan, F. (2018). Supervisor learning through collaborative video inquiry: It's not just for teacher candidates. *Contemporary Issues in Technology and Teacher Education*, *18*(3), 556–577. https://citejournal.org/volume-18/issue-3-18/general/supervisor-learning-through-collaborative-video-inquiry-its-not-just-for-teacher-candidates/

Bagherzadeh, R., & Tajeddin, Z. (2021). Teachers' curricular knowledge in teacher education programs: A case of Iran's sociocultural context. *International Journal of Society, Culture & Language*, *9*(1), 43–57. http://www.ijscl.net/article_242891.html

Bailey, K.M. (2006). *Language teacher supervision: A case-based approach*. Cambridge University Press.

Bamberg, M.G. (1997). Positioning between structure and performance. *Journal of Narrative and Life History*, *7*(1–4), 335–342. https://psycnet.apa.org/doi/10.1075/jnlh.7.42pos

Bandura, A. (1986). *Social foundations of thought and action: A social cognitive theory*. Prentice Hall.

Bandura, A. (1997). *Self-efficacy: The exercise of control*. W. H. Freeman.

Braun, V., & Clarke, V. (2006). Using thematic analysis in psychology. *Qualitative Research in Psychology*, *3*(2), 77–101. 10.1191/1478088706qp063oa

Copland, F. (2008). Deconstructing the discourse: Understanding the feedback event. In S. Garton & K. Richards (Eds.), *Professional encounters in TESOL* (pp. 5–23). Palgrave Macmillan.

Copland, F. (2010). Causes of tension in post-observation feedback in pre-service teacher training: An alternative view. *Teaching and Teacher Education*, *26*(3), 466–472. 10.1016/j.tate.2009.06.001

Copland, F. (2012). Legitimate talk in feedback conferences. *Applied Linguistics*, *33*(1), 1–20. 10.1093/applin/amr040

Copland, F., Ma, G., & Mann, S. (2009). Reflecting in and on post-observation feedback in initial teacher training on certificate courses. *English Language Teacher Education and Development*, *12*, 14–23. http://www.elted.net/issues/volume-12/index.htm

Davies, B., & Harré, R. (1999). Positioning and personhood. In R. Harré & L. Van Langenhove (Eds.), *Positioning theory: Moral contexts of intentional action* (pp. 32–52). Wiley-Blackwell.

Donaghue, H. (2015). Changing practice and enabling development: The impact of technology on teaching and language teacher education in UAE federal institutions. In T.S.C. Farrell (Ed.), *International perspectives on English language teacher education* (pp. 142–159). Palgrave Macmillan.

Faez, F., Karas, M., & Uchihara, T. (2021). Connecting language proficiency to teaching ability: A meta-analysis. *Language Teaching Research*, *25*(5), 754–777. 10.1177/1362168819868667

Fackler, S., Malmberg, L.-E., & Sammons, P. (2021). An international perspective on teacher self-efficacy: Personal, structural and environmental factors. *Teaching and Teacher Education*, *99*, 103255. 10.1016/j.tate.2020.103255

Farrell, T.S.C. (2015). Second language teacher education: A reality check. In T.S.C. Farrell (Ed.), *International perspectives on English language teacher education* (pp. 1–15). Palgrave Macmillan.

Gebhard, J.G. (1984). Models of supervision: Choices. *TESOL Quarterly*, *18*(3), 501–514. 10.2307/3586717

Gholaminejad, R. (2023). When the evil pops in: Exploring the unheard voices of teachers working in private language schools in Iran concerning supervisory observation. *International Journal of Leadership in Education*, *26*(1), 100–123. 10.1080/13603124.2020.1740795

Hyland, F., & Lo, M.M. (2006). Examining interaction in the teaching practicum: Issues of language, power and control. *Mentoring & Tutoring*, *14*(2), 163–186. 10.1080/13611260500493535

Klassen, R.M., Tze, V.M., Betts, S.M., & Gordon, K.A. (2011). Teacher efficacy research 1998–2009: Signs of progress or unfulfilled promise. *Educational Psychology Review*, *23*, 21–43. 10.1007/s10648-010-9141-8

Kurtoglu-Hooton, N. (2010). *Post-observation feedback as an instigator of learning and change: Exploring the effect of feedback through student teachers' self-reports* [Unpublished doctoral dissertation]. Aston University.

Johnson, K.E., & Golombek, P.R. (2020). Informing and transforming language teacher education pedagogy. *Language Teaching Research*, *24*(1), 116–127. 10.1177/1362168818777539

Lazarides, R., & Warner, L.M. (2020). Teacher self-efficacy. In G.W. Noblit (Ed.), *Oxford research encyclopedia: Education* (pp. 1–22). Oxford University Press.

Louw, S., Watson Todd, R., & Jimarkon, P. (2016). Teacher trainers' beliefs about feedback on teaching practice: Negotiating the tensions between authoritativeness and dialogic space. *Applied Linguistics*, *37*(6), 745–764. 10.1093/applin/amu062

Malderez, A. (2015). On mentoring in supporting (English) teacher learning: Where are we now? In D. Holló & K. Károly (Eds.), *Inspirations in foreign language teaching: Studies in language pedagogy and applied linguistics in honour of Péter Medgyes* (pp. 21–32). Pearson Education.

Markova, Z. (2021). Towards a comprehensive conceptualisation of teachers' self-efficacy beliefs. *Cambridge Journal of Education*, *51*(5), 653–671. 10.1080/0305764X.2021.1906844

Moradkhani, S., Raygan, A., & Moein, M.S. (2017). Iranian EFL teachers' reflective practices and self-efficacy: Exploring possible relationships. *System*, *65*, 1–14. 10.1016/j.system.2016.12.011

Mousavi, S.M. (2014). The effect of peer observation on Iranian EFL teachers' self-efficacy. *Procedia – Social and Behavioral Sciences*, *136*, 181–185.

Ortaçtepe, D., & Akyel, A.S. (2015). The effects of a professional development program on English as a foreign language teachers' efficacy and classroom practice. *TESOL Journal*, *6*(4), 680–706. 10.1002/tesj.185

Phan, N.T.T., & Locke, T. (2015). Sources of self-efficacy of Vietnamese EFL teachers: A qualitative study. *Teaching and Teacher Education*, *52*, 73–82. 10.1016/j.tate.2015.09.006

Pishghadam, R., & Saboori, F. (2014). A socio-cultural study of language teacher status. *International Journal of Society, Culture & Language*, 2(1), 63–72. http://www.ijscl.net/article_4520_66f844895c5607193f9be05e3fe7b5d3.pdf

Riera, G. (2011). New directions in teacher appraisal and development. In C. Coombe, L. Stephenson, & S. Abu-Rmaileh (Eds.), *Leadership and management in English language teaching* (pp. 49–66). TESOL Arabia.

Sadeghi, K., & Richards, J.C. (2016). The idea of English in Iran: An example from Urmia. *Journal of Multilingual and Multicultural Development*, 37(4), 419–434. 10.1080/01434632.2015.1080714

Tajeddin, Z., & Norouzi, M. (2022). Representation of teacher knowledge base in teacher education programs in Iran. In M.S. Khine (Ed.), *Handbook of research on teacher education* (pp. 549–569). Springer.

Tschannen-Moran, M., & Hoy, A.W. (2001). Teacher efficacy: Capturing an elusive construct. *Teaching and Teacher Education*, 17(7), 783–805. 10.1016/S0742-051X(01)00036-1

Vásquez, C. (2004). Very carefully managed: Advice and suggestions in post-observation meetings. *Linguistics and Education*, 15(1–2), 33–58. 10.1016/j.linged.2004.10.004

Walsh, S., & Mann, S. (2015). Doing reflective practice: A data-led way forward. *ELT Journal*, 69(4), 351–362. 10.1093/elt/ccv018

Walsh, S., & Mann, S. (2019). *The Routledge handbook of English language teacher education*. Routledge.

Wyatt, M. (2008). *Growth in practical knowledge and teachers' self-efficacy during an in-service BA (TESOL) programme* [Unpublished PhD dissertation]. School of Education, University of Leeds.

Wyatt, M. (2010). An English teacher's developing self-efficacy beliefs in using groupwork. *System*, 38(4), 603–613. 10.1016/j.system.2010.09.012

Wyatt, M. (2013). Overcoming low self-efficacy beliefs in teaching English to young learners. *International Journal of Qualitative Studies in Education*, 26(2), 238–255. 10.1080/09518398.2011.605082

Wyatt, M. (2015). Using qualitative research methods to assess the degree of fit between teachers' reported self-efficacy beliefs and their practical knowledge during teacher education. *Australian Journal of Teacher Education*, 40(1), 117–145. 10.14221/ajte.2015v40n1.7

Wyatt, M. (2016). Are they becoming more reflective and/or efficacious: A conceptual model mapping how teachers' self-efficacy beliefs might grow. *Educational Review*, 68(1), 114–137. 10.1080/00131911.2015.1058754

Wyatt, M. (2018). Language teachers' self-efficacy beliefs: A review of the literature (2005–2016). *Australian Journal of Teacher Education*, 43(4), 92–120. 10.14221/ajte.2018v43n4.6

Wyatt, M. (2022). Learning to use a qualitative case study approach to research language teachers' self-efficacy beliefs. In K. Dikilitaş & K.M. Reynolds (Eds.), *Research methods in language teaching and learning* (pp. 9–23). Wiley Blackwell. https://media.wiley.com/product_data/excerpt/35/11197016/1119701635-23.pdf

# 7 Support for career-long development of language teachers' self-efficacy beliefs

## Two Chinese EFL teachers' stories of professional development

*Ronggan Zhang and Judith Hanks*

## Introduction

This chapter focuses on the development of language teachers' self-efficacy (LTSE) beliefs in a rapidly changing world. Although investigations have focused on self-efficacy (Bandura, 1977), teachers' self-efficacy (Tschannen-Moran & Woolfolk Hoy, 2001), and LTSE beliefs (Wyatt, 2018) for several decades, further research is needed into how LTSE beliefs change over time in relation to teachers' lived experience in different contexts. Through such investigations, researchers can identify how teachers can be better supported.

In this chapter, we discuss two case studies of English as a Foreign Language (EFL) teachers reflecting on their career-long professional development. Using the Exploratory Practice (EP) principles (Allwright & Hanks, 2009; Hanks, 2017) as a methodological framework, we focus on teachers' developing self-efficacy beliefs against the backdrop of massive and rapid change (in EFL and more generally) in China over the past 20 years. We ask: What support did the teachers receive? What support did they value? And what support, in their view, helped to build up their self-efficacy beliefs, and thus enable positive change in their practice?

## Literature review

### Self-efficacy beliefs and language proficiency

Teachers' self-efficacy beliefs are worth exploring since they influence teachers' behaviour in the classroom and thereby, student outcomes (Pajares, 1992; Tschannen-Moran & Woolfolk Hoy, 2001; Zee & Koomen, 2016). Central to his social cognitive theory, Bandura (1986) defines self-efficacy beliefs as "people's judgments of their capabilities to organize and execute courses of action required to attain designated types of performances" (p. 391). Growing out of self-efficacy research in general education, research into LTSE beliefs has developed considerably since 2005 and "is now an

DOI: 10.4324/9781003379300-9

established domain of research" (Faez et al., 2021, p. 756). LTSE beliefs are those beliefs held by individual teachers considering "their abilities to support language learning in various task-, domain- and context-specific cognitive, metacognitive, affective and social ways" (Wyatt, 2021, p. 296).

A major focus of research into LTSE beliefs has been on the relationship between self-efficacy and language proficiency (Faez et al., 2021). The focus is necessary since, while language proficiency is a core dimension of expertise in language teaching (Richards, 2010), EFL teachers often feel insecure about their own language competencies in the face of native-speakerist discourses (Lamb & Wyatt, 2019). In the East Asian context, for instance, Chen and Goh (2011) report that their 331 participating Chinese EFL university teachers expressed frustration at perceived low self-efficacy in teaching oral English due to their self-perceived low oral English proficiency. Similarly, Hiver (2013) notes that apparent lack of *language* self-efficacy was found to be nearly synonymous with seeming lack of *teaching* self-efficacy for his seven participating Korean public school EFL teachers. Drawing on interview data with six Japanese high school EFL teachers, Thompson and Dooley (2019) conclude that language teaching efficacy has a domain related to the use of English as part of teaching. However, whereas previous research has shown that there is a positive relationship between higher levels of language proficiency and stronger LTSE beliefs (Faez et al., 2021), very little work has been done on how the relationship evolves over the span of a career.

*Career-long development of LTSE beliefs*

It is increasingly recognized that teachers' self-efficacy beliefs are fluid, context-sensitive, and open to change (Wyatt, 2018). However, given the complexities involved in their development (Tschannen-Moran & McMaster, 2009; Wyatt, 2016), much work is still needed to understand LTSE belief change processes.

Bandura (1986) suggests four principal sources of self-efficacy: mastery experience (successful task performance), vicarious experience (watching, listening to, or reading about others' experiences), verbal persuasion (being persuaded or convinced that one can master a given task), and physiological and affective states (gaining somatic information about efficacy conveyed by physiological and emotional arousal). Such experiences need to be processed, and reflection on experience is crucial (Bandura, 1986; Wyatt, 2016).

Other psychological constructs interact with self-efficacy beliefs. For example, Wyatt (2013) highlights how an Omani EFL schoolteacher overcame low self-efficacy beliefs, helped by a growth rather than a fixed mindset (Dweck, 2017). She reflected on "efficacy doubts" (Wheatley, 2002), while working in a supportive school environment that provided efficacy-building experiences (particularly mastery experiences).

Various studies have focused on changes in LTSE beliefs, such as in preservice teachers through a one-year practicum (Atay, 2007), influenced by peer coaching (one-year training programme) (Goker, 2006) or action research (14-week course) (Cabaroglu, 2014). Changes in in-service teachers' LTSE beliefs have been investigated in relation to developing practical knowledge (over a three-year part-time teacher education programme) (Wyatt, 2010), and in relation to professional identities and pedagogical practices (during a two-year writing project) (Locke et al., 2013). However, while these studies reveal positive growth processes, the time scopes considered are relatively short. Given that teacher professional development (TDP) is essentially a career-long process (Day & Sachs, 2004), research into individuals' LTSE beliefs growth over a career would enhance understanding of how teachers may be supported to sustain development.

*Support for career-long development of LTSE beliefs*

Conceptual models of LTSE beliefs growth have recently appeared (e.g., Wyatt, 2016). However, while Wyatt's model includes contextual factors, the central focus is on efficacy-building in specific tasks in relation to reflective cycles, and on how LTSE beliefs might be generalized through spiralling growth. Less attention is paid to the question: How might teachers integrate contextual support to sustain development of LTSE beliefs throughout their careers?

From an individual teacher's perspective, as a developing person embedded in the centre of context (Bronfenbrenner, 1979), self-efficacy support and other factors are interconnected in the teacher's developmental ecosystem influencing, and being influenced by, the teacher (Bronfenbrenner, 1979; van Lier, 2004). From a person-oriented ecological sustainable perspective (Zhang, 2021), Sustainable Professional Development (SPD) is needed. This concerns how individual teachers may be best supported to sustain TPD throughout their careers. Essentially, SPD proposes that:

> Supported by the joint pattern of all elements mutually supportive in the TPD ecosystem that expands and evolves progressively towards his/her ideal prospects, the schoolteacher is enabled to sustain professional development over the course of career through his/her interaction with context in a series of structurally interrelated activities, situated in his/her self-actualisation process [accompanied by role models and] paced by himself/herself with respect to his/her unique characteristics as a socially developing person in the education profession.
>
> (Zhang, 2021, p. 231)

SPD is a unified whole of three interrelated aspects. These include the teacher aspect, which concerns the teacher's characteristics as a socially developing person, including his/her physiological and affective states in Bandura's (1986) considerations of self-efficacy information. There are also the ecological and the structural aspects, respectively, concerning support at the ecosystem and the activity levels, including whether efficacy-building experiences (particularly mastery experience), vicarious experience, and verbal persuasion are provided through interrelated activities in the company of role models. In SPD, with support in place, individual teachers may integrate contextual support for self-actualization guided by their ideal career prospects, and thereby realize career-long development of self-efficacy beliefs. Therefore, considering the support provided to operationalize SPD for individual teachers' career-long development of LTSE beliefs is crucial.

One way of building LTSE beliefs is through research engagement (Cabaroglu, 2014; Wyatt, 2016; Wyatt & Dikilitaş, 2016). So, forms of practitioner research, such as Exploratory Practice (EP) (Allwright & Hanks, 2009; Hanks, 2017), may support the sustained development of LTSE beliefs. Being a form of fully inclusive practitioner research, EP is designed for sustainability through its principles:

*The "what" issues*

1 Focus on *quality of life* as the fundamental issue.
2 Work to *understand* it, before thinking about solving problems.

*The "who" issues*

3 Involve *everybody* as practitioners developing their own understandings.
4 Work to bring people *together* in a common enterprise.
5 Work cooperatively for *mutual* development.

*The "how" issues*

6 Make it a *continuous* enterprise.
7 *Minimise the burden* by integrating the work for understanding into normal pedagogic practice.
(Allwright & Hanks, 2009, p. 260, emphasis in original)

Indeed, the framework of EP principles, "encompassing quality of life, working for understanding, collegiality, and sustainability" (Hanks, 2022, p. 221), is consistent with the person-oriented ecological sustainable perspective that informs the conceptualization of SPD. For example, recounting his lived experience over a two-year EP project while teaching business English at a UK university, Banister (2019) reports that EP helped him (re-)build his practitioner self-efficacy. Banister illustrates that EP may be a form of support for sustained development of LTSE beliefs, but studies making this connection are relatively new.

In the next sections, we examine the professional development stories of two Chinese EFL school teachers from a person-oriented ecological sustainable perspective (Zhang, 2021) and use EP as a philosophical and methodological lens to aid in developing our understandings.

## Research context

The study was conducted in Chinese senior high schools. School education in China consists of 12 years/grades, generally from primary school (Grades 1–6) to junior high school (Grades 7–9) and senior high school (Grades 10–12). EFL is widely taught, although Japanese, Russian, German, French, and Spanish are also legitimate language choices (MOE, 2018). Among the various subjects taught, Chinese, Mathematics, and English are often taken by students and parents as core subjects, given that the three subjects are always included in key examinations.

While teachers in the Chinese tradition are expected to be devoted to educating and caring for the younger generation, teaching has never been among the best-paid professions. Consequently, the Chinese government has been making efforts to raise teachers' social status over the last four decades. For instance, September 10 has been celebrated as Teachers' Day since 1985 (NPC, 1993). On that day, the authorities honour outstanding teachers and make their dedication and achievements known to the public, and people commonly express their gratitude to teachers.

Massive and rapid change has taken place in China since 1978. Through continuous economic growth, the previously low-income country rose to an upper-middle-income country by 2010 (Liu, 2018). However, despite its dramatic progress overall, as a developing country with a population of 1.4 billion, China's development is unbalanced, as acknowledged by government reports (e.g., Xi, 2017) and scholarly research papers (e.g., Zhou et al., 2018). Regional and urban-rural disparities persist in economics, education, and other aspects. Co-existing with modern, developed cities like Shanghai and Shenzhen, are much less-developed rural areas. The research site of this study, Z City (pseudonym), is a southern city with moderate development, geographically distanced from more developed areas.

Against this backdrop of uneven social development in recent decades, curriculum reform bringing new educational ideals into school teachers' professional lives has been constant. The importance of enabling professional development among teachers is often acknowledged in government documents, and top-down mandatory programmes are designed and implemented alongside social change policies and curriculum reform.

In Z City, as in other parts of China, there have been interrelated systems governing professional promotion and continuing education intended to support teachers throughout their careers. The promotion system sets out the route for teachers to progress from one professional title to another, mainly from Level Two to Level One teacher, and to senior teacher and full senior teacher. Beginning teachers with bachelor's degrees usually start from Level Two, and most major in teaching a particular subject, although, after obtaining a teaching certificate, they might teach other subjects. At the same time, top-down TPD opportunities are provided by education authorities in order to help teachers qualify for promotion and realize lifelong learning opportunities.

## Methodology

In this environment and considering gaps in knowledge about the career-spans of teachers, we ask:

- How do English language teachers' self-efficacy beliefs develop dynamically over the course of a career?

We examine the lived experiences of two Chinese senior high school EFL teachers (pseudonyms: Beibei and Yaya), who were part of a larger-scale, qualitative multiple-case study (Merriam, 1998; Stake, 2006) focusing on contextual support for school teachers' professional development (Zhang, 2021). As Wyatt (2022) explains, interpretive qualitative case study has been underexploited in research into LTSE beliefs, and so this study joins the very few in the literature (e.g., Wyatt, 2010, 2013) to give "a more holistic interpretation of the complexities of the multiple realities under investigation" (Wyatt, 2022, p. 14).

### Participants

Beibei and Yaya had volunteered for the earlier study (Zhang, 2021). Both participants met the key criteria that they were senior high school teachers teaching English in the urban area of Z City, and had volunteered to participate. When interviewed, Beibei was in the 10th year of her teaching career and Yaya in the 18th year, and they were both mothers at home. Beibei graduated as an English language teaching major from a local university in 2007. She first worked as a project translator in a more developed city in the province, and then in 2009, returned to Z City to teach English at her present senior high school.

Unlike Beibei, Yaya majored in biology teaching at university but was assigned to teach English when she started her career in 2001. Subsequently, she was a teacher of English for 18 years, the first 3 years in another city of the province, and then 15 years at 2 ordinary schools in Z City. For two years during the latter period, she was re-assigned by the education authorities to teach schoolchildren Chinese in the UK, while still being affiliated to her Z City school in China as an English teacher.

*Data collection and analysis*

The data collection process was a deepening process of *understanding* the professional experiences the participants lived in their contexts. We were not attempting to solve a problem, but rather to puzzle about, work together for mutual development, and generate profound understandings of professional development over time (Allwright & Hanks, 2009; Hanks, 2017). The process started by gathering school and local contextual data through school observations and document analysis in order to understand the school and local contexts (Phase 1), and then an open-ended questionnaire was used to collect biographical data to enhance understanding of the participants' formal career experiences (Phase 2). This was followed by three waves of semi-structured interviews to generate primary data about the participants' experiences and perceptions (Phase 3). The data were collected from November 2019 to April 2020, during which time the first author (Ronggan) lived in China (mostly in Z City) and interacted with the participants and the accumulated data to develop contextually rooted understandings.

The school observation was undertaken when Ronggan was initially an outsider and was shown around by the participants. It was a wide-focused, descriptive "observation for familiarisation" (McNaughton Nicholls et al., 2014), with notes taken following an open-ended observation protocol (Creswell, 2007), in which one column recorded descriptive and the other reflective notes. Naturally occurring data (Ritchie, 2003) of TPD policy and activity documents were also collected, online from the official websites of education authorities and offline from the participants and researchers of the local education departments. Document analysis (Bowen, 2009) offered a window into the historical dimension of the local contexts beyond the immediacy of observations and interviews.

Besides generating biographical information, the open-ended questionnaire in Phase 2 was also designed to help the participants start reflecting on their lived experiences, paving the way for the interviews in the next phase of data collection. The questionnaire invited the participants to list chronologically their key professional life events and add notes next to any event they considered to be a turning point in their career lives. A sample was provided as an example for the participants to follow "so that they [knew] the kind of reply being sought" (Cohen et al., 2018, p. 475). The participants were told explicitly that they could choose to respond in

English (the language they taught) or Chinese (their native language), or both, whichever way they felt best to express themselves.

In Phase 3, three waves of semi-structured interviews were conducted. The three-wave structure allowed the participants and the researcher to maintain a sense of focus in each wave and build trust and rapport. The first wave focused on concrete details of the participants' professional lives up to the present time, the second on imagined accounts of future career prospects, and the third on in-depth perceptions of contextual support. Life maps (Neale, 2019) were used to facilitate the interviews and generate complementary data. For later interviews, the participants were asked to draw a past and a future life map, respectively called "My professional highs and lows" and "My future career prospects". The participants were provided with template sheets to draw on and a sample to show them what a life map might look like. The completed life maps then served as a reference for the participants to articulate their ideas. All the interviews had been planned to be face-to-face, but due to the outbreak of the COVID-19 pandemic, the last two waves were changed to synchronous online interviews.

The data set included contextual data from school observations and documentation, biographical data from the open-ended questionnaire, and primary data from the semi-structured interviews, as well as visual complementary data of life maps the participants drew. The different types of data from various sources allowed for triangulation (Denzin, 1970/2009) to compare and verify the participants' experiences and perceptions, as a result of which, discussion of self-efficacy (and lack thereof) emerged. We employed Template Analysis (King et al., 2018) to identify patterns emerging from the data set, and now present the findings, drawing illustrative extracts from the data as required.

## Findings

### Beibei's story: "I learned desperately"

In senior high school, Beibei met a teacher who spoke very good English and her potential in language began to show. She was then interested in English but could not do well in other subjects. The teacher was an inspiration to her, especially in spoken English:

> [...] My oral English was quite like a foreigner's. I can't say it was very good, but at least I enjoyed imitation (Beibei).

The teacher was also "like a life guide" (Beibei). With his support, Beibei said she chose without hesitation to study English at university. Beibei's university provided a context with efficacy-building elements that helped sustain her high self-efficacy, such as opportunities to interact with English native speakers:

> I felt satisfied with my academic performance, because I enjoyed hanging out with foreign teachers, and I always sat in the first row in class (Beibei).

So, Beibei was successful as an EFL learner, benefiting from efficacy-building information and contextual factors in her senior high school and university.

However, Beibei's beliefs about her language proficiency were challenged when she entered the workplace as a project translator in 2007. She encountered embarrassing moments, for instance, when she could not translate an utterance, although she understood it. She began to doubt her efficacy:

> I had thought my oral English was very good, but when I started working, I was slapped in the face, very, very hard (Beibei).

Two years later, when her company shut down the project, Beibei returned to Z City and started her teaching career, so that she could, as her parents wished, have more time to get married. As a "socially developing person" (Zhang, 2021), Beibei prioritized family factors in her job decision:

> I might be wealthy and outstanding with a successful [translator] career at the age of 30, but without a family, or even with a family, but my husband would not like me to travel often, etc. There would be lots of troubles. So I thought I'd better choose a profession good for my [future] family life. [...] It's easier to get married as a teacher. Everybody likes teachers.
>
> (Beibei)

After returning to Z City, Beibei strove to improve her English language proficiency and translation ability while busily working as an English teacher and later a young mother:

> In the first few years after my return [to the city to teach], I learned desperately. I spent three or four hours learning every day after work.
>
> (Beibei)

Beibei's "efficacy doubts" (Wheatley, 2002) after entering the workplace led her to reflect on past learning experience, and she realized that the problem might lie in her poor mastery of English grammar:

I thought over the problems. They puzzled me for a long time. I reflected on the whole process of my English learning, and asked if there was anything wrong. That's why I learned English grammar so desperately these years.

(Beibei)

Besides learning grammar by herself, Beibei made foreign friends to practise oral English, and did lots of reading: "I bought almost all the English-Chinese magazines I could get from dangdang.com, and read them all" (Beibei). She self-funded to complete many online open courses, including simultaneous interpretation classes with offline training while on holiday. She hired a private tutor to prepare her for the spoken module of IELTS (International English Language Testing System), for which she wished to score high enough to gain entry to a master's degree from abroad or teach IELTS herself someday. She also self-funded to visit the USA in 2017 with students and teachers from a language school.

As these efforts illustrate, Beibei was a very determined learner with a "growth mindset" (Dweck, 2017). She tried every means to learn and rebuild her language self-efficacy over the years, which suggests that she believed she could improve. To improve her language abilities, she used a whole range of strategies, which could be related both to her self-efficacy beliefs and to her beliefs about second language acquisition (Barcelos & Kalaja, 2011). She believed, for instance, that she could engage successfully in language learning tasks, and that practising speaking and reading autonomously would help.

Beibei's learning engendered financial issues. For example, she spent close to half her annual income on her trip to the USA and on simultaneous interpretation classes, respectively. Although Beibei considered the investment necessary and rewarding, she admitted, "I think I was a bit crazy" (Beibei). Besides financial issues, Beibei's learning also involved a balance with her family responsibilities. She tried her best to keep both in harmony. In the summer holiday of 2019, for instance, she took her translation classes in another city, but went with her husband and son: "When I went to classes, my husband took my son to play around. The child was happy, so were the adults" (Beibei).

Beibei's hard work on improving herself was not noticed or supported by the school, as she notes in response to a question about what professional support she ever received: "I don't think the school gives me any help. [I learn] all by myself. Besides, I am kind of transparent [invisible] at the school" (Beibei).

In contrast, Beibei was grateful for her family's support. Asked in which period of her professional life she felt best supported, she responded:

> I think I've got very good support from my family since I reached the age of 33. My mother-in-law was willing to look after my son, so I could pay a one-month visit to the USA. If not, I couldn't have made it.
>
> (Beibei)

Beibei's persistence in learning paid off. In 2019, her 10th year of teaching, for instance, she achieved an overall score of 7.5 for IELTS and won the first prize in a city-level teaching competition, which essentially involved giving a lesson on given content and a speech on education. Such achievements and the related mastery experiences seemed to have helped Beibei rebuild her language self-efficacy. Her LTSE beliefs also strengthened:

> Now if you ask me to tutor an undergraduate to prepare for Band 8 [the required language proficiency test for English majors in China], I think I am capable of that because my English proficiency is already very much higher than 10 years ago.
>
> (Beibei)

Positive change took place in Beibei's teaching alongside growth in LTSE and language self-efficacy beliefs. She felt that her teaching stood out as she could, for instance, provide up-to-date examples and materials from real-life experiences that her students could easily relate to. She also shared her own learning experience with her students and hoped to set an example for them, so that each of them could develop and fulfil his/her own potential (Joyce, 1980); this suggests that she wanted to be an inspiring teacher (Lamb & Wedell, 2013). She remarks:

> When a teacher keeps moving forward, his or her students would more or less do the same. I hope I can influence my students this way.
>
> (Beibei)

Looking ahead, Beibei said she had more new teaching ideas she was waiting to try out. After tutoring some IELTS students part-time, for example, she had an idea "to see if some IELTS writing techniques can be applied to English writing in the college entrance exam" (Beibei).

We now turn to a very different situation. Unlike Beibei who overcame low LTSE beliefs, Yaya continued to struggle over 18 years in teaching. Like many teachers, this was not her first choice of career and she battled with low self-efficacy. Her professional life story below offers a very different perspective of career-long development of LTSE beliefs.

*Yaya's story: "I'm actually returning to who I am"*

Yaya majored in biology teaching at university but was assigned to be an EFL teacher at the start of her career in 2001. She then worked hard to improve her English over the years. In order to obtain a professional rank in teaching English, she took her school leaders' advice and studied part time for three years, and in 2005, earned her bachelor's degree in English teaching. In 2009, "pushed" (in her words) by her friend, she signed up for teaching Chinese abroad, but her language efficacy was low: "I was well aware how bad my English was" (Yaya). So she seriously prepared herself for the selection examinations. She only slept three to four hours a night. She also paid a foreign teacher CNY250 an hour (which accumulated to a quarter of her then-monthly salary) to help improve her oral English.

After two years in the UK, Yaya's perception of her own language proficiency improved through efficacy-building experiences (particularly mastery experiences). For example, she no longer panicked when listening to English, "because [in the UK] we had colleagues from different parts of the world. They spoke all kinds of strange English" (Yaya). She also benefited from enhanced cross-cultural understanding, supported by teaching training. Asked how specifically her experience in the UK influenced her, she responded:

> At least I can understand what others write when I read an [English] article. First, I know the background well. Then we received many times of [Chinese] teaching training both in China and the UK, and my English language proficiency has improved. And, cross-cultural understanding, this is very important.
>
> (Yaya)

Yaya saw her two years in the UK as "a great turning point" in her professional life. Besides the improvement in her English, she also found that she received greater support from her school back in China: "The principal was especially kind to me. He gave me many opportunities to go outside [of the school]" (Yaya). In the city, she was invited to work for different events (e.g., as a judge for teaching competitions), and was widely acknowledged as an outstanding English teacher. Gradually her LTSE beliefs evolved in relation to how others saw her, as she notes in her response to what her experience in the UK brought her: "Kind of gilding to my name. Others would think I am the best. Then, I think, mm, yes, I'm the best" (Yaya).

However, Yaya's LTSE beliefs were still low and she did not think she was really good at English. Asked if her experience abroad made her more confident, she answered:

It's not about self-confidence. After all, English is my obvious weakness, because I was not systematically trained, I mean, for what I teach and what I do. Although my students achieved very good scores in exams, but the problem is, I'm not the kind of person who was trained formally and systematically [to be an English teacher].

(Yaya)

Although Yaya was well-recognized as an English teacher (and was also promoted to senior teacher in English soon after we met for the study), she felt that she was not good enough in English teaching because this was not her initial major, which suggests a fixed mindset (Dweck, 2017). She had to overcome the lasting sense of inadequacy over time.

On the other hand, though constrained to take on English teaching, Yaya's love for biology showed and developed whenever possible. In 2004, her school asked and Yaya accepted to join a biology teaching competition in the city, and she won the first prize. In 2016, she chose to do part-time master's study in psychology and earned her degree in 2018. Looking ahead, Yaya wished "to be the one who knows physical fitness best among English teachers" because physical fitness was fundamentally related to biology, and physical education was her best subject since childhood. To this end, she learned and obtained a physical fitness coach certificate. After 18 years of teaching English, Yaya seemed ready to return to biology in which she considered her professional potential lay, as she remarks: "As your age grows, you'll return to the field you are good at. […] so I feel I'm actually returning to who I am, the field I liked at the beginning" (Yaya).

## Discussion

The stories of Beibei and Yaya reinforce the understanding that LTSE beliefs are "fluid and context-sensitive" (Wyatt, 2018, p. 93) and open to change. We take this understanding as the starting point for a discussion of career-long development of LTSE beliefs and their support below.

As teachers' professional lives develop, LTSE beliefs evolve over time. Both Beibei and Yaya started teaching with low LTSE beliefs and kept working hard to improve themselves. Their LTSE beliefs gradually changed. They lived, however, very different experiences in their particular contexts and their LTSE beliefs developed differently. Beibei reported overcoming low LTSE beliefs, helped by a growth mindset, whereas Yaya continued to recount struggles, influenced by a fixed mindset.

To recap, Beibei displayed language potential early in senior high school and reported high self-perceptions of English language proficiency when graduating from university. However, her self-perceptions were diminished as she met with setbacks in her translator work before teaching. She then invested continuously over her teaching career in improving herself against all difficulties. She gradually managed to rebuild her language self-efficacy, and her LTSE beliefs accordingly improved, leading to transformative change in her teaching. Consistent with Wyatt's (2013) findings, Beibei's "efficacy doubts" (Wheatley, 2002), reflection, and "growth mindset" (Dweck, 2017) helped in her process of overcoming low self-efficacy. While school support was missing, Beibei received family support, which can be valuable (Brannan & Bleistein, 2012). Yaya, on the other hand, battled with a sense of weak language proficiency and reported a wide range of divergent interests (biology, physical education, and psychology).

The life stories of the two participants illustrate that the development of LTSE beliefs influences and is influenced by beliefs incorporated earlier into the belief structure (Pajares, 1992). So, Beibei's belief in her language potential dating back to her senior high school and Yaya's concern that she was not initially trained at university to be an English but rather a biology teacher were influential. These beliefs, illustrating Pajares' (1992) view that "the earlier a belief is incorporated into the belief structure, the more difficult it is to alter" (p. 325), exerted significant influence on the participants' development of LTSE beliefs.

In Yaya's case, her belief that she was a biology rather than an English major overrode her self-perceptions of improving language proficiency and kept her LTSE beliefs low, even though she gradually became well known as an excellent English teacher in the city. This finding contrasts with Akbari and Moradkhani's (2010) conclusion that academic degree does not make a difference in affecting LTSE beliefs, suggesting instead that initial teaching degree can play a role.

In Beibei's case, though, as she worked hard over the years to improve her language abilities, her LTSE beliefs were enhanced. Previous research has highlighted a positive relationship between language proficiency and LTSE beliefs (Faez & Karas, 2017; Faez et al., 2021). However, as Faez et al. (2021) note, "while language proficiency is important, there is more to teaching self-efficacy than just language proficiency" (p. 772). This is also evident in the context of this study, given the importance of earlier beliefs.

The participants' life experiences suggest that career-long development of LTSE beliefs is mediated by self-perceptions of professional potential which are consistent over past life (Zhang, 2021). Both participants formed consistent self-perceptions of professional potential in their lived experiences. Beibei developed a belief in her language potential, which guided her to study English at university and, later in her teaching career, overcome her low LTSE beliefs. Yaya consistently believed since childhood that her professional potential lay in biology-related areas. This belief gave her a sense of identity as a biology major.

To gain a deeper understanding of the participants' lived experiences, it is necessary to shift the focus from viewing them as simply language teachers to understanding them as "socially developing persons" (Zhang, 2021). Both participants noted the importance of professional development support and family support. Beibei highly valued such family support as sharing child-care responsibilities, which allowed her to have time for her professional development. As a learner of teaching (Freeman & Richards, 1996; Johnson, 2009), Yaya considered school support indispensable to her. She was supported by the school system to do part-time degree study and spend two years in the UK, and gradually developed into a qualified, and later a well-known English teacher in the city. But she also underlined the importance of a parent's role at home. The wish to be a role model for her child motivated her to pursue professional excellence. Consistent with the literature, the findings illustrate that teachers' lives at home and at school are interrelated (Day et al., 2006), and support for teachers concerns not only their professional development but also their quality of life (Allwright & Hanks, 2009; Hanks, 2017) at home.

Besides the family and school support noted above, more contextual support could be identified when the participants' life experiences were examined in relation to the three core components of context (people, place, and time) (Wedell & Malderez, 2013), each with a social and a physical aspect (Zhang, 2021). For instance, after Yaya returned from the UK, her English and teaching were recognized by people around her and the recognition helped strengthen her LTSE beliefs. Beibei was able to improve her language abilities, and hence gain higher LTSE beliefs, supported by resources available in her city at the time (e.g., English-Chinese magazines she bought online, foreigners to make friends with, and translation classes). Such support might be implicit for others but was made explicit by the participants themselves when they found it relevant to their needs as socially developing persons in the teaching profession.

Relevance (as discussed in Hanks, 2017, 2019a) seems to be an important feature of support for the development of LTSE beliefs. Efforts were made by education authorities intending to support the teachers in their contexts. However, Beibei articulated that she did not receive any support from her school over the years. It is likely that school support, though provided, was not perceived by Beibei as *relevant* to her development of professional potential in language, specifically, her improvement of language proficiency and translation abilities. In contrast, Yaya acknowledged school support as she found it relevant to her gains in language proficiency and self-efficacy. For instance, she was able to apply for a professional title in English teaching after she was supported by the school to do part-time bachelor's study in English. As these findings show, intended support efforts should first be relevant to teachers, especially to the needs they identify for themselves in the process of self-efficacy development.

Self-perceptions of language proficiency are important for the development of LTSE beliefs (Faez et al., 2021), but support for language improvement does not necessarily contribute to the sustainability of LTSE beliefs development. Yaya, for example, was supported to develop her language proficiency over 18 years. However, over the years she engaged in English learning mainly for "normative obligations" (Hiver, 2013) to comply with external pressures as an English teacher. After years of being constrained, the motivation to realize her professional potential in biology gradually took over. Yaya's story illustrates that if language self-efficacy development is inconsistent with self-perceptions of professional potential, it is unlikely to be sustained although support for language improvement is in place.

On the other hand, even without school support, teachers may invest throughout their careers in language self-efficacy development, if it is consistent with their actualization of professional potential, as in Beibei's case. In her 10-year career, Beibei was mainly guided by the belief in her language potential dating back to senior high school, although at the start of her teaching career, she was also motivated by a central need for "repairing inadequacies of the self" (Hiver, 2013, p. 215) as she perceived in her previous translator work. Although school support was not there for her, Beibei managed to overcome low LTSE beliefs and continued working hard to seek higher LTSE beliefs.

Informed by a person-oriented ecological sustainable perspective (Zhang, 2021) and the EP framework (Allwright & Hanks, 2009; Hanks, 2017), the above discussion has illustrated that support for general professional development can contribute to the development of LTSE beliefs. Teachers' lives at home and at school are interrelated, and support for teachers involves enhancing their professional development as well as their quality of life. Teachers value family and school support, and other contextual support they find relevant to them as socially developing persons in the teaching profession. While the development of LTSE beliefs is mediated by both self-perceptions of language proficiency and professional potential, mere support for language improvement might seem insufficient. This raises the question as how to support career-long development of LTSE beliefs in practice. To this end, we return to more explicitly discuss EP and its contributions.

## Pedagogical implications

Exploratory Practice (EP) provides a framework of principles which "act and interact with each other in a complex system" (Hanks, 2017, p.226), consistent with the insights discussed above. Support provided in EP is likely to be taken by teachers as relevant to their needs as socially developing persons in the profession, given that EP respects individualities and local idiosyncrasies (Allwright & Hanks, 2009). EP invites teachers to explore "puzzles" (research questions) they identify in their own classroom contexts (Hanks, 2017, 2019a). While working primarily to understand their puzzles, they integrate inquiry and pedagogy and make use of support relevant to their needs. In EP, for example, a teacher like Yaya may be encouraged to explore *why* her students did well in examinations though she was not initially trained to be an English teacher. Such reflective work on mastery experiences could potentially then impact LTSE beliefs.

Moreover, whatever puzzles Yaya chooses to explore, EP offers a context for her to relate her biology potential to her teaching of English, and reflect on how she gradually developed into a unique English teacher. In this context, both EP itself as a form of support and the support provided in the EP process are likely to help her sustain investment in LTSE beliefs development given their relevance to her self-perception of professional potential.

While career-long development of LTSE beliefs concerns sustainability, the EP principle of making the work for understanding a continuous enterprise encourages teachers to realize sustainability in their particular contexts. For example, a teacher like Beibei might want to investigate if some IELTS writing techniques can be applied to English writing in the college entrance exam. In EP, she may first be supported to understand her puzzle (e.g., IELTS and its writing techniques, and the English college entrance exam and its writing tasks), and then try integrating IELTS writing techniques into her teaching. New puzzles (e.g., how to teach IELTS writing techniques) probably follow. This may initiate a new round of exploration. With later puzzles derived or evolved from earlier ones, exploration activities are interconnected over the professional life. When activities are bound derivationally or evolutionarily, teachers are invited to engage in further activities, making sustained professional development possible (Zhang, 2021). It follows that EP provides scaffolding support for teachers to develop sustainably and thereby enables career-long self-efficacy development.

EP also increases teachers' possibilities to enjoy collegiality and have their wellbeing and esteem needs met in their professional lives. In EP, teachers are encouraged to work co-operatively for mutual development and involve everybody as practitioners in developing their own understandings. In other words, EP is a context in which teachers respect and learn from each other's uniqueness, working together to develop their own understandings rather than seeking solutions to puzzles. In EP, for example, Yaya's self-perception of professional potential is likely to be respected as she can bring in different understandings sourced from her biology knowledge, so her initial biology degree study is not a weakness but a strength for her development of LTSE beliefs. Through EP, Beibei might find like-minded colleagues who also persist in actualizing their language potential, and enjoy more collegiality than before. The way teachers work together in EP exemplifies the EP principle of working to bring people together and contributes to teachers' self-efficacy development as well as perceptions of wellbeing in their professional lives.

In sum, the pedagogical implications of this work include:

- School support can be maximized through recognition of its value
- Investigations by/for teachers can be related to everyday teaching lives via puzzling
- These investigations can develop professional potential through specific tasks to build LTSE beliefs (e.g., actively puzzling)
- Such work enhances and unlocks teachers' potential to meet the needs of their learners
- All of the above contribute to self-esteem, actualization, and ultimately quality of life and wellbeing.

## Conclusion

We have highlighted that EP enables teachers to make school (and other) support relevant to their needs and sustains investment in self-efficacy development. EP also provides opportunities for teachers to enjoy collegiality and have their wellbeing and esteem needs met. Taken together, as Hanks (2019b, p.23) notes, "Involving everyone in collegial, curious inquiry not only develops a sense of self-efficacy and wellbeing, but also enhances Quality of Life". This is consistent with the findings presented here. We therefore recommend EP as a way to support the development of language teacher self-efficacy beliefs.

We have discussed our findings from a person-oriented ecological sustainable perspective (Zhang, 2021) and suggest EP as a way to support the development of language teacher self-efficacy beliefs. We point towards future research using the EP principles of working together with teachers and learners to develop understandings of practice, and through building up a sense of self-efficacy, concurrently enhancing quality of life. Above all, we argue that there is a need to prioritize the quality of life of/for teachers and learners. The process of making the work they do relevant to their values and beliefs supports language and professional development and enhances language teacher self-efficacy.

## References

Akbari, R., & Moradkhani, S. (2010). Iranian English teachers' self-efficacy: Do academic degree and experience make a difference? *Pazhuhesh-e Zabanha-ye Khareji*, 56, 25–47.

Allwright, D., & Hanks, J. (2009). *The developing language learner: An introduction to exploratory practice*. Palgrave Macmillan. 10.1057/9780230233690

Atay, D. (2007). Beginning teacher efficacy and the practicum in an EFL context. *Teacher Development*, 11(2), 203–219. 10.1080/13664530701414720

Bandura, A. (1977). Self-efficacy: Toward a unifying theory of behavioral change. *Psychological Review*, 84(2), 191–215. 10.1037/0033-295x.84.2.191

Bandura, A. (1986). *Social foundations of thought and action: A social cognitive theory*. Prentice-Hall.

Banister, C. (2019). Rebuilding practitioner self-efficacy through learner feedback. In A. Slimani-Rolls & R. Kiely (Eds.), *Exploratory practice for continuing professional development: An innovative approach for language teachers* (pp. 135–151). Palgrave Macmillan. 10.1007/978-3-319-69763-5

Barcelos, A.M.F., & Kalaja, P. (2011). Introduction to *beliefs about SLA revisited*. *System*, 39(3), 281–289. 10.1016/j.system.2011.07.001

Bowen, G.A. (2009). Document analysis as a qualitative research method. *Qualitative Research Journal*, 9(2), 27–40. 10.3316/qrj0902027

Brannan, D., & Bleistein, T. (2012). Novice ESOL teachers' perceptions of social support networks. *TESOL Quarterly*, 46(3), 519–541. 10.1002/tesq.40

Bronfenbrenner, U. (1979). *The ecology of human development: Experiments by nature and design*. Harvard University Press.

Cabaroglu, N. (2014). Professional development through action research: Impact on self-efficacy. *System*, 44, 79–88. 10.1016/j.system.2014.03.003

Chen, Z., & Goh, C. (2011). Teaching oral English in higher education: Challenges to EFL teachers. *Teaching in Higher Education*, 16(3), 333–345. 10.1080/13562517.2010.546527

Cohen, L., Manion, L., & Morrison, K. (2018). *Research methods in education* (8th ed.). Routledge. 10.4324/9781315456539

Creswell, J.W. (2007). *Qualitative inquiry and research design: Choosing among five approaches* (2nd ed.). SAGE.

Day, C., & Sachs, J. (2004). Professionalism, performativity and empowerment: Discourses in the politics, policies and purposes of continuing professional development. In. C. Day & J. Sachs (Eds.), *International handbook on the continuing professional development of teachers* (pp. 3–32). Open University Press.

Day, C., Kington, A., Stobart, G., & Sammons, P. (2006). The personal and professional selves of teachers: Stable and unstable identities. *British Educational Research Journal*, 32(4), 601–616. 10.1080/01411920600775316

Denzin, N.K. (1970/2009). *The research act: A theoretical introduction to sociological methods*. Routledge.

Dweck, C.S. (2017). *Mindset: Changing the way you think to fulfil your potential* (Rev. ed.). Robinson.

Faez, F., & Karas, M. (2017). Connecting language proficiency to (self-reported) teaching ability: A review and analysis of research. *RELC Journal*, *48*(1), 135–151. 10.1177/0033688217694755

Faez, F., Karas, M., & Uchihara, T. (2021). Connecting language proficiency to teaching ability: A meta-analysis. *Language Teaching Research*, *25*(5), 754–777. 10.1177/1362168819868667

Freeman, D., & Richards, J.C. (Eds.). (1996). *Teacher learning in language teaching*. Cambridge University Press.

Goker, S.D. (2006). Impact of peer coaching on self-efficacy and instructional skills in TEFL teacher education. *System*, *34*(2), 239–254. 10.1016/j.system.2005.12.002

Hanks, J. (2017). *Exploratory practice in language teaching: Puzzling about principles and practices*. Palgrave Macmillan. 10.1057/978-1-137-45344-0

Hanks, J. (2019a). From research-as-practice to exploratory practice-as-research in language teaching and beyond. *Language Teaching*, *52*(2), 143–187. 10.1017/s0261444819000016

Hanks, J. (2019b). Involving everyone in enhancing quality of life in language education: Explorations and insights from praxis. *JACET International Convention Selected Papers*, *6*, 3–28. http://www.jacet.org/SelectedPapers/JACET57_2018_SP_6.pdf

Hanks, J. (2022). Integrating research into language teaching and learning: Learners and teachers as co-researchers exploring praxis. *Language Teaching*, *55*(2), 217–232. 10.1017/s026144482100032x

Hiver, P. (2013). The interplay of possible language teacher selves in professional development choices. *Language Teaching Research*, *17*(2), 210–227. 10.1177/1362168813475944

Johnson, K.E. (2009). *Second language teacher education: A sociocultural perspective*. Routledge. 10.4324/9780203878033

Joyce, B. (1980). The ecology of professional development. In. E. Hoyle & J. Megarry (Eds.), *World yearbook of education 1980: Professional development of teachers* (pp. 19–41). Kogan Page.

King, N., Brooks, J., & Tabari, S. (2018). Template analysis in business and management research. In M. Ciesielska & D. Jemielniak (Eds.), *Qualitative methods in organization studies: Volume II: Methods and possibilities* (pp. 179–206). Palgrave Macmillan. 10.1007/978-3-319-65442-3_8

Lamb, M., & Wedell, M. (2013). *Inspiring English teachers: A comparative study of learner perceptions of inspirational teaching*. British Council. https://www.teachingenglish.org.uk/sites/teacheng/files/C684%20Inspiring%20English%20Teachers_WEB_FINAL_V2.pdf

Lamb, M., & Wyatt, M. (2019). Teacher motivation: The missing ingredient in teacher education. In S. Walsh & S. Mann (Eds.), *The Routledge handbook of English language teacher education* (pp. 522–535). Routledge.

Liu, W. (2018). GDP and the new concept of development: Understanding China's changing concept of development in regards to GDP after the reform and opening-up. In R. Garnaut, L. Song & C. Fang (Eds.), *China's 40 Years of reform and development* (pp. 67–74). ANU Press.

Locke, T., Dix, S., & Whitehead, D. (2013). The impact of 'Writing Project' professional development on teachers' self-efficacy as writers and teachers of writing. *English in Australia, 48*(2), 55–69.

McNaughton Nicholls, C., Mills, L., & Kotecha, M. (2014). Observation. In J. Ritchie, J. Lewis, C. McNaughton Nicholls, & R. Ormston (Eds.), *Qualitative research practice: A guide for social science students and researchers* (pp. 242–268). SAGE.

Merriam, S.B. (1998). *Qualitative research and case study applications in education.* Jossey-Bass.

Ministry of Education (MOE), P. R. C. (2018). *Curriculum schemes for ordinary senior high schools (2017 edition) (Putong Gaozhong Kecheng Fang'an (2017 nianban))*. People's Education Press.

National People's Congress (NPC), P. R. C. (1993). Teachers Law of the People's Republic of China (Zhonghua renmin guoheguo jiaoshi fa). Retrieved 27 August 2020, from National People's Congress, http://www.npc.gov.cn/zgrdw/englishnpc/Law/2007-12/12/content_1383815.htm

Neale, B. (2019). *What is qualitative longitudinal research?* Bloomsbury Academic.

Pajares, M.F. (1992). Teachers' beliefs and educational research: Cleaning up a messy construct. *Review of Educational Research, 62*(3), 307–332. 10.3102/00346543062003307

Richards, J.C. (2010). Competence and performance in language teaching. *RELC Journal, 41*(2), 101–122. 10.1177/0033688210372953

Ritchie, J. (2003). The applications of qualitative methods to social research. In J. Ritchie & J. Lewis (Eds.), *Qualitative research practice: A guide for social science students and researchers* (pp. 24–46). SAGE.

Stake, R.E. (2006). *Multiple case study analysis.* The Guilford Press.

Thompson, G., & Dooley, K. (2019). Exploring the key domains where teacher efficacy beliefs operate for Japanese high-school English teachers. *Asia Pacific Education Review, 20*(3), 503–518. 10.1007/s12564-019-09607-y

Tschannen-Moran, M., & McMaster, P. (2009). Sources of self-efficacy: Four professional development formats and their relationship to self-efficacy and implementation of a new teaching strategy. *The Elementary School Journal, 110*(2), 228–245. 10.1086/605771

Tschannen-Moran, M., & Woolfolk Hoy, A. (2001). Teacher efficacy: Capturing an elusive construct. *Teaching and Teacher Education, 17*(7), 783–805. 10.1016/s0742-051x(01)00036-1

van Lier, L. (2004). *The ecology and semiotics of language learning: A sociocultural perspective.* Kluwer Academic.

Wedell, M., & Malderez, A. (2013). *Understanding language classroom contexts: The starting point for change.* Bloomsbury Academic.

Wheatley, K.F. (2002). The potential benefits of teacher efficacy doubts for educational reform. *Teaching and Teacher Education, 18*(1), 5–22. 10.1016/s0742-051x(01)00047-6

Wyatt, M. (2010). An English teacher's developing self-efficacy beliefs in using groupwork. *System, 38*(4), 603–613. 10.1016/j.system.2010.09.012

Wyatt, M. (2013). Overcoming low self-efficacy beliefs in teaching English to young learners. *International Journal of Qualitative Studies in Education*, 26(2), 238–255. 10.1080/09518398.2011.605082

Wyatt, M. (2016). "Are they becoming more reflective and/or efficacious?" A conceptual model mapping how teachers' self-efficacy beliefs might grow. *Educational Review*, 68(1), 114–137. 10.1080/00131911.2015.1058754

Wyatt, M. (2018). Language teachers' self-efficacy beliefs: A review of the literature (2005–2016). *The Australian Journal of Teacher Education*, 43(4), 92–120. 10.14221/ajte.2018v43n4.6

Wyatt, M. (2021). Research into second language learners' and teachers' self-efficacy beliefs: Making the connections. *TESOL Quarterly*, 55(1), 296–307. 10.1002/tesq.3010

Wyatt, M. (2022). Learning to use a qualitative case study approach to research language teachers' self-efficacy beliefs. In K. Dikilitaş & K.M. Reynolds (Eds.), *Research methods in language teaching and learning* (pp. 9–23). Wiley Blackwell.

Wyatt, M., & Dikilitaş, K. (2016). English language teachers becoming more efficacious through research engagement at their Turkish university. *Educational Action Research*, 24(4), 550–570. 10.1080/09650792.2015.1076731

Xi, J. (2017). Secure a decisive victory in building a moderately prosperous society in all respects and strive for the great success of socialism with Chinese characteristics for a new era – Speech delivered at the 19th National Congress of the Communist Party of China. *Xinhua News*. Retrieved from http://www.xinhuanet.com/english/special/2017-11/03/c_136725942.htm

Zee, M., & Koomen, H.M.Y. (2016). Teacher self-efficacy and its effects on classroom processes, student academic adjustment, and teacher well-being: A synthesis of 40 years of research. *Review of Educational Research*, 86(4), 981–1015. 10.3102/0034654315626801

Zhang, R. (2021). *Contextual support for sustainable professional development: A case study of Chinese senior high school EFL teachers* [PhD]. https://etheses.whiterose.ac.uk/31021/

Zhou, Y., Guo, Y., & Liu, Y. (2018). High-level talent flow and its influence on regional unbalanced development in China. *Applied Geography*, 91, 89–98. 10.1016/j.apgeog.2017.12.023

# 8 Growing teacher research efficacy beliefs through Exploratory Practice

An autoethnography

*Chris Banister*

## Introduction

June 2016 on the shores of the Bosphorus, in Istanbul, Turkey. I am posing for a photo with a group of colleagues outside the venue of a teacher-research conference, promoting a recently published book about teachers researching their practice. At the time, I had benefited from two years' mentoring in the principles of Exploratory Practice (EP) and had experienced its transformative impact on my continuing professional development (Slimani-Rolls & Kiely, 2019). It was these positive experiences with EP that prompted my trip to Istanbul.

After the Istanbul conference, I read and annotated one of the chapters (Wyatt, 2016) of the same teacher-research book (Artefact 8.1). This chapter discussed the psychological benefits for teachers of engaging in forms of practitioner research like EP and in it I found much that resonated with my own experiences with EP. Later, reflecting on these experiences, I wrote about "Rebuilding language teacher self-efficacy through learner feedback" (Banister, 2019). Truth be told, my understanding of Bandura's (1977) concept of self-efficacy was rudimentary at this stage. My annotations indicated that I felt that my EP work had resulted in "the development of research skills" (see the tick in Artefact 8.1, paragraph 2 below, (Wyatt, 2016, p. 5). However, my written account focused more on my efficacy gains as an early career English for Academic Purposes (EAP) teacher rather than any self-efficacy growth as a researcher of my own teaching practice.

This chapter traces my journey as a practitioner–researcher, and more specifically as an *Exploratory Practitioner,* adopting and enacting EP, from my apprenticeship through to later more assured enquiry and growth. I identify the distinct challenges EP presents for teacher–researchers and analyse the critical incidents and setbacks which, at times, threatened my burgeoning self-efficacy beliefs.

DOI: 10.4324/9781003379300-10

> [Exploratory practice] is sometimes seen as a form of action research, e.g. by Richards (2009), though Hanks (this volume) prefers to see it otherwise, as a junior member of the same rambunctious practitioner research family. Dedicated to principles such as putting the quality of life first (Allwright, 2003), exploratory practice also emphasizes making the learners central to the process. As Hanks (2015) explains, "learners are encouraged not only to investigate questions that have puzzled their teachers, but also to formulate their own questions and investigate issues themselves" (p. 118).  *T puzzle* / *L puzzles*
>
> It seems likely that engaging in action research or exploratory practice in a sustained way is likely to be a highly beneficial activity. As argued in Wyatt (2011), teachers engaging in classroom research over a period of time might gain from the development of research skills, increased awareness of the teaching / learning process, renewed enthusiasm for teaching, greater collaboration with colleagues (Atay, 2008), enhanced self-efficacy beliefs (Henson, 2001) and continuing commitment to professional development (Kirkwood and Christie, 2006). However, as has been pointed out by Borg

*Artefact 8.1* Annotated page 5 from teachers engaging in research (Wyatt, 2016, p. 5).

## Literature review

### Self-efficacy beliefs

In psychology, *self-efficacy* refers to individuals' judgements of their capabilities to plan and perform actions they consider necessary to achieve desired outcomes (Bandura, 1977). Self-efficacy beliefs explain how individuals choose activities, the effort they invest, and for how long (Bandura, 1977). *Self-efficacy beliefs* are task-, domain-, and context-specific with four sources, or influences: an individual's *mastery* experiences, the *vicarious* experiences of seeing peers succeed with the same (or comparable) tasks, an individual's physiological and *emotional* state, and social *persuasion* from "successful efficacy builders" who "structure situations ... which bring success" (Bandura, 1995, p. 4).

In Applied Linguistics, self-efficacy, alongside other theories of motivation, has shaped our understanding of language classroom life (Dörnyei, 2001). Research into *language teachers' self-efficacy* (LTSE) beliefs has distinguished *task-specific self-efficacy* (TSE), for example, a teacher's belief in their ability to apply correction techniques when learner language contains errors (Wyatt, 2018), from *global self-efficacy* (GSE), a more general self-confidence (Wyatt & Dikilitaş, 2016). TSE beliefs are flexible, dynamic, and open to change – but also somewhat fragile, whereas GSE beliefs, being less context-specific, tend towards stability (Wyatt & Dikilitaş, 2016). Complexity resides not only in TSE-GSE distinctions and efficacy's multiple sources, but also in the relationship between behaviours and an individual's feelings of efficaciousness. Low self-efficacy beliefs can cause individuals to "perceive tasks as personal threats" (Dörnyei, 2013, p. 87) and thus inhibit action, leading to task avoidance. However, a certain amount of self-doubt can play a positive role, and even, under certain conditions, facilitate self-efficacy growth (Wyatt, 2018). Conversely, there are dangers in overly high levels of efficacy; over-confidence or complacency can result in task failure and subsequent efficacy erosion (Wyatt & Dikilitaş, 2016). Studies have highlighted the value of research into LTSE beliefs and recognized that "with efficacious teachers ... many more L2 learners are likely to thrive" (Wyatt, 2021, p. 303).

An emerging strand of the literature on LTSE beliefs has begun to shed light on another category of efficacy, *teacher research efficacy* (TRE) beliefs (Wyatt & Dikilitaş, 2016). Such beliefs relate to tasks which teacher–researchers typically undertake – formulating research questions, selecting and designing suitable classroom research instruments, and disseminating findings (Wyatt & Dikilitaş, 2016), amongst others. While teacher-research has been viewed as psychologically beneficial (Wyatt, 2016), novice teacher–researchers may suffer from low TRE beliefs (Wyatt, 2018), and this was, at times, the case for me during my first efforts to enact practitioner research.

*Exploratory practice*

EP sits alongside action research as a member of the practitioner research family of enquiry (Hanks, 2017). EP represents a set of principles, "a living structure" (Dikilitaş & Hanks, 2018, p. 208), for conducting practitioner research, which is enquiry conducted by and for teachers and their students (Allwright & Hanks, 2009; Hanks, 2017). EP proposes that practitioners co-research a curiosity-led "Why?" *puzzle* about an aspect of classroom life (Dikilitaş & Hanks, 2018): "Why does peer feedback receive a lukewarm response from my learners?" (Banister, 2023) or "Why is my writing not fluent?" (Banister, 2021). As these two examples illustrate, both teachers and learners can formulate puzzles, enactments classified as *teacher-initiated* or *learner-initiated puzzling* (Kato & Hanks, 2021). Learner-initiated puzzling requires learners to identify, formulate, and explore a puzzle (via reflection, discussion, and/or research) to gain enhanced understanding of a self-selected aspect of language learning practice. This explicit positioning of learners as setters of their own research agendas is an innovation of EP, and one which distinguishes it from other practitioner research models (Allwright & Hanks, 2009; Hanks, 2017).

Underpinning EP's longer-term sustainability is its principle of integrating research into pedagogy. Therefore, Exploratory Practitioners investigate using "slightly adapted pedagogic activities that teachers and learners are familiar with" (Rangel Moraes Bezerra & Miller, 2015, p. 105), retaining the activity's original language focus while introducing an exploratory dimension designed to illuminate the puzzle. In this way, they create *Potentially Exploitable Pedagogic Activities* (PEPAs) (Hanks, 2017).

In the domain of teaching and learning EAP, Exploratory Practitioners have contributed to knowledge about motivation, Hanks describes this as a "rich area of investigation" (2022, p. 5), with studies also reporting various psychological affordances of EP itself. For example, after introducing EP, Dawson (2017) observed her learners' increasingly confident language use, Kato and Hanks (2021) found that EP's curiosity-led approach restored learners' lost self-efficacy beliefs, and Consoli (2022) reported a positive impact on learner motivation.

EP is envisioned as a collaborative endeavour, encouraging practitioners to draw on their immediate community of practice. A recent review (Hanks, 2019) also noted the existence of a wider, global EP community, encompassing teachers and learners from diverse domains and contexts across 17 countries. Exploratory Practitioners are prominent in networks promoting inclusive practitioner research, such as the International Association of Applied Linguistics' Fully Inclusive Practitioner Research (FIPR) network. It is from my position as an active member of both my local and the global EP community that, in the remainder of this chapter, I describe and analyse my developing self-efficacy beliefs as a teacher–researcher over the last eight years. I present my account as an autoethnography, a methodological choice to which I now turn.

## Research methodology

### Autoethnography

*Autoethnography* is autobiographical, qualitative research in which "stories of/about the self [are] told through the lens of culture" (Adams et al., 2015, p. 1). Autoethnographic narratives constitute borderland genres (Keles, 2022), much like EP stories. Descriptions of autoethnography as "action research for the individual" (Bochner, 2000, p. 754) highlight a shared ethos with EP and suggest autoethnography as an especially appropriate lens through which to view EP's particular challenges.

Autoethnography rejects the claims to objectivity which characterize positivist research traditions, instead celebrating selfhood and valuing the researcher's insider positioning within a community and thus, their ability to reflect on experiences and relationships to evoke "nuance, complexity, emotion, and meaning" (Adams et al., 2015, p. 32). Using narrative snapshots, or fragments of a story, autoethnography seeks to "infer trends, patterns and phenomena across a culture" (Hunter, 2020, p. 321). As with

EP, the ethos of autoethnography strongly suggests the adoption of a first-person authorship style, and in its *analytical* form, autoethnography facilitates the linking of autobiographical fragments to theory (Keles, 2022). Over the last decade, autoethnographic studies have proliferated in applied linguistics, with one review thus describing it as a "promising" methodology (Keles, 2022, p. 451). Four published autoethnographies have proven especially influential in my adoption and approach to autoethnography in this chapter.

Yazan et al.'s (2021) edited collection (in the same Routledge series as this current volume) features a range of first-hand accounts by language teaching professionals, including practitioner–researchers. In these accounts, the authors harness autoethnography to track changes in their professional identities. Meanwhile, Mumford and Dikilitas' (2020) autoethnography, in which the lead author reflects on the complexities of his multiple professional identities (EAP teacher, doctoral student) and the impact of the second author's mentoring in helping him to (re)construct a researcher identity further exemplifies the genre's potential. Then, I encountered a more personal resonance in Yazan's (2019) autoethnography. Writing from within a US higher education setting, the author presents a thoughtful narrative of his experiences as an English language learner, language teacher, and teacher educator. In Yazan's account, I found echoes of the heartfelt stories I have heard first-hand from students, friends, and family members who have faced similar struggles as teachers or learners of English. Last but by no means least, Hunter's (2020) visual autoethnography also connected powerfully. This was authored from her space as an HE academic developer, one comparably liminal in university life to that of my own in EAP. Of particular interest were the author's creative use of metaphors and images to structure her story of selfhood and her observations that engagement with a wider academic community, beyond her own institution, aided professional growth.

*Constructing my autoethnography: Narrative snapshots and journey/ travel metaphors*

In this, my autoethnography, I reflect on the changes to my TRE, my beliefs about my own efficaciousness as a teacher–researcher, as I have moved from an EP apprenticeship role to that of early career researcher. My analytical approach to autoethnography facilitates an intertwined discussion of key aspects of the EP principles and critical episodes that impacted my self-efficacy beliefs as an Exploratory Practitioner.

I view my EP work as an ongoing journey, one which has offered the opportunity to "stop, look around, and think" (Hanks, 2017, p. 274) about the landscape of my professional practice. I have therefore embedded several *travel/journey metaphors* within my narrative. After all, my professional life story includes not only physical travel – working abroad, travelling to conferences to present EP – but also psychological journeys within my professional domain – transitioning from EFL to EAP teaching, for example. I am also intrigued by the notion, from popular philosophy, that travel, at its most sublime, should be viewed as an art (de Botton, 2014), and how the motives for travel (curiosity, desire to explore) and conceptions of travel as a way to better understand *eudaimonia* or human flourishing (de Botton, 2014) seem to share so much with EP's principles. Indeed, pioneers of EP have drawn on some of these same ideas when describing its philosophical foundations (Hanks, 2017) and perceived benefits (Dawson, 2016).

Through conventional citations and direct mention, I include the voices of various EP companions (fellow Exploratory Practitioners, learners, mentors, and critical friends) as I weave a narrative which, I hope, represents "a distillation of [my EP] life so far, coloured by an anticipation of what life may hold in the future" (Muncey, 2010, p.13). Like many seasoned travellers, I have enjoyed capturing snapshots of my journey in visual form. Therefore, to aid recall, stimulate memory and track the changes in my TRE beliefs, I have revisited and re-examined a wide range of EP artefacts – not only textual, but also visual. First, I reflected extensively around three key EP tasks, gathering a collection of relevant artefacts spanning 2014–22: PEPAs, emails, journal articles, book chapters (my own and those by others mentioning me), social media posts and images, and physical artefacts (conference programmes, posters, and badges). Then I used a digital timeline to shortlist these artefacts (or images of them), positioning items chronologically and colour coding them to distinguish themes and key aspects of EP culture to which they related. Finally, I established outlines of narrative arcs for each snapshot, tracing the development in my TRE beliefs as an Exploratory Practitioner. My autoethnography below begins with a biographical sketch after which I present and frame discussion around three artefacts: a quote, a classroom activity, and a conference photograph.

I followed my institution's ethical procedures, and, in the interests of relational ethics (Adams et al., 2015), resolved to minimize potential harm by referring to individuals by name only when I was able to contact them and obtain their written permission. Otherwise, I refer to individuals by role only. All recollections are mine and represent my take on events; memory, after all, is "an instrument of simplification and selection" (de Botton, 2014, p. 15). I apologize in advance if others have viewed events differently and feel they, or their actions, have in any way been misinterpreted. I start now with an autobiographical sketch.

## My path towards EP

I grew up in eastern England in the late 1970s and early 1980s. Teaching ran in the family; both my parents were primary school teachers, and had also taught abroad, with mementoes from these times and from the family holidays we were lucky enough to enjoy scattered around our home. In the mid-1990s, I gained a degree in politics and history before completing entry-level training to teach English, and in 1998 I took a job at a private language school in Istanbul, Turkey, teaching English to adults. It was an exhilarating time – on a personal level, exploring the city's layered history, embracing a new culture, and meeting the Turkish woman who would be my future wife – and on a professional one, too – experiencing a sense of growth as a teacher as I moved from school-based teaching into freelance, in-company work.

Relocating to the UK in the mid-2000s, I secured a position at a central London language school teaching highly motivated EFL learners. The language school shared a site with several higher education colleges which eventually merged and attained private university status. By 2010, the language school had been incorporated into the new university and the 5–6 EFL teachers now shared a teaching room with two EAP lecturers. Though both EAP lecturers had previously taught at the language school, they now worked exclusively with the university students, receiving greater remuneration and additional contractual benefits. However, they often expressed frustration with their in-sessional EAP students' lack of motivation. Nonetheless, in 2012, when offered an EAP lectureship, I accepted.

I negotiated funding for part-time MA studies, and my dissertation, focusing on teachers' use of a popular academic English word list, provided my first experience of conducting traditional academic research. Despite enjoying the process and benefiting from the expert guidance of a supportive supervisor, halfway through I had concluded that research of this type was unsustainable beyond my MA due to the additional burden it would impose on top of my already high teaching workload. Meanwhile, the transition from EFL to EAP teaching (involving teaching pre-service business English as well as academic English) was proving a challenge. This was due, in part, to limited classroom contact hours, which I felt hindered rapport-building, and also, as the teachers' room talk had suggested, working with students who lacked the same high levels of motivation I had become used to at the language centre. It was while I was navigating these professional transitions that an interesting email from Dr Assia Slimani-Rolls, the research lead of our Languages and Culture Department arrived, offering the chance to participate in a Language Teacher Research (LTR) project using EP. I participated in the initial phase of this project, working alongside colleagues from foreign languages and EAP as we explored and tried to enact the EP framework over the course of 2014–16.

My results or findings, which, in line with EP's principles, I prefer to call understandings, highlight the TRE beliefs key for successful EP enquiry. In this section, I present and discuss these via a three-step approach in which I:

1 introduce a key aspect of EP,
2 link it to a reflective question about my TRE beliefs,
3 present the artefact, analysing it to spark and extend discussion.

I focus on three dimensions of my TRE beliefs. Two of these have been identified in a previous study (Wyatt & Dikilitaş, 2016, p. 5): "designing appropriate research instruments" and "producing coherent research reports". Discussion of the former centres around EP's use of PEPAs, which are familiar classroom activities given a research twist (Hanks, 2017), while discussion of the latter considers the particular challenges of making EP work public. However, the first of my three narrative snapshots centres on a conceptual dimension: understanding and enacting the full complexity of EP's notion of practice-as-research, its positioning of learners as legitimate co-researchers of their own practice (Allwright & Hanks, 2009; Hanks, 2017) and the specific challenges posed for teacher–researchers aiming to scaffold the process.

## Understandings and discussion

### Snapshot 1: At the crossroads between teacher and learner-initiated puzzling

There is a relatively modest number of published accounts of teacher–researchers reporting how their learners set and explored their own puzzles. However, learner-initiated puzzling is a key aspect of EP, one which distinguishes it from other forms of practitioner research, and, so, eventually, Exploratory Practitioners should feel efficacious in answering my first reflective question:

**Reflective question 1:** To what extent can you scaffold learner-initiated puzzling?

The quote below (Artefact 8.2), presented here as an autoethnographic artefact, concluded my written reflections as a novice Exploratory Practitioner. At the time of writing in mid-2016 (publication followed in

"Gradually, getting my students to identify their own puzzles has become a more realistic proposition ..." (Banister, 2019, p. 147)

*Artefact 8.2* Quote about learner-initiated puzzling.

Slimani-Rolls & Kiely, 2019), I found myself at a crossroads with EP. Having sustained teacher-initiated puzzling with business English groups over two years, I could now either stop doing EP, explore a new teacher-initiated puzzle, or I could embrace learner-initiated puzzling. Two elements of the quote warrant further discussion: first, my articulation of what learner-initiated puzzling would involve was incomplete – "to identify" a puzzle was a necessary starting point, but only that — further steps would be required. Second, my choice of words is tentative – "more" realistic perhaps, yet apparently not "wholly" so.

My initial experiences with EP had brought TRE beliefs gains from the mastery experiences of successfully co-researching with my students. By sharing my teacher-initiated puzzle with my learners, I accessed their insights about my puzzle, namely, why I struggled to obtain meaningful learner feedback. The process involved exposing my concerns, discussing what "meaningful" meant to me and my learners, and offering my learners the chance to air and share their own beliefs on this aspect of classroom life. After two years' fruitful enquiry, I became convinced EP had worked for me and my learners. From a self-efficacy beliefs perspective, in addition to the mastery gains, the positive emotions associated with the EP process (reconnecting with my students, empathizing, increased classroom collegiality) left me feeling efficacious about exploring future puzzles I might identify. However, I realized that while I had not consciously avoided learner-initiated puzzling, the novelty of the EP approach meant that scaffolding learner-initiated puzzling had remained terra incognita.

Speaking with two colleagues from the original LTR group, one from EAP and another a teacher of Italian, Anna Costantino, and our mentor, Dr Assia Slimani-Rolls, we discussed how to plan, execute, and embark upon a journey of learner-initiated puzzling. These discussions channelled our collective enthusiasm for EP, acted as a form of social persuasion, and harnessed the feelgood factor around the LTR project (it later received a prestigious educational award) as an emotional source of self-efficacy beliefs. The experience of conducting our own teacher-initiated enquiries was invaluable for me and it would have been hard to imagine embarking on the scaffolding of learner-initiated puzzling without having first gone through this earlier stage.

Nevertheless, many self-doubts soon resurfaced. Could I truly break down the nuances of puzzling and EP's quest for enhanced understanding and reposition myself as a successful self-efficacy beliefs builder for others? Context is a hugely significant factor in practitioner research and three local factors heightened the challenge. First, my learners, majoring in business, might be less enthusiastic puzzlers than those in fellow Exploratory Practitioners' published accounts, where some of the learner–researchers were language learning specialists themselves (Chu, 2007) or at a higher learning level, i.e., master's students (Dawson, 2017). Second, and on a related point, I doubted my ability to instil a puzzling mindset. Business study is explicitly framed around real-life case studies of problems, and a problem-based paradigm is deeply embedded. Third, the practicalities of integrating learner-initiated puzzling into a 12-week term loomed large. This was significantly less time than it had taken for me to feel efficacious with puzzling, and any scaffolding process would need to be sufficiently resilient and flexible to accommodate the messy realities of our university setting, such as late student enrolments and inconsistent attendance patterns.

Working collaboratively with an EAP colleague, I adopted a little-and-often approach, designing a staged itinerary for the introduction of EP, offering learners opportunities to research, compare, and discuss puzzles. This last point was especially important, intended as a way to create space for sharing potentially positive vicarious experiences, mirroring those enjoyed earlier by the LTR group. Use of concurrent puzzling, teachers and their learners both setting and exploring their own puzzles (Hanks, 2017), and modelling the process by presenting teacher-initiated puzzles helped establish empathy and communicated a powerful humanizing openness (Miller and Cunha, in Allwright & Hanks, 2009).

Gradually, my self-efficacy beliefs in scaffolding the process of learner-initiated puzzling grew as the fruits of learners' enquiries emerged in lively, worthwhile class discussions. These positive mastery experiences emerged as I saw learners begin to connect their puzzles with classroom activities and autonomous learning opportunities. Subsequently, with my newly enhanced TRE beliefs in this area, I set myself more challenging tasks. These involve taking the lead and advocating for learner-initiated puzzling to be embedded in the design of new academic English and professional writing courses. I believe this initiative would provide learners with opportunities to reflect on their language learning, illuminate learners' needs and help learners view our university-level business and academic English modules as distinct from their previous English language learning (Banister, 2021). I also published a paper describing some of these experiences with learner-initiated puzzling for a top-ranked EAP journal (Banister, 2021). I highlight this advocacy behaviour as evidence of high self-efficacy beliefs (Wyatt, 2018). My increased efficaciousness and my past learners' successes with EP mean that now, when I go into a new class, I see prospective learner–researchers, and wholeheartedly believe that learners can, with my support, perform the tasks which will, in turn, grow their own research self-efficacy beliefs.

It is now time to turn from learner–researchers to EP's method for integrating teaching, learning, and research, the classroom vehicles for research known as PEPAs.

## Snapshot 2: PEPAs – Research footprints in pedagogic practice

EP's innovative use of PEPAs is another key aspect of EP and one of its distinctive features, the point at which practice-as-research takes a more concrete form (Hanks, 2017). Yet some feel that PEPAs have been under-theorized (C. Crane, personal communication, 2021). The Exploratory Practitioner should be able to identify pedagogic activities, either within their syllabus or their teaching repertoire, which are ripe for exploitation as PEPAs and might illuminate their puzzle.

**Reflective question 2:** "To what extent are you confident that you can skilfully integrate practice-as-research via use of PEPAs?" (based, in part, on Wyatt & Dikilitaş, 2016, p. 569).

I start by presenting Artefact 8.3, a PEPA I designed called "Business News Around the World".

Note that the format of Artefact 8.3 was originally presented to students on an interactive digital map template from a popular online noticeboard software widely used in UK higher education teaching and learning. The format has been slightly modified in order to reproduce it here, but no content has been altered.

I have selected this PEPA because it maps neatly into the journey/travel metaphor of this autoethnography, but also as one of my most recent PEPAs. I designed and used it in the autumn of 2021 to explore a puzzle with my business English learners (Banister, 2022). The original, pre-PEPA version of the activity required learners to read a BBC article about business news and discuss the issues involved before posting written responses to a discussion forum. After several weeks' self-reflection and reading around my

---

New Delhi, Delhi, India

**New Delhi, Delhi, India**
Removal of 'illegal hawkers' from Cannaught Place. This business topic is important as it talks about the removal of hawkers, which is not right as it might be the only source of their income. I feel this is a very harsh step taken from the government's side as it might lead to starvation of many poor hawkers if the street vending they do, is their only source of income or if the hawker is the only bread-earner of the family.

The Hindu
https://www.thehindu.com/news/cities/Delhi/for-delhis-street-vendors-its-not-businessas-usual-after-hc-order/article37170126.ece 1

I think, in routine life, we tend to neglect what's going around the world, and discussing news stories from around the world in this class is an opportunity to catch up on at least some of the global happenings around the globe.

---

*Artefact 8.3* PEPA: Business News Around the World.

puzzle, "Why does it matter what business news we discuss and sources we use?", I reimagined this activity. I asked learner–researchers to:

- source a recent business news story from their own country
- summarize it on the map template
- reflect on the pros and cons for us of discussing UK-centric versus global business news stories and of using sources of business news in English versus sources in learners' first languages.

This PEPA retained the interactive and communicative elements of the original, but the new exploratory dimensions illuminated some of the tensions involved in adopting a decolonizing approach in my business English setting (see Banister, 2022, for full details).

At the outset of my EP journey, designing PEPAs initially seemed straightforward. As an experienced ELT professional, I felt highly efficacious in adapting pedagogical activities for different language learning levels, settings, and domains. Therefore, adapting an activity so that it included an exploratory dimension seemed a natural extension of this, and I was optimistic that my high TSE beliefs with regard to adapting activities would transfer to PEPA design. However, this confidence, perhaps even complacency, would soon give way to a realization that PEPA design, if it was to prove a truly sustainable approach, posed distinct challenges.

The very first PEPAs I designed, back in 2014, comprised survey-style lists of questions to which learners responded individually. Survey or questionnaire use is an established part of ELT practice, but I gradually came to realize that survey-led EP might feel somewhat mechanical. My use of surveys in my dissertation research around this time influenced my approach, but the literature on teacher-research also suggests it is common for novices to be drawn to surveys, aligning as they do with conventional conceptions of research (Smith, 2020). For truly sustainable EP, a more genuine challenge emerged: to design PEPAs that also mobilizsed my teaching artfulness. Harnessing PEPAs as "a means of creativity" (Goral, 2019, p. 173) did not happen immediately, however. I realized that my early PEPAs were somewhat clumsy additions to pedagogy rather than skilful integrations or adaptations. In the words of a colleague, I was "teaching and researching rather than researching via teaching" (Houghton, 2019, p. 157). As my mentor noted, EP's novelty meant I needed to see examples of other Exploratory Practitioners adapting their pedagogic practice to illuminate puzzles (Slimani-Rolls & Kiely, 2019). My eureka moment came while reading about Rowland's use of EP's principles to invite his students to compare their language learning experiences with extracts from ELT research articles (Rowland, 2011). The author's approach, using tried and tested reading-into-discussion ELT practice but with a creative, innovative twist, helped expand the horizons of what a PEPA could be (Banister, 2019).

By 2016, I was co-designing PEPAs with an EAP colleague whilst scaffolding learner-initiated puzzling (see first narrative snapshot). This was a crucial professional relationship in terms of my progress with EP and especially PEPA design. As colleagues, we shared many professional interests and were at a similar stage in our apprenticeship in EP. As a result, we were able to feed off each other's insights and increase self-efficacy beliefs as teacher–researchers, comparing notes as we used PEPAs with the same cohorts of business and academic English students at our institution. For example, with a new cohort, my colleague sourced a popular business text – "Start with why ... " (Sinek, 2009) and I selected an open letter to language learners about EP from Allwright (Allwright & Hanks, 2009, p. 272), one of EP's co-founders. Presenting these texts together in a jigsaw reading PEPA, we retained a communicative language focus (reading, comprehension questions, oral sharing of information pitched) whilst encouraging reflection upon and comparisons between the importance of understanding "Why?" for both business people and language learners. This collaborative approach provided opportunities to share experiences of how the PEPA had worked in class and from these debriefing discussions, mastery experiences (integrating practice-as-research), vicarious experiences (hearing about how a colleague's learners had responded), and positive emotional sources (feelings of excitement as learner-initiated puzzling became more real) gradually built TRE beliefs.

Over the next few years, I felt increasingly efficacious in designing PEPAs to creatively and skilfully explore subsequent teaching puzzles. PEPA design also began to feel more intuitive, and I am now quicker to notice opportunities to transform existing activities into PEPAs. I view PEPAs as research footprints in my teaching – the evidence of past puzzling still visible and alive within my pedagogy and, sometimes, that of colleagues. For instance, the reflective questions that formed part of a PEPA about peer teaching of vocabulary (Banister, 2018) are now integrated into a presentation template which learners are encouraged to use for this task and are also used by a colleague teaching a sister module.

When originally conceiving them, Allwright and Hanks (2009) maintained that "the range of PEPAs is only limited by the imagination" (p. 194). Looking back over 8 years of PEPA design and use, in addition to the activities mentioned above, I have adapted needs analyses, WebQuests, online polls, and even tutorials, so that now I feel strong levels of TRE beliefs in relation to this uniquely EP task. However, this took time and the ongoing challenges posed by PEPA design still feature prominently in conversations with colleagues in EP research networks.

## Snapshot 3: Pointing the way

In this final narrative snapshot, I discuss a third key aspect of EP: reporting my EP work to others. This broad area could easily constitute a whole chapter. Therefore, I limit my focus here to oral dissemination of my EP research.

**Reflective question 3:** To what extent are you able to produce coherent oral reports of your EP research? (adapted from Wyatt & Dikilitaş, 2016, p. 570) Of all my TRE beliefs, at the outset of my EP journey, I felt least efficacious in this task. If asked this question at that time, I would have responded quite negatively.

June 2016 once again, and this photo, which I posted afterwards on a professional networking platform, shows me reporting my EP research at the Teachers Research! conference in Istanbul, the same event described in the first sentence of the introduction, and so bringing us full circle in my autoethnographic narrative. Minutes before this photo was taken by an audience member, I had been listening to fellow teacher–researchers present their findings. Now, given the floor, I am pointing to my poster, reporting my EP. My right hand is in my pocket – an attempt on my part to look relaxed, when, in reality, I am anything but. In fact, orally reporting my research represented the single greatest challenge to my burgeoning TRE beliefs (Artefact 8.4).

Before my EP work, I had attended numerous conferences but never imagined speaking at one. The very thought would have inspired trepidation and I avoided this task. Whenever I have shared my anxiety around public speaking, people have often seemed confused: "As a teacher,

*Artefact 8.4* Pointing the way.

wouldn't I be used to talking in front of groups of students?" That is not how I see it. The communicative language teaching methods of my preservice training encouraged minimal, high-quality teacher talking time, a facilitation of learning (see for example, Scrivener, 2010) rather than a sage-on-the-stage approach.

Recalling the very first time I presented my EP work for the LTR project, back in 2015, a year before the Istanbul conference, I felt a sense of awkwardness standing by my EP poster before the invited audience of experienced UK-based Exploratory Practitioners and senior university colleagues. When my turn came to speak, I felt I rambled somewhat, with my negative emotions – mainly stress and embarrassment – leaking quite visibly. As a result, my already low TRE beliefs in this area suffered an initial erosion. Looking back, perhaps my TRE beliefs in other areas were insufficiently developed for me to believe I could perform this task. Nonetheless, having invested so much by this stage, dropping out of the LTR project was not something I wished to entertain and so, with the calm encouragement and persuasion of my mentor, Dr Assia Slimani-Rolls, I persevered. 2016 swiftly brought new presenting challenges; this time the group presented at two university language association events. The benefit of an additional year's EP under my belt had slowly built greater self-efficacy in terms of oral reporting, and I felt somewhat more comfortable at the extended sound of my own voice. Equally important for my burgeoning self-efficacy beliefs was the chance to talk from slides rather than a poster. Unlike posters, I was familiar with designing and using slides in my teaching. Although my use of slides in the classroom was different, tending towards short bursts, slide design and use scaffolded me as I found visuals and ways to use text which assisted me in better explaining the complexities of EP as method alongside the focus of my own enquiry. My growing self-efficacy beliefs in this area also reflected a belief that my enhanced understanding of my puzzle was now, at this later stage (now two years in), truly worth sharing. It had also helped that colleagues from the LTR group, like me new to disseminating, had shared their own anxieties with aspects of presenting. These vicarious experiences reflected a growing collegiality amongst the group.

Shortly afterwards, and wanting to build my TRE beliefs further, I recall my excitement upon identifying the Istanbul event for further dissemination. I was now relishing the challenge and ready to go it alone. So, with the ongoing and generous support of my mentor, I obtained funding. It helped that the conference venue in Istanbul was one I knew well. In fact, I had lived in this part of the city almost 20 years earlier. By contrast, the Teachers Research! conference format was decidedly unfamiliar. Uniquely, everyone attending would be both an audience member and a presenter of their own practitioner research, including EP. Presenters received a short, dedicated timeslot to showcase their investigations, with time set aside afterwards for questions and audience interaction. This time, redoubling my efforts, and with the benefit of successful presenting experiences to draw on, I summarized my own research much more coherently and genuinely enjoyed the ad-hoc interactions with fellow teacher–researchers and keynote speakers, amongst whom were pioneer Exploratory Practitioners.

Teachers Research! was to prove pivotal. My involvement in the event deepened over subsequent years. I took on an organizing role in 2017 and co-delivered an EP workshop in 2018. My GSE beliefs as a teacher–researcher grew sufficiently for me to accept a role moderating and writing up online discussions of research for a teacher's association group. This had a positive knock-on impact on my self-efficacy beliefs, developing through the spirals of growth described in the literature (Bandura, 1977).

Presenting my EP at live events over 2016–22 has provided further vicarious experiences which have boosted my TRE beliefs. Observing other speakers, I noticed how pedagogic trends towards interactive classroom approaches were, to some extent, being mirrored in the conference domain, with audience involvement and a workshop style that plays more to my facilitatory strengths increasingly preferred. Nevertheless, sometimes audience attendance or interaction disappointed, and on such occasions, my TRE beliefs temporarily came under threat again and self-doubts began to re-emerge. Sometimes events at which I chose to share oral reports of my EP proved unsuitable, but I learnt to consider this all part of my dissemination literacy. Also, luckily for me, the wider EP community is extremely supportive. Drs Assia Slimani-Rolls and Judith Hanks, EP pioneers, and others influential in the wider field of practitioner research such as Dr Kenan Dikilitaş, have consistently been generous with their time and wise words of guidance. Knowing they have faced many similar challenges to my own has made all of these individuals, alongside other colleagues from my institution, the FIPR group and beyond, effective efficacy builders. Their social persuasion shared in personal correspondence, online meetings, and ad-hoc chats has bolstered my self-efficacy beliefs and encouraged me to share my EP reports. Thus, I have developed my professional network and enhanced my professional standing, receiving invitations to talk about EP at several schools and university language centres, all of which further nurtured my TRE beliefs.

Apparent to a more experienced EP scholar who has attended these talks is that my "local presentations at CPD workshops led to greater confidence" (Hanks, 2022, p. 8); yet these efficacy gains were hard won. An indication that I had developed some level of mastery in the task of verbally sharing EP research followed a 2017 talk when an audience member contacted me to praise my presentation delivery, structure, and content, stating her intention to emulate my approaches when reporting her own research.

I have learnt much from audience feedback, including what to spend more time explaining, what is of most interest to different audiences, and where greater rigour might be valuable.

Of all the aspects of EP discussed in this chapter, sharing my research orally is the area where social persuasion has proved most vital in building my initially low TRE beliefs and where the emotional dimension of TRE beliefs has seemed to come most to the fore. As I have mentioned, efficacy builders have included my mentors, LTR colleagues, and fellow Exploratory Practitioners, but individuals beyond these communities have also been instrumental. Two (now former) colleagues, both outside the original group of language teacher–researchers, Jonathan Beaton and Tatiana Suarez, have emerged as especially trusted critical friends over the last eight years. Their constructive feedback, whether commenting on slides and proposed structure for oral presentations of my EP work or patiently discussing and helping me making sense of my post-reporting reflections, has grown my TRE beliefs further and, on a personal level, been genuinely and deeply appreciated.

One final reflection: by choosing to share this photo of myself orally reporting my EP, both here in this chapter and on social media several years ago, I was/am enacting my recently established researcher identity (Hunter, 2020), which, in turn, reflects my enhanced global sense of self-efficacy following my eight-year EP journey. My TRE beliefs in this area started at such a low level that, despite the undoubted efficacy gains, it still feels more fragile than in the other areas I have discussed. So I have consciously endeavoured to maintain it by regularly reporting my EP orally to maintain my TRE beliefs at a high level (avoiding avoidance!) by, for example, disseminating at online events during the recent pandemic. Terra incognita remains, however; I have not yet managed to organize sharing a platform with my learner–researchers and reporting our EP work together as fellow Exploratory Practitioners have done in oral (Dar, 2012) or in written form (Dawson, 2017).

## Implications for practitioner–researchers and conclusions

I present three key implications intended to be useful for fellow/prospective Exploratory Practitioners. They could also be interpreted for use with other models of PR.

### *Learner-initiated puzzling*

Embrace learner-initiated puzzling as this represents a deeper enactment of the EP principles. If new to EP, consider a round of teacher-initiated puzzling before moving towards concurrent puzzling to establish a sense of inter-practitioner empathy. Avoid underestimating your learners' potential as learner–researchers. Early on, enquire about learners' experiences and preconceptions of research via a needs analysis, and follow-up by classroom discussion. Dispel preconceptions which conflict with instilling a puzzling mindset and scaffold learner-initiated puzzling via activities that open up spaces for learner–researchers to experience mastery, vicarious and emotional sources of efficacy building.

*PEPAs*

When planning PEPAs, identify opportunities to harness your teacherly creativity and, indeed, your learners' creativity as learners. When designing PEPAs, consider your full teaching repertoire and allow learners some choice in their responses (written/spoken text, visual, and multi-media/digital means). Collaborating with like-minded colleagues on PEPA design can generate momentum, spark breakthroughs, and expand the dataset.

When approaching learners, consider how you will introduce and explain EP's aims. Anticipate how your learners may view a learner-researcher role. For example, in a university context, learners' expectations of a research element to their learning may be exploited. Also, remember that not all learners will necessarily be comfortable with you using data they provide in responses to PEPAs. Be ready to explain the value of exploring puzzles and to gain informed consent to aid later dissemination. Ultimately, bundling research and practice together means that the Exploratory Practitioner must be prepared to exclude individuals' data from any dataset whilst still ensuring that all learners can participate fully in class for language learning purposes. Early attention to ethics and these practicalities will pay dividends later, leaving you better placed to ensure the research process is rigorous in terms of data collection and analysis, and thus more likely to boost the self-efficacy beliefs of all involved.

*Oral reporting*

Help make EP a visible endeavour – not only for the potential professional development advantages this may bring you as an individual practitioner, but also to serve as inspiration and, in turn, point the way for others. Remember that oral reporting takes more than one form and oral presentations are only one of these. Choose the methods or tools that you feel most comfortable with (e.g., poster presentations, slides, and online talks – live or pre-recorded). Think of oral reporting as an opportunity to learn from audience feedback and, if like me, you struggle to envisage yourself in a presenter role, remember that current best practice in oral dissemination of research often aims towards interactivity and audience engagement. As such, it is a task most teachers will have mastery experiences upon which to grow their self-efficacy beliefs.

Finally, for support with all the above, engage with the wider EP community. The FIPR website has contact details: https://www.fullyinclusivepr.com/exploratory-practice.html

In this chapter, I have explained how a combination of the experiences identified by Bandura (1977) (mastery, vicarious, persuasion, and emotional) fostered my efficacy growth as a teacher–researcher and enabled me to overcome threats to TRE beliefs that emerged. My TRE beliefs were boosted in all three key aspects of EP discussed. When scaffolding learner-initiated puzzling, mastery experiences with teacher-initiated puzzling were especially potent. While designing and using PEPAs, vicarious experiences proved invaluable and when sharing oral reports of EP, social persuasion and emotional influences were prominent efficacy builders. Evident throughout my account is what Wyatt and Dikilitas (2016, p. 5) describe as the "uneven nature" of TRE beliefs growth. My initial TRE beliefs were high in relation to PEPA design (though this proved somewhat illusory), yet noticeably low for sharing oral reports of EP. Nonetheless, my reconceptualization of my learners as co-researchers and my ability to support them in their EP enquiries, the research footprints left by PEPAs as I integrated research into pedagogy, and last, but not least, the oral reports I have shared of my EP, all suggest enhanced TRE beliefs, albeit with scope for further development.

The autoethnographic approach has aided me in tracing my efficacy development as a teacher–researcher and prompted additional layers of reflection. Therefore, I would recommend autoethnography to others researching the development of TRE beliefs.

The professional lives of ELT professionals are complex and multifaceted and so it is likely that my TRE beliefs will have been impacted by factors other than EP. But through engagement with EP's principles and the varied research journeys prompted by the approach, I have been able to explore previously submerged aspects of classroom life and simultaneously grow my efficacy beliefs as a teacher–researcher.

## References

Adams, T. E., Holman Jones, S. L., & Ellis, C. (2015). *Autoethnography*. Oxford University Press.

Allwright, D., & Hanks, J. (2009). *The developing language learner: An introduction to exploratory practice*. Palgrave Macmillan.

Bandura, A. (1977). *Social learning theory*. Prentice Hall.

Bandura, A. (Ed.). (1995). *Self-efficacy in changing societies*. Cambridge University Press.

Banister, C. (2018). Exploring teacher and learner perceptions of the value of peer-teaching vocabulary: Convergences and divergences. In G. Barkhuizen, A. Burns, K. Dikilitaş, & M. Wyatt (Eds.), *Empowering teacher researchers, empowering learners*. (pp. 121–128). IATEFL.

Banister, C. (2019). Rebuilding practitioner self-efficacy through learner feedback. In A. Slimani-Rolls & R. Kiely (Eds.), *Exploratory practice for continuing professional development: An innovative approach for language teachers* (pp. 135–151). Palgrave Macmillan.

Banister, C. (2021). Harnessing learner research agendas to continuously explore EAP learners' needs. *Journal of English for Academic Purposes, 51*, 100980. 10.1016/j.jeap.2021.100980

Banister, C. (2022). Decolonizing business English: Exploring classroom ideologies. *ELT Journal*. 10.1093/elt/ccac043

Banister, C. (2023). Exploring peer feedback processes and peer feedback meta-dialogues with learners of academic and business English. *Language Teaching Research*, 136216882095222. 10.1177/1362168820952222

Bochner, A. P. (2000). Criteria against ourselves. *Qualitative Inquiry, 6*(2), 266–272. 10.1177/107780040000600209

Chu, P. (2007). How students react to the power and responsibility of being decision makers in their own learning. *Language Teaching Research, 11*(2), 225–241. 10.1177/1362168806070746l3

Consoli, S. (2022). Practitioner research in a UK pre-sessional: The synergy between Exploratory Practice and student motivation. *Journal of English for Academic Purposes, 57*, 101108. 10.1016/j.jeap.2022.101108

Crane, C. (2021). Re: PEPA Survey Draft for feedback—Thank you!! [Personal communication].

Dar, Y. (2012). Exploratory practice: Investigating my own classroom pedagogy. *ELT Research, 26*, 8–10.

Dawson, S. (2016). *The language learning lives of English for Academic Purposes learners: From puzzlement to understanding and beyond in inclusive practitioner research* [Unpublished doctoral dissertation]. University of Manchester. https://www.research.manchester.ac.uk/portal/files/84022142/FULL_TEXT.PDF

Dawson, S. (2017). EAP learners explore their language learning lives through Exploratory Practice. In T. Stewart (Ed.), *TESOL Voices: Insider Accounts of Classroom Life*. TESOL Press.

de Botton, A. (2014). *The art of travel*. Hamish Hamilton.

Dikilitaş, K., & Hanks, J. (Eds.). (2018). *Developing language teachers with exploratory practice*. Springer International Publishing. 10.1007/978-3-319-75735-3

Dörnyei, Z. (2001). *Motivational strategies in the language classroom*. Cambridge University Press.

Goral, M. (2019). Insight into learner-generated materials. In A. Slimani-Rolls & R. Kiely (Eds.), *Exploratory Practice for continuing professional development: An innovative approach for language teachers* (pp. 169–183). Springer International Publishing: Imprint: Palgrave Macmillan.

Hanks, J. (2022). De-mystifying the nimbus of research: Re-igniting practitioners' interest in exploring EAP. *Journal of English for Academic Purposes, 60*, 101176. 10.1016/j.jeap.2022.101176

Hanks, J. (2017). *Exploratory practice in language teaching: Puzzling about principles and practices*. Palgrave Macmillan.

Hanks, J. (2019). From research-as-practice to exploratory practice-as-research in language teaching and beyond. *Language Teaching*, 52(02), 143–187. 10.1017/S0261444819000016

Houghton, J. (2019). Gaining deeper understanding of teaching speaking skills from collaborative inquiry. In A. Slimani-Rolls & R. Kiely (Eds.), *Exploratory practice for continuing professional development: An innovative approach for language teachers* (pp. 153–167). Springer International Publishing: Imprint: Palgrave Macmillan.

Hunter, A. (2020). Snapshots of selfhood: Curating academic identity through visual autoethnography. *International Journal for Academic Development*, 25(4), 310–323. 10.1080/1360144X.2020.1755865

Kato, Y., & Hanks, J. (2021). Learner-initiated exploratory practice: Revisiting curiosity. *ELT Journal*. 10.1093/elt/ccab039

Keles, U. (2022). Autoethnography as a recent methodology in applied linguistics: A methodological review. *The Qualitative Report*. 10.46743/2160-3715/2022.5131

Mumford, S., & Dikilitaş, K. (2020). The autoethnography of an [Re]-emerging researcher identity and its impact on EAP teaching pedagogy. In. B. Yazan & K. Lindahl (Eds.), *Language teacher identity in TESOL teacher education and practice as identity work*. (pp. 271–276). Routledge.

Muncey, T. (2010). *Creating autoethnographies—SAGE research methods*. https://methods.sagepub.com/book/creating-autoethnographies

Rangel Moraes Bezerra, I. C., & Miller, I. K. de. (2015). Exploratory practice and new literacy studies: Building epistemological connections. *Pensares Em Revista*, 0(6). 10.12957/pr.2015.18426

Rowland, L. (2011). Lessons about learning: Comparing learner experiences with language research. *Language Teaching Research*, 15(2), 254–267. 10.1177/1362168810388726

Scrivener, J. (2010). *Learning teaching: A guidebook for English language teachers* (2. ed., [Nachdr.]). Macmillan.

Sinek, S. (2009). *Start with why: How great leaders inspire everyone to take action*. Portfolio.

Slimani-Rolls, A., & Kiely, R. (2019). *Exploratory practice for continuing professional development: An innovative approach for language teachers* (1st ed. 2019). Springer International Publishing: Imprint: Palgrave Macmillan.

Smith, R. (2020). *Mentoring teachers to research their classrooms: A practical handbook*. British Council. https://www.britishcouncil.in/sites/default/files/mentoring_teachers_to_research_their_classrooms_a_practical_handbook.pdf

Wyatt, M. (2016). Engaging language teachers in research: achieving psychological and educational benefits. In K. Dikilitaş, M. Wyatt, J. Hanks, & D. Bullock (Eds.),*Teachers Engaging in Research*. (pp. 3–18). IATEFL.

Wyatt, M. (2018). *Language Teachers' self-efficacy beliefs: An introduction* (pp. 122–140). Multilingual Matters. https://www.degruyter.com/document/doi/10.21832/9781783099467-012/html

Wyatt, M. (2021). Research into second language learners' and teachers' self-efficacy beliefs: Making the connections. *TESOL Quarterly*, 55(1), 296–307. 10.1002/tesq.3010

Wyatt, M., & Dikilitaş, K. (2016). English language teachers becoming more efficacious through research engagement at their Turkish university. *Educational Action Research*, *24*(4), 550–570. 10.1080/09650792.2015.1076731

Yazan, B. (2019). An autoethnography of a language teacher educator: Wrestling with ideologies and identity positions. *Teacher Education Quarterly*, *46*(3), 34–56. https://www.jstor.org/stable/26746049.

Yazan, B. , Canagarajah, A. S. , & Jain, R. (Eds.). (2021). *Autoethnographies in ELT: Transnational identities, pedagogies, and practices*. Routledge.

Part 3

# Investigating domain-specific dimensions of English language learners' and teachers' self-efficacy beliefs

# 9 "I'm not a walking dictionary"
## Unpacking English language teachers' self-efficacy beliefs about teaching vocabulary

*Ben Naismith and Leo Selivan*

### Introduction

Language teachers' self-efficacy (LTSE) beliefs encompass all of the many ways in which teachers view their own capabilities to support language learning, whether through cognitive, metacognitive, affective, or social means (Wyatt, 2010). Importantly, these beliefs are task-, domain-, and context-specific (Wyatt, 2021), interacting with language teachers' beliefs about their own language awareness (Wyatt & Dikilitaş, 2021). Although research into LTSE beliefs and teacher cognition in general has burgeoned in recent years (see Wyatt, 2018, for a review), to date few studies have addressed specific language domains. What is more, the focus of such studies has primarily been on grammar and literacy, rather than vocabulary,[1] despite the central role of vocabulary in language acquisition (Nation, 2013).

Why do LTSE beliefs about vocabulary merit closer examination? Admittedly, nearly everything that goes on in the language classroom involves vocabulary and contributes to vocabulary acquisition. However, for vocabulary growth to occur efficiently, exposure to rich input is not sufficient; there has to be a principled approach to vocabulary teaching. Obviously, such teaching is affected not only by teachers' knowledge about vocabulary and vocabulary pedagogy, but also by a number of variables. Such variables include beliefs, attitudes, experience, identity constructions, and more pertinently, self-efficacy (Newton, 2020).

At present, however, little is known about language teachers' cognitions regarding vocabulary teaching and, in particular, about their self-efficacy beliefs, which mediate how knowledge is transformed into action. Consequently, it is imperative to identify the concerns and challenges of teachers in relation to LTSE beliefs about vocabulary so that future training and professional development can be informed by teachers' context-specific needs together with lexical research findings. In doing so, the goal is to enable positive transformative change that in turn will improve the quality of learning for students.

DOI: 10.4324/9781003379300-12

## Background

In the literature on teacher knowledge, a distinction is normally made between subject matter knowledge – knowing the content of what is taught – and pedagogic knowledge – how it is taught (Shulman, 1987). A similar distinction is made in vocabulary research literature (Webb, 2020), which broadly divides research studies into those exploring vocabulary description, teaching/learning, and assessment. Based on the view that teaching and assessment should be integrated (William, 2011), teaching/learning and assessment can be subsumed under one category: pedagogy. Although in the daily practice of teaching these knowledge bases are inextricably linked and used simultaneously (Tsui, 2003), it is helpful to look separately at these two cornerstones of teachers' professional knowledge: "the how" (pedagogy) and "the what" (content). We now look briefly at each of these components in relation to vocabulary before examining how they relate to teachers' beliefs and classroom practices.

### *Teaching vocabulary: How to teach*

The topic of vocabulary pedagogy extends far beyond the scope of this one section (see Zwier & Boers, 2022, for an overview). Here, we briefly touch on a selection of key issues relevant to the current study. To start, a large vocabulary is necessary in order to effectively operate in English, estimated at several thousand word families depending on the language activity (Schmitt et al., 2017). Obviously, it is impossible to reach such goals in the classroom given that class time is limited (Newton, 2020); that is why setting vocabulary learning priorities is key.

One popular way of prioritizing vocabulary for teaching purposes is frequency. Corpus-based research has highlighted the importance of distinguishing between high-, mid-, and low-frequency vocabulary (Schmitt & Schmitt, 2014). A direct corollary of this strand of research is the proliferation of frequency lists which teachers can consult to inform vocabulary selection (see Selivan, 2022, for an overview). Frequency information is also provided in learner's dictionaries. The process of selecting what vocabulary to focus on, therefore, has never been easier, provided teachers know where to look.

The importance of frequently reviewing, recycling, and practising vocabulary has been another dominant theme in second language (L2) vocabulary research. The consensus is that frequent encounters with new vocabulary – whether single words or chunks – are necessary to ensure retention (Laufer & Rozovski-Roitblat, 2011). Review of new vocabulary can take many forms (e.g., gap-fills, use of flashcards, etc.), all of which have been shown to be beneficial for vocabulary learning and retention (Laufer, 2020).

One quandary that has been addressed by research is the use of the learners' first language (L1), which for many years was considered undesirable (Laufer & Nation, 2012). Recent reappraisal of the role of the L1 (Kerr, 2014) has had an impact on vocabulary teaching too, and there is evidence that the use of L1 is effective for clarifying meaning and focusing on interlingual differences. While there are many ways of clarifying the meaning of new items, Nation (2003) notes that translation is usually the most effective one because of the clarity and familiarity of translations. Comparing and contrasting between English and the L1 may be particularly suitable for the learning of L2 collocations which are not congruent with their L1 counterparts (Laufer & Girsai, 2008). No less importantly, learners themselves respond positively to the incorporation of their L1 in the classroom (Brooks-Lewis, 2009).

To sum up, effective vocabulary teaching prioritizes vocabulary based on frequency, provides frequent repetition through classroom activities, and creates opportunities for recycling. The use of the L1, previously discouraged, is now supported by research, especially when it is used as a quick way of unlocking the meaning of new words or for contrastive analysis.

*Teaching vocabulary: What to teach*

We now turn to the domain of content knowledge, that is, what is involved in knowing vocabulary. The knowledge of a word has many facets. In his well-known framework, Nation (2001) breaks down word knowledge into nine aspects grouped under *form* (pronunciation, spelling, word parts), *meaning* (form-meaning link, concept and referents, associations), and *use* (grammatical functions, collocations, constraints on use). Covering all nine aspects for every new item taught in class may seem overly ambitious; however, this list should be seen as an inventory of all aspects that comprise word knowledge and not as a checklist. Ultimately, not all aspects are equally important for all lexical items or useful for learners at every level or in every context.

Another inventory by Hoey (2003) also consists of nine aspects, albeit with certain differences. While Nation includes spelling and the knowledge of word parts, Hoey places more importance on contextual and co-textual properties. According to Hoey (2005), when we encounter a word we make a mental note of the contexts and co-texts in which it occurs. These patterns of occurrence, which include fixed and semi-fixed expressions the word appears in, constitute an inextricable part of word knowledge.

*Teaching vocabulary: What teachers believe and what they do*

While vocabulary acquisition has been extensively researched, not all findings are taken up by practitioners. Rossiter et al. (2016) surveyed 30 Canadian

English language teachers of adults and found several discrepancies between teacher beliefs, practices, and research findings. These discrepancies mainly concern the setting of instructional priorities, vocabulary learning strategies, and teaching techniques. Although the majority of the respondents were aware of corpora and corpus-based frequency lists, they were less likely to promote dictionary use or display important words and chunks in the classroom, both of which are practices proven to be beneficial for learners.

Even when teachers consider certain strategies or techniques to be important, they do not always practise what they preach. In Niu and Andrews's (2012) case study of tertiary-level instructors in China, all four participants unanimously believed that students should guess the meaning of new words, even though the strategy was rarely employed in their observed lessons. Other inconsistencies between beliefs and practices concerned dictionary use and self-study: these strategies were marginally used despite teachers' beliefs indicating their perceived utility. These incongruencies between reported beliefs and classroom practice can be accounted for by the dynamic, emergent, socially-constructed, and contextually-situated nature of teachers' beliefs (Barcelos & Kalaja, 2011). Various contextual factors such as classroom reality, institutional culture, and curricular constraints may cause teachers to deviate from or modify their beliefs.

Similar explanations for why teachers' practices may not reflect their beliefs have been put forward by other small-scale studies, conducted in Iran (Gerami & Noordin, 2013), Indonesia (Hermagustiana et al., 2017), and Argentina (Lopez-Barrios, 2021). All three studies revealed a number of incongruencies between teachers' self-reported beliefs and their pedagogical practices caused by "impeding factors" (Hermagustiana et al., 2017, p. 40). At the same time, many practices observed during the lessons were consistent with the teachers' beliefs. The participants in all three studies stressed the importance of focusing not only on word meanings but on other aspects of word knowledge, such as pronunciation and word parts, and this belief was reflected to some extent in the observed classes.

When it comes to the use of L1, most participants in Niu and Andrews's (2012) study resorted to translation when it was called for, for example when it was easier to convey a concept without recourse to a long-winded definition in English. L1 use alongside other techniques for clarifying meaning was also reported in the three studies mentioned above. Not all teachers enthusiastically embrace L1 use, however. Wach and Monroy (2020) uncovered some interesting differences in beliefs about L1 use among Spanish and Polish teachers-in-training, which again point to contextual mediation of teachers' belief systems, in this case, different educational cultures in the two countries. While the Spanish participants did not dismiss or reject the use of L1 as a teaching resource, they did not recognize the various functions it can serve in the classroom. The Polish participants, on the other hand, had a generally more favourable attitude towards the role of L1 in the classroom and acknowledged its usefulness as a scaffolding tool.

Most of the research reviewed here has been limited to one or two countries and has been largely qualitative in nature, relying on interviews and classroom observations. One notable exception that used a combination of quantitative and qualitative instruments is Gao and Ma's (2011) study consisting of a questionnaire followed by in-depth interviews. The questionnaire revealed that Chinese teachers placed greater emphasis on learning vocabulary through linguistic context whereas their Hong Kong counterparts prioritized memorization. The follow-up interviews then sought to explain the differences in these beliefs, which were again attributed to social/contextual factors, such as fewer opportunities for L2 use outside the classroom in mainland China. Such mixed-method studies are critical when providing a deeper understanding of teachers' experiences (Wyatt, 2014).

This section has focused on the relationship between teachers' beliefs and vocabulary pedagogy. We are not aware of any extant research distinctly focused on the relationship between teachers' beliefs and lexical awareness. Parallel research on grammar instruction (Wyatt & Dikilitaş, 2021) and pronunciation instruction (Zhang, 2018) has shown that there is a correlation between teachers' awareness of these systems and their self-efficacy beliefs. The question remains as to whether this correlation would hold for vocabulary instruction.

### *Current study*

The studies reviewed above present some incongruencies between teachers' beliefs and practice; however, none of the research has focused on teachers' beliefs in their abilities to effectively teach vocabulary, that is, their self-efficacy beliefs. Investigating these beliefs is important because there are tangible consequences for teachers' classroom practice. For example, if teachers lack confidence in responding to "difficult" vocabulary questions from their learners, will they simply panic, avoid giving learners opportunities to ask them questions, or request to teach lower-level courses?

To clarify the key concepts explored in this study, moving forward we use the following terms in relation to vocabulary:

- *Pedagogic confidence:* Language teachers' self-efficacy beliefs in their own abilities to successfully employ pedagogic techniques and strategies. Examples of such techniques include identifying vocabulary errors or presenting new vocabulary items in context.
- *Lexical awareness:* Language teachers' knowledge and meta-knowledge of different components of vocabulary items, including the ability to

recognize and name them for pedagogic purposes, for example, being able to recognize and name the part-of-speech of words. Lexical awareness therefore extends beyond procedural knowledge (how to use vocabulary proficiently) which all expert speakers possess. Lexical awareness is not a type of self-efficacy belief; rather, it is measurable teacher knowledge.
- *Knowledge confidence:* A type of self-efficacy belief closely connected to the concept of lexical awareness. Essentially, it is language teachers' confidence in their own lexical awareness so that they can effectively teach this content to their learners.
- *Overall vocabulary teaching confidence:* A holistic LTSE belief teachers possess about their overall ability to effectively teach vocabulary, encompassing both pedagogic confidence and knowledge confidence.

Exploring the interplay of these concepts, the current study addresses four research questions:

RQ1 Which aspects of vocabulary pedagogy are teachers most and least confident in, and is there an underlying factor structure for these LTSE beliefs?
RQ2 Which aspects of vocabulary knowledge are teachers most and least confident in?
RQ3 To what extent are teachers lexically aware of different types of vocabulary?
RQ4 To what extent do aspects of pedagogic confidence, knowledge confidence, and lexical awareness predict overall vocabulary teaching confidence?

## Methodology

A mixed-methods approach was adopted using an explanatory sequential design consisting of two principal stages (Creswell & Plano Clark, 2011). First, (mostly) quantitative data were collected from an online survey. Then a subset of the respondents were interviewed to better understand their LTSE beliefs and to further explore the statistical patterns that emerged from the quantitative data. The multi-phase design of the study was selected to provide greater explanatory power and validity through triangulation of the multiple data types (Bryman, 2006).

### Instruments

The primary data collection instrument was a survey created using Google Forms (Appendix A), using the survey from Wyatt and Dikilitaş (2021) on grammar LTSE beliefs as a model. After piloting, the survey was reduced to four sections and 52 items:

1 *Pedagogic confidence*: 15 questions asking teachers to indicate their degree of confidence with regard to various vocabulary teaching techniques. Some questions related to the practices for teaching vocabulary described earlier, such as vocabulary selection, use of L1, and recycling vocabulary. Other questions related to areas normally covered in initial teacher training courses, which we drew from the CELTA syllabus (Cambridge English, 2021). These included the ability to clarify relevant aspects of meaning and form, provide clear contexts and a communicative focus, and identify and correct learner errors. In addition, several questions reflected language teaching methodologies with particular relevance to vocabulary teaching, namely, the Lexical Approach (Lewis, 1993, 1997), which gives prominence to lexical chunks, and Dogme ELT (Meddings & Thornbury, 2009), with its emphasis on responsive teaching and reformulation. Finally, there was a 16th question asking about teachers' overall confidence in teaching vocabulary. Responses were recorded on a 5-point Likert scale.
2 *Knowledge confidence*: 12 questions asking teachers to indicate their degree of confidence in teaching various aspects of vocabulary knowledge, for example, collocations. To devise the list of questions for this section, we combined Hoey's (2003) list with its emphasis on co-textual and contextual aspects and Nation's (2001, 2013) framework, which includes spelling and word parts. Responses were recorded on a 5-point Likert scale.
3 *Lexical awareness*: a short coursebook passage presented to participants (adapted from Graham-Marr et al., 2023). Ten questions followed to assess participants' awareness and ability to identify vocabulary for teaching purposes, for example, identifying a multi-word verb or an item suitable to pre-teach for a learner at level C1 on the Common European Framework of Reference (CEFR; Council of Europe, 2001).
4 *Personal information*: 14 questions to elicit demographic information and information about teaching experience, English proficiency, education, and training.

For the follow-up interviews, a semi-structured format was used, consisting of five predetermined questions plus additional questions to probe the participants' responses. Interviews lasted between 30 and 35 minutes and were all conducted by the same researcher over Zoom. Following the interviews, transcripts and researcher notes were analysed and discussed in relation to the findings from the survey. All interviewee names were anonymized.

## Participants

To recruit participants for the study, the researchers shared the survey through their social media accounts. This form of convenience sampling is widely used in L2 research (Dörnyei, 2007) because it is practical for both researchers and respondents. However, online surveys cannot access the entire desired population, in this case English language teachers of adults, as there is inherently auto selection bias with only more motivated teachers taking the time to respond, as well as those known to the researchers. As a result, the sample cannot be considered representative of the English language teaching (ELT) community as a whole, but rather, a subpopulation with particular characteristics.

In total, 143 people responded to the survey; seven agreed to be interviewed. One respondent who selected "Not applicable" for all teaching-related questions was omitted. From the 142 valid responses, a relatively homogenous profile emerged with respect to expertise (Table 9.1). These

*Table 9.1* Characteristics of participants

| n = 142 | n | % |  | n | % |
|---|---|---|---|---|---|
| Gender |  |  | Education |  |  |
| Female | 94 | 66.2 | High school | 7 | 4.9 |
| Male | 44 | 31.0 | Bachelor's | 41 | 28.9 |
| Unknown | 4 | 3.8 | Master's | 71 | 50.0 |
|  |  |  | Doctoral | 23 | 16.2 |
| Age |  |  |  |  |  |
| 20–29 | 9 | 6.3 | Teacher qual. |  |  |
| 30–39 | 38 | 26.8 | Certificate | 41 | 28.9 |
| 40–49 | 46 | 32.4 | Diploma | 42 | 29.6 |
| 50–59 | 21 | 14.8 | National qual. | 32 | 22.5 |
| 60–69 | 26 | 18.3 | None | 9 | 6.3 |
| 70+ | 2 | 1.4 | Rel. degree | 18 | 12.7 |
| L1 |  |  | Teaching exp. |  |  |
| English | 83 | 58.5 | < 1 | 2 | 1.4 |
| Other | 59 | 41.5 | 1–2 | 2 | 1.4 |
|  |  |  | 3–5 | 14 | 9.9 |
| English prof. |  |  | 6–10 | 21 | 14.8 |
| CEFR B1 | 1 | 0.7 | 11–20 | 56 | 39.4 |
| CEFR B2 | 4 | 2.8 | > 20 | 47 | 33.1 |
| CEFR C1 | 23 | 16.2 |  |  |  |
| CEFR C2 | 114 | 80.3 | Vocab. training |  |  |
|  |  |  | Formal | 105 | 73.9 |
| Primary context |  |  | Informal | 27 | 19.0 |
| Mix of classes | 45 | 31.7 | None | 10 | 7.0 |
| General English | 45 | 31.7 |  |  |  |
| EAP | 29 | 20.4 |  |  |  |
| ESP | 11 | 7.7 |  |  |  |
| Exam prep | 7 | 4.9 |  |  |  |
| Teacher training | 4 | 2.8 |  |  |  |
| YLs | 1 | 0.7 |  |  |  |

participants are highly experienced, with 93.7% over the age of 30 and 87.3% possessing 6+ years of teaching experience. They are also highly trained, with 95.1% possessing a university degree (and 66.2% a graduate degree), 93.7% possessing a teaching qualification, and 92.9% having undergone some sort of formal training for teaching vocabulary. Regarding English proficiency, 80.3% self-reported as being at CEFR level C2 (and 96.5% at either C1 or C2).

This participant pool therefore necessitates careful interpretation of the data: any conclusions proposed are in reference to this type of teacher who makes up only a fraction of the global ELT community. Other demographics were more heterogeneous: geographically, the teachers have a range of L1s (19 languages) and teach a variety of class types.

*Data analysis*

The quantitative data was first grouped to produce more meaningful statistics. For the survey section related to pedagogic confidence (RQ1), exploratory factor analysis (EFA) was performed with the scores from the 15 items to uncover potential latent dimensions elicited by these questions. The factorability and sampling adequacy of these data were checked using the psych package in R (Revelle, 2022; KMO = 0.894, Bartlett: $\chi^2(105)$ = 1013.4, $p < .001$). Next, Scree and Parallel analysis plots suggested a three-factor solution, with all three factors having eigenvalues over one. The factor analysis was carried out using principal axis factoring and oblique rotation because of the underlying assumption that the variables are correlated (Costello & Osborne, 2005). Mean confidence scores for each factor were then obtained.

To group the scores of the section on knowledge confidence (RQ2), mean scores were calculated for items related to the aspects of form, meaning, and use. For the lexical awareness section (RQ3), a total lexical awareness score of 0–10 was tallied by awarding each correct item one point. More than one answer could be provided, and the point was awarded as long as one of these was unambiguously correct. To calculate the total score all unique responses ($n$ = 247) were independently graded by both researchers and then compared, showing substantial agreement (κ = 0.77), followed by discussion to resolve discrepancies.

Using these aggregate scores, a linear regression model was created to test which variables predict teachers' overall vocabulary teaching confidence[2] (RQ4). The model was created in the R environment (R Core Team, 2022), and all assumptions listed in Levshina (2015) were checked and met through plotting and statistical tests. All variables of interest were included in the model, with theoretically motivated interaction terms added if they were found to be significant and improved model fit. The relative importance of the regressors was calculated using the relaimpo package (Groemping, 2006).

## Findings

We present the findings in the order of the research questions, interspersing insights from the qualitative data throughout.

**RQ1:** In the tallied descriptive statistics for the pedagogic confidence survey items (Table 9.2), pedagogic confidence items have a high, narrow range from 3.70–4.51 ($M = 4.27$, $SD = 0.73$). These means closely align with the overall vocabulary teaching confidence indicated in item P16. Teachers appeared least confident in selecting vocabulary items to teach, selecting texts to use based on vocabulary, and using learners' L1 to support learning.

*Table 9.2* Mean and standard deviations for pedagogic confidence survey items

| Item | Description (Confidence in …) | Mean | SD |
|---|---|---|---|
| P1 | Presenting new vocabulary items in natural examples | 4.37 | 0.74 |
| P2 | Encouraging students to write full sentences with new vocabulary items | 4.16 | 0.94 |
| P3 | Encouraging students to notice and record "chunks" | 4.13 | 0.86 |
| P4 | Providing varied vocabulary practice | 4.05 | 0.84 |
| P5 | Identifying and correcting vocabulary errors in student production | 4.41 | 0.76 |
| P6 | Helping students to reformulate their production | 4.11 | 0.95 |
| P7 | Assessing students' use of vocabulary in speaking and writing | 4.18 | 0.88 |
| P8 | Deciding which vocabulary items to teach based on frequency | 3.84 | 0.90 |
| P9 | Deciding which materials/texts to use based on vocabulary difficulty | 3.98 | 0.84 |
| P10 | Using a variety of ways to present/clarify vocabulary meaning | 4.29 | 0.87 |
| P11 | Using learners' first language to support vocabulary learning | 3.70 | 1.27 |
| P12 | Answering students' questions about vocabulary meaning | 4.47 | 0.68 |
| P13 | Answering students' questions about vocabulary form | 4.51 | 0.70 |
| P14 | Answering students' questions about vocabulary use | 4.21 | 0.80 |
| P15 | Recycling/reviewing previously taught vocabulary in a variety of ways | 4.09 | 0.85 |
| P total | Mean confidence of items P1-P15 | 4.17 | 0.22 |
| P16 | Overall vocabulary teaching confidence | 4.27 | 0.73 |
| Factor 1 | Presenting, practising, and correcting | 4.2 | 0.63 |
| Factor 2 | Responsively using teacher vocabulary knowledge | 4.34 | 0.65 |
| Factor 3 | Making vocabulary-based selections | 3.91 | 0.77 |

*Note:* Pedagogic confidence scores are on a scale of 1–5.

In the follow-up interviews, participants were asked how they select lexis before reading or listening tasks. Responses included the students' needs, the topic of the lesson, or items that seemed to pose difficulty during the task. Asking students themselves to decide what items they would like to focus on was also mentioned by Alistair (based in the UK). Only one interviewee, Anita (based in Poland), mentioned consulting online learner's dictionaries to help with vocabulary selection. Although other interviewees mentioned consulting dictionaries, only one teacher, Gabriella (based in Honduras), encourages her students to look up words themselves. This trend is generally in line with Rossiter et al.'s (2016) and Niu and Andrews's (2012) findings, which show that teachers could do more to promote dictionary use among students.

With respect to the underlying factor structure, the three factors in the EFA consist of eight, four, and two survey items, respectively (Table 9.3). In addition, one survey item (P11) did not load on to any factor. The other 14 items all show loadings over 0.4, above the suggested minimum rule-of-thumb of 0.32 (Tabachnick & Fidell, 2001). The three factors cumulatively explain 55% of the variance in responses (Factor 1 = 25%, Factor 2 = 20%, Factor 3 = 10%).

For Factor 1, we propose the label of *Presenting, practising, and correcting*. This factor contains teaching techniques relating to presenting

*Table 9.3* Exploratory factor analysis of pedagogic confidence survey items

| Item | PA 1 | PA 2 | PA 3 |
|---|---|---|---|
| *Factor 1: Presenting, practising, and correcting* | | | |
| P4 | **0.76** | 0.06 | −0.06 |
| P10 | **0.75** | 0.01 | −0.07 |
| P1 | **0.72** | −0.04 | 0.56 |
| P2 | **0.69** | 0.07 | 0.58 |
| P15 | **0.60** | 0.16 | −0.05 |
| P6 | **0.55** | −0.06 | 0.35 |
| P5 | **0.45** | 0.37 | 0.07 |
| P3 | **0.40** | 0.03 | 0.34 |
| *Factor 2: Responsively using teacher vocabulary knowledge* | | | |
| P13 | −0.02 | **0.91** | −0.04 |
| P12 | −0.02 | **0.88** | 0.00 |
| P14 | 0.10 | **0.74** | 0.07 |
| P7 | 0.15 | **0.50** | 0.16 |
| *Factor 3: Making vocabulary-based selections* | | | |
| P8 | −0.06 | 0.04 | **0.74** |
| P9 | 0.17 | 0.10 | **0.59** |
| *No factor* | | | |
| P11 | −0.25 | 0.22 | 0.30 |

*Note:* Figures in bold represent the highest factor loading for each survey item.

vocabulary (e.g., P1 and P10); practising vocabulary (e.g., P2 and P4); and correcting vocabulary (e.g., P5 and P6). Taken together, these elements of vocabulary teaching all relate to concrete techniques, often deductive in nature, for conveying information about vocabulary and ensuring that this information is put into productive practice.

For Factor 2, we propose the label of *Responsively using teacher vocabulary knowledge*. This factor includes answering students' questions about vocabulary meaning, form, and use (P12, P13, P14), as well as assessing students' use of vocabulary (P7). For all of these teaching competencies, there are two elements. First, it requires teachers to be confident in their own vocabulary knowledge to the extent that they can clarify doubts or assess learners' needs with respect to different elements of vocabulary. Second, there is an element of responsiveness as answering student questions and classroom assessment often take place in real time, potentially in relation to unanticipated emergent language. This difficulty, acknowledged in the interviews, could be overcome by consulting a reliable source or getting students to look up lexical information themselves. Referring specifically to emergent language, one interviewee (Carlos) admitted to often looking up difficult vocabulary items, particularly idiomatic expressions, on his phone in class, which is a self-efficacious coping strategy.

For Factor 3, we suggest the label *Making vocabulary-based selections*. This factor contains only two items, P8 and P9. Clearly, there is an element of decision making for both these competencies, with the decisions typically occurring outside the classroom. In addition, two other items from Factor 1, P1 and P2, cross-load on Factor 3, though the relationship to this secondary factor is less apparent though potentially still related to vocabulary planning. We posit that confidence with these skills is unique in that they are not classroom teaching skills but instead require the ability (and desire) to research vocabulary, often using online tools. Interviews confirm that some teachers are willing to go this extra mile: three interviewees mentioned online dictionary consultation, either for verifying the suitability of certain items for different CEFR levels (Anita), for dealing with emergent language (Carlos), or for investigating vocabulary ahead of the lessons (Anita and Olha).

Finally, the one survey item that did not belong to any factor related to using learners' L1 to support vocabulary learning (P11). One potential explanation is that this skill can be equally applied to all three factors. After all, it is possible for teachers to use their learners' L1 when presenting new vocabulary, for example, by providing or eliciting a translation. Yet it is equally plausible for a teacher to answer questions or select vocabulary to teach bearing in mind the learners' L1, for example, highlighting a false cognate. This competency may also be distinct due to its polarizing nature. As previously noted, the use of translation and learners' L1s in language teaching has long been a hotly debated topic. It was found in the interviews that most teachers working in English as a Foreign Language contexts do not shy away from L1 use. Some interviewees acknowledge it as another tool in their arsenal, for example, Irene, who said she often uses contrastive analysis between English and other languages. Depending on the lesson aims, Gabriella also often gets her students to make cross-linguistic and cross-cultural comparisons. Generally speaking, the surveyed teachers resort to L1 use as a backup (Alistair and Zara). It should be noted, however, that this practice is context-specific and related to the existence of a shared L1; this item, therefore, may have less perceived relevance for some respondents.

**RQ2:** In the knowledge confidence section (Table 9.4), teachers were less confident about teaching aspects of vocabulary use ($M = 3.97$, $SD = 0.76$) compared to aspects of meaning and form, especially idioms/semi-fixed expressions (K8) and text positions of words (K12). However, overall, scores in this section were still high with a range of 3.80–4.53 ($M = 4.21$, $SD = 0.26$).

That confidence in all three categories was still relatively high points to considerable self-efficacy among the respondents with regard to teacher vocabulary knowledge. The qualitative data largely corroborates this finding with interviewees pointing to "Use" as the area posing the most difficulty. Two teachers, Carlos (Brazil) and Irene (Greece), attributed slightly lower confidence in "Use" to the fact that English is their L2; however, Zara (USA) also admitted that "Use" was the most difficult aspect despite having English as her L1.

*Table 9.4* Mean and standard deviations for knowledge confidence survey items

| Item | Vocabulary aspect | Category | Mean | SD |
|---|---|---|---|---|
| K1 | Meaning | Meaning | 4.49 | 0.64 |
| K2 | Pronunciation | Form | 4.53 | 0.64 |
| K3 | Spelling | Form | 4.51 | 0.64 |
| K4 | Part of speech | Form | 4.51 | 0.71 |
| K5 | Affixation | Form | 4.42 | 0.76 |
| K6 | Genre | Use | 4.06 | 0.79 |
| K7 | Collocations | Use | 4.08 | 0.81 |
| K8 | Idioms and semi-fixed expressions | Use | 3.90 | 0.89 |
| K9 | Associations and connotations | Meaning | 4.04 | 0.87 |
| K10 | Synonymy | Meaning | 4.20 | 0.74 |
| K11 | Grammatical patterns | Use | 4.03 | 0.91 |
| K12 | Text position | Use | 3.80 | 0.95 |
| K total | Mean confidence of items K1-K12 | | 4.21 | 0.26 |
| K form | Mean confidence of form-related items | | 4.49 | 0.53 |
| K meaning | Mean confidence of meaning-related items | | 4.24 | 0.65 |
| K use | Mean confidence of use-related items | | 3.97 | 0.76 |

*Note:* Knowledge confidence scores are on a scale of 1–5.

"Use" encompasses a wide array of collocations, idioms, and semi-fixed expressions; familiarity with all these lexical items might be an elusive goal, even for expert speakers. As Anita laconically put it, "You're not a walking dictionary". Indeed, Faez et al.'s (2021) findings indicate that language proficiency is not the most crucial component of teachers' self-efficacy; rather, self-efficacious teachers will know where to look when occasionally stumped by a student's question. Both Anita and Carlos reported that students' questions regarding vocabulary use often have them reaching for a dictionary. Anita referred to this as "a human factor".

"Use", however, was not the only category mentioned by interviewees. Anita also pointed out "Form" as an area she feels slightly less confident in. For example, teaching pronunciation (spoken form) is an area where L2 speakers can experience imposter syndrome due to the prevalence and prestige of certain varieties. Zara, on the other hand, identified "Form" as the area she is confident in thanks to her background in linguistics.

**RQ3:** On the lexical awareness task (Table 9.5), respondents correctly identified 80% of items ($M$ = 0.80, $SD$ = 0.20). Notably, accuracy in identifying semi-fixed expressions was significantly lower than for all other items at 50%. The next lowest was accuracy in identifying vocabulary for pre-teaching purposes at CEFR levels B2 (65%) and C1 (79%).

Trying to explain the difficulty in identifying a semi-fixed expression in the text (e.g., *from the comfort of your [home/office/sofa]*), Zara attributed this challenge to the greater emphasis placed on idioms and collocations in teacher preparation. Alistair referred to this item as "a grey area", which is notoriously difficult to pin down, asking "How fixed should a fixed expression be?". Echoing this view, Olha also described semi-fixed expressions as vague and "a bit tricky".

*Table 9.5* Mean and standard deviations for the lexical awareness task items

| Item | Description (item to identify) | Mean | SD |
| --- | --- | --- | --- |
| L1 | Informal vocabulary item | 0.82 | 0.38 |
| L2 | Item with multiple meanings | 0.87 | 0.33 |
| L3 | Collocation | 0.82 | 0.38 |
| L4 | Semi-fixed expression | 0.50 | 0.50 |
| L5 | Multi-word verb | 0.89 | 0.31 |
| L6 | Idiom | 0.92 | 0.28 |
| L7 | Discourse marker | 0.91 | 0.29 |
| L8 | Item to pre-teach for a learner at CEFR B1 | 0.83 | 0.38 |
| L9 | Item to pre-teach for a learner at CEFR B2 | 0.65 | 0.48 |
| L10 | Item to pre-teach for a learner at CEFR C1 | 0.79 | 0.41 |
| L total | Mean of items L1–L10 | 0.80 | 0.20 |

*Note:* Lexical awareness item scores are the proportion correct.

The other items with relatively low scores in the lexical awareness section were words at different CEFR levels for pre-teaching purposes. Interestingly, in the open-ended section of the questionnaire, many participants questioned the implicit assumption that lexis should be pre-taught before a reading or listening task. However, six out of seven teachers who were interviewed agreed, by and large, that some pre-teaching is generally called for. Gabriella was the only dissenting voice; she felt that pre-teaching lexis creates too much of a structure for students and does them a disservice by not preparing them for the spontaneity of real life.

**RQ4:** The linear regression model (Table 9.6) brings together data from the three survey sections to predict overall vocabulary teaching confidence. The results of this analysis indicate that all three pedagogic confidence factors were significant, such that higher confidence in each of these areas predicted higher overall vocabulary teaching confidence when taking all other variables into account. Recall, the three factors were *Presenting, practising, and correcting, Responsively using teacher vocabulary knowledge,* and *Making vocabulary-based selections*. In particular, the first two factors had the greatest effect, accounting for 19.3% and 14.3% of variance, respectively.

In contrast, the picture painted by the knowledge confidence variables in the model is less straightforward. "Meaning" and "Use" confidence were not significant by themselves, and unexpectedly, "Form" had a *negative* estimate in the model. We see no intuitive explanation for this finding. One tentative hypothesis is that teachers with more confidence in their knowledge of vocabulary form are more aware of the challenges of teaching

*Table 9.6* Linear regression of variables predicting overall vocabulary teaching confidence

| Predictors | Estimate | SE | t value | p | lmg |
|---|---|---|---|---|---|
| (Intercept) | −1.257 | 0.960 | −1.309 | 0.193 | – |
| Pedagogic confidence – factor 1 | 0.546 | 0.107 | 5.106 | <0.001*** | 0.193 |
| Pedagogic confidence – factor 2 | 0.356 | 0.094 | 3.791 | <0.001*** | 0.143 |
| Pedagogic confidence – factor 3 | 0.654 | 0.203 | 3.225 | 0.002** | 0.062 |
| Lexical awareness | 0.311 | 0.101 | 3.085 | 0.002** | 0.001 |
| Knowledge confidence – form | −0.255 | 0.115 | −2.215 | 0.028* | 0.026 |
| Knowledge confidence – meaning | −0.060 | 0.134 | −0.448 | 0.655 | 0.047 |
| Knowledge confidence – use | 0.140 | 0.113 | 1.236 | 0.219 | 0.065 |
| Lexical awareness: factor 3 interaction | −0.080 | 0.026 | −3.119 | 0.002** | 0.039 |

Notes:
\* $p < .05$, \*\* $p < .01$, \*\*\* $p < .001$
Model formula: lm(formula = overall_conf ~ factor 1 + factor 2 + factor 3 + lexical_awareness + form + meaning + use + lexical_awareness:factor 3).

vocabulary. Indeed, Olha said that she makes a point of explicitly teaching other aspects of word knowledge, such as collocation, often overlooking pronunciation. Commenting on whether this indicates a lack of confidence, she noted, somewhat tongue-in-cheek: "I don't lack confidence in teaching [pronunciation]; I lack confidence in remembering to teach it".

As for lexical awareness, in line with initial expectations, there was a significant positive relationship with higher lexical awareness scores predicting higher overall vocabulary teaching confidence. However, there was also a significant negative interaction between lexical awareness scores and Factor 3 pedagogic confidence scores. This negative interaction suggests that the sum of the individual effects is greater than their combined effect. Speculatively, having confidence in making vocabulary-based selections and being more lexically aware might be somewhat overlapping traits in teachers and do not provide any additional boost to overall vocabulary teaching confidence. Overall, the model had an adjusted $R^2$ of 0.55.

In the interviews, when asked what contributes more to teachers' confidence in teaching vocabulary – pedagogic knowledge or content knowledge – most participants were hesitant to commit to one or the other. Nonetheless, pedagogic knowledge seems to tip the scales somewhat, as evidenced by Carlos's comment:

> Knowing how to approach certain lexical items with students could help teachers to develop their confidence more than having a deeper understanding of the items themselves. Obviously both are equally important.

Anita puts it down to frequent practice teachers get themselves while practising vocabulary with students:

> I would say techniques contribute more to teachers' confidence in teaching vocabulary. If you teach vocabulary to students and do many exercises with them, you're more likely to gain confidence in teaching it.

Other teachers considered a sound knowledge base more important. Olha emphasized the importance of preparation before teaching vocabulary, particularly clarifying meaning and especially for higher levels. Such preparation would, presumably, put teachers on solid ground when answering students' questions about the form, meaning, and use (Factor 2). Reflecting on his experience as a teacher trainer, Alistair also pointed out the difficulty teachers may experience when teaching vocabulary at higher levels and cautiously noted it might particularly affect the confidence of L2 English-speaking teachers. Ultimately, according to Alistair, it is vocabulary knowledge that is more important.

## Conclusions and pedagogical implications

The study presented in this chapter explored LTSE beliefs with respect to pedagogic confidence, knowledge confidence, and lexical awareness. The survey and interview data suggest that LTSE beliefs in the broad categories of *Presenting and practising vocabulary* and *Responsively using teacher vocabulary knowledge* are the key contributors to the teachers' perceived vocabulary teaching confidence. In contrast, confidence in *Making vocabulary-based selections* and lexical awareness were significant but less powerful factors.

In terms of teaching various aspects of vocabulary knowledge, the teachers were slightly less confident with the aspects under the "Use" heading compared to "Meaning" or "Form". Lack of confidence in this area might result in avoidance behaviour; however, self-efficacious teachers, who are aware of the inherent difficulty of these aspects, employ coping strategies, such as researching target items thoroughly before the lesson or consulting authoritative online sources on the spot. The finding that "Use" is the most difficult category is also reflected in the lexical awareness task, where a semi-fixed expression was the item most participants had difficulty identifying. The importance of units of language beyond single words is probably one of the most important insights gained in the last 30 years in the field of vocabulary instruction. Usually referred to as *chunks* or *lexical chunks* in pedagogical literature (Dellar & Walkley, 2016; Selivan, 2018), their ubiquity was brought to the fore by corpus linguistics, particularly Sinclair (1991), and popularized in ELT with the Lexical Approach (Lewis, 1993, 1997). It seems, though, that while collocations have established themselves in the ELT canon, semi-fixed expressions remain in relative obscurity, possibly due to their elusive nature. Although they do not impact overall vocabulary teaching confidence, there is clearly a case for devoting more attention to what one interviewee referred to as the grey area that lies between fixed expressions and free combinations of words.

Importantly, these findings should be considered in light of certain limitations regarding the participant pool. For one, although the survey was answered by a sufficient number of teachers ($n = 142$) for reliable statistical analysis, there was limited interview uptake ($n = 7$). As a result, not all quantitative trends could be fully explored. In addition, the sample of teachers answering the survey is not representative of the ELT population as a whole, instead skewing towards more experienced, expert teachers. These characteristics likely account in part for the relatively high and restricted range of self-reported LTSE beliefs. It seems logical that teachers with lower teaching confidence would be less likely to complete an optional survey about their LTSE beliefs. One teacher, Anita, exemplifies the positive LTSE beliefs of the respondents in her description of her teaching philosophy:

It's perfectly fine. That's what I tell my students right when we start the course, you know. I tell them, "Okay, guys, you are people. I am a person as well. I'm not a robot. I may forget something, and it's okay". It would always have a human factor. So in case I don't remember something, I want to check it. It's not because maybe I don't remember. Maybe I do. I just want to double check, so that you [students] wouldn't learn something in the wrong way.

This attitude, we argue, is admirable, and one that teacher preparation courses would do well to try to instill as it balances teaching confidence with the awareness that no language teacher can ever know everything about a language. By better understanding the vocabulary LTSE beliefs of expert teachers such as Anita, the current study contributes to our understanding of the multifaceted nature of LTSE vocabulary teaching beliefs and the factors which impact them.

## Notes

1 The terms *vocabulary* and *lexis* are used interchangeably throughout this chapter. When describing the work of others, we aim to maintain the original wording (e.g., *lexis* when describing the Lexical Approach), and in all other cases consistency, clarity, and naturalness guide our decisions as to which word to use.
2 Demographic data was analysed but a discussion of these findings is beyond the scope of the study reported here.

## References

Barcelos, A.M.F., & Kalaja, P. (2011). Introduction to beliefs about SLA revisited. *System*, *39*(3), 281–289. 10.1016/j.system.2011.07.001

Brooks-Lewis, K.A. (2009). Adult learners' perceptions of the incorporation of their L1 in foreign language teaching and learning. *Applied Linguistics*, *30*(2), 216–235. 10.1093/applin/amn051

Bryman, A. (2006). Integrating quantitative and qualitative research: How is it done? *Qualitative Research*, *6*(1), 97–113. 10.1177/1468794106058877

Cambridge English. (2021). *CELTA (Certificate in Teaching English to Speakers of Other Languages): Syllabus and assessment guidelines*. Retrieved November 5, 2022, from www.cambridgeenglish.org/Images/21816-celta-syllabus.pdf

Costello, A.B., & Osborne, J.W. (2005). Best practices in exploratory factor analysis: Four recommendations for getting the most from your analysis. *Practical Assessment, Research & Evaluation*, *10*(7), 1–9. 10.7275/jyj1-4868

Council of Europe. (2001). *Common European framework of reference for languages: Learning, teaching, assessment*. Council of Europe Publishing.

Creswell, J.W., & Plano Clark, V.L. (2011). *Designing and conducting mixed methods research*. SAGE Publications.

Dellar H., & Walkley, A. (2016). *Teaching lexically*. Delta Publishing.

Dörnyei, Z. (2007). *Research methods in applied linguistics*. Oxford University Press.
Faez, F., Karas, M., & Uchihara, T. (2021). Connecting language proficiency to teaching ability: A meta-analysis. *Language Teaching Research, 25*(5), 754–777. 10.1177/1362168819868667
Gao, X., & Ma, Q. (2011). Vocabulary learning and teaching beliefs of pre-service and in-service teachers in Hong Kong and mainland China. *Language Awareness, 20*(4), 327–342. 10.1080/09658416.2011.579977
Gerami, M.R., & Noordin, N.B. (2013). Teacher cognition in foreign language vocabulary teaching: A study of Iranian high school EFL teachers. *Theory & Practice in Language Studies, 3*(9), 1531–1545. 10.4304/tpls.3.9.1531-1545
Graham-Marr, A., Beaudry, Y., Naismith, B., & Castro Urbina, A. (2023). *World Voices 4*. ABAX Publishing. https://www.abax.co.jp/product/226
Groemping, U. (2007). Relative importance for linear regression in R: The package relaimpo. *Journal of Statistical Software, 17*(1), 1–27. 10.18637/jss.v017.i01
Hermagustiana, I., Hamra, A., Rahman, Q., & Salija, K. (2017). Reflection of teacher cognition in EFL vocabulary instructional practices in Indonesia. *International Journal of English Linguistics, 7*(5), 34–45. 10.5539/ijel.v7n5p34
Hoey, M. (2003). What's in a word? *English Teaching Professional, 27*, 5–8.
Hoey, M. (2005). *Lexical priming: A new theory of words and language*. Routledge.
Kerr, P. (2014). *Translation and own-language activities*. Cambridge University Press.
Laufer, B. (2020). Evaluating exercises for learning vocabulary. In S. Webb (Ed.), *The Routledge handbook of vocabulary studies* (pp. 351–368). Routledge.
Laufer, B., & Girsai, N. (2008). Form-focused instruction in second language vocabulary learning: A case for contrastive analysis and translation. *Applied Linguistics, 29*, 694–716. 10.1093/applin/amn018
Laufer, B., & Nation, I.S.P. (2012). Vocabulary. In S.M. Gass, & A. Mackey (Eds.), *The Routledge handbook of second language acquisition* (pp. 163–176). Routledge.
Laufer, B., & Rozovski-Roitblat, B. (2011). Incidental vocabulary acquisition: The effects of task type, word occurrence and their combination. *Language Teaching Research, 15*(4), 391–411. 10.1177/1362168811412019
Lewis, M. (1993). *The Lexical Approach: the state of ELT and a way forward*. Language Teaching Publications.
Lewis, M. (1997). *Implementing the Lexical Approach: Putting theory into practice*. Language Teaching Publications.
Levshina, N. (2015). *How to do linguistics with R: Data exploration and statistical analysis*. John Benjamins. 10.1075/z.195
López-Barrios, M., San Martín, M.G., & Villanueva de Debat, E. (2021). EFL vocabulary teaching beliefs and practices: The case of two teachers in Argentina. *TESOL Journal, 12*(1). 10.1002/tesj.533
Meddings, L., & Thornbury, S. (2009). *Teaching unplugged*. Delta Publishing.
Nation, I.S.P. (2001). *Learning vocabulary in another language*. Cambridge University Press.

Nation, I.S.P. (2003). The role of the first language in foreign language learning. *Asian EFL Journal*, 5, 1–8. 10.26686/wgtn.12560333.v1

Nation, I.S.P. (2013). *Learning vocabulary in another language* (2nd ed.). Cambridge University Press.

Newton, J. (2020). Approaches to learning vocabulary inside the classroom. In. S. Webb (Ed.), *The Routledge handbook of vocabulary studies* (pp. 255–270). Routledge.

Niu, R., & Andrews, S. (2012). Commonalities and discrepancies in L2 teachers' beliefs and practices about vocabulary pedagogy: A small culture perspective. *TESOL Journal*, 6, 134–154. http://tesol-international-journal.com/wp-content/uploads/2013/11/A9_V6.pdf

R Core Team (2022). R: A language and environment for statistical computing. *R Foundation for Statistical Computing*. https://www.R-project.org/

Revelle, W. (2022). *Psych: Procedures for psychological, psychometric, and personality research*. Northwestern University. https://CRAN.R-project.org/package=psych

Rossiter, M.J., Abbott, M.L., & Kushnir, A. (2016). L2 vocabulary research and instructional practices: Where are the gaps?. *TESL-EJ*, 20(1), 1–16. 10.2307/3585941

Schmitt, N., & Schmitt, D. (2014). A reassessment of frequency and vocabulary size in L2 vocabulary teaching. *Language Teaching*, 47(4), 484–503. 10.1017/S0261444812000018

Schmitt, N., Cobb, T., Horst, M., & Schmitt, D. (2017). How much vocabulary is needed to use English? Replication of van Zeeland & Schmitt (2012), Nation (2006) and Cobb (2007). *Language Teaching*, 50(2), 212–226. 10.1017/S0261444815000075

Selivan, L. (2018). *Lexical grammar: Activities for teaching chunks and exploring patterns*. Cambridge University Press.

Selivan, L. (2022). Corpus linguistics and vocabulary teaching. In. K. Harrington, & P. Ronan (Eds). *Demystifying corpus linguistics for English language teaching* (Chapter 8). Palgrave Macmillan.

Shulman, L.S. (1987). Knowledge and teaching: Foundations of the new reform. *Harvard Educational Review*, 57, 1–22. 10.17763/haer.57.1.j463w79r56455411

Sinclair, J. (1991). *Corpus, concordance, collocation*. Oxford University Press.

Tabachnick, B.G., & Fidell, L.S. (2001). *Using multivariate statistics*. Allyn and Bacon.

Tsui, A. (2003). *Understanding expertise in teaching: Case studies of second language teachers*. Cambridge University Press.

Wach, A., & Monroy, F. (2020). Beliefs about L1 use in teaching English: A comparative study of Polish and Spanish teacher-trainees. *Language Teaching Research*, 24(6), 855–873. 10.1177/1362168819830422

Webb, S. (2020). Introduction. In. S. Webb (Ed.), *The Routledge handbook of vocabulary studies* (pp. 1–12). Routledge.

William, D. (2011). *Embedded formative assessment*. Solution Tree.

Wyatt, M. (2010). An English teacher's developing self-efficacy beliefs in using groupwork. *System*, 38(4), 603–613. 10.1016/j.system.2010.09.012

Wyatt, M. (2014). Towards a re-conceptualization of teachers' self-efficacy beliefs: Tackling enduring problems with the quantitative research and moving on. *International Journal of Research & Method in Education*, 37(2), 166–189. 10.1080/1743727X.2012.742050

Wyatt, M. (2018). Language teachers' self-efficacy beliefs: A review of the literature (2005–2016). *Australian Journal of Teacher Education*, 43(4), 92–120. 10.14221/ajte.2018v43n4.6

Wyatt, M. (2021). Research into second language learners' and teachers' self-efficacy beliefs: Making the connections. *TESOL Quarterly*, 55(1), 296–307. 10.1002/tesq.3010

Wyatt, M., & Dikilitaş, K. (2021). English language teachers' self-efficacy beliefs for grammar instruction: implications for teacher educators. *The Language Learning Journal*, 49(5), 541–553. 10.1080/09571736.2019.1642943

Zhang, B. (2018). English language teachers' required knowledge and self-efficacy beliefs about pronunciation instruction. *Electronic Thesis and Dissertation Repository*, 5290. https://ir.lib.uwo.ca/etd/5290

Zwier, L.J., & Boers, F. (2022). *English L2 vocabulary learning and teaching: Concepts, principles, and pedagogy.* Routledge. 10.4324/9781003172994

## Appendix A: Survey items

1. Vocabulary teaching

Please indicate your degree of self-confidence with regard to each of the following aspects of vocabulary teaching:

1 Not at all confident
2 Not very confident
3 Moderately confident
4 Very confident
5 Completely confident

1. presenting new vocabulary items in natural examples (e.g., in full sentences)
2. encouraging students to write full sentences with new vocabulary items
3. encouraging students to notice and record 'chunks' (e.g., collocations, semi-fixed expressions, idioms)
4. providing varied vocabulary practice
5. identifying and correcting vocabulary errors in student production
6. helping students to reformulate their production so that they can express their intended meaning
7. assessing students' use of vocabulary in speaking and writing
8. deciding which vocabulary items to teach based on frequency
9. deciding which materials/texts to use based on vocabulary difficulty
10. using a variety of ways to present/clarify vocabulary meaning (e.g., realia, images, synonyms, etc.)
11. using learners' first language to support vocabulary learning (e.g., contrastive analysis, translation)
12. answering students' questions about vocabulary meaning
13. answering students' questions about vocabulary form (e.g., pronunciation, spelling, word formation)
14. answering students' questions about vocabulary use (e.g., register, collocations, grammatical patterns)
15. recycling/reviewing previously taught vocabulary in a variety of ways
16. teaching vocabulary (overall)

2. Vocabulary knowledge

Please indicate your degree of self-confidence with regard to teaching each of the following aspects of vocabulary knowledge:

1 Not at all confident

2 Not very confident
3 Moderately confident
4 Very confident
5 Completely confident

1 What does the word mean?
2 How is the word pronounced?
3 How is the word spelled?
4 What part of speech is the word?
5 What word parts are recognizable (e.g., prefixes)?
6 Is the word restricted to specific contexts and genres?
7 What are the word's collocations?
8 What idioms and semi-fixed expressions does the word appear in?
9 What are the word's associations or connotations?
10 What other words can be used instead?
11 What grammatical patterns is the word likely to appear in/with?
12 What positions in a text is the word likely to appear in?

3. Identifying vocabulary for teaching purposes

Read the short text below and identify the vocabulary items from the text which you might teach.

Example:
Question: a formal vocabulary item
Answer: "trauma"

Shopping at the mall is my worst nightmare. For a start, there's the trauma of finding parking. Then, there are the crowds, the noise, the smells – shopping at a mall is always an overwhelming and exhausting ordeal. I used to run around like a headless chicken, but thanks to the rise in online shopping, I can now get almost anything from the comfort of my home. Searching for products online is a breeze – all I have to do is type into a search bar to find what I need, and I'm good to go. A few days later my purchases are dropped off on my doorstep. Phew! Nothing beats online shopping!

*Adapted with permission from World Voices 4 (ABAX publishing)*

NB. More than one answer is possible for each question.

1 an informal vocabulary item
2 an item with multiple meanings
3 a collocation

4 a semi-fixed expression
5 a multi-word verb (e.g., a phrasal verb)
6 an idiom
7 a discourse marker
8 an item to pre-teach for a learner at CEFR B1
9 an item to pre-teach for a learner at CEFR B2 (different from the previous answer)
10 an item to pre-teach for a learner at CEFR C1 (different from the previous two answers)

## Appendix B: Interview questions

1 Do you think it's important to pre-teach lexis before a reading/listening task? Why (not)?
2 How do you select which lexis to focus on after reading/listening? Do you pre-select lexis before reading/listening tasks? How do you decide which items require additional practice?
3 Would you say you have a good degree of confidence across all 3 aspects: meaning/form/use? Which one do you find the most challenging (and why)?
4 On the questionnaire, were there any types of lexical items (e.g., discourse markers) that were new to you or that you do not normally consider important? Were there any specific items that were challenging in that section?
5 Do you use learners' L1 to support vocabulary teaching? Why (not)? In what ways?
6 Which do you think contributes more to teachers' confidence in teaching vocabulary: the knowledge of vocabulary (e.g., what is a collocation? how frequent is the word? etc.) or the techniques used (e.g., having a variety of practice tasks, review activities, error correction, etc.)? Why?

# 10 An exploratory study on teachers' and learners' self-efficacy beliefs for English as a foreign language listening in Algeria

*Keltoum Mansouri, Suzanne Graham, and Naomi Flynn*

## Introduction

The concept of self-efficacy in education in general and in language teaching and learning in particular has received increasing attention in the last two decades. Its interest to researchers most likely stems from its ability to predict various behavioural, cognitive, and affective outcomes. Yet even though some studies (e.g., Hoang, 2018; Xue, 2022) suggest that there exists a relationship between language teachers' self-efficacy (LTSE) beliefs and language learners' self-efficacy (LLSE) beliefs, research into LTSE and LLSE has developed separately (Wyatt, 2021). This is the case even though teachers and learners are evidently both core, interconnected elements in the language classroom and their belief patterns are likely to shape what happens in their environment. Furthermore, while recent years have seen an increase in research into second-language listening, most investigations of L2 listening self-efficacy (e.g., Graham & Macaro, 2008) have focused on learners rather than on teachers. This chapter brings together these two key groups and reports on a study exploring teachers' and learners' self-efficacy beliefs in the teaching and learning of listening to English as a foreign language (EFL) learners, and more precisely with regards to listening strategies and metacognition. The study's findings regarding the relationship between teacher and learner self-efficacy and outcomes in listening are discussed in terms of self-efficacy theory and classroom implications.

## Literature review

From the diverse body of research into listening in a second language (L2), at least two conclusions may be drawn. The first is that L2 listening is challenging for both learners (Graham, 2006) and teachers (Graham & Santos, 2015), partly because of the covert nature of listening comprehension, which takes place without any external manifestation, making it seem outside learners' and teachers' control and hence a potential source of anxiety (Arnold, 2000; Mills et al., 2006). In Graham (2006), learners of French expressed doubts about being able to cope with the speed of delivery of spoken input and segment it, difficulties echoed by Chinese learners of English in Goh (2000), for whom overall understanding was also an issue even if individual words were understood. Second-language listening requires the careful integration of bottom-up (linguistic) and top-down (non-linguistic) information and strategies.

That leads to a second conclusion that has been put forward, namely, that how well learners comprehend spoken L2 input is related to their use of listening strategies, which one may define as "the ways in which listeners manage real-time interactions with spoken text to achieve comprehension" (Bao & Guan, 2019, n.p). This "managing" of the listening process in turn encompasses metacognition, which includes not only "awareness of the cognitive processes involved in comprehension", but also "the capacity to oversee, regulate, and direct these processes" (Vandergrift & Baker, 2015, p. 395). This capacity may include the use of metacognitive strategies such as planning, monitoring, and evaluating both listening comprehension and the use of cognitive listening strategies, such as translation and drawing on prior knowledge to work out the meaning of the input (Vandergrift, 2003).

The extent to which metacognition is responsible for how well learners listen has received research attention for the past 30 years or so, with some studies conducting correlational analyses to assess the relationship between metacognition (assessed through questionnaires) and listening comprehension (Lau, 2017). Others have analysed qualitative reports to compare the metacognitive strategy use of so-called "good" and "not so good" listeners (Vandergrift, 2003). Both of these research approaches, however, tend to overlook the influence of other factors that might be of equal or greater importance, such as vocabulary knowledge, which more recent studies have taken into consideration using techniques such as Structural Equation Modelling. While this kind of analysis has increasingly shown that the contribution of metacognitive knowledge to listening outcomes diminishes when vocabulary knowledge is also accounted for (Wallace, 2022), there is still evidence that it is an important factor in explaining how well learners listen (Vafaee & Suzuki, 2020).

Metacognition has also been found to be related to other variables that have been studied individually in respect of their relationship with listening comprehension, such as self-efficacy. This is defined as the belief in "one's capabilities to organize and execute the courses of action required to produce given attainments" (Bandura, 1997, p.3). As well as being significantly related to listening proficiency (Mills et al., 2006; Razmi et al. 2021; Tabrizi & Saeidi, 2015), L2 listening self-efficacy has been found to be related to listening strategy use in general and metacognitive strategy use in particular. This has not only been through correlational studies (Kassem, 2015; Wong, 2005) but perhaps more convincingly from interventions to improve listening strategy use that also strengthen listening self-efficacy beliefs (Graham & Macaro, 2008). The intervention implemented by these authors focused on making high school learners of French, with previously low listening self-efficacy beliefs, more metacognitively aware of the listening process, better able to exert control over the listening task by using listening strategies skilfully, and more perceptive of the link between strategy application and listening outcomes. Likewise, a recent study by Xu et al. (2021) with tertiary learners of English in China found that listeners with high self-efficacy beliefs demonstrated frequent use of listening strategies, and that strategy-based instruction boosted learners' self-efficacy. The relationship between metacognition and self-efficacy can be explained through reference to the framework of self-regulated learning, which has been used to suggest that metacognitive strategies mediate between L2 self-efficacy beliefs and attainment (Teng et al., 2021). If we view self-efficacy as the belief that we can "organize and execute the courses of action required to produce given attainments" (Bandura 1997, p. 3), that is, control of how we perform on activities, then it has clear links with metacognition, the ability to control, direct, or organize cognition. In other words, self-efficacious people are likely to be able to use metacognitive strategies, which they believe they can muster to achieve desired outcomes and hence persist with the challenges that they may encounter (Pajares, 2009). It should be noted, however, that in another study (Simasangyaporn, 2016), not only was there a fairly modest albeit statistically significant relationship between listening proficiency and self-efficacy but also a metacognitive listening intervention had no significant impact on listening self-efficacy beliefs, suggesting further research is needed.

One factor that has been considered less frequently in relation to L2 listening is the teacher. This is surprising, given that the instructional approaches teachers take to L2 listening would be expected to have an impact on learners' listening development. Such approaches are in turn likely related to teachers' beliefs about L2 listening, including their self-efficacy beliefs, defined by Wyatt (2018a, p. 136) as teachers' "beliefs in their abilities to support language learning in various task-, domain- and context-specific cognitive, metacognitive, affective and social ways". While literature in mainstream, first-language education has found that teachers with higher self-efficacy are more likely to persevere in learning how to use new teaching approaches, with a concomitant impact on learners' outcomes (Cantrell et al., 2013), research into second-language teacher self-efficacy is less plentiful. The task- and domain-specific nature of self-efficacy beliefs, however, means that studies that focus on teachers of particular curriculum areas are needed, and indeed language teacher self-efficacy has been an area of rapid growth along with a focus on teachers' sense of efficacy for specific aspects of their work (Wyatt, 2018b). In his review of 115 studies between 2005 and 2016, Wyatt (2018b) discussed several studies focusing on more specific aspects of LTSE beliefs, including reading skills development (Karimi et al., 2016), and writing instruction (Locke & Johnston, 2016). No study of LTSE beliefs for developing listening proficiency is included in the review, however.

Furthermore, within the research literature, there is also only a limited number of studies exploring language teachers' beliefs about listening or about how they approach listening in their practice. While it has been claimed that teachers, across different contexts, take a "comprehension approach" (Field, 2008, p. 7), in which learners' understanding is "tested" but listening skills are rarely "taught", empirical evidence to support these claims is more limited but growing. This is especially the case in research in Asian contexts that have illuminated which aspects of listening teachers prioritize. For example, Siegel (2014) indicated that EFL teachers in Japan focused more on comprehension questions than other aspects of listening instruction. Meanwhile, in studies involving teachers in England and Brazil (Graham et al., 2014; Graham & Santos, 2015; Santos & Graham, 2018), it was found that language teachers focused more on the product rather than the process of listening.

Contradictory aspects between teachers' stated beliefs and their stated practices have also been identified (Graham et al., 2014). On the one hand, the majority of 115 teacher respondents to a questionnaire stated that the main purpose of conducting listening activities in class was "To teach learners how to listen more effectively". On the other hand, in responses to other parts of the questionnaire, there was very little indication of teachers reporting that they actually taught listeners how to listen more effectively, that they modelled any listening strategies, or that they encouraged learners to reflect on how to listen (Graham et al., 2014). Classroom observations and teacher interviews then allowed Graham and Santos (2015) to elaborate on these findings. Teachers tended to conceptualize "effective listening" as learners answering comprehension questions correctly, seemingly because of curriculum requirements. However, while one of the 13 teachers interviewed saw teaching listening as unproblematic and was confident in her own approach because she saw listening as a "passive activity, there's not a lot of effort required" (p. 84), a key theme to emerge was that most teachers saw listening as a "problem". They felt that this was something that caused learners difficulties and frustrations that they as teachers were unsure how to resolve.

Factors teachers mentioned in Graham and Santos (2015) as undermining their confidence in developing learners' listening competence included inadequate materials, examination requirements, and learners' own lack of proficiency. Similarly, Wyatt (2018b) highlighted school policies (Wyatt, 2010), limited course material (Ganjabi et al., 2013), and student language difficulties (Siwatu, 2011) as barriers to language teachers' overall self-efficacy. By contrast, enabling factors included in-service teacher education (Wyatt, 2013), observing similar others implementing teaching practices successfully (Phan & Locke, 2015), and having a stronger theoretical rationale for one's classroom practices (Karimi et al., 2016). Again, this has echoes in findings relating to teachers' beliefs about listening, in that Graham and Santos (2020) showed how one teacher went some way to becoming more confident in providing listening instruction after research-based in-service professional development. The latter activity helped her strengthen her rationale for how listening should and could be taught and also provided opportunities for "mastery experiences". These experiences are viewed by Bandura (1994) as constituting an important source of self-efficacy, especially where they involve succeeding on a challenging task rather than an easier one, and the individual perceives that success originates in their own actions and behaviours.

The above review indicates that alongside a sizeable literature on learner listening proficiency and metacognition, we have fewer insights into teachers' self-efficacy and teachers' beliefs about L2 listening. Studies have also tended to consider these areas separately, rather than offering a more holistic picture that gives an understanding of the relationship between learner and teacher variables. This chapter therefore explores these issues of teacher and learner self-efficacy for listening in Algeria, in the context of learning EFL, where those wishing to study English at university have to demonstrate a minimum competence level in an examination (approximately B2 level on the CEFR) taken prior to university. This gate-keeping examination, however, assesses reading, writing, and grammar only. By contrast, listening and speaking are the focus of the Oral Expression module taken as a fundamental module in the first year at university, for which students' previous education provides little real preparation. A further issue is that, within the institution the study below focuses upon, anecdotal evidence suggests that listening receives little particular focus in the Oral Expression module and is not supported by a detailed syllabus or materials. As in Azzi's (2012) study with Algerian teachers, training in developing learners' communicative skills such as listening has been limited. Hence issues of teacher and learner self-efficacy for listening are a concern and are explored below through the following questions:

1 In the context of Algerian university EFL classes, what is the relationship between teachers' self-efficacy for listening instruction, learners' listening self-efficacy, and also learners' listening outcomes?
2 How do teachers view L2 listening instruction and what factors do they perceive as important for their self-efficacy beliefs in that area?
3 How do learners of different levels of proficiency and self-efficacy approach L2 listening?

The first research question was approached through correlational analysis from questionnaire data. Questions 2 and 3 then provide further insights, through an exploration of interview data.

## Research methodology

This chapter draws on data from a larger study in which teachers and learners went on to take part in an intervention in which teachers were given research-informed training by the first author to enable them to provide their learners with metacognition and strategy-based listening instruction. The impact of this instruction on learners' and teachers' self-efficacy beliefs and learners' listening proficiency was then assessed. This chapter explores the relationship between those variables prior to the intervention.

### Participants

The participants spoke Tamazight and Algerian Arabic as their first languages. The former is an indigenous language, spoken by the minority. The latter, spoken by the majority, is a combination of basic Arabic vocabulary and some loanwords from Tamazight, French, Spanish, and Turkish. English in this context is the third language learnt in schools after Standard Arabic and French.

Data were collected through convenience sampling from 186 Algerian EFL freshmen (28 male, 158 female), who were taught in 10 classes by 10 teachers (3 male, 7 female) from 2 different universities. The participants had been working together for a semester. The teachers were of differing teaching experiences, age, and educational levels (Table 10.1).

### Data collection tools

A mixed-method approach was followed, using a questionnaire and interviews with both teachers and learners to explore their self-efficacy beliefs. Data on learners' listening proficiency were obtained through a listening test.

*Table 10.1* Teachers' demographic information

|  |  | *Frequency* |
|---|---|---|
| Gender | Female | 07 |
|  | Male | 03 |
| English teaching experience | > 15 | 02 |
|  | 5 to 15yrs | 04 |
|  | < 5yrs | 04 |
| Highest educational degree | Master's | 08 |
|  | Bachelor's | 02 |

The teacher questionnaire investigated the sense of efficacy for teaching English listening comprehension and was called the "teacher self-efficacy beliefs about listening inventory" (TSEBLI). In developing the instrument, the researchers drew on existing general teachers' self-efficacy scales (Dellinger et al., 2008; Tschannen-Moran & Hoy, 2001; Tschannen-Moran & Johnson, 2011), and made it more domain- and task-specific, in line with recent trends (see Chapter 2 of this volume for a discussion of these trends). The TSEBLI consisted of 23 items rated on an 11-point Likert scale from 0% (I absolutely can't do this) to 100% (I absolutely can do this) (all items are given in the Results section, Table 10.4). The items covered different aspects of a lesson focused on listening, including instruction and management, development of listening strategies and metacognition, learners' listening and self-efficacy, and so on. Overall, these aspects were categorized theoretically into two main sub-sections (the sample being too small for Exploratory Factor Analysis): self-efficacy in instructional strategies and classroom management (10 items), and self-efficacy in relation to learners' listening development (13 items). The overall Cronbach's alpha of the scale was .95; alphas of .84 and .95 emerged for the first and the second sub-sections, respectively. A percentage score for each item was used in the analysis in addition to a composite self-efficacy score that was calculated, first, using the mean of the 23 items combined, and second, using the mean of each-sub-scale expressed as a percentage.

Semi-structured interviews were conducted with all the teachers after they completed the questionnaire. The interviews offered qualitative insights into teachers' beliefs about listening, including their stated rationale for teaching listening and how confident they felt about doing that. The interviews also aimed to gain in-depth insights into the areas covered in the TSEBLI and the reasons behind their ratings for certain items. The interviews lasted approximately 30 minutes for each teacher and were audio recorded and transcribed by the first author, who used Thematic Analysis (Braun & Clarke, 2013) to identify patterns of meaning and themes related to the research questions. Participants' quotes are used verbatim in the extracts below and may include errors. They have not been corrected to maintain authenticity.

The learner questionnaire – "learner self-efficacy beliefs about listening inventory" (LSEBLI) – investigated learners' self-efficacy beliefs for certain tasks related to listening in English. It consisted of 13 items rated on an 11-point Likert scale from 0% (I absolutely can't do this) to 100% (I absolutely can do this) (all items are given in the Results section, Table 10.4). It was based on the instrument used in Graham and Macaro (2008), with other items added by the first author to fit the study focus (metacognition and strategy use). Using factor analysis (KMO = .89, $p < .001$), the questionnaire items were categorized into two main sub-sections: self-efficacy for general listening development (eight items), and self-efficacy for metacognition regarding listening development (five items). The overall Cronbach's alpha of the LSEBLI was .83; alphas of .86 and .81 emerged for the first and the second sub-sections, respectively. A percentage score for each item was used in the analysis in addition to a composite self-efficacy score, which was calculated, first, using the mean of the 13 items combined, and second, using the mean of each sub-scale expressed as a percentage.

The listening test, 35 questions in five sections, assessed a wide range of listening skills: comprehending the gist, comprehending specific details, identifying speakers' opinions and attitudes, and following an argument. It was adapted from English language tests by Cambridge English Language Assessment (IELTS, 2015; Preliminary English Test, 2010) targeted at participants at a similar overall level of language proficiency to those involved in this study. The Cronbach's alpha for the test was .90 and scores were converted to percentages for data analysis. The test was taken in the language laboratories where regular classes were taking place.

Semi-structured interviews were also conducted with 20 learners after they completed the LSEBLI. Following Graham et al. (2020) and Staples and Biber (2015), a hierarchical cluster analysis of learner self-efficacy beliefs and listening test scores for the whole sample was undertaken. This revealed four clusters or groups of learners: two where learners' scores on both self-efficacy beliefs and listening "matched" (high/high, or low/low) and two where they did not (high/low, low/high) (Table 10.2).

Two learners from each group were interviewed in order to give further insights into the relationship between listening proficiency and self-efficacy beliefs. The mean scores for self-efficacy beliefs and listening proficiency were used to form two categories for each variable: high (above the mean) and low (below the mean). The recorded interviews (20 minutes) asked learners to reflect on their experience of listening to English in class, and also why they had responded to different questionnaire items in the way that they had. After being transcribed by the first author, the interviews were analysed qualitatively through thematic analysis.

*Table 10.2* Levels of listening proficiency and self-efficacy of learners involved in the interviews

|  | Listening proficiency (n) | Self-efficacy (n) |
| --- | --- | --- |
| High | 15 | 10 |
| Low | 5 | 10 |

## Results

We now present the results, addressing our research questions.

### *Relationship between teachers' self-efficacy for instruction, learners' listening outcomes, and learners' listening self-efficacy beliefs*

Table 10.3 presents the correlations between the variables. It shows that, on the one hand, both teachers and learners reported having a moderately positive level of self-efficacy in teaching and learning English listening, respectively, even though mean scores for listening comprehension were below 50% and therefore could be seen as low. The large Standard Deviations also indicate much variability within participants for the three variables. Meanwhile, on the other hand, correlation results revealed a positive, significant, though moderate relationship between learners' self-efficacy beliefs and their listening proficiency. However, both learner variables had a weak, non-significant relationship with teachers' self-efficacy. These findings were then explored further through the interview data with both groups, as discussed below.

### *Teachers' views on L2 listening instruction and factors they perceived as important for their self-efficacy in that area*

Teacher responses to the TSEBLI indicated that they had a relatively high level of overall self-efficacy but more so for teaching and managing the listening lesson than for influencing learners' listening development (Table 10.4).

In respect of instructional strategies, teachers reported having the highest level of self-efficacy for clarifying the goal of each listening task (item 13) and making their listening instruction understandable (item 21), and the lowest level for implementing new methods to teach listening (item 10) and teaching listening strategies (item 15). Regarding learners' listening development, reported levels of self-efficacy were very similar across all items, but highest for providing learners with opportunities to practise listening outside

*Table 10.3* Descriptive statistics and correlations for overall teachers' self-efficacy, learners' self-efficacy, and learners' listening proficiency

|  | Mean (%) | SD | Correlation 1 | 2 | 3 |
|---|---|---|---|---|---|
| Teacher self-efficacy | 67.15 | 13.74 | 1 | .05 | .06 |
| Learner self-efficacy | 65.81 | 15.16 |  | 1 | .38** |
| Learner listening proficiency | 41.39 | 18.28 |  |  | 1 |

*Notes:*
** Indicates a significance level at .01.

Table 10.4 Descriptive statistics, individual aspects of teachers' self-efficacy

| Scale | Items | | M (%) | SD | Min (%) | Max (%) |
|---|---|---|---|---|---|---|
| Instructional strategies and classroom management | 13. | Clarify the goal of each listening task | 81.50 | 11.57 | 60 | 100 |
| | 21. | Make my listening instruction understandable | 80.86 | 13.44 | 50 | 100 |
| | 14. | Achieve the objective I have set for listening | 78.97 | 13.81 | 60 | 100 |
| | 9. | Manage the listening session if unexpected student behaviour occurs | 74.35 | 16.79 | 40 | 100 |
| | 2. | Use the allocated time for listening activities appropriately | 71.98 | 17.82 | 40 | 100 |
| | 1. | Select relevant teaching listening materials appropriate to all students' language level | 71.45 | 18.67 | 40 | 100 |
| | 3. | Plan the listening course effectively | 69.73 | 16.93 | 40 | 100 |
| | 23 | Use a variety of listening activities to assess students' listening proficiency. | 67.52 | 26.57 | 20 | 100 |
| | 10. | Implement new methods to teach listening | 59.83 | 20.28 | 30 | 90 |
| | 15. | Teach listening strategies effectively | 59.89 | 22.39 | 20 | 90 |
| | Total | | 71.61 | 11.73 | 55 | 91 |
| Learners' listening development | 5. | Provide students with opportunities to practise listening outside classroom | 69.24 | 22.93 | 20 | 100 |
| | 8. | Improve students' listening proficiency | 68.87 | 13.12 | 50 | 90 |

| | | | | | |
|---|---|---|---|---|---|
| 4. | Provide students with feedback on their listening performance | 68.49 | 19.99 | 40 | 100 |
| 6. | Maintain high levels of students' motivation and engagement in listening tasks | 68.44 | 17.24 | 40 | 100 |
| 12. | Persist with students whose listening is not improving | 67.79 | 18.68 | 30 | 90 |
| 7. | Foster interaction among students | 66.45 | 21.08 | 40 | 100 |
| 22. | Raise students' awareness of the nature of the listening process | 62.79 | 20.42 | 30 | 100 |
| 18. | Improve students' sense of efficacy for listening | 62.04 | 16.21 | 30 | 90 |
| 20. | Raise students' awareness of the different types of listening task demands | 61.45 | 25.15 | 20 | 100 |
| 11. | Persist with students who are unmotivated when listening | 59.89 | 20.69 | 30 | 90 |
| 17. | Evaluate students' use of listening strategies | 58.76 | 20.19 | 20 | 90 |
| 19. | Provide students with opportunities to reflect on their way of processing listening input | 57.47 | 28.27 | 00 | 90 |
| 16. | Develop students' effective use of listening strategies | 56.77 | 22.38 | 20 | 90 |
| Total | | 63.73 | 16.16 | 30.77 | 92.31 |

the classroom (item 5) and lowest for developing learners' effective use of strategies (item 16).

These areas of relatively lower self-efficacy were reflected in the interviews with teachers. Firstly, while teachers claimed they did teach listening as a skill in its own right, they all reportedly did so by exposing learners to spoken language as much as possible and testing their comprehension, in order to develop their vocabulary and speaking. There was very little evidence of teachers seeking to systematically develop listening as a skill. Likewise, when teachers were asked about teaching different strategies to help learners build their awareness of the listening process and hence to manage it, some demonstrated limited or no awareness of listening strategies; for example, Leila commented: "*Honestly, I am not aware what are listening strategies*".

Furthermore, clarifying their responses to the TSEBLI, teachers attributed their perceived ability to teach listening effectively to two main themes: individual and contextual.

*Theme 1: Individual factors*

The participants considered their own learning experience a key factor influencing their practice and hence their self-efficacy to teach listening, in the sense that they constructed their knowledge based on the way they had been taught. They reported that this knowledge was reflected in their practice (lesson planning, class management, and so on) and they found it difficult to conceive of any other way to approach listening. For instance, Joseph reported: " … . *I don't think there is another way to address the lab session except for this way, and I think all teachers do the same thing. I was taught the same way*".

Teachers' apparent lack of knowledge about how to teach listening also emerged as an important individual factor. Thus, Leila demonstrated her lack of self-efficacy in selecting appropriate teaching materials, evaluating learners' performance, and improving their understanding of spoken English, stating: "*sometimes they [materials] don't work and each time I keep changing my mind about what to use … . I cannot evaluate them … . I don't know how … . I know that I can't improve their comprehension*".

For other teachers, lack of knowledge about how to teach listening was attributed to their own lack of interest and experience. For example, Sarah commented: "*I don't have the techniques to teach listening, simply because it is not my area of interest … I am not sure I can improve their listening comprehension*".

*Theme 2: Contextual factors*

The influence of contextual factors emerged as a theme from the interview data; contextual factors appeared to add to teachers' sense of challenge in teaching listening. These factors were related mainly to the department where they worked but also to their students.

DEPARTMENT-RELATED FACTORS

The lack of a syllabus and teaching materials for listening development was felt to have a direct influence on their practice and an indirect one on their self-efficacy beliefs. This was because it made it difficult for them to decide on the content and objectives of lessons. Azzah commented: " ...*with lack of the teaching materials I am sometimes undecisive how and what should I choose as activities, and whether they are relevant or not*".

Despite not having a common syllabus and encountering different challenges in preparing lessons, the majority of teachers stated that they did not collaborate with their colleagues to share their experiences and knowledge to address these issues. For example, one stated: " … . *each one of us is using his/her own method and materials*", "*I prepare my own lessons and I do not even know the teachers who are teaching the same module as I work as a part-time teacher*".

LEARNER-RELATED FACTORS

As another part of the teaching context, learner-related factors were commonly cited. First, the heterogeneity of classes posed challenges. Teachers mentioned that teaching learners with different proficiency levels, including those with too low levels for university study, made it difficult to select teaching materials to suit all learners. One reported: "*the challenge is that the students are not of the same level … … Sometimes, some just rely on their classmates' answers to give an answer without comprehending …* ". Another teacher added: "*that is why I could not decide on what to teach. Honestly, sometimes what I prepare works and sometimes does not*".

Second, learner motivation and autonomy were also raised as factors affecting teachers' own motivation and practice. Some teachers felt less able to persist with unmotivated learners, even when they tried approaches such as varying the sources and types of teaching materials. Azzah claimed … . "*some students are not really interested. Motivating students and engaging them in the tasks is difficult … . some students just don't care… … even if I use songs which they are normally interested in but, some of them are just bored no matter what type or topic of the songs is.*" Zeena further added: "*some students are all the time passive and I just become like them … … I can't motivate the whole class … . I can't persist, if I do, I'll lose my motivation … . the students get affected if the teacher is not motivated.*"

Teachers also viewed learners as lacking in autonomy both inside and outside the classroom, in that they made no effort to develop their listening comprehension and did not appreciate their teachers' efforts. They also claimed that learners had become used to a teacher-centred approach from their prior experience at secondary schools, which then affected their autonomy. As Aisha explained, "*they are not confident … . they were not taught to be independent by their previous teachers*", with Jacob adding: " … . *language students do not even try to make efforts to understand [a new word] … . they are not equipped with problem-solving skills …* ".

Thus, although teachers reported moderately positive self-efficacy beliefs for teaching listening in the questionnaire, the interviews revealed that various factors, personal and contextual (both department and learner-related), seem to influence their sense of efficacy negatively.

*How learners of different levels of proficiency and self-efficacy approach L2 listening*

Learner responses to the LSEBLI indicated a relatively high level of self-efficacy in understanding spoken English, but more so for general listening development than for metacognition regarding listening development (Table 10.5). Regarding the former, learners reported having the highest level of self-efficacy in understanding the gist of aural material (item 3), and the lowest level in recognizing words in connected speech (item 4). For metacognition regarding listening development, self-efficacy was lowest for item 7 (planning effectively how they are going to listen) and highest for persisting with listening despite the difficulties encountered in understanding (item 6).

The interviews with learners provided more insights into their beliefs about the listening process and their self-efficacy beliefs for listening. Firstly, they mentioned that the listening classes they attended allowed them to hear more authentic English, learn more vocabulary, and practise speaking. None mentioned that the classes improved their listening.

Following Graham et al. (2020), who identified different learner profiles in respect of combinations of self-efficacy, strategy use and language proficiency, learners' scores on the LSEBLI and on the listening test suggested that they could be divided into four groups (Figure 10.1). The interview transcripts were then analysed to gain more fine-grained insights into the different combinations of attainment and self-efficacy levels, from which the group labels shown in Figure 10.1 were derived.

The Achieving group involved eight learners, who scored highly on both listening and self-efficacy, the latter especially regarding their ability to persist in listening despite comprehension difficulties and to use a range of strategies to solve these problems. Hence these learners possessed a degree of self-direction and confidence in controlling their comprehension. One learner, for example, explained:

Table 10.5 Descriptive statistics, individual aspects of learner self-efficacy

| Scale | Items | M (%) | SD | Min (%) | Max (%) |
|---|---|---|---|---|---|
| General listening development | 3. Understand the gist (main idea) of what I hear | 81.29 | 17.65 | 30 | 100 |
| | 1. Develop my ability to understand spoken English | 77.58 | 20.32 | 20 | 100 |
| | 11. Listen to English without panicking | 70.91 | 24.55 | 00 | 100 |
| | 2. Understand the details of what I hear | 64.73 | 20.37 | 20 | 100 |
| | 5. Recognize opinions expressed by speakers while listening | 64.62 | 21.18 | 10 | 100 |
| | 10. Get the meaning of unknown or incomprehensible words | 62.41 | 23.55 | 00 | 100 |
| | 8. Understand a passage without transcripts | 61.23 | 21.33 | 10 | 100 |
| | 4. Identify words in connected (fast) speech | 56.45 | 22.73 | 00 | 100 |
| | Total | 67.41 | 15.45 | 28.75 | 100 |
| Metacognition for listening development | 6. Continue listening even if I find difficulties understanding | 69.83 | 28.35 | 00 | 100 |
| | 13. Evaluate how effectively I am listening | 67.20 | 23.28 | 00 | 100 |
| | 9. Use different sources of information to understand what I am listening to | 66.72 | 24.39 | 00 | 100 |
| | 12. Control how I am listening | 63.81 | 24.49 | 10 | 100 |
| | 7. Plan effectively how I am going to listen | 48.65 | 27.36 | 00 | 100 |
| | Total | 63.25 | 18.73 | 10 | 100 |

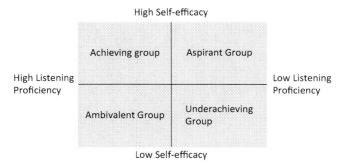

*Figure 10.1* Learner groups.

> *The first thing is I concentrate and use the knowledge I already have about the topic; I try to relate words together to understand the general idea. Similar words between English and French also help me understand. I also focus on the words I know, if there's any word I do not understand I can guess its meaning from the context.*

However, these learners felt they were less successful in planning how to listen effectively, claiming that they were unaware of how they should plan (reflecting perhaps the low mean score for "planning" in the LSEBLI overall). One explained: "*I don't have a particular plan, and I do not know what to do, I just improvise*". It is possible, of course, that for such learners planning was not deemed necessary and that the process of listening well had become automatic for them. Likewise, although some of these learners reported being unaware of what form evaluation should take, they insisted that they were able to assess their understanding. As one put it: "*I don't know how to evaluate … … but I would not say I can't evaluate because it's just I do not know how*".

There were only two learners in the Aspirant group, with low levels of listening proficiency but high levels of self-efficacy, the latter perhaps arising from their reported use of strategies to assist comprehension. However, these strategies were restricted mainly to translation and identification of English/French cognates: "*I translate to French or Arabic, and if I encounter shared words with French, it would facilitate comprehension for me*". Moreover, the learners claimed they persisted in listening despite finding it difficult, because of their interest and motivation to learn English. One explained: "*It happened several times that I couldn't understand what is said in the audio … … but I keep listening … I like English and I want to improve my language and listening*". The learners also reported planning, but for general understanding only: "*I can have an overall plan for understanding only the main idea … … I mainly concentrate on the words I know, then I gather them to construct meaning"*. Overall, the learners' willingness, determination, and love for the language, despite their limited knowledge of the listening process and the strategies required to manage it, seemed to boost their sense of efficacy, helping them to aspire to reach their goal of improving their language proficiency in general and listening in particular.

The Ambivalent group consisted of seven learners with high levels of listening proficiency but low levels of self-efficacy. They explained that they lacked awareness of how they should approach listening tasks and they appeared to blame their teachers for not guiding them in that respect. Even though they reported using a range of strategies, most seemed unaware of what the term strategy meant. They commented that the listening materials they encountered seemed irrelevant, very simple linguistically, and with uninteresting content. Consequently, they doubted whether they would be able to or even wish to persist if faced with more challenging listening material. As one learner explained: *"I think it depends on the topic of the audio, if it is interesting to me, I would continue listening despite the difficulties, but if it is not, I am not sure I would carry on listening"*. This view was shared by another learner: *"I am not sure about this; I have not experienced it [difficulty in understanding] so far, all the listening passages that we are exposed in the classroom are simple"*.

The last group, the Underachieving group, low on both listening proficiency and self-efficacy, comprised three learners who had little if any awareness of strategic listening, especially in relation to planning and evaluation. They also referred to their perceived inability to use listening strategies to overcome difficulties in comprehending, ascribing this to their poor listening proficiency. One affirmed: *"I know that I can't, because my listening is not good"*, while another demonstrated a very limited number of strategies, *"generally, I'd translate or ask a classmate or the teacher"*. Furthermore, the learners emphasized how difficult it was to follow what they were listening to because their attention wandered and they experienced a high level of anxiety. As one learner explained: *"I don't understand everything, and most of the time I miss some parts … … . I can't catch what they are saying … . I feel anxious even before listening"*. Overall, self-efficacy beliefs for this group seemed to be affected strongly by the outcomes of their previous listening experiences.

The qualitative data thus helped to explain the correlational findings established for Research Question 1. Learners with similar levels of self-efficacy could have different levels of listening proficiency and vice versa, with greater use and awareness of strategies seeming to boost self-efficacy beliefs but having a varying impact on listening outcomes depending on how effectively any strategies were employed.

## Discussion

The initial correlational analysis indicated that there was no statistically significant relationship between teachers' self-efficacy beliefs and scores for learners' listening comprehension and learners' self-efficacy beliefs, as measured quantitatively. The qualitative data, however, suggested that these areas were inter-related. Teachers reported that their ability to teach listening was indeed related to learner factors, especially learners' level of language proficiency, motivation, and autonomy, echoing in part the findings of Siwatu (2011) in respect of teachers perceiving learner lower language proficiency as a barrier to their own self-efficacy development.

Another discrepancy to emerge was that the quantitative findings suggested that, overall, teachers perceived themselves as fairly highly self-efficacious in terms of instructional strategies and classroom management. This may be because they judged their ability to teach listening in terms of their own narrower curriculum goals, which in turn appeared to also stem from their own learning experiences, a relationship suggested by Barnard and Burns (2012). From the interviews, it was evident that teachers conceived of listening as comprehension activities to test learners' understanding of a range of topics and a means to develop learners' vocabulary and speaking skills. There was very little evidence, if any, of them seeking to systematically develop listening as a skill. This finding perhaps supports Siegel's (2015) claim that listening instructors tend to lack a firmly established approach involving selecting pedagogical activities to teach listening as a skill in its own right. Indeed, the interviews showed teachers to have lower levels of self-efficacy for teaching listening when it came to improving learners' proficiency or strategy use. They underlined the challenges they encountered, notably regarding the selection of the listening materials relevant to the learners' language level.

The participants thus often attributed their difficulties to external factors, such as the heterogeneity of classes in terms of learners' language proficiency, lack of pre- or in-service training, and lack of syllabus, echoing the wider literature on LTSE beliefs (Wyatt, 2018b). Lower levels of self-efficacy also emerged in respect of teaching listening strategies and implementing novel teaching methods, echoing in part the contention of Cantrell et al. (2013) that less self-efficacious teachers are less likely to be open to learn and use new teaching methods.

Turning to learners, they demonstrated a low level of listening proficiency, and a somewhat higher level of self-efficacy in the questionnaire. The correlational analysis showed a positive, significant, albeit moderate relationship between their listening proficiency and their listening self-efficacy, similar to what was found by Simasangyaporn (2016) with learners of English in Thailand. Qualitative data from the interviews with the learners provided further insights into this finding. On the one hand, they highlighted that in many areas of listening, they reflected on their previous experiences, mastery experiences, positive or negative, to judge their ability to execute a particular listening task effectively. This is in line with Bandura's (1994) view that people's previous mastery experiences are very likely to influence their sense of efficacy. On the other hand, there was not always a clear-cut relationship between listening proficiency and listening self-efficacy, which seemed to be affected by metacognition and strategy use, particularly where there was a mismatch between self-efficacy beliefs and listening proficiency levels, as in the Aspirant and Ambivalent groups. The self-efficacy of the former group was perhaps boosted by their attempts to employ some listening strategies, possibly as a result of their stated strong desire to learn English and to develop listening in particular. Such strategies were, however, not used effectively enough or with enough metacognitive control to result in higher listening proficiency.

Furthermore, learners like teachers referred to external factors that could influence their listening self-efficacy beliefs. These included teacher practices, such as their use of less interesting and engaging materials and lack of support for developing effective listening strategies. Arguably, it may be that such a teaching approach did little to persuade learners, either that their teachers had confidence in their instructional abilities or that they themselves could get better at listening.

## Pedagogical implications and conclusions

In this study, self-efficacy beliefs appeared to manifest differently in different participants. While teachers' learning and teaching experiences were central factors underpinning how confident they felt in teaching listening, other factors were also found to influence these beliefs. Schools or department-related factors, such as lack of syllabus, collaboration, and teaching resources, were perceived as threats to their confidence to teach effectively. Of no less importance were learner-related factors, such as language level, motivation, and autonomy.

A discrepancy between teachers' self-efficacy reported in the questionnaire and the interviews was found. While they reported a moderately positive level of self-efficacy in the questionnaire, the interview analysis showed them not to be very confident. This inconsistency in the findings suggests a need to gather data through a range of different methods and to discuss discrepancies with participants themselves. The questionnaire and interviews also revealed that teachers felt less confident in developing learners' use of listening strategies and were unaware of any particular form of listening pedagogy. Taken together, and echoing Graham and Santos (2015), these results suggest a need for pre-/in-service teacher training regarding the systematic teaching of listening, focusing on metacognition and strategy use.

While there was a significant, moderate relationship between learners' listening scores and their listening self-efficacy beliefs, the interview data suggested that the relationship was complex, and perhaps underpinned by the extent to which learners were able to use metacognitive strategies that they believed would help them achieve desired outcomes (Pajares, 2009). That suggests that there is a place for targeted listening instruction. Such instruction should:

- raise learners' awareness of the process of listening
- teach strategic listening and metacognition through relevant content
- provide adequate feedback

Such an approach is also supported by studies reviewed earlier in this chapter, with benefits for both listening self-efficacy and listening proficiency (e.g., Graham & Macaro, 2008).

The language classroom is a complex environment, where teacher and learner factors interact in sometimes complex ways. Both groups, however, require the provision of quality training to ensure knowledge, self-efficacy, and skills development. Finally, as the study's findings are exploratory, further empirical investigations into teacher and learner self-efficacy beliefs for listening are needed.

**References**

Arnold, J. (2000). Seeing through listening comprehension exam anxiety. *TESOL Quarterly, 34*(4), 777–786. 10.2307/3587791

Azzi, M. (2012). The new pedagogical practices within the LMD system: Perceptions of EFL faculty members. *Procedia Social and Behavioral Sciences, 69,* 1004–1013. 10.1016/j.sbspro.2012.12.027

Bandura, A. (1997). *Self-efficacy: The exercise of control.* Freeman.

Bandura, A. (1994). Self-efficacy. In V. S. Ramachandran (Ed.), *Encyclopedia of human behavior* (vol. 4, pp. 71–81). Academic Press.

Bao, D., & Guan, C. (2019). Listening strategies. In J. I. Liontas (Ed.), *The TESOL encyclopedia of english language teaching* (1st ed.). John Wiley & Sons. 10.1002/9781118784235.eelt0588

Barnard, R., & Burns, A. (2012). *Researching language teacher cognition and practice: International case studies.* Multilingualism Matters.

Braun, V., & Clarke, V. (2013). *Successful qualitative research: A practical guide for beginners.* SAGE Publications.

Cantrell, S. C., Almasi, J. F., Carter, J. C., & Rintamaa, M. (2013). Reading intervention in middle and high schools: Implementation fidelity, teacher efficacy, and student achievement. *Reading Psychology, 34*(1), 26–58. 10.1080/02702711. 2011.577695

Dellinger, A. B., Bobbett, J. J., Olivier, D. F., & Ellett, C. D. (2008). Measuring teachers' self-efficacy beliefs: Development and use of the TEBS-Self. *Teaching and Teacher Education, 24*(3), 751–766. 10.1016/j.tate.2007.02.010

Field, J. (2008). *Listening in the language classroom.* Cambridge University Press

Ganjabi, M., Jafarigohar, M., Soleimani, H., & Iravani, H. (2013). Investigating the role of self-efficacy in manipulating textbooks: A matter of Iranian language teachers. *International Journal of Applied Linguistics & English Literature, 2*(6), 76–87. 10.7575/aiac.ijalel.v.2n.6p.76

Goh, C. (2000). A cognitive perspective on language learners' listening comprehension problems. *System, 28*, 55–75. 10.1016/S0346-251X(99)00060-3

Graham, S. (2006). Listening comprehension: The learners' perspective. *System, 34*(2), 165–182. 10.1016/j.system.2005.11.00

Graham, S., & Macaro, E. (2008). Strategy instruction in listening for lower-intermediate learners of French. *Language Learning, 58*(4), 747–783. 10.1111/j.1467-9922.2008.00478.x

Graham, S., & Santos, D. (2015). *Strategies for second language listening: Current scenarios and improved pedagogy.* Palgrave Macmillan.

Graham, S., & Santos, D. (2020) Becoming a good teacher of listening. In C. Griffiths & Z. Tajeddin (Eds.), *Lessons from good language teachers* (pp. 246–259). Cambridge University Press.

Graham, S., Santos, D., & Francis-Brophy, E. (2014). Teacher beliefs about listening in a foreign language. *Teaching and Teacher Education, 40*, 44–60. 10.1016/j.tate.2014.01.007

Graham, S., Woore, R., Porter, A., Courtney, L., & Savory, C. (2020). Navigating the challenges of L2 reading: Self-efficacy, self-regulatory reading strategies, and learner profiles. *The Modern Language Journal, 104*, 693–714. 10.1111/modl.12670

Hoang, T. (2018). Teacher self-efficacy research in English as a foreign language contexts: A systematic review. *Asia TEFL, 15*(4), 976–990. 10.18823/asiatefl.2018.15.4.6.976

Karimi, M. N., Abdullahi, K., & Haghighi, J. K. (2016). English as a foreign language teachers' self-efficacy as a determinant of correspondence between their professed orientations towards reading and their reading instructional practices. *Innovation in Language Learning and Teaching, 10*(3), 155–170. 10.1080/17501229.2014.920847

Kassem, H. M. (2015). The Relationship between listening strategies used by Egyptian EFL college sophomores and their listening comprehension and self-efficacy. *English Language Teaching, 8*(2), 153–169. 10.5539/elt.v8n2p153

Lau, K. L. (2017). Strategy use, listening problems, and motivation of high-and low-proficiency Chinese listeners. *The Journal of Educational Research, 110*, 503–514. 10.1080/00220671.2015.1134421

Locke, T., & Johnston, M. (2016). Developing an individual and collective self-efficacy scale for the teaching of writing in high schools. *Assessing Writing, 28*, 1–14. 10.1016/j.asw.2016.01.001

Mills, N., Pajares, F., & Herron, C. (2006). A reevaluation of the role of anxiety: Self-efficacy, anxiety, and their relation to reading and listening proficiency. *Foreign Language Annals, 39*(2), 276–295. 10.1111/j.1944-9720.2006.tb02266.x

Pajares, F. (2009). Motivational role of self-efficacy beliefs in self-regulated learning. In D. H. Schunk & B. J. Zimmerman (Eds.), *Motivation and self-regulated learning: Theory, research, and applications* (pp. 111–139). Routledge.

Phan, N. T. T. & Locke, T. (2015). Sources of self-efficacy of Vietnamese EFL teachers: A qualitative study. *Teaching and Teacher Education, 52,* 73–82. 10.1016/j.tate.2015.09.006

Razmi, M. H., Jabbari, A. A., & Zare, S. (2021). An investigation into perfectionism, self-efficacy, metacognitive strategy use, and second language listening comprehension: A path analysis approach. *Journal of Teaching Language Skills, 40,* 119–159. 10.22099/jtls.2021.40272.2977

Santos, D., & Graham, S. (2018). What teachers say about listening and its pedagogy: A comparison between two countries. In A. Burns & J. Siegel (Eds.), *International perspectives on teaching the four skills in ELT* (pp. 21–35). Palgrave Macmillan. 10.1007/978-3-319-63444-9_2

Siegel, J. (2014). Exploring L2 listening instruction: Examinations of practice. *ELT Journal.* 10.1093/elt/cct058

Siegel, J. (2015). *Exploring listening strategy instruction through action research.* Palgrave MacMillan.

Simasangyaporn, N. (2016). The effect of listening strategy instruction on Thai learners' self-efficacy, English listening comprehension and reported use of listening strategies. (PhD), Reading, Retrieved from http://centaur.reading.ac.uk/68649/1/21028113_Simasangyaporn_thesis.pdf

Siwatu, K. O. (2011). Preservice teachers' sense of preparedness and self-efficacy to teach in America's urban and suburban schools: Does context matter?, *Teaching and Teacher Education, 27,* 357–365. 10.1016/j.tate.2010.09.004

Staples, S., & Biber, D. (2015). Cluster analysis. In L. Plonsky (Ed.), *Advancing quantitative methods in second language research* (pp. 243–274). Routledge.

Tabrizi, H. M., & Saeidi, M. (2015). The relationship among Iranian EFL learners' self-efficacy, autonomy and listening comprehension ability. *English Language Teaching.* 10.5539/elt.v8n12p158

Teng, M. F., Wang, C., & Wu, J. G. (2021). Metacognitive strategies, language learning motivation, self-efficacy belief, and English achievement during remote learning: A structural equation modelling approach. *RELC Journal,* 1–19. 10.1177/00336882211040268

Tschannen-Moran, M., & Hoy, A. W. (2001). Teacher efficacy: Capturing an elusive construct. *Teaching and Teacher Education, 17*(7), 783–805. 10.1016/S0742-051X(01)00036-1

Tschannen-Moran, M., & Johnson, D. (2011). Exploring literacy teachers' self-efficacy beliefs: Potential sources at play. *Teaching and Teacher Education, 27,* 751–761. 10.1016/j.tate.2010.12.005

Vafaee, P., & Suzuki, Y. (2020). The relative significance of syntactic knowledge and vocabulary knowledge in second language listening ability. *Studies in Second Language Acquisition, 42,* 383–410. 10.1017/S0272263119000676

Vandergrift, L. (2003). Orchestrating strategy use: Toward a model of the skilled second language listener. *Language Learning, 53,* 463–496. 10.1111/1467-9922.00232

Vandergrift, L., & Baker, S. (2015). Learner variables in second language listening comprehension: An exploratory path analysis. *Language Learning*, *65*, 390–416. 10.1111/lang.12105

Wallace, M. P. (2022). Individual differences in second language listening: Examining the role of knowledge, metacognitive awareness, memory, and attention. *Language Learning*, *72*, 5–44. 10.1111/lang.12424

Wong, M. S. L. (2005). Language learning strategies and language self-efficacy: Investigating the relationship in Malaysia. *RELC Journal*, *36*, 245–269. 10.1177/0033688205060050

Wyatt, M. (2010). An English teacher's developing self-efficacy beliefs in using groupwork. *System*, *38*(4), 603–613. 10.1016/j.system.2010.09.012

Wyatt, M. (2013). Overcoming low self-efficacy beliefs in teaching English to young learners. *International Journal of Qualitative Studies in Education*, *26*(2), 238–255. 10.1080/09518398.2011.605082

Wyatt, M. (2018a). Language teachers' self-efficacy beliefs: An introduction. In S. Mercer & A. Kostoulas (Eds.), *Language teacher psychology*. Multilingualism Matters.

Wyatt, M. (2018b). Language teachers' self-efficacy beliefs: A review of the literature (2005–2016). *Australian Journal of Teacher Education*, *43*(4), 92–120. 10.14221/ajte.2018v43n4.6

Wyatt, M. (2021). Research into second language learners' and teachers' self-efficacy beliefs: Making the connections. *TESOL Quarterly*, *55*(1), 296–307. 10.1002/tesq.3010

Xu, J., Fan, J., & Luo, K. (2021). Exploring L2 listening instruction, self-efficacy, and strategy use: A mediation analysis. *Frontiers in Psychology*, *12*, 758757. 10.3389/fpsyg.2021.758757

Xue, Y. (2022). The role of EFL teachers' self-efficacy and emotional resilience in appraisal of learners' success. *Frontiers in Psychology*. 10.3389/fpsyg.2021.817388

# 11 Changes in the academic writing self-efficacy beliefs of students in transition from high school to an English medium instruction university programme in Japan

*Oliver Hadingham and Gene Thompson*

## Introduction

English Medium Instruction (EMI) has swiftly become a central feature of higher education globally and students' ability to cope with the transition to EMI tertiary study is an emerging research focus. EMI refers to the teaching of academic subjects (e.g., history, engineering, science) via English in countries where English is not the primary locally used language (Macaro et al., 2018). Language learning is generally not a stated educational goal for EMI (Curle et al., 2020); however, it is often desired and anticipated (Pecorari & Malmstrom, 2018) and can represent a key reason to embark on EMI study. Research has suggested that learners who choose to study via EMI at university may have dual purposes of improving their English and studying content via English (see Galloway et al., 2017). EMI provision is gaining traction across Asia (Macaro et al., 2018), particularly in Japan (Bradford, 2020), the setting of the current study. Due to governmental support, EMI programmes are being offered at around 40% of universities in Japan (Bradford et al., 2022).

The rapid growth of EMI has outstripped empirical research (Macaro et al., 2018); however, extant research indicates that many university students have little prior exposure to English-medium classes before entering university (see Curle et al., 2020), and many EMI programmes fail to specify any English language proficiency attainment for enrolment or set them purposely low to attract applicants (Irie, 2019). This issue is particularly common in Japan (Bradford, 2020), where students transitioning to EMI programmes are faced with a taxing adjustment (Richards & Pun, 2021). Studies on school-university "transition" thus far have revealed that writing academically is a key difficulty for students entering EMI programmes, although language-related "challenges" may also be discipline-specific (Curle et al., 2020).

DOI: 10.4324/9781003379300-14

Research into EMI learner self-efficacy has suggested that learner beliefs may contribute to success in EMI study (e.g., Soruç et al., 2022; Thompson et al., 2022a, 2022b) as stronger self-efficacy is associated with greater effort in relation to the challenges of studying via a second language (Thompson et al., 2022a). Thus far, however, few studies have examined learners' self-efficacy beliefs as they transition to EMI learning contexts. This suggests that research is needed into the nature, strength, and development of EMI students' academic self-efficacy beliefs, and how these beliefs link with the academic difficulties experienced at EMI transition. The current study responds by examining the self-efficacy beliefs of freshman EMI students at a university in Japan with respect to academic writing during their first semester of transitioning to an EMI social science degree programme.

## Background to the study

Self-efficacy research probes beliefs about the ability to "organize and execute the course of action required to produce given attainments" (Bandura, 1997, p. 3). People feel efficacious towards different tasks under different circumstances. Research has shown that self-efficacy beliefs mediate the choices, effort, and motivation of students (Pajares, 1996). Self-efficacy beliefs are both changeable and malleable (Bong & Skaalvik, 2003), indicating that if teachers can help their learners to develop skills and stronger self-beliefs, students may be better placed to invest time and put forth greater effort into their studies.

Meta-analyses from the field of educational psychology demonstrate that self-efficacy is strongly related to academic performance (e.g., Stajkovic et al., 2018). Studies have also shown that the self-efficacy beliefs of L2 language learners are positively related to achievement (Mills et al., 2007). Researchers probing L2 English writing self-efficacy (e.g., Wang & Sun, 2020) have revealed that L2 writing self-efficacy predicts L2 writing outcomes. For example, a recent meta-analysis of 76 studies relating to L1 and L2 English writing self-efficacy (Sun et al., 2021) indicated that the relationship between writing self-efficacy and writing achievement ($r = .441$) is stronger for L2 writers than for L1 writers ($r = .233$).

Research into L2 writing self-efficacy in English for Academic Purposes (EAP) in East Asian contexts is growing. A study of master's students in China (Zhang, 2018) suggested initial low self-efficacy stemmed from limited experience of academic writing and low English proficiency. However, students' self-efficacy beliefs did strengthen over the one-semester EAP course, with the goal-oriented pedagogy seen as fuelling it. A recent study (Zhou et al., 2022) identified a strengthening of engineering students' self-efficacy beliefs regarding source use, supported by an EAP course that facilitated sufficient mastery experiences.

However, the Japan EAP context is less researched. Nevertheless, Ruegg's (2018) pre-/post-treatment questionnaire revealed that over a one-year period students who received teacher feedback on essay drafts increased their writing self-efficacy more than those who only received peer feedback. Moreover, a study of an EMI support programme (Thompson, 2018) found that business students' self-efficacy beliefs differed according to the type of EAP task/activity. Past experiences seemingly weighed heavily on students' beliefs, with self-efficacy weaker for tasks deemed difficult and for those where limited practice was available.

Self-efficacy research has recently extended to EMI contexts, with links found between learners' self-efficacy beliefs and success (e.g., Soruç et al., 2022; Thompson et al., 2022a, 2022b). For example, in one study from Japan, Thompson et al. (2022a) found that self-efficacy, alongside L2 proficiency, was a direct predictor of success in an International Business course for students enroled in a bilingual business programme. Another study from Japan revealed a positive relationship (albeit weak) between self-efficacy beliefs and academic achievement in an undergraduate finance course (Thompson et al., 2022b).

Elsewhere, limited L2 proficiency has been found to have a negative impact. EMI learners in China were found to have lower self-efficacy beliefs for their ability to achieve a high grade in an EMI course than in a Chinese-medium course (Rose et al., 2020). A study of writing self-efficacy beliefs among freshman EMI physics students in Finland ($n = 74$) (Mendoza et al., 2022) revealed that students with higher self-efficacy beliefs were concerned less with the mechanics of academic writing than with the writing process generally; those with lower levels of self-efficacy stressed linguistic difficulties, their limited experience, and a desire for feedback.

Research into EMI self-efficacy thus far (e.g., Soruç et al., 2022; Thompson et al., 2022a, 2022b) has tended to be cross-sectional in nature, that is, studies have examined a one-time 'snapshot' of self-efficacy and have not explored the potential for efficacy change over time. Another limitation is the usage of general measures of self-efficacy (e.g., Thompson et al. 2022a), rather than task-specific measures, as recommended and used in other studies (Mills et al., 2007; Thompson, 2018; Wyatt, 2022). The current study addresses these limitations by longitudinally exploring self-efficacy development towards academic writing.

This focus could be valuable, since research has indicated that language-related challenges surround the school-university transition for EMI students (Curle et al., 2020). Among specific language-related EMI challenges, academic writing is among the most keenly felt by university students (Evans & Morrison, 2011), although, in certain contexts, listening and reading may present more difficulties (Curle et al., 2020). Consequently, language support is becoming a core feature of EMI degree programmes. The nature, length, availability, and content of support courses vary depending on the support model chosen by the university (Richards & Pun, 2021) but most provide EAP and sometimes English for Specific Purposes (ESP) courses geared towards giving students "enough English, and the right English, to succeed in learning their subjects through the medium of English" (Hyland & Hamp-Lyons, 2002, p. 2).

Academic writing tuition features heavily in such support programmes (Curle et al., 2020). This is understandable given its centrality to university study and the challenge of meeting specific linguistic and disciplinary demands. Writing within the social sciences (including in the EMI major of the participants in the present study) blends empiricism and interpretation, and involves much synthesis and analysis (Hyland, 2006). Learning to craft writing into such a genre is no easy task. As Hyland (2015, p. 57) reminds us, academic writing is "no one's first language". Students transitioning to EMI study might therefore not feel particularly efficacious about writing academically via their L2.

Such concerns may be justified. According to Hinkel (2011, p. 535), "shortfalls of writers' language proficiencies and restricted linguistic repertoire ... significantly undermine L2 writers' ability to produce high-quality text". For Japanese L2 English students, this issue may be compounded by the fact that writing remains a neglected skill in Japan's English language curriculum (Yasuda, 2014) as high school curricula are geared towards the L2 reading and listening demands of the high-stakes university entrance exams. Accordingly, students have limited exposure to writing multiple-paragraph compositions (Kobayashi & Rinnert, 2002) and scant writing instruction (Hirose, 2005). As a result, it is hardly surprising that 72% of high school students from 6 universities across Japan ($n = 481$) felt unprepared for university written tasks (Yasuda, 2014). Given the importance of perceptions of past successful performance (i.e., enactive mastery) in developing self-efficacy beliefs (Bandura, 1997), students transitioning to EMI learning contexts may have very few actual experiences of academic writing, let alone experiences perceived to be successful. This makes the transition experience of key importance as it may be a vital source of information driving efficacy beliefs development. The current study addresses this issue by examining EMI learners' self-efficacy beliefs towards academic writing during their transition to EMI study.

Few studies have explored Japanese learner self-efficacy in a longitudinal fashion. An intervention study of reading (McLean & Poulshock, 2018) traced efficacy beliefs over an eight-week treatment period, finding that those students who set a word target appeared to become more self-efficacious readers. Leeming (2017) examined L2 speaking self-efficacy beliefs over eight time-points through a freshman academic year. Overall, speaking self-efficacy beliefs strengthened, although there was marked variation between students' initial self-efficacy and its development trajectory. Those of lower language proficiency started with weaker self-efficacy but after one academic year, their self-efficacy had surpassed that of their more linguistically proficient peers. Leeming attributes this to the generally low self-efficacy levels among participants at enrolment, a consequence of not gaining much L2 speaking practice at high school, making gains relatively easy from such a low base. A structured syllabus, regular positive feedback, and a general acclimatization to university life may also have contributed to self-efficacy beliefs growth. These studies have shown how self-efficacy beliefs change for Japanese language learners. However, there is a lack of longitudinal research on writing in this national context.

In summary, the current study addresses the following gaps in the research literature. Although there is a large amount of research into EMI learners' beliefs and attitudes, including self-efficacy, there are few longitudinal studies, and more research is needed into the experience of learners transitioning to EMI (Macaro et al., 2018). Research into EMI learners thus far has been limited by cross-sectional designs and the usage of general measures of self-efficacy lacking in domain- and task-specificity (e.g., Soruç et al., 2022; Thompson et al., 2022a, 2022b). Self-efficacy beliefs appear as one variable among others in shaping EMI success; however, few studies have addressed how efficacy beliefs may change or develop for learners entering EMI contexts, particularly with respect to writing among students in Japan. The current study addresses these gaps by exploring the development of EMI learners' self-efficacy beliefs towards writing during transition to EMI. It addresses the following research questions:

1 To what extent does academic writing self-efficacy change over the first semester for students transitioning to EMI?
2 How do students perceive their efficacy to change over the first semester of their transition to an EMI learning environment?

## Methodology

This study adopts a longitudinal, mixed methods design in which quantitative and qualitative data sources were gathered simultaneously and analysed in parallel. This offered a means of obtaining complementary data that can "yield deeper, broader, and more insightful" analyses (Greene, 2015, p. 614), thereby strengthening the credibility of findings (Creswell, 2022). It draws on questionnaire data collected at four time-points from 40 students, interview data collected at three time-points and analysis of journal entries completed by students across the semester. This study is focused on the learners' first semester after entering the EMI university due to findings

*Academic writing self-efficacy at an EMI university in Japan* 225

from previous studies (e.g., Aizawa & Rose, 2020) that suggest that transitional challenges may be strongest during this initial semester.

*Setting and participants*

A total of 40 first-year undergraduate students from a social sciences EMI programme at a private university in Tokyo agreed to participate in the study (see Table 11.1). The university is considered relatively prestigious; it was established more than 100 years ago and has an acceptance rate of approximately 12–15% of entrance examination test takers. All participants were L1 Japanese speakers who had received six years of L2 English language instruction at L1-mediated high schools in Japan. Participants provided their scores on the Computerized Assessment System for English Communication (CASEC) test taken at entry, ranging from CEFR A2 to CEFR B2. Most had a CEFR level of B1 ($n = 21$) and B2 ($n = 15$), although a small number ($n = 4$) tested at the A2 level. Students in the EMI programme complete a preparatory curriculum of EAP courses during their first year before starting EMI study in their second year. All freshmen take two academic writing classes per week during their first university semester, alongside other skills-focused classes on reading, listening, and speaking.

*Instruments and data collection*

The study analyses the following sets of data, which were collected at various points during the first semester:

- 'EMI Writing Self-efficacy Scale' at four time-points Self-efficacy beliefs for 23 academic writing ($n = 40$)
- nine journal entries throughout the semester ($n = 40$)
- three semi-structured interviews with nine students at three time-points ($n = 9$)

*Table 11.1* Participant demographics

| Variable | Survey/journal participants (n = 40) Group | n | Ratio | Interview participants (n = 9) Group | n | Ratio |
|---|---|---|---|---|---|---|
| Gender | Female | 23 | 57% | Female | 6 | 66.6% |
|  | Male | 17 | 43% | Male | 3 | 33.3% |
| Age | 18 | 18 | 45% | 18 | 5 | 55% |
|  | 19 | 22 | 55% | 19 | 4 | 45% |
| English proficiency level (based on CASEC score) | A2 | 4 | 10% | A2 | 1 | 10% |
|  | B1 | 21 | 52.5% | B1 | 4 | 45% |
|  | B2 | 15 | 37.5% | B2 | 4 | 45% |

The *EMI Writing Self-efficacy Scale* was administered at four time-points (T1-4) through the semester (Weeks 3, 7, 10, 14). The 23-item scale (Table 11.2) was adapted from the 15-item Writing Challenges scale used in prominent EMI transition studies (e.g., Evans & Morrison, 2011; Aizawa & Rose, 2020). Items were changed by writing them in a 'can do' format, following Bandura (2006), and participants were asked to express their confidence towards each task on a 0–100 response scale. Eight additional items (16–23) were added, based on feedback and consultation from 10 EAP and content faculty members of the institution, who were considered experts with respect to the learning context (see Thompson, 2020, for a discussion of how an expert panel can be utilized to support scale design). The additional items (e.g., item 23 on specialist academic vocabulary) represent skills considered important for the learners in this context. After piloting the survey with 20 students from a previous cohort at the institution, the survey was administered to participants in the current study electronically via *Qualtrics* at each of the four time-points. Internal reliability of the scale was evaluated using

*Table 11.2* Self-efficacy beliefs for 23 academic writing skills

| Academic writing skill<br>To what extent do you believe you can successfully …? | T1 | T2 | T3 | T4 |
|---|---|---|---|---|
| | | Mean scores | | |
| Plan written assignments | 48.02 | 49.56 | 46.34 | 48.02 |
| Express ideas in correct English | 41.59 | 48.17 | 44.51 | 44.22 |
| Revise written work | 46.71 | 50.54 | 44.54 | 46.34 |
| Use appropriate academic style | 43.46 | 46 | 42.27 | 43.56 |
| Write a bibliography references section | 47.81 | 47.42 | 41.98 | 43.73 |
| Proofread written work | 51.85 | 48.44 | 48.49 | 44.9 |
| Refer to sources in written work | 52.32 | 55 | 44.44 | 46.59 |
| Summarize and paraphrase ideas in sources | 50.34 | 44.27 | 42.88 | 45.42 |
| Organize ideas in coherent paragraphs | 47.68 | 46.85 | 42.49 | 44.34 |
| Express ideas clearly and logically | 45.85 | 47.88 | 41.44 | 42.22 |
| Link ideas from different sources | 53.02 | 53.02 | 45.46 | 49.15 |
| Write the introduction to an assignment | 51.88 | 50.39 | 47.02 | 49.02 |
| Write the body of an assignment | 49.12 | 49.68 | 45.61 | 46.93 |
| Write the conclusion to an assignment | 51.59 | 52.54 | 49.66 | 48.49 |
| Link sentences smoothly | 46.1 | 43.2 | 42.29 | 48.24 |
| Quote from sources | 53.29 | 48.63 | 48.671 | 48.61 |
| Use evidence to support your ideas | 51.22 | 52.2 | 46.02 | 43.78 |
| Use reporting verbs and nouns to introduce information from sources | 43.78 | 43.78 | 43.05 | 44.85 |
| Give an appropriate title | 53.46 | 53.15 | 53.68 | 55.32 |
| Explain ideas and issues in the essay | 50.54 | 53.05 | 47.24 | 48.83 |
| Use your professor's comments and feedback | 56.29 | 60.9 | 54.29 | 56.76 |
| Use academic vocabulary in your essay | 41.71 | 43.56 | 40.9 | 40.05 |
| Use social science vocabulary in your essay | 38.17 | 40.12 | 40.49 | 40.39 |

Cronbach's alpha coefficient procedure, showing a value of .96 (time-point 1); .96 (time-point 2); .98 (time-point 3); and .98 (time-point 4).

Participants completed 9 journal entries of 200–300 words focused on their perceptions of their writing development, and all agreed to allow the first researcher to analyse these in the current study. The regular recording and reflection on everyday experiences and thoughts across time provided a "contextualized and individualized account" (Rose, 2019, p. 349) of student perceptions. The journals explored two themes. "Event contingent" journal entries captured feelings, thoughts, and experiences of a particular event (e.g., a graded written task, a new skill practised) as close to the corresponding class or homework activities as permitted (Rose, 2019). An example of an event contingent theme is the following journal prompt used: *How do you feel after getting back your first graded report this morning? How has the feedback and grade influenced your confidence about your writing skills?* (Week 7 – Journal 4). "Interval contingent" entries charted perceptions and beliefs at a key point of the semester (e.g., the halfway stage, the final week). For instance, one interval contingent journal theme used the following prompt: *You have reached the end of your first university semester. How confident are you now as an essay writer compared to your first week at university?* (Week 14 – Journal 9).

A total of nine students were selected and agreed to participate in semi-structured interviews conducted at three time-points through the semester, using prompts/questions from Aizawa and Rose (2020), such as "*What are some of the difficulties in taking university courses in English?*" and "*Which aspects of academic English would you like to improve the most? Why?*" The selection of interview participants ($n = 9$) was "information-oriented" (Brinkmann, 2013), that is guided by the desire to capture the experiences of students of differing proficiency levels, and therefore the interview participant demographics generally align with those from the wider sample (Table 11.1). Interviews were conducted in remote format, recorded, and transcribed verbatim by the first author of the study. Illustrative examples presented below have been edited to correct grammatical errors for reader-friendliness.

*Data analyses*

To respond to research question 1, descriptive statistics were produced for the questionnaire responses from each time-point for each of the 23 items and analysed in terms of the strength of students' writing self-efficacy beliefs for different skills. The average value for the entire scale for each participant at each time-point was calculated, alongside descriptive statistics and boxplots for the average at each time-point. A repeated-measures ANOVA analysis was conducted to explore whether there was a significant change in writing self-efficacy beliefs (on average for the entire group) over the semester. The dataset was also examined to identify patterns for each student, and these were grouped together based on common elements (e.g., consistent growth).

To respond to research question 2 and gain a deeper understanding of results from the quantitative analyses, a qualitative content analysis was conducted on the journal and interview data due to the need for "context-sensitive interpretation of data" (Selvi, 2019, p. 443) and the demonstrated utility of this analytical method in prior studies of student self-efficacy beliefs (e.g., Thompson et al., 2022b). Coding was carried out using NVivo 12 Pro. Initial deductive coding was conducted by coding via categories from existing research (e.g., Aizawa & Rose, 2020). Codes were then grouped into themes in an inductive manner to show patterns across the dataset.

## Results

### Research question 1: To what extent does academic writing self-efficacy change over the first semester for students transitioning to EMI?

Table 11.2 shows the overall mean self-efficacy scores for each of the 23 academic writing skills. Generally, there was a pattern of weakening/fluctuating efficacy over the course of the semester for each of the efficacy items. At each time-point, self-efficacy beliefs were strongest towards using one's professor's comments and feedback. Student efficacy beliefs were generally weakest towards using academic and social science vocabulary.

As shown in Table 11.3, a similar pattern of fluctuating self-efficacy was observed in the average value of self-efficacy for the academic writing scale over the four time-points. Efficacy initially rose slightly, then fell at the mid-semester, before rising slightly again at Time 4. Overall, average student self-efficacy fell over the course of the semester, with a value of 47.70 at Time 4 in comparison to 51.06 at the start of the semester. As shown by minimum and maximum scores and the range at each time-point, there was a wide variation in self-efficacy amongst the participants.

A repeated-measures ANOVA (analysis of variance) was conducted to observe trends in average self-efficacy over the four time-points. Assumptions were confirmed: No outliers were identified, and there were no variables with Skew or Kurtosis values above 2 (Table 11.3), indicating no substantial

*Table 11.3* Descriptive statistics for writing self-efficacy by time-point

| Time-point | n | Mean | SD | Median | Min | Max | Range | Skew | Kurtosis |
|---|---|---|---|---|---|---|---|---|---|
| T1 | 40 | 51.06 | 11.84 | 51.74 | 19.35 | 84.70 | 65.34 | .22 | 1.88 |
| T2 | 40 | 51.33 | 12.73 | 54.13 | 16.00 | 72.65 | 56.65 | .91 | -.88 |
| T3 | 40 | 46.81 | 14.30 | 49.22 | 16.22 | 74.65 | 58.43 | .61 | -.21 |
| T4 | 40 | 47.70 | 15.0 | 48.43 | 19.09 | 78.00 | 58.91 | .17 | .57 |

*Academic writing self-efficacy at an EMI university in Japan* 229

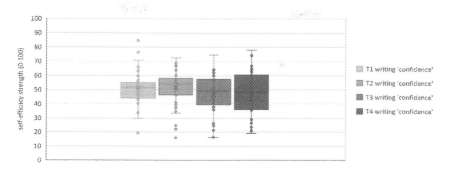

*Figure 11.1* Boxplot graphs for writing self-efficacy mean scores.

departure from normality. The six values identified as outliers, as shown in Figure 11.1, did not have $z$ scores above 3, and were included in the study following Leys et al. (2013). Mauchly's Test of Sphericity indicated the assumption of sphericity had been violated, $\chi 2(5) = 23.364$, $p = < .001$. Therefore, a Greenhouse–Geisser correction was applied ($\varepsilon = 0.606$). No statistically significant changes in "writing self-efficacy" over time were identified, $F(2.104, 82.046) = 1.534$, p .221, partial $\eta 2 = 0.038$.

However, as shown by the boxplots for each time-point (Figure 11.1), there was a growing variation in average self-efficacy belief values as the semester unfolded, indicated by a widening in the standard deviation values for the mean scores at each time-point (Table 11.3). As the boxplot graphs reveal, at Times 1 and 2, although mean self-efficacy score were higher ($M = 51.06/51.33$) there was less variation in students' self-efficacy beliefs ($SD = 11.84/12.73$) than at Times 3 and 4, where there was much wider variation ($SD = 14.30/15$). This implies that some students experienced a strengthening of writing self-efficacy beliefs, and others a weakening.

Patterns of change for each student were examined revealing four patterns of efficacy change for the student cohort: Consistent fall ($n = 2$, T1–T4 avg. change = –20); Fluctuating downward ($n = 23$, T1–T4 avg. change = –16); Fluctuating up ($n = 14$, T1–T4 avg. change = 18); and Consistent growth ($n = 1$, T1–T4 avg. change = 22). Most students had fluctuating efficacy, with 23 moving in a downwards direction (i.e., experiencing growth between at least two time-points but overall falling across the semester) and 14 moving in a positive direction from T1 to T4 (i.e., experiencing a fall between at least two time-points but overall increasing across the semester). Although the results from Table 11.3 indicate that efficacy was generally falling for most students over the semester, it is important to note that only 11 of the 40 students rated their efficacy lowest at T4. A total of 10 students had their lowest rating at T1, 7 at T2, and 12 at T3.

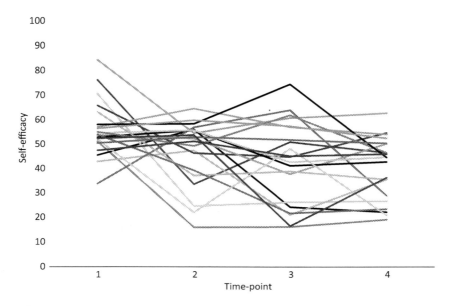

*Figure 11.2* Pattern of efficacy change for "Fluctuating downward" group.

The mid-semester time-points were commonly the low point for student self-efficacy; approximately three-quarters of the participants reported stronger efficacy at T4 from their lowest point in the semester. To represent this pattern, Figure 11.2 shows the individual variations for those in the "Fluctuating downward" group, while Figure 11.3 represents those in the "Fluctuating up" group.

***Research question 2: How do students perceive their efficacy change over the first semester of their transition to an EMI learning environment?-***

Findings from the qualitative content analysis of journals and interviews revealed similar patterns to the quantitative analyses presented above. Regarding specific dimensions of academic writing, student self-efficacy beliefs were weakest towards writing long essays (journals: $n = 26$), the novelty of using an academic style (journals: $n = 13$/interviews: $n = 9$), and the vocabulary-intensive nature of academic writing ($n = 36/n = 12$). The EAP course did not transform students' self-efficacy beliefs but rather led many to reflect upon their skills and assumptions about the challenge of university-level writing, and their lack of skills and preparedness towards the task. Contextual and individual factors (primarily reflections upon personal experiences) had a bearing on the degree of perceived change in self-efficacy

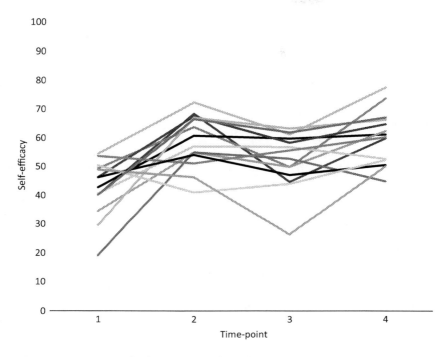

*Figure 11.3* Pattern of efficacy change for "Fluctuating up" group.

beliefs experienced. Broadly, two trends emerged in the dataset: (1) Some students appeared to have underestimated the difficulty of academic writing and been over-efficacious; (2) others perceived themselves to be coping (often imperfectly) with the demands of academic writing at the university level, resulting in perceptions of skills development and stronger self-beliefs. We report results below using illustrative examples with the participant number, CEFR level of language proficiency (e.g., B1), source of information (e.g., journal entry 1 = J1), and grouping (e.g., fluctuating down).

*Theme 1: Underestimating the difficulty of academic writing*

The first key theme relates to student perceptions of task difficulty and their capability to deal with academic writing challenges. This was commonly identified in the fluctuating down group with one student noting in her third journal entry that she was "saddened by the many things I can't do" (Student 5, A2, J3, fluctuating down). As the semester progressed, several students focused on the gaps between their experiences at high school and academic writing at the university level, discussing differences as they noticed the changed pedagogy and expectations. For example, Student 25 (B2, J6, fluctuating down) explained that:

> in high school, the topic of essays that teachers gave me was too easy for me and I felt a little bored. I had a lot of time to spare. In contrast to them, the topic of academic writing in college is too hard for me to finish with plenty of time. So, I cannot state my purpose and ideas clearly.

Other students discussed other differences between their experience of writing at high school and university, suggesting that the onus at university was more on to "find and solve problems myself using facts as evidence" (Student 23, B2, fluctuating down), making the task more difficult than they had expected.

As was shown in Table 11.3 above, there was fluctuation in self-efficacy at different time-points, with student efficacy weakening from T2 to T3 on average. This period matched with the structure in the course from paragraph writing to essay writing, leading many students to reassess their efficacy due to a stronger understanding of the difficulty of specific tasks such as smoothly connecting ideas, quoting outside sources, and referencing sources. For example, one participant explained:

> I may be confused about the way of writing an English essay and reference list. For example, in a long English essay, I often miss what I intend to convey to the reader ... I have little confidence in my writing an English final essay (Student 24, B2, J9, fluctuating down).

Another participant discussed their difficulty with using outside sources:

> Another reason which explains my confidence going down is the aspect of using sources ... I thought summarizing and quoting are easy at first because I experienced and practiced that when I was a high school student. But I was wrong. Therefore, I will have to practice those aspects harder. It makes my confidence less but it could be a chance to improve myself (Student 11, B2, J9, fluctuating down).

In summary, this theme captured a perception in respondents that the reality of academic writing was more difficult than anticipated. As shown below, this did not prevent them from also perceiving a sense of efficacy development. Two forces appeared to be at work as students both grappled with their understanding of the requirements of academic writing and developed skills to tackle them.

## Theme 2: Perceiving skill development (and stronger self-efficacy)

The second theme concerns the pattern of development in academic writing self-efficacy beliefs. Students generally attributed a strengthening of their self-efficacy beliefs to their enhanced skills as writers (e.g., greater competence at writing in a disciplinary-specific way, knowing how to cite sources correctly) and the practice activities (e.g., source integration tasks, paraphrasing exercises). Interestingly, many students considered writing the journal as an aid in their efficacy development. Within this theme, there were two common elements, with students suggesting that they were (1) coping (imperfectly) with the demands of academic writing; yet still (2) nevertheless perceived their skills to be improving.

For some, perceived developments in self-efficacy beliefs had a brittle quality. Many students still battled with negative physiological arousal: "My confidence in academic writing skills developed a little compared to myself in April, but I am feeling a little nervous, too" (Student 10, J9, fluctuating down); "I became more confident than at the beginning, but I still have a lot of anxiety" (Student 5, A2, J3, fluctuating down). Nearing the semester halfway mark students felt their self-efficacy beliefs had strengthened but only incrementally. One student explained their doubts as they perceived development in their skills but still grappled with the difficulty of the task:

> I understand what academic writing is and how to write it, but I'm not used to it because I've only written it for a few months. There are many academic writing rules, and I haven't learned the rules yet, so it's too academic [i.e., too theoretical] for me. Writing is still difficult and it seems difficult to be confident (Student 5, A2, J6, fluctuating down).

Others similarly acknowledged that their increased familiarity with academic writing had strengthened their self-efficacy beliefs. As Student 30 (B1, J6, fluctuating down) admitted, through this course "I gradually comprehend how to write". One of her peers explained,

> I have confidence about academic writing because I get used to academic writing ... I overcame some difficulties so that I can hold I am confident about academic writing (Student 19, B1, J9, fluctuating up).

By the end of the semester, many students recognized a strengthening of self-efficacy beliefs "little by little" (Student 33, B2, J9, fluctuating up), albeit often partial and specific to certain task-based aspects of academic writing. One student admitted that as she began to enjoy the process of writing academically her "academic writing confidence developed" (Student 20, B2, J9, fluctuating up). Student 36 (A2, J9, fluctuating up) confessed he still did not enjoy writing but acknowledged that his writing self-efficacy beliefs had developed incrementally as he had "challenged [i.e., practised] many tasks to improve [his] writing skills".

In summary, the qualitative data reveals that students sensed that developing writing self-efficacy was a gradual and piecemeal process, with many reassessing their efficacy as they experienced the reality of writing at the university level. Although the survey averages were relatively similar, journal entries indicate perceptions of increasing confidence overall. An adjustment journey had begun:

> I felt that the contents of class were above my ability and spent days challenging myself. As a result, I can now write an academic essay by using my developed skills and it gives me more confidence in Week 13 (Student 17, B1, J9, fluctuating down).

## Discussion

The findings suggest that the transition to academic writing at the university level led to re-evaluations and fluctuations in self-efficacy beliefs for the students in this study over the semester. Similar to Thompson (2018), two key factors were identified for the students in this study, as the learners (1) reassessed their efficacy against the difficulty of the task and (2) perceived positive growth in their self-efficacy beliefs from practice activities. The combination of these two factors led to average values of self-efficacy weakening through the second half of the semester for the group overall, with greater variation appearing in self-efficacy between participants.

Self-efficacy beliefs are rooted in experience; they are "not fabricated out of thin air" (Bandura, 1997, p. 60). Findings indicate that the relatively stronger initial self-efficacy ratings from some students were based on cognitive assessment of tasks largely based on their school writing experiences. As their preparatory writing course was initially geared to mastering the paragraph, students may have equated their perceptions of success (i.e., mastery experiences) from writing paragraphs at the high school level with stronger judgments of self-efficacy beliefs. However, this early self-efficacy had an elevated quality for some participants, as students were not fully aware of the actual demands of academic writing. As Bandura (1997, p. 83) has pointed out, "ambiguity about task demands adds an element of uncertainty in the appraisal of personal efficacy". Their perceptions of success were limited initially, and task difficulty was partially deduced "from the perceived similarity to other activities for which the difficulty and requisite skills are better known" (1997, p. 83).

Evidence of a selective attention to elements of the paragraph compositions already mastered at school was apparent from journal entries, with many mentioning how confident they were in structuring a paragraph. Yet students gradually realized it was imperative for university writers to integrate and cite evidence and analyse and explain ideas, aspects not covered in the high school syllabus. Students' self-efficacy beliefs had a "hollow" nature at Times 1 and 2 as they were unaware of academic expectations; they may have also been basing their efficacy expectations on previous social comparisons from high school that did not translate to the relatively prestigious university environment they entered. Students appear to have underestimated the task demands, and this may explain the discrepancy between self-efficacy beliefs and performance in the graded tasks. An illustration comes from Student 13 (B2, J2, fluctuating down) who believed his "vocabulary" would be the key to his likely success. However, as the semester unfolded, he gradually found that vocabulary could be more challenging to *use* within academic essays. His self-efficacy was founded on his mastery experiences at school and inadequate knowledge of the performance level required of academic writing study. These findings provide evidence to support frameworks of efficacy assessment (e.g., Thompson, 2020) that emphasize the evaluation of task difficulty as a key initial step when assessing efficacy towards different tasks. It appears that familiarity with the task and knowledge of what is required for a successful performance are crucial for individuals aiming to accurately assess their self-efficacy beliefs.

Previous studies of EAP learners transitioning to EMI study have shown that *specific* task experience is an important source of information for efficacy development (Evans & Morrison, 2011; Thompson, 2018). Our results support such findings; as students tackled more specific academic skills (e.g., paraphrasing, summarizing, source integration, and citation), the true demands and expectations of university writing tasks became clearer. This fuelled changes in their writing self-efficacy beliefs, which students attributed to skills development from practice activities (i.e., mastery experiences) and feedback (i.e., social persuasion). In other words, when more challenging tasks were completed and feedback had been received, students' task-based confidence appeared to stabilize, strengthen, or weaken.

Overall, the semester appeared to be a period for students of identifying and re-appraising their skills against new demands. As the boxplot charts (Figure 11.1) of student averages make clear, students' self-efficacy beliefs became less uniform over the semester as they brought together more information about the different task demands and the skills that they perceived available to them. The efficacy "doubts" (Wyatt, 2014) that students experienced during this time led to efficacy beliefs bottoming out at timepoints 2 and 3 as the demands of academic writing were clarified, and performance feedback was received. For most students, the semester concluded with positive perceptions of competence towards specific tasks, leading to perceptions of efficacy development in their final journal entries.

These findings demonstrate, therefore, the value of a longitudinal design as a way of capturing the dynamic nature of efficacy assessment and development in contexts where self-efficacy beliefs for academic writing might fluctuate, for example in Japan as students transition to university.

## Pedagogical implications and conclusion

In tracing the trajectories of self-efficacy beliefs, our findings reveal how essential academic language support is for students embarking on EMI. For example, given the consistent weakness of student self-efficacy beliefs found in this study towards content-specific terms and vocabulary, one implication is that greater specificity is needed in EMI preparation programmes such as the one examined here. EAP provision is often criticized for being too generic (Galloway & Ruegg, 2020), and students may need opportunities to interact with content-specific terms bespoke to their specific field of study to develop their self-efficacy beliefs in creating academic texts. This may help lower proficiency students to navigate the transition to full EMI study (Rose, 2021), which is particularly pertinent in the Japanese context, where students less linguistically proficient may be joining EMI programmes.

Another pedagogic implication is that the instructional order may influence the developmental timeframe: the jump from instruction focused on writing at the paragraph level to the essay level may be greater than anticipated. The current course was structured around firstly a focus on the paragraph, then a progression to the academic essay, likely as a means of reducing student anxiety by reviewing their knowledge about writing. However, for many students, the paragraph was a text type they were already very familiar with from high school. Consequently, it was not until the middle of the semester that students had a better understanding of the true demands of academic writing. This questions whether such an ordering reduces anxiety or only moves it to a later point for many learners.

Findings revealed that students in transition often feel uneasy, confused, and unsure about their capabilities to succeed in writing effectively for English-medium social science courses. So, it is important to find ways to reduce anxiety. EMI preparation programmes may also benefit from an awareness that there are additional ways to enhance students' "learning potential" (Macaro, 2022, p. 77) beyond skills instruction. For example, studies have shown that strategy training may enhance writing strategy use and writing performance (e.g., DeSilva, 2015). Few studies thus far have examined the potential of efficacy forming "affordances" (Thompson, 2018) in EAP classrooms; however, research from other fields (e.g., Huang & Mayer, 2019) has indicated that small additions can be made to lesson materials that may result in stronger learner self-efficacy beliefs and retention of knowledge. For example, short explanations can be added to task instructions that may encourage a growth mindset and reduce anxiety (i.e., reduce the impact of negative affective states) (Huang & Mayer, 2019). Integrating self-efficacy training within support programmes may also help students confront linguistic challenges and eventually handle full EMI content courses (Thompson et al., 2022a). This is especially pertinent for students at lower proficiency levels, whose more pronounced language-related EMI transition difficulties may well result in lower self-efficacy beliefs.

Interestingly, several students in the current study discussed the value of the journal activities as a source of information informing their perceptions of efficacy change (and growth). One interpretation is that the journal provided students with an opportunity to simultaneously (1) practise their writing skills and (2) reflect upon their skills. As Bandura (1997, p. 51) has stated, "efficacy beliefs are structured by experience and reflective thought". Reflection appears to be a crucial element for the cognitive processing of efficacy-forming information (Wyatt, 2014), and these tasks appear to have provided a context for these learners to address each of these points. Moreover, as Mendoza et al. (2022) have pointed out, student journals may prove a useful resource for instructors, in helping identify students who need different types of support (i.e., with weak self-efficacy beliefs or experiencing anxiety). Our findings indicate the necessity of understanding the past experiences of learners and their emotional state of mind, as these factors may influence the extent to which learners find certain tasks challenging. This insight highlights an area for future researchers to investigate.

## References

Aizawa, I., & Rose, H. (2020). High school to university transitional challenges in English medium instruction in Japan. *System*, *95*, 102390. 10.1016/j.system.2020.102390

Bandura, A. (1997). *Self-efficacy: The exercise of control*. W.H Freeman and Company.

Bandura, A. (2006). Guide for creating self-efficacy scales. In F. Pajares, & T. Urdan (Eds.), *Self-efficacy beliefs of adolescents* (pp. 307–338). Information Age Publishing.

Bong, M., & Skaalvik, E. M. (2003). Academic self-concept and self-efficacy: How different are they really? *Educational Psychology Review*, *15*, 1–40. 10.1023/A:1021302408382

Bradford A. (2020) Internationalizing Japan's undergraduate education through english medium instruction. In S. Dimova, & J. Kling (Eds.), *Integrating content and language in multilingual universities* (pp. 53–74). Springer.

Bradford, A., Ishikura, Y., & Brown, H. (2022). Sustaining internationalization: English-medium programs in Japan. *International Higher Education*, *110*, 15–16. 10.36197/IHE.2022.110.07

Brinkmann, S. (2013). *Qualitative interviewing.* Oxford University Press.
Creswell, J. W. (2022). *A concise introduction to mixed methods research.* SAGE.
Curle, S., Sahan, K., Jablonkai, R., Mittelmeier, J., & Veitch, A. (2020). English in higher education – English medium Part 1: Literature review. In N. Galloway (Ed.), *English in higher education.* British Council.
De Silva, R. (2015). Writing strategy instruction: Its impact on writing in a second language for academic purposes. *Language Teaching Research, 19*(3), 301–323. 10.1177/1362168814541738
Evans, S., & Morrison, B. (2011) Meeting the challenges of English-medium higher education: The first-year experience in Hong Kong. *English for Specific Purposes, 30*(3), 198–208. 10.1016/j.esp.2011.01.001
Galloway, N., Kriukow, J., & Numajiri, T. (2017). *Internationalisation, higher education and the growing demand for English: An investigation into the English medium of instruction (EMI) movement in China and Japan.* British Council. https://www.teachingenglish.org.uk/sites/teacheng/files/H035 ELTRA Internationalisation_HE_and the growing demand for English A4_FINAL_WEB.pdf
Galloway, N., & Ruegg, R. (2020). The provision of student support on English Medium Instruction programmes in Japan and China. *Journal of English for Academic Purposes, 45*, 100846. 10.1016/j.jeap.2020.100846
Greene, J. C. (2015). Preserving distinctions within the multi-method and mixed method research merger. In S. N. Hesse-Biber, & B. Johnson (Eds.), *The Oxford handbook of multimethod and mixed methods research inquiry* (pp. 606–615). Oxford University Press.
Hinkel, E. (2011). What research on second language writing tells us and what it doesn't. In E. Hinkel (Ed.), *Handbook of Research in Second language teaching and learning* (pp. 523–538). Routledge.
Hirose, K. (2005). *Product and process in the L1 and L2 writing of Japanese students of English.* Keisuisha.
Huang, X., & Mayer, R. E. (2019). Adding self-efficacy features to an online statistics lesson. *Journal of Educational Computing Research, 57*(4), 1003–1037. 10.1177/0735633118771085
Hyland, K. (2006). *English for academic purposes: An advanced coursebook.* Routledge.
Hyland, K. (2015) *Academic publishing: Issues and challenges in the construction of knowledge.* Oxford University Press.
Hyland, K., & Hamp-Lyons, L. (2002). EAP: Issues and directions. *Journal of English for Academic Purposes, 1*(1), 1–12. 10.1016/s1475-1585(02)00002-4
Irie, K. (2019). An insider's view: Launching a university program. In H. Reinders, S. Ryan, & S. Nakamura (Eds.), *Innovation in language teaching and learning: The case of Japan* (pp. 211–232). Palgrave Macmillan.
Kobayashi, H., & Rinnert, C. (2002). High school student perceptions of first language literacy instruction: Implications for second language writing. *Journal of Second Language Writing, 11*(2), 91–116.
Leeming, P. (2017). A longitudinal investigation into English speaking self-efficacy in a Japanese language classroom. *Asian-Pacific Journal of Second and Foreign Language Education, 2*(1), 1–18. 10.1186/s40862-017-0035-x

Leys, C., Ley, C., Klein, O., Bernard, P., & Licata, L. (2013). Detecting outliers: Do not use standard deviation around the mean, use absolute deviation around the median. *Journal of Experimental Social Psychology, 49*, 764–766. 10.1016/j.jesp.2013.03.013

Macaro, E. (2022). Learner strategies in an English Medium Instruction context. In D. B. Sabato, & B. Hughes (Eds.), *Multilingual perspectives from Europe and beyond on Language policy and practice* (pp. 63–82). Routledge.

Macaro, E., Curle, S., Pun, J., An, J., & Dearden, J. (2018). A systematic review of English medium instruction in higher education. *Language Teaching, 51*(1), 36–76. 10.1017/S0261444817000350

McLean, S., & Poulshock, J. (2018). Increasing reading self-efficacy and reading amount in EFL learners with word-targets. *Reading in a Foreign Language, 30*(1), 76–91.

Mendoza, L., Lehtonen, T., Lindblom-Ylänne, S., & Hyytinen, H. (2022). Exploring first-year university students' learning journals: Conceptions of second language self-concept and self-efficacy for academic writing. *System, 106*. 10.1016/j.system.2022.102759

Mills, N., Pajares, F., & Herron, C. (2007). Self-efficacy of college intermediate French students: Relation to achievement and motivation. *Language Learning, 57*(3), 417–442. 10.1111/j.1467-9922.2007.00421.x

Pajares, F. (1996). Self-Efficacy Beliefs in Academic Settings. *Review of Educational Research, 66*(4), 543–578. 10.2307/1170653

Pecorari, D., & Malmström, H. (2018). At the crossroads of TESOL and English medium instruction. *TESOL Quarterly, 52*(3), 497–515. 10.1002/tesq.470

Richards, J. C., & Pun, J. (2021). A typology of English-medium instruction. *RELC Journal*, 003368822096858. 10.1177/0033688220968584

Rose, H. (2019). Diaries and journals: collecting insider perspectives in second language research. In J. McKinley & H. Rose (Eds.), *The Routledge handbook of research methods in applied linguistics* (pp. 348–359). Routledge.

Rose, H. (2021). Students' language-related challenges of studying through English: What EMI teachers can do. In D. Lasagabaster, & A. Doiz (Eds.), *Language use in English-medium instruction at university: International perspectives on teacher practice* (pp. 145–166). Routledge.

Rose, H., McKinley, J., Xu, X., & Zhou, S. (2020). *Investigating policy and implementation of English medium instruction in higher education institutions in China*. British Council. https://www.teachingenglish.org.uk/publications/case-studies-insights-and-research/investigating-policy-and-implementation-english-0

Ruegg, R. (2018). The effect of peer and teacher feedback on changes in EFL students' writing self-efficacy. *The Language Learning Journal, 46*(2), 87–102. 10.1080/09571736.2014.958190

Selvi, A. F. (2019). Qualitative content analysis. In J. McKinley, & H. Rose (Eds.), *The Routledge handbook of research methods in applied linguistics* (pp. 440–452). Routledge.

Soruç, A., Pawlak, M., Yuksel, D., & Horzum, B. (2022). Investigating the impact of linguistic and non-linguistic factors on EMI academic success. *System, 107*, 102794. 10.1016/j.system.2022.102794

Stajkovic, A. D., Bandura, A., Locke, E. A., Lee, D., & Sergent, K. (2018). Test of three conceptual models of influence of the big five personality traits and self-efficacy on academic performance: A meta-analytic path-analysis. *Personality and Individual Differences*, *120*, 238–245. 10.1016/j.paid.2017.08.014

Sun, T., Wang, C., Lambert, R. G., & Liu, L. (2021). Relationship between Second Language English writing self-efficacy and achievement: A meta-regression analysis. *Journal of Second Language Writing*, *53*. 10.1016/j.jslw.2021.100817

Thompson, G. (2018). Insights for efficacy development from an exploration of Japanese business management students' EAP self-efficacy beliefs. *The Asian ESP Journal*, *14*(7.1), 244–284.

Thompson, G. (2020). *Exploring language teacher efficacy in Japan*. Multilingual Matters.

Thompson, G., Aizawa, I., Curle, S., & Rose, H. (2022a). Exploring the role of self-efficacy beliefs and learner success in English medium instruction. *International Journal of Bilingual Education and Bilingualism*, *25*(1), 196–209. 10.1080/13670050.2019.1651819

Thompson, G., Takezawa, N., & Rose, H. (2022b). Investigating self-beliefs and success for English medium instruction learners studying finance. *Journal of Education for Business*, *97*(4), 220–227. 10.1080/08832323.2021.1924108

Wang, C., & Sun, T. (2020). Relationship between self-efficacy and language proficiency: A meta-analysis. *System*, *95*, 102366. 10.1016/j.system.2020.102366

Wyatt, M. (2014) Towards a re-conceptualization of teachers' self-efficacy beliefs: Tackling enduring problems with the quantitative research and moving on. *International Journal of Research & Method in Education*, *37*(2), 166–189.

Wyatt, M. (2022). Self-efficacy. In S. Li, P. Hiver, & M. Papi (Eds.), *The Routledge handbook of second language acquisition and individual differences* (pp. 207–219). Routledge.

Yasuda, S. (2014). Issues in teaching and learning EFL writing in East Asian contexts: The case of Japan. *Asian EFL Journal*, *16*(4), 150–187.

Zhang, Y. (2018). Exploring EFL learners' self-efficacy in academic writing based on process-genre approach. *English Language Teaching*, *11*(6), 115–124. 10.5539/elt.v11n6p115

Zhou, Q., Chen, L., & Hou, X. (2022). Exploring Chinese EFL undergraduates' writing from sources: Self-efficacy and performance. *Assessing Writing*, *54*, 100663. 10.1016/j.asw.2022.100663

# 12 Exploring language self-efficacy beliefs and technology-based learning strategies in an increasingly digitalized world

*Nalan Şan and Derin Atay*

## Introduction

The thorny issue of what predicts success in second language (L2) learning contexts has been widely raised and extensively debated among scholars around the world. A growing body of research highlights the significance of individual differences (ID) in L2 attainment (Li et al., 2022). The scope of ID encompasses L2 learners' motivation, age of onset, aptitude, personality traits, learning styles, willingness to communicate as well as language self-efficacy (LSE) beliefs and language learning strategies.

Self-efficacy beliefs are defined as "beliefs in one's capabilities to organize and execute the courses of action required to produce given attainments" in Bandura's self-efficacy theory (Bandura, 1997, p. 3). When this definition is adapted to L2 learning contexts, it leads to the inescapable interpretation that students' self-efficacy is construed by their own beliefs in their ability to organize and apply the most appropriate learning strategies so as to attain their L2 language goals. These goals relate to the subtleties of each fundamental language skill, namely reading, writing, speaking, and listening in the L2. However, language learners may feel more efficacious in some skills than others, as revealed by various studies (Li & Wang, 2010; Mills et al., 2006), and their LSE beliefs in each skill may have been influenced by technology-based self-regulated English learning strategies, which are essential in today's rapidly digitalized world. Consequently, this relationship requires exploration.

### Language self-efficacy beliefs of L2 learners and technology-based learning strategies

Bandura (1997) postulated that self-efficacy is informed by four primary sources, namely: *enactive mastery experience*, previous successful experiences with the task; *verbal persuasion*, positive comments from significant others regarding one's performance; *vicarious experience*, observed performance of others on a similar task; and *affective factors* associated with performing a task.

DOI: 10.4324/9781003379300-15

According to Bandura (2006), these four sources influence one's perceived self-efficacy, which then acts as an agent during the learning process to influence performance. People with high self-efficacy choose to perform more challenging tasks. They set themselves higher goals and stick to them. Actions are pre-shaped in thought, and once an action has been taken, highly self-efficacious people invest more effort and persist longer than those low in self-efficacy. When setbacks occur, they recover more quickly and remain committed to their goals.

Self-efficacy influences the choices students make and the effort they put into their performance (Boekaerts & Cascallar, 2006), and a positive link has been found between students' self-efficacy beliefs and their self-regulation, both variables being predictive of their academic achievement (Diseth, 2011; Yusuf, 2011). Students with high self-efficacy set higher goals, invest more effort, choose more effective strategies, and seek more tangible solutions to accomplish the task. By contrast, inefficacious students may easily be defeated by obstacles in the learning process (Diseth, 2011; Magogwe & Oliver, 2007; Pajares, 2001).

Positive relationships between the use of self-regulated learning (SRL) strategies and L2 self-efficacy beliefs have been found in the field of second language acquisition (SLA) as well (Anam & Stracke, 2020; Liem et al., 2008; Wang & Pape, 2005). Recently, in a number of studies, the Questionnaire of English Self-efficacy (developed by Wang et al., 2013) was used to measure specifically L2 learners' self-efficacy in all four skills. Results showed that highly/medially efficacious L2 students reported more frequent use of SRL strategies compared to students with low LSE beliefs (Kim et al., 2015). Students with high self-efficacy beliefs reported self-evaluating, seeking social assistance, keeping records, and monitoring strategy use more fully than students with low self-efficacy profiles (Wang & Bai, 2017).

Most of these studies were carried out in traditional classroom-based learning environments. However, as a context-specific construct, self-regulation may manifest differently in the management of online learning resources. Consequently, students' self-regulatory processes in online learning environments may differ from those in conventional classroom-based settings (Benson, 2001; Zheng et al., 2018). Technology-based English SRL strategies, e.g., using online translation websites or dictionaries and reading online texts with interactive answer keys and hyperlinked glossaries, are actions adopted by English language learners expanding their English learning in technology-using conditions (An et al., 2021).

However, so far only a few empirical investigations have been conducted into the relationship between English language learners' self-regulation and their self-efficacy in online settings. These investigations include Su et al.'s (2018) study with Chinese L2 learners, which highlighted the positive role of learners' online self-regulation strategies, i.e., self-evaluation, environment structuring, and goal-setting strategies, in explaining their English LSE beliefs. Pan's (2020) recent research indicates that motivation mediates relationships between technological self-efficacy beliefs, technology acceptance, and attitudes toward technology-based self-directed learning. In Pan's study, students with greater technology acceptance and technological self-efficacy were more positive toward technology-based self-directed learning. In another recent study, Teng and Yang (2022) identified a positive and significant correlation among L2 learners' metacognition, motivation, online learning, and self-efficacy. Metacognition and motivation had a joint mediating role in shaping self-efficacy beliefs, which impacted English learning achievement in online learning environments.

We believe that the use of technology-based self-regulated English learning strategies can also help with task management in language learning and, hence, may be a mediating factor in LSE beliefs. Since self-efficacy has been found to act as an intermediary between learners' aptitude, previous accomplishments, and subsequent performances (Bandura, 2006), it is extremely meaningful to do further research on learners' LSE beliefs and ways to develop these beliefs in different L2 educational settings, especially in novel technology-based self-regulated English learning environments. Combining LSE beliefs research with technology-assisted self-regulation is also highly meaningful because, in our current rapidly digitalizing education environment, the use of technology not only leads to more self-regulated L2 learners in and outside class but also has a considerable impact on their LSE beliefs.

This study aims to investigate the LSE beliefs and technology-assisted SRL strategy-use levels of Turkish undergraduate students and uncover underlying factors that affect these L2 learners' LSE beliefs and their technology-based self-regulated English learning strategy use. Thus, the research questions are as follows:

1 What are the English language self-efficacy levels of Turkish L2 learners within the context of hybrid English education at the tertiary level?
2 What are their levels of technology-based self-regulated English learning strategy use?
3 Is there a correlation between learners' English language self-efficacy beliefs and technology-based self-regulated English learning strategies?
4 What are the factors that affect learners' English language self-efficacy beliefs and technology-based self-regulated English learning strategies?

## Methodology

### Participants and setting

With the abrupt and ill-prepared transition to online education in the second term of the 2019–2020 academic year, online language education was adopted in all universities in Türkiye. In the English foundation year of a competitive state university in Istanbul, where the present study took place, the L2 instructors were required to provide online English courses, by devising a variety of online activities and using technological education tools.

At the beginning of the 2021 fall semester, the university started offering hybrid education: traditional face-to-face teaching started with a curriculum that had newly been adapted to include digital education tools and flipped online grammar instruction in addition to completely online reading classes with an instructor. That is to say, B1 and B1+ learners, as defined by the Common European Framework of Reference (CEFR) at the foundation year of this university, took 12 hours of traditional face-to-face main course classes that integrated all 4 skills of the English language and four hours of traditional face-to-face writing classes on a weekly basis. Furthermore, they had four hours of flipped online grammar instruction through YouTube videos, interactive PowerPoint presentations, and such digital education tools as Quizlet, Kahoot, Quizziz, Google Jamboard, Jeopardy Games, Wordwall, and Bamboozle. They also had four hours of online reading classes per week with their reading instructor through Zoom. Such a radical transition in the curriculum required new ways of interacting with technology for which many students might have felt ill-equipped. This, in turn, may have influenced their self-efficacy beliefs and their technology-assisted SRL strategy-use levels.

The study was conducted in four classes, two B1 and two B1+ levels with a total of 94 students, all Turkish students with an age range from 18 to 21. Since only volunteer students participated in the data collection, 84 participants completed the Questionnaire of English Self-Efficacy (QESE) (Wang et al., 2013) and 81 participants completed the Technology-based Self-regulated English Learning Strategies Questionnaire (An et al., 2021).

### Data collection tools and analyses

An explanatory sequential mixed method approach was implemented in this study; for the first three research questions, data were collected by means of the Questionnaire of English Self-Efficacy (QESE) (Wang et al., 2013) and the Technology-based Self-regulated English Learning Strategies Questionnaire (TSRLSQ) (An et al., 2021). The QESE consists of 32 items and was specifically developed to assess the English self-efficacy of language learners in four fundamental language skills with eight items each on a five-point Likert scale from 1 ("I cannot do it at all") to 5 ("I can do it very well"). It measures (a) self-efficacy for listening (8 items); (b) self-efficacy for speaking (8 items); (c) self-efficacy for reading (8 items); and (d) self-efficacy for writing (8 items). (See Appendix 1 for the items for speaking and reading.) Each item asks students to make judgments about their capabilities to accomplish certain tasks using English in listening, speaking, reading, and writing contexts. Meanwhile, the TSRLSQ was designed to assess learners' SRL strategy use in technology-assisted language learning with 26 items on a 5-point Likert scale.

Both questionnaires were kept in their original English versions, without any changes, as the students' proficiency levels (B1 and B1+) were adequate to fully comprehend and complete them. The overall reliability coefficient, Cronbach Alpha, obtained for the QESE questionnaire was .94 while it was .85 for the TSRLSQ.

A convenience sampling technique was adopted when picking the participants to complete the two online questionnaires. Volunteer students completed the online Google form versions of both questionnaires in the second semester of the academic year 2021–2022. The questionnaires were given on two different days so as not to overwhelm the students, and the researchers answered the students' questions about questionnaire items to clear up any possible confusion. The quantitative data were analysed using SPSS, by running descriptive and correlational inferential statistical analysis to reveal frequency tables and produce bar charts.

Data for the fourth research question came from focus-group interviews conducted with 30 students. A purposeful sampling technique was adopted when choosing the 15 students with the lowest LSE and technology-based SRL beliefs in the entire participant pool of 84 learners, and 15 students with the strongest beliefs. Each focus group included 5 students from either group at a time. A total of six interviews was conducted over Zoom. The main objective of these interviews was to have in-depth information about the underlying reasons for their LSE beliefs and SRL strategies. The interviewer, who was also the first author of this study, kept a meticulous record of how many students in each focus group actually agreed with certain statements, e.g., regarding limited input and output outside class leading to low LSE beliefs.

The interviews were conducted in participants' L1 in order to achieve mutual trust and to eliminate any possible misunderstandings due to a language barrier. The transcripts of these interviews were subsequently translated into English and the qualitative data was analysed using inductive thematic analysis. According to Braun and Clarke (2006), inductive thematic analysis involves a process of coding the data without trying to fit it into a pre-existing coding frame or the researcher's analytic preconceptions. This kind of qualitative analysis was adopted because we were trying to explore the underlying reasons for the learners' high and low levels of LSE and technology-based strategy use without a pre-existing theoretical frame. As per their own requests, participants' real names were never disclosed in the study.

## Results

### What are the English language self-efficacy levels of Turkish L2 learners within the context of hybrid English education at tertiary level?

To begin to address our first research question, the skills-based LSE levels of the participants are presented in Table 12.1.

*Table 12.1* Students' self-efficacy beliefs for each skill

|  | *Minimum* | *Maximum* | *Mean* | *Std. Deviation* |
|---|---|---|---|---|
| Listening efficacy | 2 | 5 | 3.48 | 0.57 |
| Speaking efficacy | 2 | 5 | 3.72 | 0.56 |
| Reading efficacy | 1 | 5 | 3.55 | 0.55 |
| Writing efficacy | 2 | 5 | 3.82 | 0.62 |
| Valid N (listwise) | 84 | | | |

Since the QESE questionnaire has four sub-dimensions for each language skill, with each comprising of eight items on a five-point Likert scale, the score for each sub-dimension ranges from 0 to 5. Students' listening self-efficacy is the lowest with a mean of 3.48 when compared to their LSE beliefs in speaking, reading, and writing, even though the mean differences are minor, while their writing self-efficacy is comparatively high with a mean of 3.82. However, standard deviation is also highest for writing efficacy, which means the data are more spread out between a minimum of 2 and a maximum of 5. Overall, students' LSE levels are higher for the productive skills while their LSE levels are comparatively lower for the receptive skills. We now examine these differences further, focusing on listening and writing (the lowest and highest) for reasons of space, and then possible reasons for these differences. We focus on listening first. Item-based results are presented in Table 12.2.

*Table 12.2* Students' self-efficacy beliefs for listening

|  | *Minimum* | *Maximum* | *Mean* | *Std. Deviation* |
|---|---|---|---|---|
| 1. Can you understand stories told in English? | 2 | 5 | 3.71 | .65 |
| 2. Can you understand American English TV programs? | 2 | 5 | 3.54 | .73 |

(*Continued*)

*Table 12.2* (Continued)

|  | Minimum | Maximum | Mean | Std. Deviation |
|---|---|---|---|---|
| 3. Can you understand radio programs in English-speaking countries? | 1 | 5 | 3.08 | .86 |
| 4. Can you understand English TV programs? | 2 | 5 | 3.40 | .79 |
| 5. If your teacher gives you an audio-recorded English dialogue about school life. can you understand it? | 2 | 5 | 3.93 | .59 |
| 6. Can you understand English movies without Turkish subtitles? | 1 | 5 | 3.32 | .86 |
| 7. Can you understand English songs? | 1 | 5 | 3.24 | .87 |
| 8. Can you understand telephone numbers spoken in English? | 2 | 5 | 3.67 | .89 |
| Valid N (listwise) 84 | | | | |

It can be seen that students mostly struggle with the comprehension of such authentic input as American and British radio programmes, TV programmes, songs, and movies without Turkish subtitles. However, they feel more self-efficacious about the English input that has been custom tailored for educational purposes and used in the classroom. The highest self-efficacy level was found in the writing skill, and Table 12.3 presents item-based results for this skill.

*Table 12.3* Students' self-efficacy beliefs for writing

|  | Minimum | Maximum | Mean | Std. Deviation |
|---|---|---|---|---|
| 25. If you have access to the Internet, can you release news on the Internet (e.g., Facebook. Twitter. blogs)? | 1 | 5 | 3.43 | .94 |
| 26. Can you write English compositions assigned by your teachers? | 1 | 5 | 3.60 | .74 |
| 27. Can you leave a message to your classmates in English? | 2 | 5 | 3.86 | .73 |
| 28. Can you make new sentences with the words just learned? | 1 | 5 | 3.74 | .83 |
| 29. Can you send emails in English? | 1 | 5 | 3.57 | .96 |

(*Continued*)

*Table 12.3* (Continued)

|  | Minimum | Maximum | Mean | Std. Deviation |
|---|---|---|---|---|
| 30. Can you make sentences with English idiomatic phrases? | 1 | 5 | 2.79 | .85 |
| 31. Can you write diaries in English? | 1 | 5 | 3.31 | .89 |
| 32. Can you write an article in about two pages about your English teacher in English? | 1 | 5 | 2.87 | .90 |
| Valid N (listwise) 84 | | | | |

Table 12.3 shows that the learners have lower writing efficacy levels regarding the use of English idiomatic phrases and writing an article about their English teacher. Their writing efficacy is comparatively higher when it comes to leaving a message to their classmates in English and making new sentences with the words they have just learnt, which are the tasks in which they have more control over the language or vocabulary needed.

So, even though the mean differences are minor, participants' listening self-efficacy is comparatively the lowest among the four skills while their writing self-efficacy is comparatively the highest. As to why, learners' vicarious and mastery experiences may play an essential role in improving their L2 writing self-efficacy beliefs (Han & Hiver, 2018). Since these participants have already proved that they can write at B1 level English proficiency in previous level placement exams at the locally prestigious institution, this kind of mastery experience may have boosted their writing self-efficacy. Similarly, students in a Japanese context (Chapter 11 of this volume) can be self-efficacious in their writing abilities early in their studies.

Meanwhile, regarding L2 listening skills, Chen (2009) found in a Taiwanese context that the most significant sources of self-efficacy included social persuasion and mastery experiences. Given that tasks perceived as overly challenging can lead to negative self-appraisals (Bandura, 1986), it is worth considering the institutional exam format employed in this context. Anecdotal evidence suggests that listening to a lengthy lecture and taking extensive notes renders even B1 learners rather pessimistic in the face of listening tasks. Similarly, in an Algerian context (see Chapter 10 of this volume), the assessment of listening at university can cause anxiety.

### What are their levels of technology-based self-regulated English learning strategy use?

The levels of the learners' technology-based SRL strategies are revealed below. The TSRLSQ questionnaire (An et al., 2021) has a total of 26 items:

## Language self-efficacy and technology-based learning strategies 249

motivational regulation strategies (9 items), goal-setting and learning evaluation strategies (5 items), social strategies (4 items), technology-based English song and movie learning strategies (5 items) and technology-based vocabulary learning strategies (3 items). Tables 12.4–12.8 show item-based descriptive analysis of these five sub-dimensions. A five-point Likert scale was used.

Table 12.4 shows that the participants mostly use technology to help them sustain or enhance interest in learning English while they do not as

*Table 12.4* Students' motivational regulation strategies

| | Minimum | Maximum | Mean | Std. Deviation |
|---|---|---|---|---|
| 1. I select and use appropriate technological tools to improve the areas I'm weak in. | 1 | 5 | 3.69 | .80 |
| 2. I use technologies outside the classroom to access authentic materials in English. | 1 | 5 | 3.57 | .96 |
| 3. I search related materials online when I have difficulties in the process of studying English. | 1 | 5 | 3.72 | .91 |
| 4. I seek opportunities through technological resources to practice my oral English. | 1 | 5 | 3.01 | 1.00 |
| 5. I use technologies to help me sustain/enhance interest in learning English. | 1 | 5 | 3.74 | .78 |
| 6. I use technologies (APPs or websites) to make the English learning task more interesting. | 1 | 5 | 3.44 | .94 |
| 7. I use mobile devices to enhance my willingness to participate in English social events. | 1 | 5 | 3.15 | 1.03 |
| 8. Sometimes I look through the visual and vivid courseware to arouse my interest in English learning. | 1 | 5 | 3.02 | 1.01 |
| 9. When I feel bored with learning English, I adopt technological resources to decrease the boredom and increase the enjoyment. | 1 | 5 | 3.36 | .953 |
| Valid N (listwise) 81 | | | | |

often seek opportunities through technological resources to practise their oral English.

According to Table 12.5, students do not listen to radio broadcasts much or set and monitor technology-assisted English learning goals. However, they do reflect on the effectiveness of using technologies for English learning. This may be due to many English teachers introducing digital education tools for English learning at the institution throughout the semester.

*Table 12.5* Students' use of goal-setting and learning evaluation strategies

|  | *Minimum* | *Maximum* | *Mean* | *Std. Deviation* |
|---|---|---|---|---|
| 10. I listen to English radio broadcasts (e.g., VOA and BBC) to improve my English proficiency. | 1 | 5 | 2.67 | 1.29 |
| 11. At the beginning of the semester, I set technology-assisted English learning goals. | 1 | 5 | 2.74 | .99 |
| 12. I often monitor my technology-assisted English learning progress. | 1 | 5 | 2.98 | .94 |
| 13. I reflect on the effectiveness of using technologies for English learning. | 1 | 5 | 3.57 | .87 |
| 14. I adjust my English learning plans in response to different technology-assisted learning activities. | 1 | 5 | 3.07 | .87 |
| Valid N (listwise) 81 |  |  |  |  |

Table 12.6 shows that the students are generally capable of implementing social strategies regarding technology use.

*Table 12.6* Students' use of social strategies

|  | *Minimum* | *Maximum* | *Mean* | *Std. Deviation* |
|---|---|---|---|---|
| 15. I seek advice on how to use technologies effectively for English language learning. | 1 | 5 | 3.49 | .86 |
| 16. I seek opportunities to talk with native English | 1 | 5 | 3.16 | 1.10 |

(*Continued*)

*Language self-efficacy and technology-based learning strategies* 251

*Table 12.6* (Continued)

|  | Minimum | Maximum | Mean | Std. Deviation |
|---|---|---|---|---|
| speakers through technological tools. | | | | |
| 17. When I have problems in English learning, I ask my teacher for help through technological tools. | 1 | 5 | 3.31 | .98 |
| 18. I share my problems with my classmates online so we can solve our problems together. | 1 | 5 | 3.22 | 1.22 |
| Valid N (listwise) 81 | | | | |

According to Table 12.7, students tend to adopt strategies for technology-based English song and movie learning. The mean scores for this sub-dimension are comparatively high. This may be mostly due to the ease of access to such modern streaming channels as Netflix and Amazon Prime in Türkiye.

*Table 12.7* Students' strategies for technology-based English song and movie learning

|  | Minimum | Maximum | Mean | Std. Deviation |
|---|---|---|---|---|
| 19. I "copy" useful words and expressions in English movies or programs. | 1 | 5 | 3.90 | .84 |
| 20. I practice saying new expressions in English movies or programs to myself. | 1 | 5 | 3.88 | .90 |
| 21. I listen to English songs to help me remember words. | 1 | 5 | 3.73 | 1.14 |
| 22. I use technologies (e.g., English movies) to learn more about English and the culture. | 2 | 5 | 4.22 | .67 |
| 23. I use technologies to connect English learning with my personal interest (e.g., playing English games. or listening and singing English songs). | 2 | 5 | 4.04 | .79 |
| Valid N (listwise) 81 | | | | |

Table 12.8 demonstrates that most learners use online dictionaries and such lexical applications as Quizlet to persist in their English learning goals, which is not surprising when we consider that the institutional curriculum has recently instigated the use of these digital lexical resources for all levels.

*Table 12.8* Students' technology-based vocabulary learning strategies

|  | Minimum | Maximum | Mean | Std. Deviation |
|---|---|---|---|---|
| 24. I use lexical apps (i.e., Quizlet) to help me memorize new words. | 1 | 5 | 3.64 | 1.08 |
| 25. I use online dictionaries to check English words. | 2 | 5 | 4.51 | .74 |
| 26. I use technologies (e.g., vocabulary apps) to help me persist in my English learning goals. | 1 | 5 | 3.67 | 1.01 |
| Valid N (listwise) 81 | | | | |

### Is there a correlation between learners' English language self-efficacy beliefs and technology-based self-regulated English learning strategies?

Pearson's correlation analysis was conducted to reveal correlations between English LSE beliefs and technology-based SRL strategies. A modest but statistically significant positive correlation ($r = .46$) was found, suggesting that the stronger the English LSE levels, the higher the technology-based SRL strategy use, as Table 12.9 reveals.

*Table 12.9* Correlations between English language self-efficacy beliefs and technology-based self-regulated English learning strategies

|  |  | LSE | Technology-based SRL Strategy |
|---|---|---|---|
| LSE | Pearson Correlation | 1 | .467** |
|  | Sig. (2-tailed) |  | .000 |
|  | N | 67 | 67 |
| Technology-based SRL Strategy | Pearson Correlation | .467** | 1 |
|  | Sig. (2-tailed) | .000 |  |
|  | N | 67 | 67 |

**Correlation is significant at the 0.01 level (two tailed).

*Language self-efficacy and technology-based learning strategies* 253

***What are the factors that affect learners' low English language self-efficacy beliefs and technology-based self-regulated English learning strategies?***

Inductive content analysis of qualitative data gathered from learners with low LSE levels and technology-based strategy use revealed four overarching themes: (1) limited oral and written input and practice, (2) inability to travel overseas, (3) negative personal educational background experiences, and (4) difficulty in vocabulary retrieval. The guiding questions of the focus-group interviews can be found in Appendix 2.

1 *Limited oral and written input and output:* All 15 participants highlighted that they had limited chance to receive oral and written input outside the classroom and practise their speaking and writing skills.

- I think I can improve my self-confidence by getting more exposure to the language outside the class, especially if the majority speaks English (Participant A).
- A lot of repetition and increased practice would definitely help (increase my self-efficacy beliefs) (Participant B).
- I need to be in a place where people speak English more. I just use it in the class, which is not enough. Maybe digital platforms can open up some speaking opportunities, I don't know (Participant C).
- I mostly speak Turkish even in class. Only if I had more opportunities to speak and write in English, it would really help (Participant D).

2 *Limited opportunities to travel overseas:* Eight participants pointed out financial problems and familial obligations as the main obstacles in the path of their freedom of travel.

- If only I had the chance to live abroad for a while ... Everything would be completely different (Participant E).
- English must be part of my life, but it's just not. You need to go abroad for that, I mean to make it an integral part of my life so that I can truly believe in myself. Now I keep thinking in Turkish, it is literally impossible to change the language of my thoughts unless I travel overseas (Participant F).
- Virtual travel is always an option, but it lacks the same human interaction. It's just not the same (Participant E).

3 *Educational background:* Five participants mentioned their personal education backgrounds with reference to a sense of learnt helplessness or previous attempts that ended in total failure to account for their low LSE beliefs.

- I think I have a terrible English learning history. My English learning endeavours have always ended up in a dead-end street and I have no

reason to believe that it will end in a different way this year, with or without Quizlet or Kahoot (Participant K).
- The English classes that I have attended so far have made me believe that I will never ever master the ability to understand what is being said or written completely (Participants G and H).

4 *Difficulty in vocabulary retrieval*: Four participants pointed out that they are experiencing immense difficulties in vocabulary retrieval, which leads to low LSE beliefs.
- When I speak, it really demoralizes me when I can't find a particular word in the middle of the conversation. At that moment, my confidence is completely shattered into pieces. It requires time to look up the words even in digital dictionaries, you can't really keep up with a fluent person (Participants I and J).

**What are the factors that affect learners' high English language self-efficacy beliefs and technology-based self-regulated English learning strategies?**

The overarching themes to account for high LSE levels and technology-based strategy use were (1) L2 learning enjoyment, (2) low anxiety levels, (3) ID, (4) online gaming, and (5) high technology-based SRL strategy use outside class.

1 *L2 learning enjoyment*: Eight participants who had high overall LSE beliefs in all four skills of the English language mentioned that learning English is inherently enjoyable for them.
- Learning English, especially speaking, is so much fun. Experimenting with the new words is like solving a puzzle. I love doing that and when I do things that I love this much, I am usually successful (Participant O).
- I feel relaxed and happy when I am able to do the language tasks in class. After handling such tasks easily, I take pleasure in learning this language. I have started believing that I can handle real-life conversations with native speakers as well (Participant P).
- The English language sounds so nice and smooth. I like American culture as well. These particular things help me enjoy the learning process itself. I do believe that I have high aptitude for learning English (Participant Q).

2 *Low anxiety levels:* Five participants reported that they hardly ever feel tense or anxious when they are required to do productive tasks in English. As a result, they have a stronger sense of perceived competence in the language.
- I often feel really relaxed while speaking English, as if I am speaking Turkish (the participant's L1), you know. In my opinion, this has a lot to do with my self-confidence (Participant R).

- I am almost never afraid to make mistakes. Why would I be? How can I learn without making any mistakes? Who has ever learnt anything without making many mistakes first? I am not nervous at all, even before exams. I think I will pull through (Participant S).

3 *Individual differences*: Four participants' ID features such as language learning aptitude, increased and intentional attempts to practise English outside class, a wide social circle that includes native speakers of English and personality traits such as being a self-assertive person in general contributed to the high levels of their LSE beliefs.

- Overall, I do believe that I can achieve anything that I do. I guess you can say that I am a very self-assertive person. Besides, I have always believed that I have a thing for learning languages. It has always come easy for me (Participants T and U).

4 *Online gaming*: Nine participants mentioned that regular online gaming contributed substantially to their high LSE beliefs. They further explained that online gaming creates a sense of comradery as they raid in cyber dungeons together with people from all over the world and they exchange instant text messages in the chat box of the platform, or they sometimes talk out loud using their headphones and microphones to carry out these online attacks more successfully in the game. These online gaming practices improve their lexicon and help them gain a sense of achievement in simultaneous real-life conversations with foreigners from various different countries.

- I realized that I am perfectly capable of communicating with people from Japan, Korea, or China in English. I have even made several close friends in online games. This helped a lot. Once I started believing that I am able to communicate in English with people from other countries, you know, not just Turkish people, my grades improved too (Participant V).
- That sense of being an essential part of a group in online games, it is really amazing. I often forget which language I am using as the message itself is more important. I've gotta do what you've gotta do (Participant X).

5 *High technology-based SRL strategy use outside class*: Fourteen out of fifteen participants mentioned various different technology-based strategies that they use outside class as the source of their high LSE beliefs. Some of them were highly self-regulated. In other words, they purposefully looked for digital tools to overcome their particular weaknesses in certain linguistic aspects and used these digital tools on a regular basis to improve their overall LSE beliefs and language proficiency over the course of the entire academic year. For the majority of them (12 out of

14), the verbal appraisal of their teachers when they noticed they use these tools regularly also encouraged them to keep using such tools.

- Online apps are a big advantage. The language of my phone has been English for a long time now. Our teacher suggested that at the beginning of the year; he was so happy when he saw I actually took his advice (Participant Y)
- If I feel that I have fallen behind in terms of vocabulary, I use Quizlet. If I get a low grade from the reading part of the cumulative exam, I do online reading on the British Council's free Learn English website. (Participants R, P, O, and V).

Among the above-mentioned themes, L2 learning enjoyment and low anxiety levels are both affective indicators identified by Bandura (1997) as contributing to the formation of positive self-efficacy beliefs. Moreover, increased and intentional attempts to practise English outside class and in a wide English-speaking social circle suggest high self-efficacy in beneficial socio-constructivist L2 learning practices. In relation to this, online gaming and high technology-based SRL strategy use outside class are prominent contributing factors to learners' high LSE levels since they are practical and essential elements of novel hybrid education practices in the class as well.

## Discussion

To summarize our key findings, quantitative data revealed that, among the four skills, participants' listening self-efficacy is comparatively the lowest while their writing self-efficacy is comparatively the highest, even though the mean differences are minor. Graham (2011) contends that "low self-efficacy may be particularly acute in second language listening" (p. 114) and asserts the underlying reason may be listening being less controllable than other skills; if the speech is too fast, a significant message being shared can be irrevocably lost (Wyatt, 2022). High writing efficacy can be attributed to previous mastery experiences of the high proficiency learners in this study. In previous research, mastery experiences were also found influential in the writing performance of doctoral students, who were more efficacious than those studying for master's degrees (Ho, 2016).

Overall, students' LSE levels are higher for the productive skills while their LSE levels are comparatively lower for the receptive skills. This may be attributed to the testing system of the institution where the study was conducted because listening is tested in two phases: first, the students take notes under predetermined titles as they listen to a lengthy lecture (approximately 13–15 minutes long) and then they answer multiple choice questions using their own notes. This testing procedure generally results in lower grades for the listening part of the assessment and this kind of negative mastery experience is known to lead to lower LSE levels (Bandura, 1997). However, the lower scores on listening can also partly, perhaps, be attributed to Wang et al.'s (2013) scale; for example, while the listening items pertained to understanding unknown/unfamiliar TV/radio programmes, the writing items related to familiar tasks, e.g., writing an email. It is also noteworthy that participants' speaking efficacy was slightly higher than their reading and listening efficacy. This might again be due to the nature of the scale as it inquiries into practical, everyday speaking tasks, e.g., introducing yourself, your university/teacher, telling a story, which may not be so challenging for B1/B1+ learners.

The second set of quantitative data showed that technology-based goal-setting strategies were comparatively poor, as the students did not often set and monitor technology-assisted English learning goals. However, their technology-based motivational, social, song/movie, and vocabulary learning strategy use was widespread, as they mostly use technology to help them sustain or enhance interest in learning English and also reflect on the effectiveness of using technologies for English learning. This may be due to many English teachers and curricular policies introducing and facilitating the effective use of digital education tools for English learning at the institution throughout the semester. Previous research (Carneiro et al., 2007) also indicates that digital education tools help learners plan their learning process effectively and manage their resources on their own outside the class, and students can easily reflect on and evaluate their own learning behaviour and outcomes thanks to the use of modern technology.

As for the third research question, the modest positive correlation between learners' LSE beliefs and technology-based SRL strategies suggests that learners' technology-based SRL strategy use can have a mediating effect on their levels of LSE beliefs in digital learning environments. These findings corroborate Wang et al.'s (2013) study that indicated statistically significant relationships between self-efficacy beliefs, use of SRL strategies, and English language test scores. Similarly, Teng and Yang's (2022) findings showed a positive and significant correlation among L2 learners' motivation, metacognition, online learning, and self-efficacy beliefs and also indicate that metacognition and motivation jointly mediate the influences of self-efficacy beliefs on English learning achievement in online learning environments.

The qualitative data from focus-group interviews demonstrate that the students with high LSE beliefs tend to enjoy the L2 learning process as well as online gaming, have low language anxiety, high technology-based SRL strategy use outside class, and present with beneficial ID features. These features include high perceived language learning aptitude, increased and intentional attempts to practise English outside class, and a wide social circle that includes native speakers of English. Since previous research indicates that strong LSE beliefs are also indicative of higher success and L2 proficiency (Mills et al., 2006, 2007), B1 and B1+ learners in this study may have also benefited from their favourable proficiency levels, which may have boosted their LSE beliefs through curriculum and classroom practices to begin with. Similarly, Su et al.'s (2018) results highlighted the positive role of learners' self-evaluation, environment structuring, and goal setting for explaining English LSE beliefs. In this study, the participants structured their immediate environment through digital means, which in turn boosted their LSE beliefs. Lai et al.'s (2018) research indicates that entertainment and information-oriented technological experiences were influenced directly by perceived ease of the technological experience for language learning. Perceived usefulness of educational technologies and entertainment through English songs, movies, and online gaming were also frequently mentioned by the participants in this study as underlying factors for the development of high LSE beliefs.

## Pedagogical implications and conclusions

This study uncovered a definitive link, indicated by a modest but significant positive correlation between high self-efficacy levels and technology-based SRL strategy use. This finding was supported by the qualitative data from interviews since 15 participants with the highest LSE beliefs not only reported using a wide range of digital education strategies but also clearly indicated that the use of such technologies contributed considerably to their high LSE levels. Most of these participants self-regulated in terms of using technology to help them sustain enhanced interest in learning their L2; they purposefully searched for digital tools to deal with their shortcomings in particular linguistic areas or skills and used these digital tools regularly to boost their overall LSE beliefs and L2 proficiency throughout the entire academic year. Pan's (2020) recent research also indicates positive relationships between learning motivation, technological self-efficacy beliefs, technology acceptance, and attitudes toward technology-based self-directed learning. In this study, students with greater technology acceptance and technological self-efficacy showed more favourable attitudes toward technology-based self-directed learning. Thus, a direct pedagogical implication would be to encourage learners to develop greater technology acceptance and build increased technological self-efficacy beliefs. This could be achieved through modelling the use of the latest and most efficient digital learning tools in class by language teachers. This strategy would be appropriate in a close-knit learning culture, such as that of Türkiye, where verbal persuasion (Bandura, 1997) and role modeling by a teacher can be primary pedagogical driving sources, strengthening learners' perseverance in tackling language learning goals and strengthening their LSE beliefs. In such a context, verbal appraisal and role modeling by an L2 teacher can very beneficially encourage efficient educational technology use, which may facilitate self-regulated language learning in the long term.

Previous research also highlights that L2 learners' self-efficacy beliefs in various different L2 contexts have an impact on their motivation and learning performance in varied language domains (Hsieh & Kang 2010; Mills et al., 2006, 2007; Tilfarlioğlu & Ciftci, 2011; Wang et al., 2009). The findings of the current study corroborated this particular impact because the participants with higher LSE levels in the productive skills of the English language also reported possessing higher L2 learning enjoyment and higher language learning aptitude. They also reported making a greater number of intentional attempts to practise English outside class, which indicates strong motivation and can lead to improved learning performance. Therefore, while motivation is sometimes neglected, boosting the LSE beliefs of L2 learners should be among the primary pedagogical objectives of a given curriculum.

Another significant finding of this study was that learners with high levels of LSE tended to display more fully articulated metacognition, control, and knowledge of effective learning strategies, a relationship which was previously pointed out in Graham and Macaro's (2008) study as well. In this study, the participants with high levels of LSE tended to use more technology-based motivational regulation strategies, which included online gaming, using mobile applications developed for language learning purposes, and listening to mainstream broadcasting channels. It is essential to note here that this relationship between LSE beliefs and technology-based learning strategies is not linear. Bekleyen and Hayta's (2015) findings have already revealed that various different types of mobile phone-assisted language learning strategies help learners to improve their English proficiency. The participants in this study contended that such technology-based self-regulatory strategies improved not only their English proficiency but also strengthened their LSE beliefs. This inevitably leads to the conclusion that self-efficacy and self-regulation can be aided by technology to a great extent in the rapidly digitalizing language learning environments prevalent in foundation programmes at tertiary level in Türkiye.

As for the weak LSE beliefs, it was also observed during the interviews that learners had come to possess a sense of perceived incompetence due to their previous negative mastery experiences and vicarious experiences, in Bandura's (1997) terms. Other significant reasons for low LSE beliefs included limited oral and written input and practice, the inability to travel overseas mostly due to financial burdens, challenging personal educational backgrounds, and difficulty in vocabulary retrieval. Such learners need encouragement to help them believe they can succeed.

Participants with strong LSE beliefs reported hardly ever feeling tense or anxious when they were required to do productive tasks in English. As a result, they have a stronger sense of perceived competence in the language. In Bandura's (1997) terms, their affective indicators acted as a source of high LSE beliefs. Moreover, when language teachers noticed the regular use of digital tools, they also encouraged the participants to keep using such tools. Bandura (1997) refers to this phenomenon as verbal persuasion, which is a key source of LSE beliefs.

Learners with weak LSE beliefs mostly complained in the interviews about an overwhelming difficulty in vocabulary retrieval during real-life communication. Their self-regulation regarding social strategy use, and goal setting and evaluation strategy use, was also relatively lower than their peers with high LSE beliefs. They referred to limited oral and written input and practice as well as their inability to travel overseas as the primary sources of their low LSE beliefs while admitting that they did not really use mobile devices to participate in English social events; this is an indication of low technology-based self-regulatory social strategy use. Furthermore, the participants with lower LSE beliefs reported not being able to set realistic learning goals for themselves and evaluate their own learning process in a healthy way as they mostly mentioned a sense of learned helplessness and desperation due to their previous failures in their language learning background. Such learners need support so that they gain positive mastery experiences in interacting with technologies for English learning, which they can then be encouraged to reflect upon.

Overall, besides uncovering the complex and non-linear relationship between Turkish students' LSE levels, their technology-based strategy use and self-regulation at tertiary level, the current study has identified several major factors underlying high and low LSE levels. Based on our own findings, we believe that improving L2 students' technology-based SRL strategy use may have a considerable impact on their LSE beliefs, in reducing language anxiety and increasing enjoyment both in and outside the classroom.

As for the limitations, the current study was conducted only with B1 and B1+ level students. Students from lower proficiency levels may have lower LSE beliefs and different justifications for their LSE beliefs. Furthermore, the students were still in the process of getting used to technology-based SRL strategies since the hybrid curriculum was implemented at the beginning of the academic year. Their technology-assisted SRL strategy use may have improved considerably since. Thus, further study is needed to investigate the transition from analogue modes of learning that have been used in traditional public high schools in Türkiye to the regular and consistent use of technology-assisted SRL strategies at university that clearly help increase LSE levels.

# References

An, Z., Wang, C., Li, S., Gan, Z., & Li, H. (2021). Technology-assisted self-regulated English language learning: Associations with English language self-efficacy, English enjoyment, and learning outcomes. *Frontiers in Psychology, 11*, 3763. 10.3389/fpsyg.2020.558466

Anam, S.U., & Stracke, E. (2020). The role of self-efficacy beliefs in learning English as a foreign language among young Indonesians. *TESOL Journal, 11*(1), e00440. 10.1002/tesj.440

Bandura, A. (1986). *Social foundations of thought and action: A social cognitive theory*. Prentice Hall.

Bandura, A. (1997). *Self-efficacy: The exercise of control*. W.H. Freeman and Company.

Bandura, A. (2006). Adolescent development from an agentic perspective. In. F. Pajares, & T. Urdan (Eds.), *Self-efficacy beliefs of adolescents* (pp. 1–43). Information Age Publishing.

Bekleyen, N., & Hayta, F. (2015). Language learning in new era: Do mobile phones help?. In A. Akbarov (Ed.), *The practice of foreign language teaching: Theories and applications* (pp. 434–445). Cambridge Scholars Publishing.

Benson, P. (2001). *Teaching and researching learner autonomy in language learning*. Longman.

Braun, V. & Clarke, V. (2006). Using thematic analysis in psychology. *Qualitative Research in Psychology, 3*(2), 77–101. 10.1191/1478088706qp063oa

Boekaerts, M., & Cascallar, E. (2006). How far have we moved toward the integration of theory and practice in self-regulation?. *Educational Psychology Review, 18*, 199–210. 10.1007/s10648-006-9013-4

Carneiro, R., Lefrere, P., & Steffens, K. (2007). *Self-regulated learning in technology enhanced learning environments: A European review*. Kaleidoscope Network of Excellence. Available online at: http://www.lmi.ub.es/taconet/documents/srlinteles3.pdf

Chen, A.H. (2009). Listening strategy instruction: Exploring Taiwanese college students' strategy development. *Asian EFL Journal, 11*(2), 54–85.

Diseth, Å. (2011). Self-efficacy, goal orientations and learning strategies as mediators between preceding and subsequent academic achievement. *Learning and Individual Differences, 21*(2), 191–195. 10.1016/j.lindif.2011.01.003

Graham, S. (2011) Self-efficacy and academic listening. *Journal of English for Academic Purposes, 10*, 113–117. 10.1016/j.jeap.2011.04.001

Graham, S., & Macaro, E. (2008). Strategy instruction in listening for lower-intermediate learners of French. *Language learning, 58*(4), 747–783. 10.1111/j.1467-9922.2008.00478.x

Han, J., & Hiver, P. (2018). Genre-based L2 writing instruction and writing-specific psychological factors: The dynamics of change. *Journal of Second Language Writing, 40*, 44–59. 10.1016/j.jslw.2018.03.001

Hsieh, P.P., & Kang, H.S. (2010). Attribution and self-efficacy and their inter-relationship in the Korean EFL context. *Language Learning, 60*(3), 606–627. 10.1111/j.1467-9922.2010.00570.x

Ho, M. -C. (2016). Exploring writing anxiety and self-efficacy among EFL graduate students in Taiwan. *Higher Education Studies*, 6(1), 24–39. 10.5539/hes.v6n1p24

Kim, D.-H., Wang, C., Ahn, H. S., & Bong, M. (2015). English language learners' self-efficacy profiles and relationship with self-regulated learning strategies. *Learning and Individual Differences*, 38, 136–142.

Lai, C., Hu, X., & Lyu, B. (2018). Understanding the nature of learners' out of-class language learning experience with technology. *Computer-assisted Language Learning*, 31, 114–143. 10.1080/09588221.2017.1391293

Li, Y., & Wang, C. (2010). An empirical study of reading self-efficacy and the use of reading strategies in the Chinese EFL context. *Asian EFL Journal*, 12(2), 144–162.

Li, S., Hiver, P., & Papi, M. (Eds.). (2022). *The Routledge handbook of second language acquisition and individual differences*. Taylor & Francis 10.4324/9781 003270546

Liem, A.D., Lau, S., & Nie, Y. (2008). The role of self-efficacy, task value, and achievement goals in predicting learning strategies, task disengagement, peer relationship, and achievement outcome. *Contemporary Educational Psychology*, 33(4), 486–512. 10.1016/j.cedpsych.2007.08.001

Magogwe, J.M., & Oliver, R. (2007). The relationship between language learning strategies, proficiency, age and self-efficacy beliefs: A study of language learners in Botswana. *System*, 35(3), 338–352. 10.1016/j.system.2007.01.003

Mills, N., Pajares, F., & Herron, C. (2006). A reevaluation of the role of anxiety: Self-efficacy, anxiety, and their relation to reading and listening proficiency. *Foreign Language Annals*, 39(2), 276–295. 10.1111/j.1944-9720.2006. tb02266.x

Mills, N.A., Pajares, F., & Herron, C. (2007) Self-efficacy of college intermediate French students: Relation to achievement and motivation. *Language Learning*, 57(3), 417–442. 10.1111/j.1467-9922.2007.00421.x

Pan, X. (2020). Technology acceptance, technological self-efficacy, and attitude toward technology-based self-directed learning: learning motivation as a mediator. *Frontiers in Psychology*, 11, 564294. 10.3389/fpsyg.2020.564294

Pajares, F. (2001). Toward a positive psychology of academic motivation: The role of self-efficacy beliefs. *The Journal of Educational Research*, 95, 27–35. https:// www.tandfonline.com/doi/abs/10.1080/00220670109598780

Su, Y., Zheng, C., Liang, J.-C., & Tsai, C.C. (2018). Examining the relationship between English language learners' online self-regulation and their self-efficacy. *The Australasian Journal of Educational Technology*, 34, 105–121. 10.14742/ ajet.3548

Teng, M.F., & Yang, Z. (2022). Metacognition, motivation, self-efficacy belief, and English learning achievement in online learning: Longitudinal mediation modeling approach. *Innovation in Language Learning and Teaching*, 1–17. 10.1 080/17501229.2022.2144327

Tilfarlioğlu, F.T., & Ciftci, F.S. (2011). Supporting self-efficacy and learner autonomy in relation to academic success in EFL classrooms (a case study). *Theory and Practice in Language Studies*, 1(10), 1284–1294. 10.4304/tpls.1.10. 1284-1294

Wang, C., & Bai, B. (2017). Validating the instruments to measure ESL/EFL learners' self-efficacy beliefs and self-regulated learning strategies. *TESOL Quarterly*, *51*(4), 931–947. 10.1002/tesq.355

Wang, C., & Pape, S.J. (2005). Self-efficacy beliefs and self-regulated learning strategies in learning English as a second language: Four case studies. *The CATESOL Journal*, *17*(1), 76–90.

Wang, C., Schwab, G., Fenn, P., & Chang, M. (2013). Self-efficacy and self-regulated learning strategies for English language learners: Comparison between Chinese and German college students. *Journal of Educational and Developmental Psychology*, *3*(1), 173–191. 10.5539/jedp.v3n1p173

Wang, J., Spencer, K., & Xing, M. (2009). Metacognitive beliefs and strategies in learning Chinese as a foreign language. *System*, *37*, 46–56. 10.1016/j.system.2008.05.001

Wyatt, M. (2022). Self-efficacy. In. S. Li, P. Hiver, & M. Papi (Eds.), *The Routledge handbook of second language acquisition and individual differences* (pp. 207–219). Routledge. 10.4324/9781003270546-17

Yusuf, M. (2011). The impact of self-efficacy, achievement motivation, and self-regulated learning strategies on students' academic achievement. *Procedia-Social and Behavioral Sciences*, *15*, 2623–2626. 10.1016/j.sbspro.2011.04.158

Zheng, C., Liang, J. C., Li, M., & Tsai, C. C. (2018). The relationship between English language learners' motivation and online self-regulation: A structural equation modelling approach. *System*, *76*, 144–157. https://doi.org/10.1016/j.system.2018.05.003

## Appendix 1: Part of the Questionnaire of English Self-Efficacy (speaking and reading items only)

### Speaking Efficacy
9. Can you introduce your university in English?
10. Can you tell the directions to your classroom from your home/dormitory in English?
11. Can you tell a story in English?
12. Can you ask questions to your teachers in English?
13. Can you introduce your English teacher in English?
14. Can you discuss in English with your classmates some topics assuming all of you are interested?
15. Can you answer your teachers' questions in English?
16. Can you introduce yourself in English?

### Reading efficacy
17. Can you finish your homework of English reading independently?
18. When you read English articles, can you guess the meaning of unknown words?
19. Can you understand the English news on the Internet?
20. Can you read English short novels?
21. Can you read English newspapers?
22. Can you find the meaning of new words by using English-English dictionaries?
23. Can you understand English articles about Turkish culture?
24. Can you understand new reading materials (e.g., news from the Time magazine) selected by your instructor?

## Appendix 2: Guiding questions and prompts for focus-group interviews

1. English Language Self-Efficacy
2. What makes you more or less self-efficacious about your writing and speaking abilities in English?
3. Do you feel self-efficacious when you read or listen to English texts? Why or why not?
4. What makes you more or less self-efficacious about your reading and listening abilities in English?
5. Technology-based Self-regulated Learning Strategy Use
6. Do you think technology helps you learn English more efficiently? Why or why not?
7. What kind of digital education tools or platforms do you use? How, when and why do you use these?

# Epilogue

# 13 Researching the self-efficacy beliefs of language learners and teachers
## The roads ahead

*Farahnaz Faez and Mark Wyatt*

**Introduction**

This volume has presented cutting-edge research from around the world into language learners' self-efficacy (LLSE) and language teachers' self-efficacy (LTSE) beliefs. We conclude the volume by highlighting key themes that have emerged within and across the various studies, followed by pointing the way towards further research, proposing a research agenda.

In an era of accountability and increased demand for highly effective teachers and enhanced learning outcomes, researching LTSE and LLSE beliefs is crucial. Teacher efficacy does not determine teacher effectiveness but is considered a strong variable that impacts teacher behaviour and student outcomes (Bandura, 1997). Stronger efficacy beliefs can lead to increased teaching effectiveness and strengthened learning outcomes, thereby being a significant factor that needs to be considered in education.

Researching and understanding second/foreign LLSE and LTSE beliefs has developed significantly in the past two decades. This progress is evident through contributions included in this volume and trends that we highlight in this epilogue. Following our introduction, this edited volume included 11 chapters, 9 of which presented empirical data gathered from learners and teachers in a variety of national contexts such as Algeria, Brazil, Bulgaria, China, Greece, Honduras, Iran, Italy, Japan, Poland, Türkiye, the UK, and Vietnam. Adding to the international flavour of the volume, the editors are based in Canada and the UAE, while contributing authors include graduates of American, Australian, British, and Canadian universities. Some chapters reflect international collaboration, for example, with co-authors from China and the UK (Chapter 7). Both English as a foreign language (EFL) and English as a second language (ESL) contexts are represented, as are a variety of types of institution, including schools and universities.

Chapters 2 and 3 are syntheses. Chapter 2 is a broad synthesis of survey instruments used in quantitative/mixed methods LTSE beliefs research, while Chapter 3 is a synthesis of LTSE beliefs research conducted in one

DOI: 10.4324/9781003379300-17

country, Türkiye. The sheer number of studies included in these 2 syntheses, 83 studies in Chapter 2 and 76 studies in Chapter 3, shows the increasing interest in research on LTSE beliefs over the past two decades.

In Parts 2 and 3 of this volume, nine empirical studies are included. Part 2 features five qualitative studies. This is novel, since previous syntheses of research on LTSE beliefs have highlighted a dearth of qualitative studies in the field (Wyatt, 2015, forthcoming). The number of participants in these studies ranges from a single participant (Chapter 4) to 19 – 15 teachers and 4 supervisors (Chapter 6). Participants include so-called "native speakers" (Chapter 5), which is striking since LTSE beliefs research to date has predominantly focused on the so-called "non-native" teachers[1] in EFL contexts (Wyatt, 2018). The variety in the qualitative research methodologies utilized in these chapters also deserves attention. Single and multi-case studies (Chapters 4 and 5), discourse analysis (Chapter 6), narrative case study (Chapter 7), and autoethnography (Chapter 8) have all been featured in these contributions.

The third section of the volume features four mixed methods studies examining domain-specific areas of LLSE and LTSE beliefs that are novel in various ways. For example, research on LTSE beliefs in the sub-areas of language teaching has been limited so far to grammar (Wyatt & Dikilitaş, 2019) and pronunciation (Zhang, 2018). However, this volume also features studies on vocabulary (Chapter 9) and listening (Chapter 10). The latter study is also novel in focusing both on LTSE and LLSE beliefs. Meanwhile, the studies of LLSE beliefs focused on academic writing (Chapter 11) and technology-based learning strategies (Chapter 12) are also innovative in different ways. For example, Chapter 11 is longitudinal, following students through a semester, while Chapter 12 considers LLSE beliefs in a hybrid learning environment of the type that will likely become increasingly common post-pandemic.

## Emerging trends in LTSE beliefs research

We now report on the trends that have emerged from studies included in this volume as well as research on LTSE beliefs in the past two decades more broadly.

One trend that has been emphasized in research on LTSE beliefs in this volume and recent studies is the dynamic, fluid, situated, and somewhat multiple nature of LTSE beliefs. Wyatt (2021) defines LTSE beliefs as "teachers' beliefs in their abilities to support language learning in various task-, domain- and context-specific cognitive, metacognitive, affective and social ways" (p. 296). This definition suggests that self-efficacy beliefs are not fixed or static and can change across time and space and should therefore be examined in the contexts in which they are negotiated. This trend is exemplified in several qualitative studies in this volume. Markova (Chapter 4) shows the formation and development of her participant's LTSE beliefs and in doing so reveals the shifting nature of LTSE beliefs impacted by a practicum experience. Donohue (Chapter 5) shows the dynamic and fluctuating nature of five novice teachers' LTSE beliefs due to the task-, domain-, and context-specific factors they encounter in their first year of teaching. In Chapter 6, Tajeddin and Tadayon's discourse analysis of teacher–supervisor post-observation conversations highlights how teachers express their LTSE beliefs in dialogue with their supervisors, which might lead to re-appraisals of these beliefs. Zhang and Hanks (Chapter 7) show the development of two teachers' LTSE beliefs over the course of their careers and highlight the fluid and somewhat multiple nature of LTSE beliefs. Moreover, while the dynamicity and fluidity of LTSE beliefs can better be exemplified through qualitative studies, Hadingham and Thompson (Chapter 11) capture this dynamicity through a longitudinal mixed methods study. They examine LLSE beliefs in relation to writing self-efficacy at four time-points throughout one semester and reveal how LLSE beliefs fluctuate across time.

Another trend that is emerging from recent studies is greater attention to the role of reflection in strengthening LTSE beliefs, as illustrated by conceptual models (e.g., Markova, 2021; Wyatt, 2016) and empirical research findings (e.g., Moradkhani et al., 2017) that suggest that more efficacious EFL teachers are also more reflective. So, it is interesting that, of the total 76 studies included in the synthesis of studies from Türkiye (Chapter 3), 6 studies used some form of reflective research tools. Several studies in this volume exemplify how research engagement (Chapter 8) and reflection (Chapters 4, 6, and 7) play a central role in efficacy building. A clear pedagogical implication, then, is that given the central role of reflection and research engagement in strengthening LTSE beliefs, inviting teachers to engage in reflecting on their experiences, philosophies, principles, and practices (after Farrell, 2016) can be encouraged to further develop their efficacy beliefs. Also, supporting and promoting practitioner research opportunities for teachers can provide motivating efficacy-building opportunities. However, while there is no doubt that reflective skills should be fostered in teacher education programmes and through professional development activities, ways to do so effectively remain a work in progress, so that Chapters 7 and 8 offer some guidance here.

Another prominent trend in LTSE beliefs research is working towards understanding the role of language proficiency and content knowledge. In a meta-analysis of 19 studies published in the past 2 decades, Faez et al. (2021) report a positive yet moderate relationship between language proficiency and LTSE beliefs. This suggests that language proficiency plays an important role in strengthening LTSE beliefs. Moderator analysis showed that studies that used domain-specific instruments to measure LTSE beliefs were more strongly correlated with LTSE beliefs than those that did not. However, while there were insufficient studies that used domain-specific instruments (only 3 of the 19) to draw conclusive results about the contribution of language proficiency to LTSE beliefs using domain-specific measures, the trend towards using more domain-specific survey instruments evident in this volume (Chapters 9 and 10) suggests that perhaps more reliable conclusions can be drawn in the future. Qualitative studies in this volume (Chapters 4 and 7) also shed light on the relationship between language proficiency and LLSE/LTSE beliefs. Given the positive association identified, it seems essential to provide opportunities for teachers to enhance their language proficiency, especially in targeted domain-specific areas such as classroom proficiency (Karas, 2019) or English-for-teaching (Freeman, 2017).

Finally, general broad surveys like Tschannen-Moran and Woolfolk Hoy's (2001) widely recognized and repeatedly used Teacher Sense of Efficacy Scale (TSES), cannot accurately capture LTSE beliefs. While 65 out of 83 quantitative studies to date (see Chapter 2) have used the TSES in its original form (N = 50), or a modified version of it (N = 15), the trend is to use more task-, domain-, and context-specific survey instruments. This trend is evident in Chapters 9–12 of this volume; each study generated and/or adapted surveys specific to the task and domain under investigation.

## Future research

Despite the progress in researching LTSE and LLSE beliefs that has been made to date, as evidenced by contributing chapters to this volume, the field will still benefit further from understanding how to best assess or measure LTSE and LLSE beliefs. Considerations that should inform the design of quantitative research include: what type of scale and items to include, the optimal balance between global and more task-, domain-, and context-specific items, and the ideal Likert scale to use. However, once these issues are addressed, there are also still valid concerns about the trustworthiness of self-reported data. Hence, in the following, we outline some directions for future research.

Firstly, regarding one key theme, while the importance of language proficiency is undeniable for LTSE beliefs, there are several dimensions of language proficiency that particularly deserve further research. Language proficiency is not easy to define and is contextually bound. The issue of what level and type of proficiency is required for optimal levels of LTSE is a complicated matter, as different contexts and purposes require different types and levels of proficiency. In Zhang's (2018) study, pronunciation proficiency correlated with LTSE beliefs for providing pronunciation instruction, but general proficiency did not. Similarly, in Karas' (2019) study, classroom proficiency was a significant predictor of LTSE beliefs, while general proficiency, as measured by the Common European Framework (CEFR), was not. There have been calls to acknowledge the significance of classroom proficiency or English-for-teaching (Freeman, 2017; Richards, 2017) for English teachers, and we would argue that investigating the contribution of general proficiency or classroom proficiency to LTSE beliefs is a clear future research direction. Research is needed since, while language proficiency is intertwined with LTSE beliefs in complex ways, there are insufficient studies at present that have looked at the needs for different types of proficiency for task-, domain-, and context-specific areas of language teaching.

However, there is a danger that an over-emphasis on teachers' language proficiency might tend to promote the native-speakerism ideology (Holliday, 2006), i.e., the erroneous perception that native speakers are better language teachers by virtue of their linguistic identity. This ideology has been challenged, and there is increasing recognition that knowledge of an additional language tends to boost efficacy levels (Karas & Faez, 2021; see also Chapter 3). Hence one area that should be considered for further research is examining the relationships among general proficiency, classroom proficiency, linguistic identities, target language use, language awareness, and LTSE beliefs, and the way they interact with levels of students in the classrooms taught.

The other issue concerning language proficiency relates to the construct of proficiency itself and how it is assessed. In language classrooms, language serves both as the medium of instruction and the content of the classroom (Freeman, 2016). Therefore, the issue of whether language proficiency should be incorporated as part of the LTSE scale or measured separately deserves attention. As noted in Chapter 2, there is a wide discrepancy in the field as to how language proficiency has been incorporated in LTSE survey instruments and/or measured separately. While early scales predominantly measured language proficiency separately (Faez et al., 2021), others, particularly recent ones, have somehow incorporated proficiency as part of their LTSE survey instrument. Some examples include L2 Self-Confidence (Nishino, 2012), Language Proficiency (Cooke & Faez, 2018), Classroom Proficiency (Karas, 2019), and Using English (Thomson & Woodman, 2019).

Similar to language proficiency, teaching efficacy is difficult to define and assess as it is also culturally and contextually bound (Faez et al., 2021). Also, related to survey instruments for evaluating LTSE beliefs is the issue of what subscales or factors surveys should include. Are there factor structures that are integral to LTSE beliefs? And others that are more domain and context-specific? As discussed, some form of language proficiency has featured in many survey instruments. Also, Culture has featured prominently (e.g., Swanson, 2012; Karas, 2019), sometimes as cultural knowledge (Cooke & Faez, 2018; Parks, 2021). Moreover, L2 instructional strategies and student engagement have also been incorporated in several surveys, whereas other factors such as Communicative Language Teaching (Nishino, 2012; Hoang & Wyatt, 2021), Materials Development (Karas, 2019; Hoang & Wyatt, 2021), and Classroom Management (Akbari & Tavassoli, 2014) seem to be more context-bound (see Chapter 2 for a full discussion).

Other considerations related to survey instrument development for evaluating LTSE beliefs are scale length and how wide Likert scales should be, and/or how they impact levels of self-reported efficacy. Swanson's (2010a, 2010b, 2012, 2013, 2014) studies report higher levels of LTSE beliefs using a 101-point scale. The question is: does using wider range scales impact self-reported levels of efficacy or are there other factors involved (context, participant, etc.)? Also related to this issue is whether even number or odd number-point scales should be used. With 'even number-point' Likert scales, there is no mid-point. Odd number-point scales may encourage the tendency for the mid-point to be over-used.

Evidently, more research is needed to address the optimal balance between more global versus task-, domain-, and context-specific items. As Wyatt (2014) points out, when items are produced from a global perspective, they are less predictive of actual behaviour, and it is difficult to understand what teachers are actually evaluating themselves on. When items are too specific, it is difficult to provide a complete picture of overall efficacy. Hence, better understanding of the optimal balance between the more global and the more task-, domain-, and context-specific items can be valuable in the field.

The other area that deserves attention is acknowledging limitations of self-reported data both in evaluating efficacy beliefs and in measuring language proficiency. However, Faez et al. (2021) compared studies that used self-reported proficiency measures and objective measures of proficiency and reported no significant difference between both groups of studies. Nevertheless, only three studies in their meta-analytic study had used objective measures, while there are concerns that self-reported proficiency evaluations are notoriously inaccurate (e.g., Trofimovich et al., 2016). Future research should examine this issue and whether the same perspective holds true for self-reported LTSE beliefs. Few studies have examined how self-reported levels of LTSE beliefs corroborate with the evaluation of others. Thus, future research in this area would be useful.

Also related to methodological quality is the importance of following recommended practices in quantitative studies and reporting reliability coefficients and employing factor analysis. Even if established measures such as the TSES (Tschannen-Moran & Woolfolk Hoy, 2001) or an adapted version are being used, it is important not to assume that self-efficacy measures and their factor structure will work in the same way in different contexts as they did in the original study. In fact, it is important to see how the factor structure will compare with the results of the original study and with different studies. However, a large number of participants is required to conduct factor analytic procedures to examine the construct validity of the new or adapted LTSE survey instruments, which is something that should be borne in mind.

While most recommendations in this section so far have centred on quantitative studies, it is important to note that quantitative measures cannot capture the fluid and dynamic nature of LTSE beliefs in the same in-depth way that qualitative studies can. Also, the nuances regarding which specific teaching tasks one feels more-or-less efficacious about cannot be captured by quantitative research methods. Therefore, purely qualitative studies or mixed methods studies are valuable for this reason, as the studies in this volume demonstrate.

To gain a full picture of LTSE beliefs data, triangulation is also important. While most studies employ interviews as it is the most convenient and feasible method of data collection, observational data have been quite rare. For example, of the 76 studies reviewed in Chapter 3, only three included observational data. Yet such data can be valuable to support triangulation processes (Stake, 1995), including "methodological triangulation to compare the teachers' words with their actions or with their written plans, reports and reflections [and] data source triangulation to compare changes in reported cognitions or observed behaviour over time" (Wyatt, 2015, p. 138). Notably, nearly all of the qualitative and mixed methods studies in this volume employ triangulation processes. Despite this, however, it can be challenging for researchers to incorporate observations in research designs, particularly when separated from the contexts of the teachers and learners they are investigating. This might suggest that self-observation, as in autoethnographic accounts of self-development, such as in Chapter 8, might be encouraged more to advance understanding of change processes shaped by efficacy-building experiences.

Much of the above is focused more on LTSE than LLSE beliefs, but researchers working primarily in the former field can learn much from the latter. As highlighted as well in Chapter 1 and evident in Chapters 10–12, feeling efficacious in different domain- and task-specific elements of their language learning can be highly beneficial for students. This understanding has resulted in the development of highly principled teaching practices, as researchers have explored the links between effective learning strategies and LLSE beliefs. Insights from this field suggest it can be highly advantageous if teachers feel efficacious about providing contextually appropriate learning opportunities to provide win–win situations for everyone. There are implications then, regarding the efficacy building that can take place through teacher education, with opportunities to experience success, benefit from finely attuned input, and receive sensitive mentoring needed.

## Note

1 For a discussion of the terms "native" and "non-native" speakers, which we dislike for the pejorative associations with the latter, please see Chapter 1.

## References

Akbari, R., & Tavassoli, K. (2014). Developing an ELT context-specific teacher efficacy instrument. *RELC Journal*, *45*(1), 27–50. https://doi.org/10.1177/0033688214523345

Bandura, A. (1997). *Self-efficacy: The exercise of control*. Freeman.

Cooke, S., & Faez, F. (2018). Self-efficacy beliefs of novice French as a second language teachers: A case study of Ontario teachers. *Canadian Journal of Applied Linguistics*, *21*(2), 1–18. https://www.erudit.org/en/journals/cjal/1900-v1-n1-cjal04434/1057963ar.pdf

Faez, F., Karas, M., & Uchihara, T. (2021). Connecting language proficiency to teaching ability: A meta-analysis. *Language Teaching Research*, *25*(5), 754–777. 10.1177/1362168819868667

Farrell, T.S.C. (2016). Anniversary article: The practices of encouraging TESOL teachers to engage in reflective practice: An appraisal of recent research contributions. *Language Teaching Research*, *20*(2), 223–247. https://doi.org/10.1177/1362168815617335

Freeman, D. (2016). *Educating second language teachers: The same things done differently*. Oxford University Press.

Freeman, D. (2017). The case for teachers' classroom English proficiency. *RELC Journal*, *48*(1), 31–52. 10.1177/0033688217691073

Hoang, T., & Wyatt, M. (2021). Exploring the self-efficacy beliefs of Vietnamese pre-service teachers of English as a foreign language. *System*, *96*(102422), 1–14. First published online 25/11/2020. 10.1016/j.system.2020.102422

Holliday, A. (2006). Native-speakerism. *ELT Journal*, *60*(4), 385–387.

Karas, M. (2019). *English language teacher self-efficacy beliefs* [Unpublished doctoral dissertation]. Western University.

Karas, M., & Faez, F. (2021). Self-efficacy of English language teachers in Ontario: The impact of language proficiency, teaching qualifications, linguistic identity, and teaching experience. *The Canadian Modern Language Review*, *77*(2), 110–128. 10.3138/cmlr-2020-0012

Markova, Z. (2021). Towards a comprehensive conceptualisation of teachers' self-efficacy beliefs. *Cambridge Journal of Education*, *51*, 653–671. 10.1080/0305764x.2021.1906844

Moradkhani, S., Raygan, A., & Moein, M.S. (2017). Iranian EFL teachers' reflective practices and self-efficacy: Exploring possible relationships. *System*, 65, 1–14. https://doi.org/10.1016/j.system.2016.12.011

Nishino, T. (2012). Modeling teacher beliefs and practices in context: A multimethods approach. *The Modern Language Journal*, 96(3), 380–399. 10.1111/j.1540-4781.2012.01364.x

Parks, P. (2021). *Should I stay, or should I go? A mixed method study of pre-service English second language teacher efficacy-identity development in Quebec.* [Unpublished doctoral dissertation]. McGill University.

Richards, J.C. (2017). Teaching English through English: Proficiency, pedagogy and performance. *RELC Journal*, 48(1), 7–30. 10.1177/0033688217690059

Stake, R.E. (1995). *The art of case study research.* Sage.

Swanson, P. (2010a). Teacher efficacy and attrition: Helping students at introductory levels of language instruction appears critical. *Hispania*, 93(2), 305–321.

Swanson, P. (2010b). Efficacy and language teacher attrition: A case for mentorship beyond the classroom. *NECTFL Review*, 66, 48–72.

Swanson, P. (2012). Second/foreign language teacher efficacy and its relationship to professional attrition. *The Canadian Modern Language Review*, 68(1), 78–101. doi: 10.3138/cmlr.68.1.078

Swanson, P. (2013). From teacher training through the first year on the job: Changes in foreign language teacher efficacy. *Electronic Journal of Foreign Language Teaching*, 10(1), 5–16.

Swanson, P. (2014). The power of belief: Spanish teachers' sense of efficacy and student performance on the National Spanish Examinations. *Hispania*, 97(1), 5–20.

Thompson, G., & Woodman, K. (2019). Exploring Japanese high school English teachers' foreign language teacher efficacy beliefs. *Asia-Pacific Journal of Teacher Education*, 47(1), 48–65. doi: 10.1080/1359866X.2018.1498062

Trofimovich, P., Isaacs, T., Kennedy, S., Saito, K., & Crowther, D. (2016). Flawed self-assessment: Investigating self- and other perception of second language speech. *Bilingualism: Language and Cognition*, 19, 122–140. https://doi.org/10.1017/S1366728914000832

Tschannen-Moran, M., & Woolfolk Hoy, A. (2001). Teacher efficacy: Capturing an elusive construct. *Teaching and Teacher Education*, 17, 783–805. https://doi.org/10.1016/S0742-051X(01)00036-1

Wyatt, M. (2014). Towards a re-conceptualization of teachers' self-efficacy beliefs: tackling enduring problems with the quantitative research and moving on. *International Journal of Research and Method in Education*, 37(2), 166–189. https://doi.org/10.1080/1743727X.2012.742050

Wyatt, M. (2015). Using qualitative research methods to assess the degree of fit between teachers' reported self-efficacy beliefs and their practical knowledge during teacher education. *Australian Journal of Teacher Education*, 40(1), Art 7, 1–30. http://ro.ecu.edu.au/ajte/vol40/iss1/7/

Wyatt, M. (2016). "Are they becoming more reflective and/or efficacious?" A conceptual model mapping how teachers' self-efficacy beliefs might grow. *Educational Review*, 68(1), 114–137. https://doi.org/10.1080/00131911.2015.1058754

Wyatt, M.(forthcoming). Language teachers' self-efficacy beliefs (2010–2020): A systematic review. In Z. Tajeddin & T.S.C. Farrell (Eds.), *Handbook of language teacher education: Critical reviews and research syntheses*. Springer.

Wyatt, M. (2018). Language teachers' self-efficacy beliefs: An introduction. In S. Mercer & A. Kostoulas (Eds.), *Language teacher psychology* (pp. 122–140). Multilingual Matters.

Wyatt, M. (2021). Research Into Second Language Learners' and Teachers' Self-Efficacy Beliefs: Making the Connections. *TESOL Quarterly*, 55, 296–307. 10.1002/tesq.3010

Wyatt, M., & Dikilitaş, K. (2019). English language teachers' self-efficacy beliefs for grammar instruction: implications for teacher educators. *The Language Learning Journal*, 49, 541–553. 10.1080/09571736.2019.1642943

Zhang, B. (2018). *English language teachers' required knowledge and self-efficacy beliefs about pronunciation instruction* [Unpublished master's thesis]. University of Western Ontario.

# Index

academic writing self-efficacy beliefs 220–237; boxplot graphs for *229*; descriptive statistics for **228**; difficulty of 231–232; history 221–224; methodology 224–228; overview 220–221; results 228–234; self-efficacy beliefs for **226**; skill development 233–234
academic writing tuition 223
Achieving group 210
affective states 70, 82, 111, 127, 129, 237
agent-means beliefs 67
Agheshteh, H. 121
Akbari, R. 31, 35, 39, 139
Akyel, A. S. 54
Alagözlü, N. 49, 56
Alıcı, D. 57
Allwright, D. 160
Ambivalent group 213, 215
Anderson, J. 90, 101
Andrews, S. 176, 183
Askham, J. 91
Aspirant group 212, 215
Atay, D. 54, 68
autoethnography 151–153
Azzi, M. 201

Bandura, A. 1–2, 68, 70, 105, 148, 166, 201, 215, 226, 234, 237, 241–242, 256, 259–260; principal sources of self-efficacy 127; Social Cognitive Theory 45, 110–111, 126
Banister, C. 9, 129–130

Barnard, R. 214
Beaton, Jonathan 164
Bekleyen, N. 259
Borg, M. 103
Braun, V. 245
Burns, A. 214

Cabaroglu, N. 9, 54
Çakır, Ö. 57
Cambridge Certificate in Teaching English to Speakers of Other Languages (CELTA) 11, 90–91, 94, 103
Can, S. 49
Caner, M. 56
Cantrell, S. C. 214
Çapan, S. A. 54
career-long development: case studies 133–138; of language teachers' self-efficacy (LTSE) beliefs 126–143; methodology 131–133; pedagogical implications 141–143; research context 130–131; support for 126–143
Chacón, C.T. 22, 27, 52–53
Chen, A.H. 248
Chen, Z. 127
China: EFL 130–131; EMI learners in 222; school education 130–131; tertiary learners of English in 199; tertiary-level instructors in 176
Choi, E. 22, 53
Clarke, V. 245
coding scheme 25

## Index

cognitive listening 198
Common European Framework of Reference (CEFR) 244, 271
communicative language teaching (CLT) 31, 53, 162, 272; -based teaching practices 55; pre-service training 162
Computerized Assessment System for English Communication (CASEC) 225
Consoli, S. 151
Cooke, S. 31
corrective feedback 69–70
Costantino, Anna 156
culture: and autoethnography 151; Confucian heritage 4; EP 153; and language 31; and LTE programmes 39; Western 6

Daloğlu, A. 49
Dawson, S. 151
Dellinger, A.B. 3
Dikilitaş, K. 9, 23, 31, 39, 56, 152, 163, 166, 178
Dinçer, R. 55
Doğan, C. 53
Dolgun, H. 56
Dooley, K. 127

effective listening 200, 215
efficacy doubts 127, 139
Ekizler, F. 57
enactive mastery experience 2, 7, 54, 68–70, 75–82, 241
English as a foreign language (EFL) 197, 267; Algerian university 201; novice teachers self-efficacy beliefs 87–106; teachers in Japan 200; transitioning to EAP teaching 153–154; Turkish context 44–60
English as a Second Language (ESL) 58, 267
English for Academic Purposes (EAP) 148, 154–155, 221–222, 236
English for Specific Purposes (ESP) courses 223
English language learners: and teachers' self-efficacy beliefs 1–14
English language teaching (ELT) 46–47, 87, 131, 180

English Medium Instruction (EMI) 13, 220–237; data analyses 227–228; data collection 225–227; history 221–224; instruments 225–227; methodology 224–228; overview 220–221; results 228–234; setting and participants 225, **225**; writing self-efficacy scale 226
Eslami, Z. R. 53
exploratory factor analysis (EFA) 181, 183, **183**
Exploratory Practice (EP) 148–166; described 150–151; implications for practitioner–researchers 164–166; literature review 149–151; overview 148; principles 126, 129, 141–143; research methodology 151–155; understandings 155–164

Fackler, S. 122
Faez, F. 5, 7, 8, 31, 38, 52, 58, 59, 186, 269, 272
Farrell, T.S.C. 112
Fatahi, A. 53
focus-group interviews 49–50
Freeman, D. 39
frequency: importance of 174; information 174
Fully Inclusive Practitioner Research (FIPR) 151, 166

Gao, X. 177
Gebhard, J.G. 112
Gholaminejad, R. 121
global self-efficacy (GSE) 149, 163
Goh, C. 127, 198
Graham, S. 1, 198, 200–201, 204, 210, 215, 256
grammar-translation method (GTM) 53, 58
Greenhouse–Geisser correction 229

Hanks, J. 151, 160, 163, 269
Hayta, F. 259
high technology-based SRL strategy 255–256
Hinkel, E. 223
Hiver, P. 127

Hoang, T. 5, 31, 39, 68
Hoey, M. 175
Holliday, A. 6
Howard, E.A. 90, 101
Hoy, A.W. 46, 91, 105
Huangfu, W. 32
Hunter, A. 152
Hyland, F. 112
Hyland, K. 223

imposter syndrome 7
İnceçay, G. 50
individual differences 255
interview 196
Irie, K. 5

James, William 1
Japan: EFL teachers in 200; EMI university in 220–237; foreign English teachers in 38

Karas, M. 5, 8, 32, 38, 39, 52, 58, 271
Kato, Y. 151
Keşli Dollar, Y. 50
Kiely, R. 91
Kiss, T. 101
Kissau, S. 31, 36, 38
Klassen, R.M. 38, 105
knowledge confidence 178, 179, **185**
Kurt, G. 54

L2 learning enjoyment 254
Lai, C. 258
language learners' self-efficacy (LLSE) beliefs 3–4; characteristics of research 5–6; data collection tools 202–204; descriptive statistics **211**; for English as a foreign language (EFL) 197–216; literature review 197–202; research methodology 202–204, 267–274; results 205–213
language learning 220
language self-efficacy (LSE) beliefs 241–260; methodology 245–246; overview 241–243; results 246–256
Language Teacher Research (LTR) 154, 156, 157
language teachers' self-efficacy (LTSE) beliefs 3–4, 89–92, 149–150, 173–190; about specific domains of teaching and L2 instruction 55–56; background 174–178; career-long development of 127–130; characteristics of research 6–9; classroom practices 53; comparison of 56–57; contextual factors 208–209; current study 177–178; data analysis 181–182; data collection tools 202–204; department-related factors 209; descriptive statistics **206–207**; development of 53–55; Emerging trends in 268–270; for English as a foreign language (EFL) 197–216; findings 182–188; individual factors **206–207**, 208; learner-related factors 209–210; literature review 197–202; methodology 178–182; overview 173; participants **180**, 180–181; pedagogical implications 59–60, 189–190; pedagogic confidence 177, 179, **182**; in relation to different factors 51–53; research methodology 202–204, 267–274; results 205–213; support for career-long development of 126–143; surveying 49; teacher-supervisor post-observation conferences in Iran 110–122; teaching vocabulary 174–177; in Turkish EFL context 44–60, **50**
learner groups *212*
learner-initiated puzzling 150, 155–157, 164–165
learner self-efficacy beliefs about listening inventory (LSEBLI) 203, 204, 210, 212
Lee, J. 22, 53
Lee, J.A. 38
Leeming, P. 223
Levshina, N. 181
lexical awareness 177–178, 179, **186**
Leys, C. 229
Linguistics and Language Behaviour Abstracts (LLBA) 24

Lipsey, M. 47
listening: cognitive 198; effective 200; metacognitive 198–199; outcomes 205; proficiency 200; proficiency and self-efficacy **204**, 210–213; second-language (L2) 197–199, 201, 205–208; self-efficacy beliefs 205
Lo, M.M. 112
low anxiety levels 254–255
low self-efficacy 150
LTSE scales 26, 27–32, **28–30**; categorizing levels of self-efficacy 36; levels of self-efficacy across **35**, 35–36
LTSE surveys 21–40; discussion 36–38; literature review 21–24; methodology 24–26; overview 21; pedagogical implications 38–39; results 26–36; and TSES 21–22

Ma, Q. 177
Maslow, A.H. 1
mastery experiences 127, 201
Mauchly's Test of Sphericity 229
Medgyes, P. 101
Mehrpur, S. 121
Mendoza, L. 237
metacognitive listening 198–199
Mills, N.A. 5
Mızrak, P. 51
Modified TSES 23, 27, 34–35
Monroy, F. 176
Moradkhani, S. 111, 139
Mumford, S. 152

Nation, I.S.P. 175
native-speakerism 6–7
Nishino, T. 31
Niu, R. 176, 183
Norris, J. M. 47
novice EFL teachers' self-efficacy beliefs 87–106; context-specific impacts **103**, 103–104; discussion 99–104; domain-specific impacts 101–103, **102**; overview 87–92; pedagogical implications 104–106; research methodology 92–93; results 93–99; social support 104; task-specific factors 99–101, **100**

Onbaşı, M. 56
online gaming 255
oral reporting 165–166
Original TSES 22, 27, 32–34, **33**, **34**, 38
Ortaçtepe, D. 54
Ortega, L. 47
overall vocabulary teaching confidence 178
Oxford, R. 5

Pajares, F.M. 4
Pan, X. 243, 258
Parks, P. 34
pedagogical implications: career-long development 141–143; LTSE beliefs 59–60; LTSE surveys 38–39; novice EFL teachers' self-efficacy beliefs 104–106; PLTSE beliefs 83–84; post-observation conferences 121–122
pedagogic confidence 177, 179, **182**
personal information 179
physiological and affective states 127
post-observation conferences (POCs): audio-recorded 113; feedback in 111–112; LTSE beliefs 110–122; overview 110; pedagogical implications 121–122; teacher-supervisor in Iran 110–122; TSE beliefs about instructional strategies 114–118; TSE beliefs about student engagement 118–120
Potentially Exploitable Pedagogic Activities (PEPAs) 151, 158–160, 165
Praver, M. 38
pre-service language teachers (PLTSE) beliefs 67–84; cultivating high 74–80; data collection and analysis 72–74; literature review 68–70; overcoming doubts 77–80; pedagogical implications 83–84; research context 70–71; research methodology 71–72
professional development: Chinese EFL teachers' stories of 126–143; self-efficacy beliefs and language proficiency 126–127

ProQuest Dissertations 24
ProQuest Education 24

Questionnaire of English Self-Efficacy (QESE) 242, 244, 246

reading efficacy 264
relevance, and LTSE beliefs 140
Rogers, C.R. 1
Rossiter, M.J. 175, 183
Rotter, J. 3
Ruegg, R. 222

Şahin, F. E. 54, 68
Santos, D. 200–201, 215
school-university transition 220
Schunk, D.H. 1
Second/Foreign Language Teacher Efficacy Scale (S/FLTES) 27, 36
second-language (L2): English writing self-efficacy 221; individual differences (ID) in 241; listening 197–199, 201, 205–208; Self-Confidence 31; self-efficacy scales 23; teaching self-efficacy 35–36
second language acquisition (SLA) 242
self-concept: *vs.* self-efficacy beliefs 2
self-efficacy beliefs 13, 148, 149–150; Bandura on 2–3; defined 67, 241; for each skill **246**; language learners' 3–4; and language proficiency 126–127; for listening 205, **247**; novice EFL teachers 87–106; *vs.* self-concept 2; *vs.* self-esteem 1–2; teachers 1–14; for writing **247–248**; *see also* academic writing self-efficacy beliefs
self-esteem: *vs.* self-efficacy beliefs 1–2
self-perceptions of language proficiency, and LTSE beliefs 141
self-regulated learning (SRL) 5, 242–244, 252
semi-structured interviews 203
Senior, R. 90
Serin, N. 58
short initial teacher education courses (SITECs) 90–92, 105
Siegel, J. 200, 214
Simasangyaporn, N. 214
Siwatu, K. O. 214
Slimani-Rolls, Assia 156, 162, 163

Social Cognitive Theory 45, 110–111, 126
social persuasion 84n1
speaking efficacy 264
Spero, R.B. 91, 105
Structural Equation Modelling 198
students' learning evaluation strategies **250**
students' motivational regulation strategies **249**
students' self-efficacy beliefs: for each skill **246**; for listening **247**; for writing **247–248**
students' strategies for technology-based English song and movie learning **251**
students' technology-based vocabulary learning strategies **252**
students' use of goal-setting **250**
students' use of social strategies **251**
Su, Y. 242, 258
Suarez, Tatiana 164
Sun, T. 5, 6
Sustainable Professional Development (SPD) 128–130
Swanson, P. 27, 31, 35

Taşçı, Ç. 51–52
task-specific self-efficacy (TSE) beliefs 149
Tavassoli, K. 31, 35, 39
teacher-initiated puzzling 150, 155–157
teacher professional development (TDP) 128
teacher research self-efficacy (TRE) beliefs 9, 150, 155–156, 161–162
teacher self-efficacy beliefs about listening inventory (TSEBLI) 203, 205
teachers' self-efficacy (TSE) beliefs 45; about instructional strategies 114–118; about student engagement 118–120; and English language learners 1–14; and research 3–4; sources 111
Teachers' Sense of Efficacy Scale (TSES) 4, 21, 36–38, 46, 68, 270; 3-factor structure 36–37; and LTSE researchers 21–22; subscales to 22–23

Teaching English as a Foreign Language (TEFL) 112
teaching English to young learners (TEYL) 55
teaching vocabulary 173–177
technological pedagogical content knowledge (TPACK) 55
technology-based learning strategies 241–260; affecting factors 252–256; learners' English language self-efficacy and 252, **252**; methodology 244–246; overview 241–243; results 246–256
Technology-based Self-regulated English Learning Strategies Questionnaire (TSRLSQ) 244–245; levels of 248–250
Teng, M.F. 243, 257
Thompson, G. 5, 31, 38, 127, 222, 234
Tschannen-Moran, M. 3, 21, 23, 26, 46, 57, 68, 111, 270
Turkish EFL context: literature review 45–46; LTSE beliefs in 44–60, **48**; overview 44–45; research methodology 46–48; results 48–57

Ucar, H. 49
Underachieving group 213
Üstünbaş, Ü. 49, 56
Uztosun, M. S. 56

Valeo, A. 59
verbal persuasion 127, 241
vicarious experience 127
vocabulary 190n1; LTSE beliefs about 173; LTSE beliefs for 12; pedagogy 173; PEPA about peer teaching of 160; and teaching 173–177; teaching aspects of 12; teaching confidence 178

Wach, A. 176
Wang, C. 5, 6, 257
Weiner, B. 1
Wilson, D. B. 47
Woodman, K. 31, 38
Woolfolk Hoy, A. 3, 21, 26, 57, 68, 111, 270
Wyatt, M. 2–3, 9, 23, 31, 36, 39, 46, 56–57, 68, 89, 166, 178, 199–200, 268, 272

Xu, J. 199

Yang, Z. 243, 257
Yaylı, D. 57
Yazan, B. 152
Yazıcı Bozkaya, M. 49
Yüksel, H. G. 50, 53

Zhang, B. 23, 31, 39, 269, 270
Zonoubi, R. 101

Printed in the United States
by Baker & Taylor Publisher Services